CERES™
Celestial Legend
Volume 10: Monster
Shôjo Edition

STORY & ART BY YÛ WATASE

English Adaptation/Gary Leach

Translation/Lillian Olsen
Touch–Up Art & Lettering/Melanie Lewis
Cover & Graphic Design/Hidemi Sahara
Editor/Avery Gotoh
Supervising Editor/Frances E. Wall

Managing Editor/Annette Roman
Director of Production/Noboru Watanabe
Editorial Director/Alvin Lu
Sr. Director of Licensing & Acquisitions/Rika Inouye
Vice President of Sales & Marketing/Liza Coppola
Executive Vice President/Hyoe Narita
Publisher/Seiji Horibuchi

© 1997 Yuu Watase/Shogakukan, Inc. First published by Shogakukan, Inc. in Japan as "Ayashi no Ceres."
New and adapted artwork and text © 2005 VIZ, LLC. The CERES: CELESTIAL LEGEND logo is a trademark of VIZ, LLC.
All rights reserved. The stories, characters, and incidents mentioned in this publication are entirely fictional.

Printed in Canada

Published by VIZ, LLC
P.O. Box 77010 • San Francisco CA 94107

Shôjo Edition

10 9 8 7 6 5 4 3 2 1

First printing, January 2005

store.viz.com

www.viz.com

www.animerica-mag.com

VIZ GRAPHIC NOVEL

CERES
Celestial Legend
Vol. 10: Monster

Story and Art by
Yû Watase

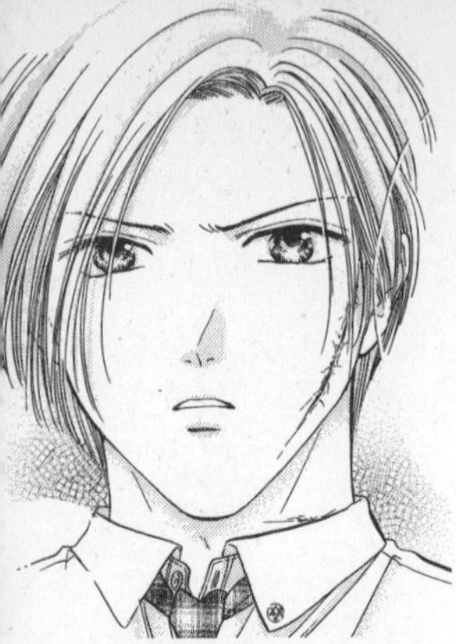

AKI MIKAGE: Aya's twin brother. While the consciousness of Ceres is taking over Aya, Aki is showing signs of bearing the consciousness of the founder (progenitor) of the Mikage family line. Placed under confinement by the Mikage family to keep him separated from Aya, still nothing will keep him from her....

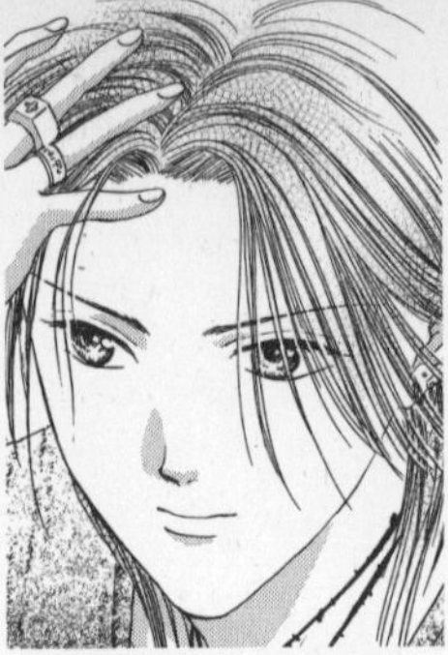

SHURO: Surviving member of the beautiful, androgynous Japan pop duo, GeSANG. A woman (with ten'nyo ancestry) passing as a man, her agent's urging prompts Shuro to consider a return to the pop-music scene, this time as a solo act.

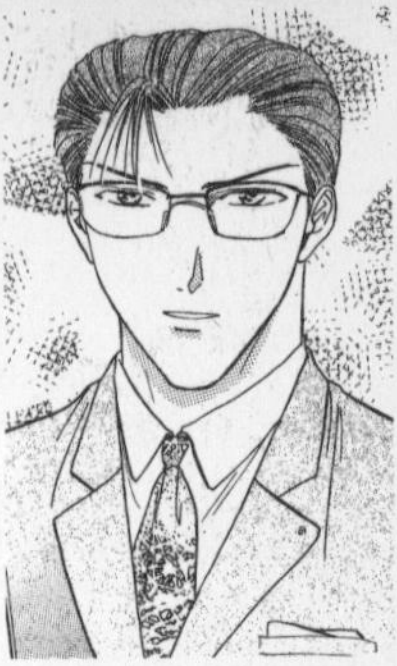

KAGAMI: Although the Mikage family wants to kill off Ceres through Aya, Kagami—head of Mikage International's research and development department—has put into motion his own agenda: C-Project, a plan to gather descendants of ten'nyo and use their power.

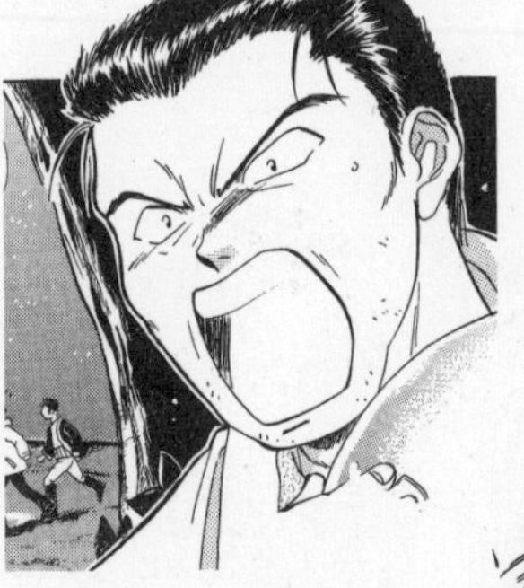

DR. KUROZUKA: A gruff-talking country doctor who's also endlessly kind, "Kurozuka-sensei" will later play an important role in both Tôya and Aya's future lives.

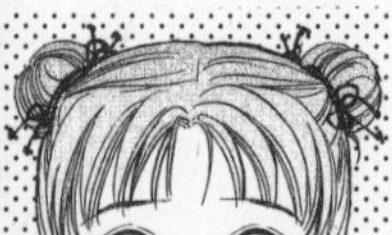

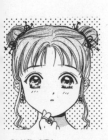

CHIDORI: Awakened to her own, unsuspected celestial powers only after her younger brother was put in mortal danger, Chidori Kuruma was at first another target of Kagami's, but was spared by the compassion of Tôya. Deceptively young in appearance (she looks like a grade-schooler but is actually in high school, just like Aya), Chidori has since decided to help Aya and the others in the search for Ceres' missing hagoromo.

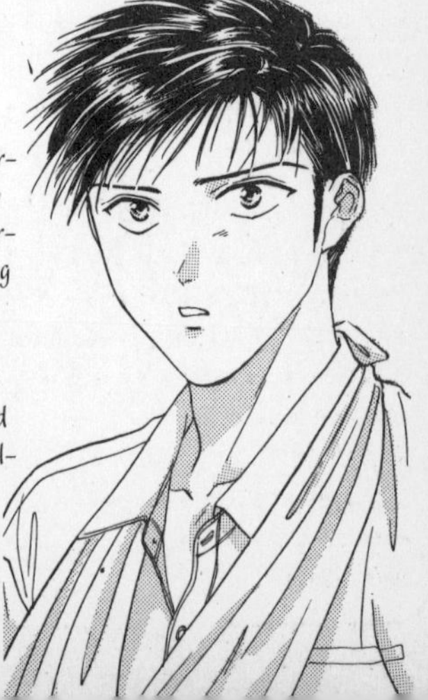

YÛHI: Sixteen-year-old brother-in-law to Suzumi. A skilled martial artist and aspiring chef, Yûhi has been asked (ordered, more like) to serve as Aya's watchful protector and guardian...his own feelings for her notwithstanding.

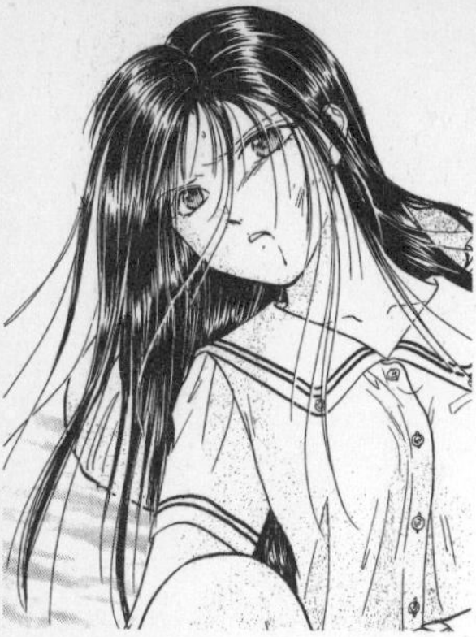

TÔYA: Aya's mysterious lover; he must keep himself away from Aya as he tries to center himself after a long period of amnesia. Cruelly toyed with by Kagami and the false memories he implanted, Tôya is no longer sure who or even what he is. One thing is for sure, though—he still has strong feelings for Aya.

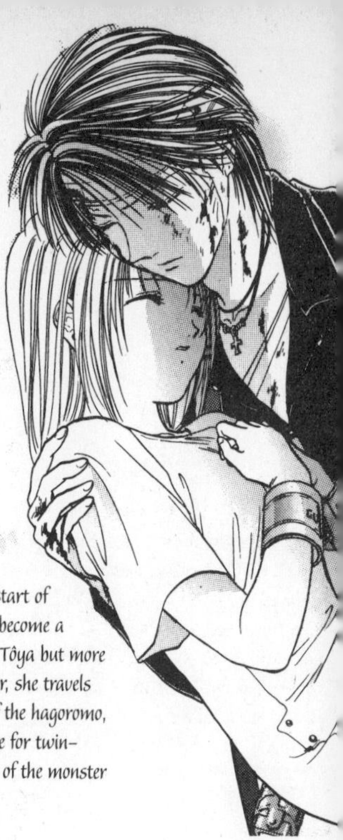

CERES: Once upon a time...long, long ago...a ten'nyo named Ceres descended to Earth. Her hagoromo or "feathered robes" stolen, Ceres—unable to return to the heavens—was forced by the human thief to become his wife and bear his children...thus beginning the Mikage family line. Awakened after aeons of waiting—and anger—Ceres wants her hagoromo back and vows to use all her celestial powers to avenge herself against the descendants of the man who wronged her.

AYA MIKAGE: Sixteen years old at the start of the story, Aya has since become a woman. Separated from Tôya but more in love with him than ever, she travels across Japan in search of the hagoromo, trying to reconcile her love for twin-brother Aki with her fear of the monster he's since become.

SUZUMI: Instructor of traditional Japanese dance and descendant of ten'nyo or "celestial maidens" herself. A big sister figure, Suzumi has welcomed Aya into her household and is more than happy to provide her with all the protection, assistance and support that she can.

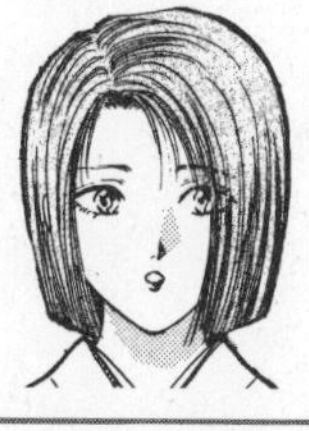

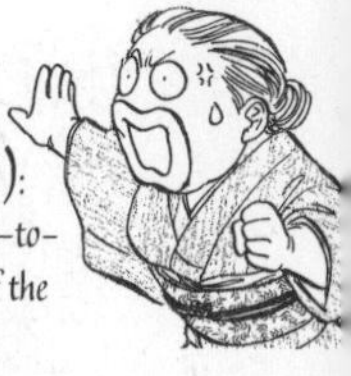

MRS. Q (ODA-KYÛ): Eccentric yet loyal-to-a-fault servant of the Aogiri household.

You may have noticed some unfamiliar people and things mentioned in CERES. VIZ left these Japanese pop-culture references as they originally appeared in the manga series. Here's an explanation for those who may not be so J-Pop savvy:

Page 9: "Safety First." A familiar (you might say ubiquitous) slogan found on construction sites in Japan, the characters for "Anzen Dai'ichi" and a green "cross" adorn the hardhats of workers, as well.

Page 24: "Hit me with a mop, you—!" If you're relatively new to anime and manga, this may come as a huge shock, but in Japan—unlike in the U.S.—students are expected to be responsible for the cleaning of their own classrooms. This is why the girl on this page (who doesn't look at all like a janitor, does she?) is carrying a mop.

Page 45: Yû Yû Kyûbin. A play, perhaps, on Japan's "Yû-Pack" consumer delivery service, the "yû" in Yû Yû Kyûbin recalls not only the "Yû" of Yû Watase and her famous series, Fushigi Yûgi, but also, in its doubling, suggests the famous panda "Ling Ling" (the small cartoon of the panda on Aya's birthday box doesn't hurt, either).

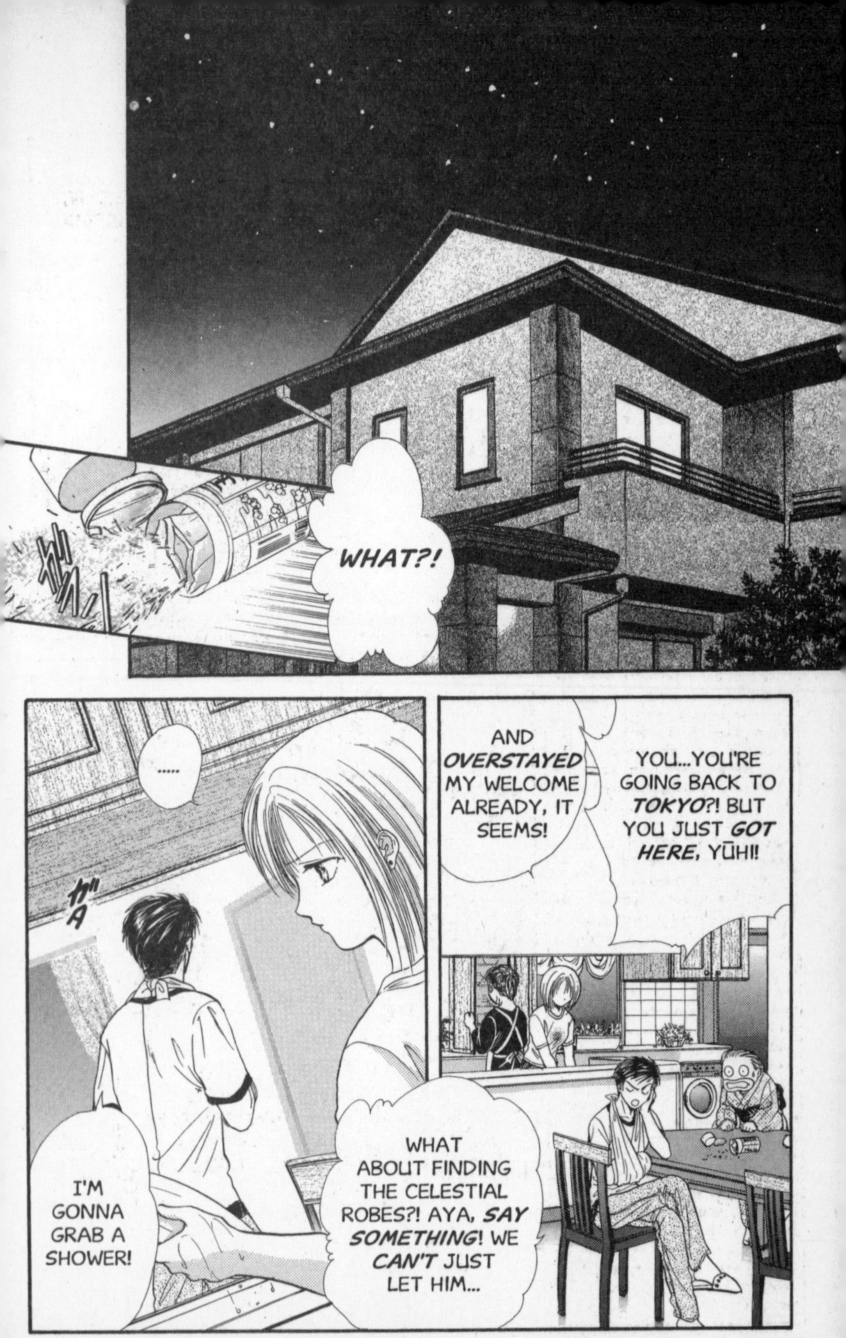
WHAT?!
YOU...YOU'RE GOING BACK TO *TOKYO*?! BUT YOU JUST *GOT HERE*, YŪHI!
AND *OVERSTAYED* MY WELCOME ALREADY, IT SEEMS!
.....
WHAT ABOUT FINDING THE CELESTIAL ROBES?! AYA, *SAY SOMETHING*! WE *CAN'T* JUST LET HIM...
I'M GONNA GRAB A SHOWER!

Ceres: 10

Hey! Watase, here. So another year's come and gone—and now it's 1999. I'm doubtful the predictions of Nostradamus are about to come true, though. If you ask me, my opinion is that Japan's about to face **social** collapse—that is, unless we can come up with a national vision and rebuild the country—and **soon.** Whoa! Serious way to start off a sidebar, huh?

I do want to thank everyone who bought the **Ceres** calendar. I hear it was practically sold-out... thank you for your support! I have a computer with all sorts of graphics programs, but still I painted and cut out everything by hand. ◡̈ Back when I first started out, I was told by the editors that color art wasn't my forte (truth? I just hated the work), so, I did always want one day to get better at it, and that's why I wanted to do it this time by hand. I **am** enjoying color art more these days. Maybe it's because I personally like the color-scheme for **Ceres.**

Apparently a lot of people have been a bit shy about displaying the May/June image of a nude Ceres. ◡̈ It's **supposed** to be **artistic!** But I guess it **can** look like a center-fold, depending. ◡̈ I put so much effort into drawing the bark on that pine tree, though.... Is it my drawing style that makes it look indecent? Many past editors have remarked that the girls I draw are "realistic and curvaceous." ◡̈ "The breasts look so soft," they say, that they "want to reach out and touch them"...and then they go on about the sexuality of girls who've yet to reach adulthood. Um, hello...? ◡̈ Hmm. I used to hate girls in shōjo manga who had matchsticks for legs...so, back when I was in junior high, I practiced drawing realistic female bodies. The thing is, I'd wanted to work for a shōnen magazine. ◡̈ I'm a woman, but half the time, when I'm drawing, I try to think like a man—and that's why there are some suggestive shots, sometimes. ◡̈ Plus, I **am** trying to make the illustrations for **Ceres** erotic on purpose (why?), so a certain amount of sexiness is necessary. Seriously, it's not supposed to be indecent. I guess eroticism isn't something you can just crank out on demand.

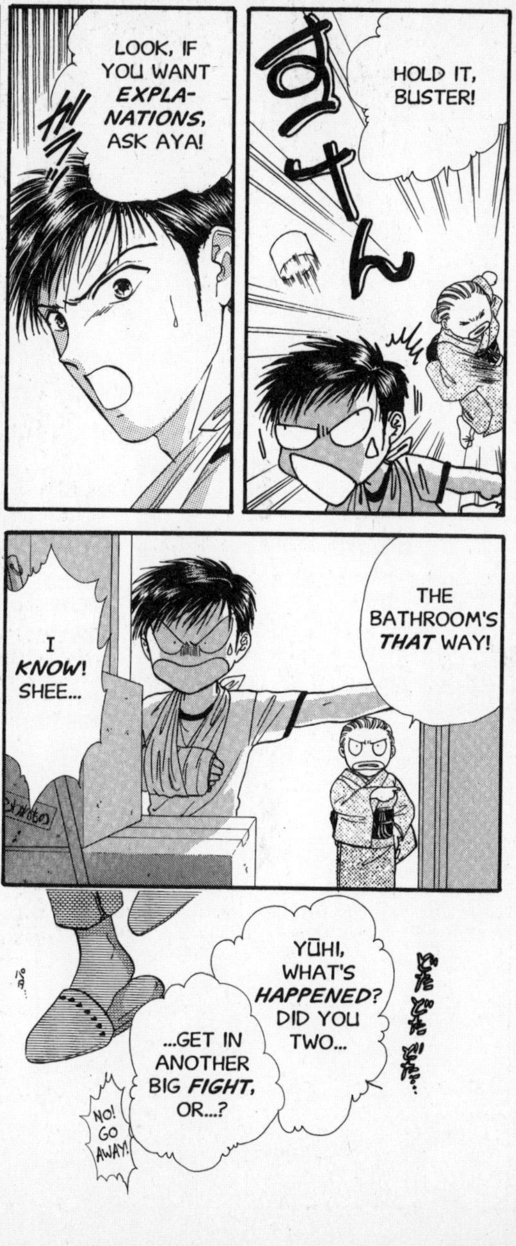

HOLD IT, BUSTER!
LOOK, IF YOU WANT *EXPLANATIONS,* ASK AYA!
THE BATHROOM'S *THAT* WAY!
I *KNOW!* SHEE...
YŪHI, WHAT'S *HAPPENED?* DID YOU TWO...
...GET IN ANOTHER BIG *FIGHT,* OR...?
NO! GO AWAY!

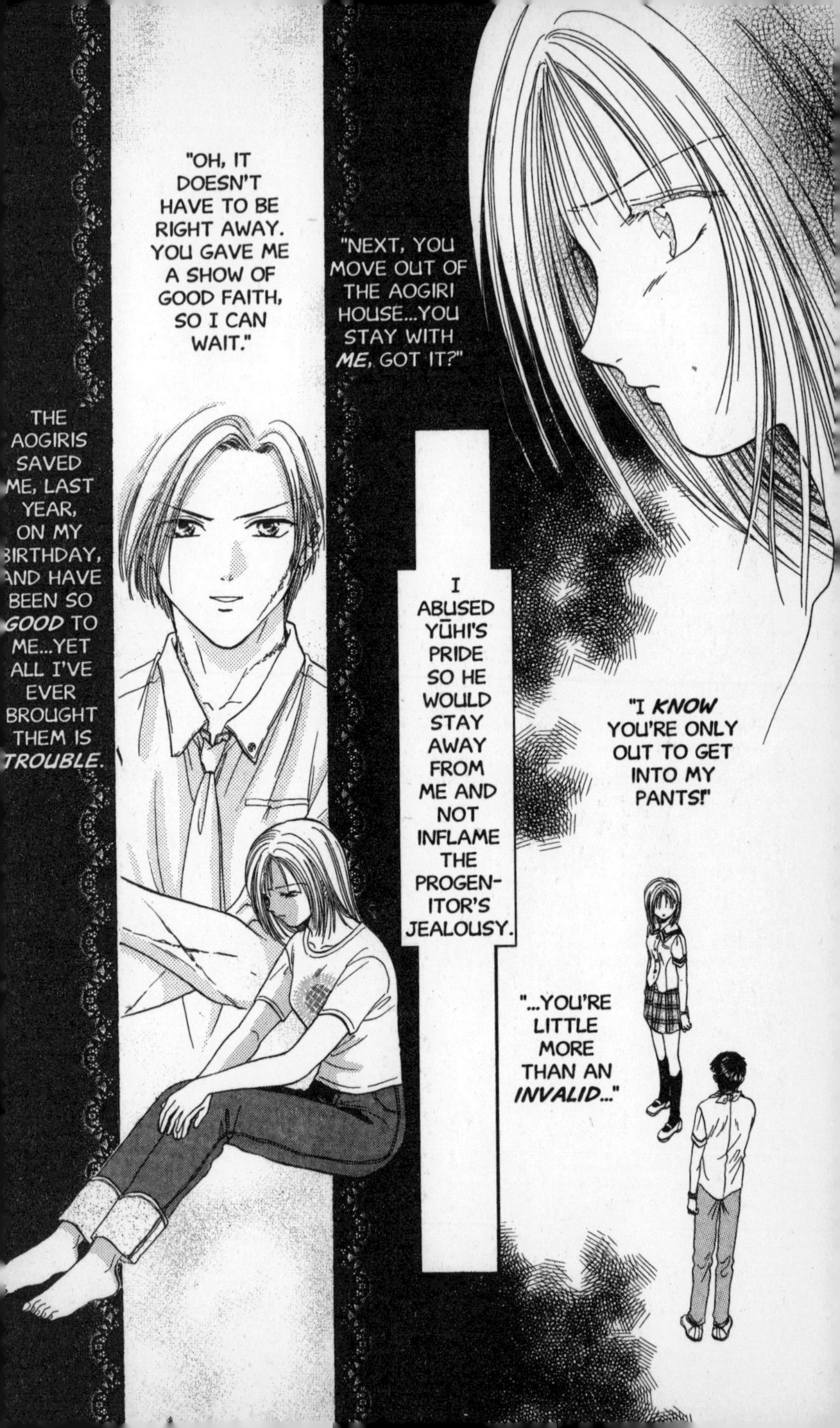
"I *KNOW* YOU'RE ONLY OUT TO GET INTO MY PANTS!"
"...YOU'RE LITTLE MORE THAN AN *INVALID*..."
"NEXT, YOU MOVE OUT OF THE AOGIRI HOUSE...YOU STAY WITH *ME*, GOT IT?"
I ABUSED YŪHI'S PRIDE SO HE WOULD STAY AWAY FROM ME AND NOT INFLAME THE PROGEN-ITOR'S JEALOUSY.
"OH, IT DOESN'T HAVE TO BE RIGHT AWAY. YOU GAVE ME A SHOW OF GOOD FAITH, SO I CAN WAIT."
THE AOGIRIS SAVED ME, LAST YEAR, ON MY BIRTHDAY, AND HAVE BEEN SO *GOOD* TO ME...YET ALL I'VE EVER BROUGHT THEM IS *TROUBLE*.

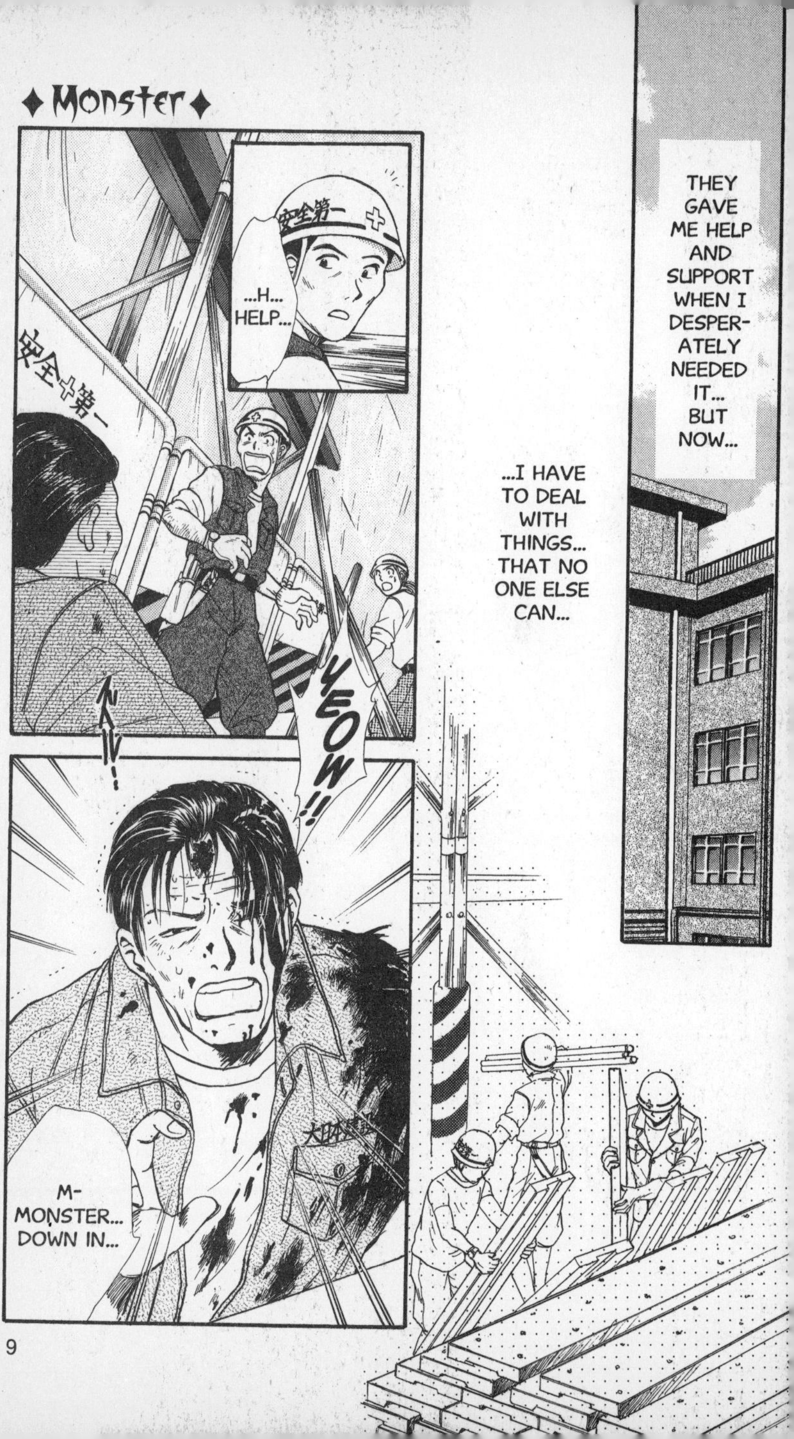
THEY GAVE ME HELP AND SUPPORT WHEN I DESPERATELY NEEDED IT... BUT NOW...
...I HAVE TO DEAL WITH THINGS... THAT NO ONE ELSE CAN...
安全第一
...H... HELP...
YEOW!!
M-MONSTER... DOWN IN...

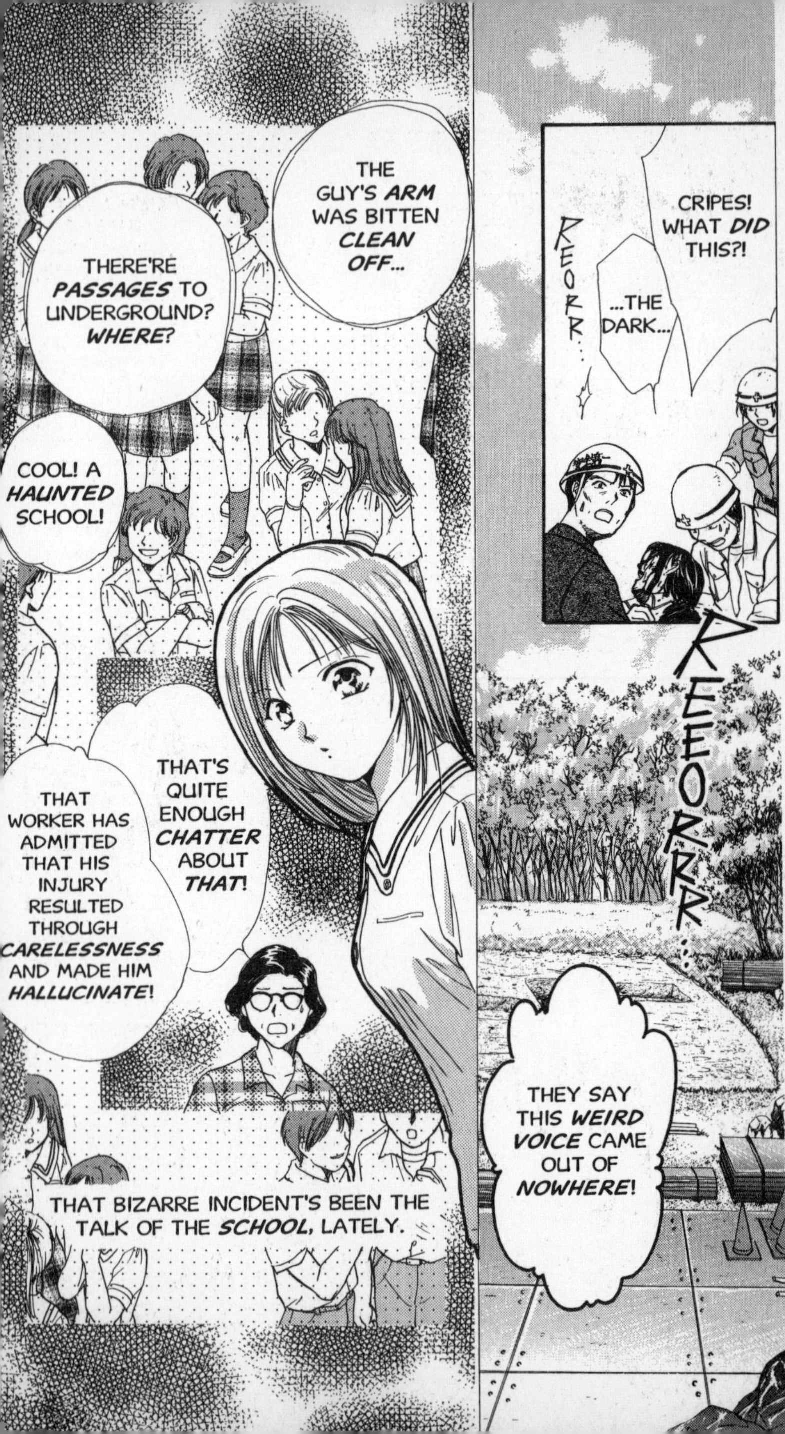
CRIPES! WHAT DID THIS?!
...THE DARK...
REORRR...
REEORRR...
THEY SAY THIS WEIRD VOICE CAME OUT OF NOWHERE!
THE GUY'S ARM WAS BITTEN CLEAN OFF...
THERE'RE PASSAGES TO UNDERGROUND? WHERE?
COOL! A HAUNTED SCHOOL!
THAT'S QUITE ENOUGH CHATTER ABOUT THAT!
THAT WORKER HAS ADMITTED THAT HIS INJURY RESULTED THROUGH CARELESSNESS AND MADE HIM HALLUCINATE!
THAT BIZARRE INCIDENT'S BEEN THE TALK OF THE SCHOOL, LATELY.

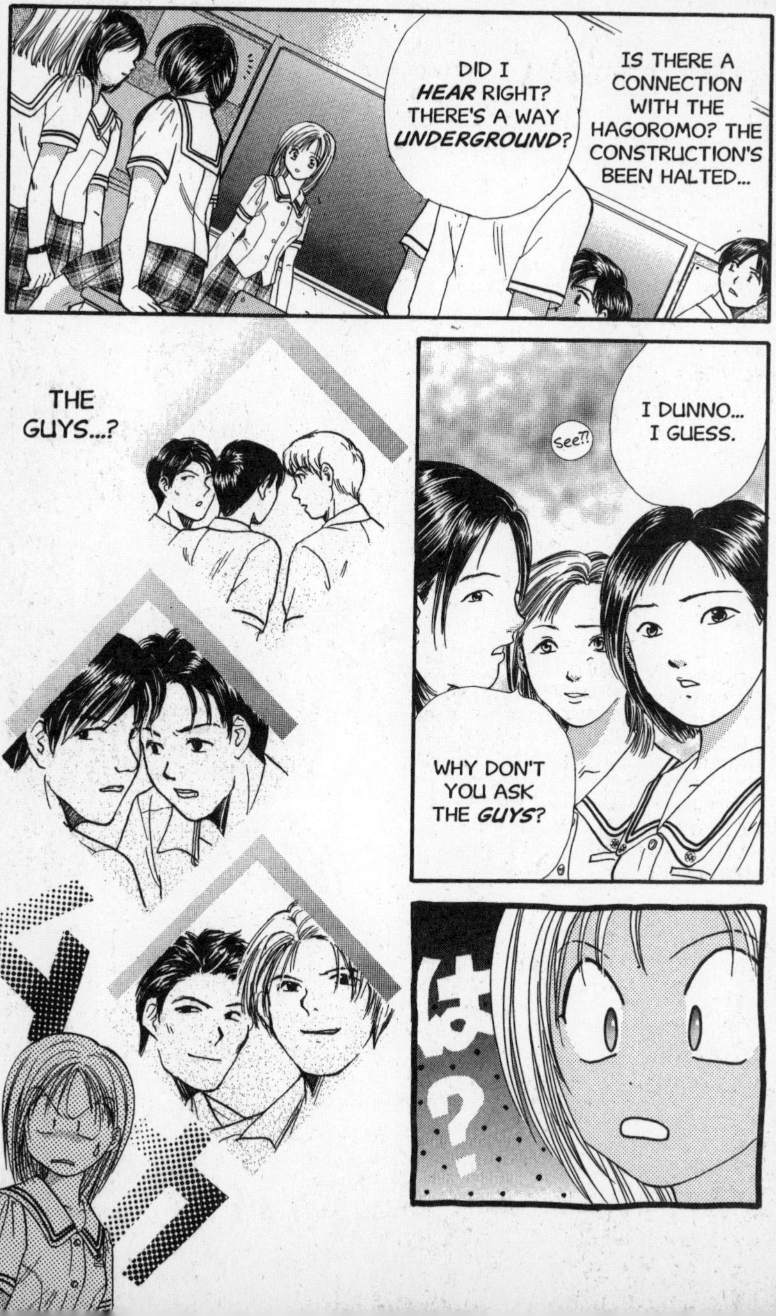
DID I *HEAR* RIGHT? THERE'S A WAY *UNDERGROUND*?
IS THERE A CONNECTION WITH THE HAGOROMO? THE CONSTRUCTION'S BEEN HALTED...
I DUNNO... I GUESS.
See??
WHY DON'T YOU ASK THE *GUYS*?
THE GUYS...?
は?

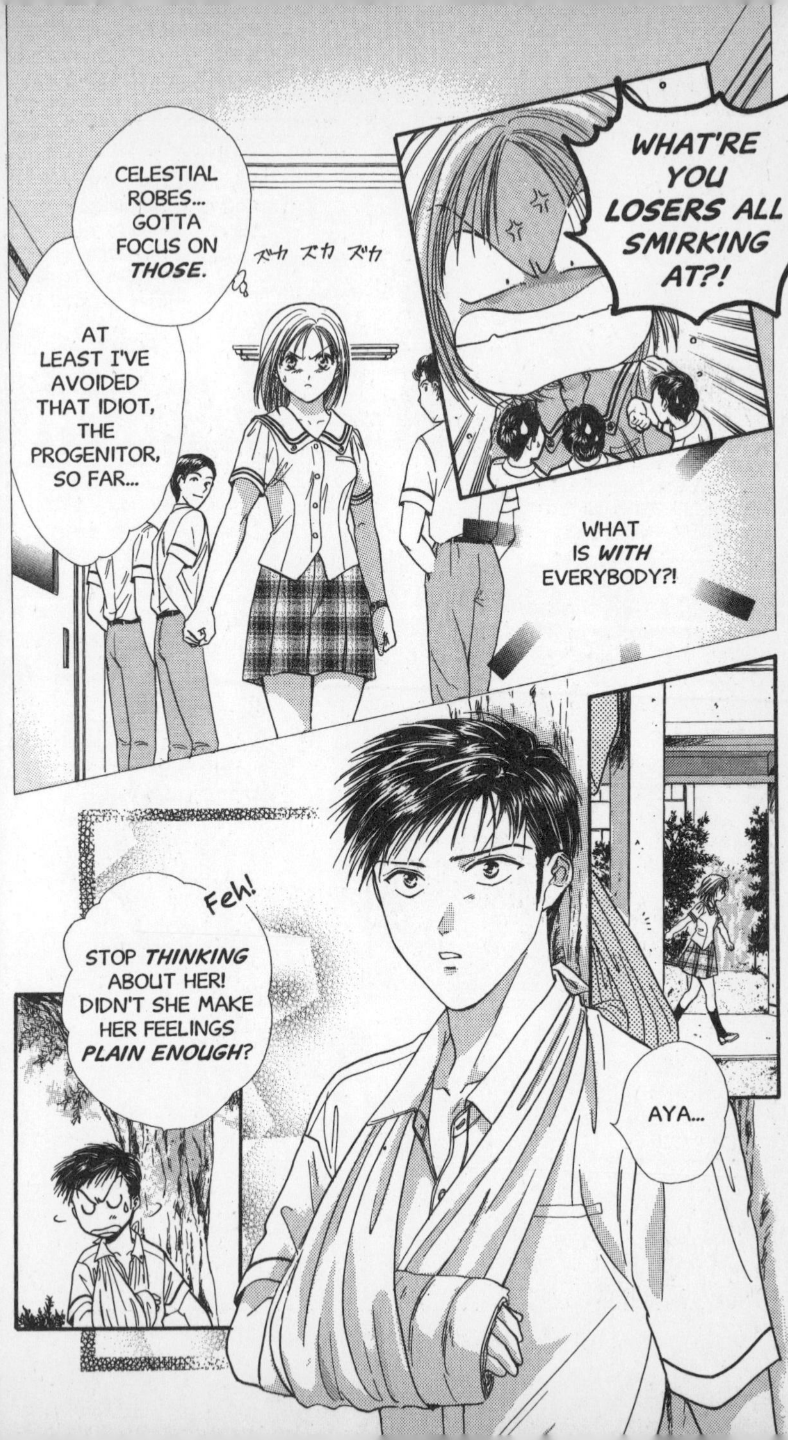
WHAT'RE YOU LOSERS ALL SMIRKING AT?!
CELESTIAL ROBES... GOTTA FOCUS ON THOSE.
ズカ ズカ ズカ
AT LEAST I'VE AVOIDED THAT IDIOT, THE PROGENITOR, SO FAR...
WHAT IS WITH EVERYBODY?!
AYA...
Feh!
STOP THINKING ABOUT HER! DIDN'T SHE MAKE HER FEELINGS PLAIN ENOUGH?

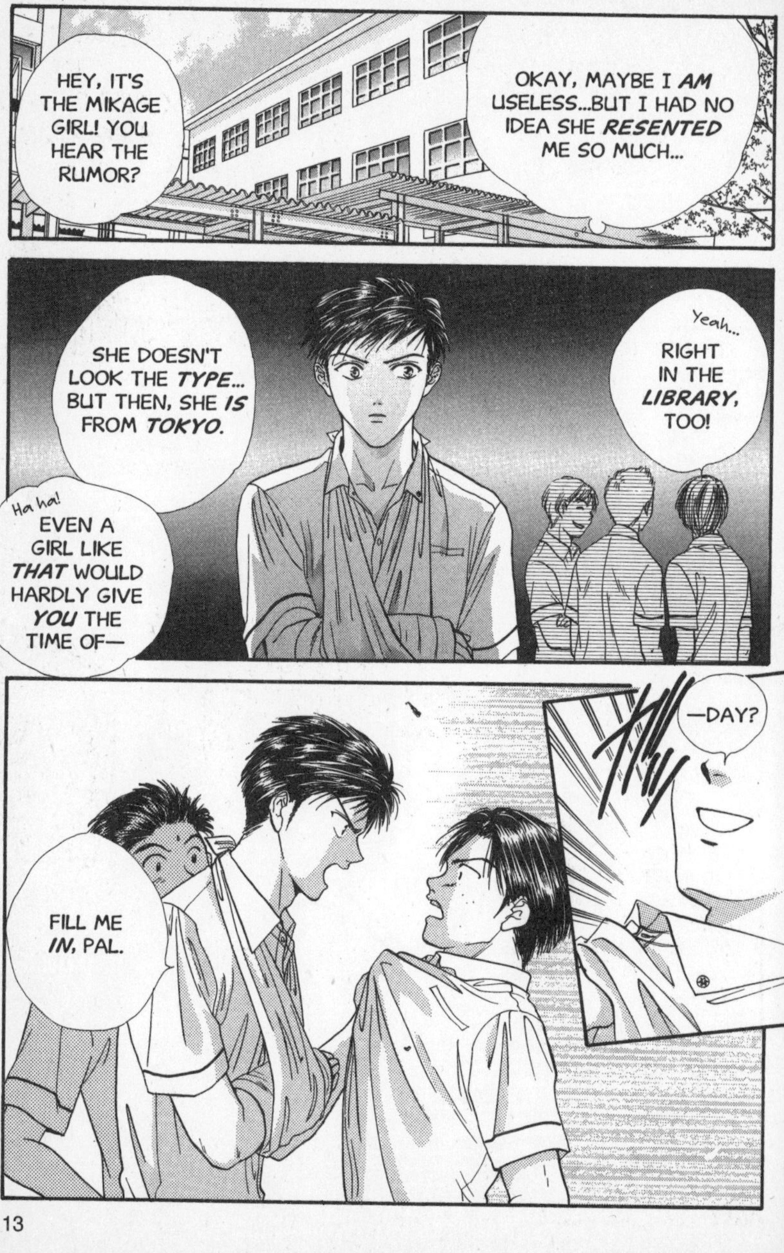
OKAY, MAYBE I *AM* USELESS...BUT I HAD NO IDEA SHE *RESENTED* ME SO MUCH...
HEY, IT'S THE MIKAGE GIRL! YOU HEAR THE RUMOR?
Yeah...
RIGHT IN THE *LIBRARY*, TOO!
SHE DOESN'T LOOK THE *TYPE*... BUT THEN, SHE *IS* FROM *TOKYO*.
Ha ha!
EVEN A GIRL LIKE *THAT* WOULD HARDLY GIVE *YOU* THE TIME OF—
—DAY?
FILL ME *IN*, PAL.

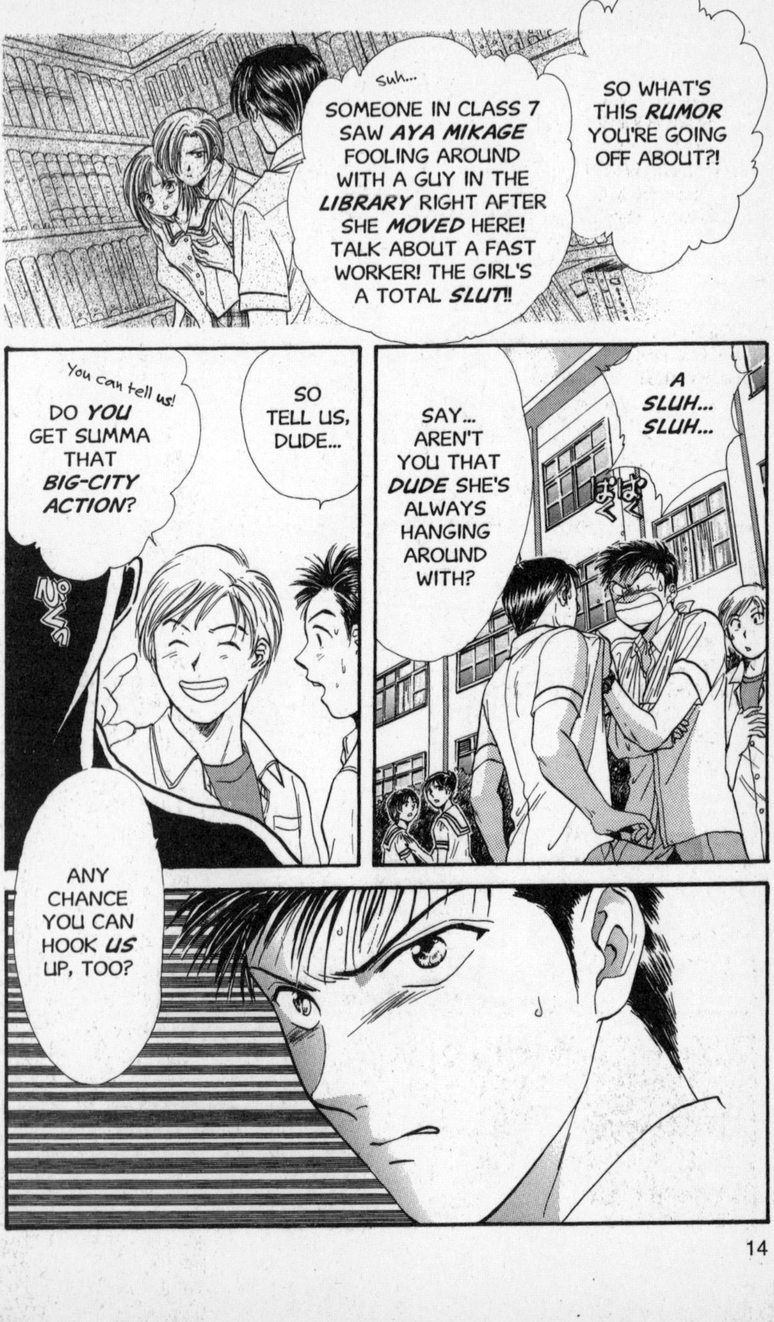
SO WHAT'S THIS RUMOR YOU'RE GOING OFF ABOUT?!
Suh...
SOMEONE IN CLASS 7 SAW AYA MIKAGE FOOLING AROUND WITH A GUY IN THE LIBRARY RIGHT AFTER SHE MOVED HERE! TALK ABOUT A FAST WORKER! THE GIRL'S A TOTAL SLUT!!
A SLUH... SLUH...
ぱくぱく
SAY... AREN'T YOU THAT DUDE SHE'S ALWAYS HANGING AROUND WITH?
SO TELL US, DUDE...
You can tell us!
DO YOU GET SUMMA THAT BIG-CITY ACTION?
ANY CHANCE YOU CAN HOOK US UP, TOO?

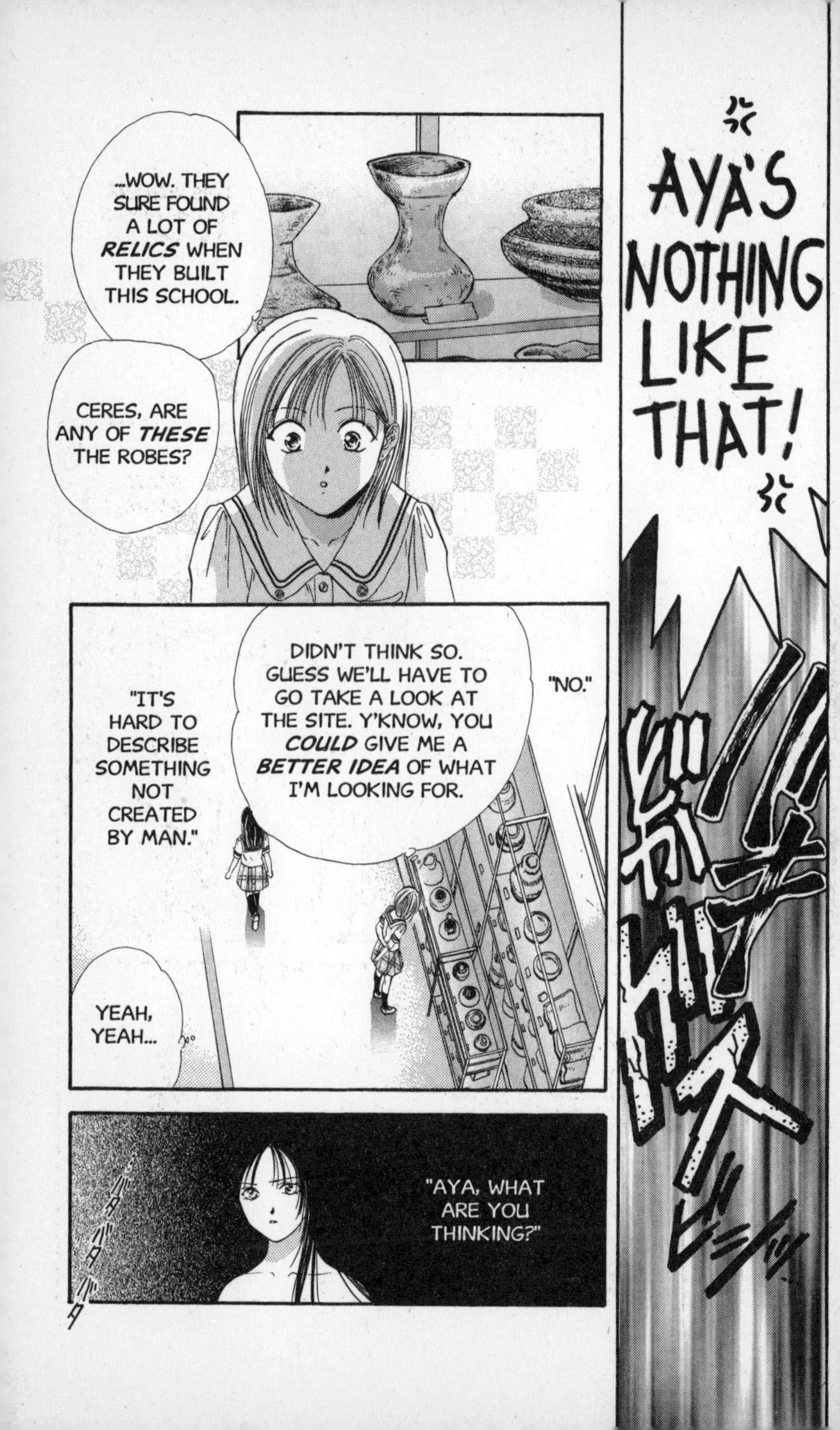
AYA'S NOTHING LIKE THAT!
...WOW. THEY SURE FOUND A LOT OF *RELICS* WHEN THEY BUILT THIS SCHOOL.
CERES, ARE ANY OF *THESE* THE ROBES?
"NO."
DIDN'T THINK SO. GUESS WE'LL HAVE TO GO TAKE A LOOK AT THE SITE. Y'KNOW, YOU *COULD* GIVE ME A *BETTER IDEA* OF WHAT I'M LOOKING FOR.
"IT'S HARD TO DESCRIBE SOMETHING NOT CREATED BY MAN."
YEAH, YEAH...
"AYA, WHAT ARE YOU THINKING?"

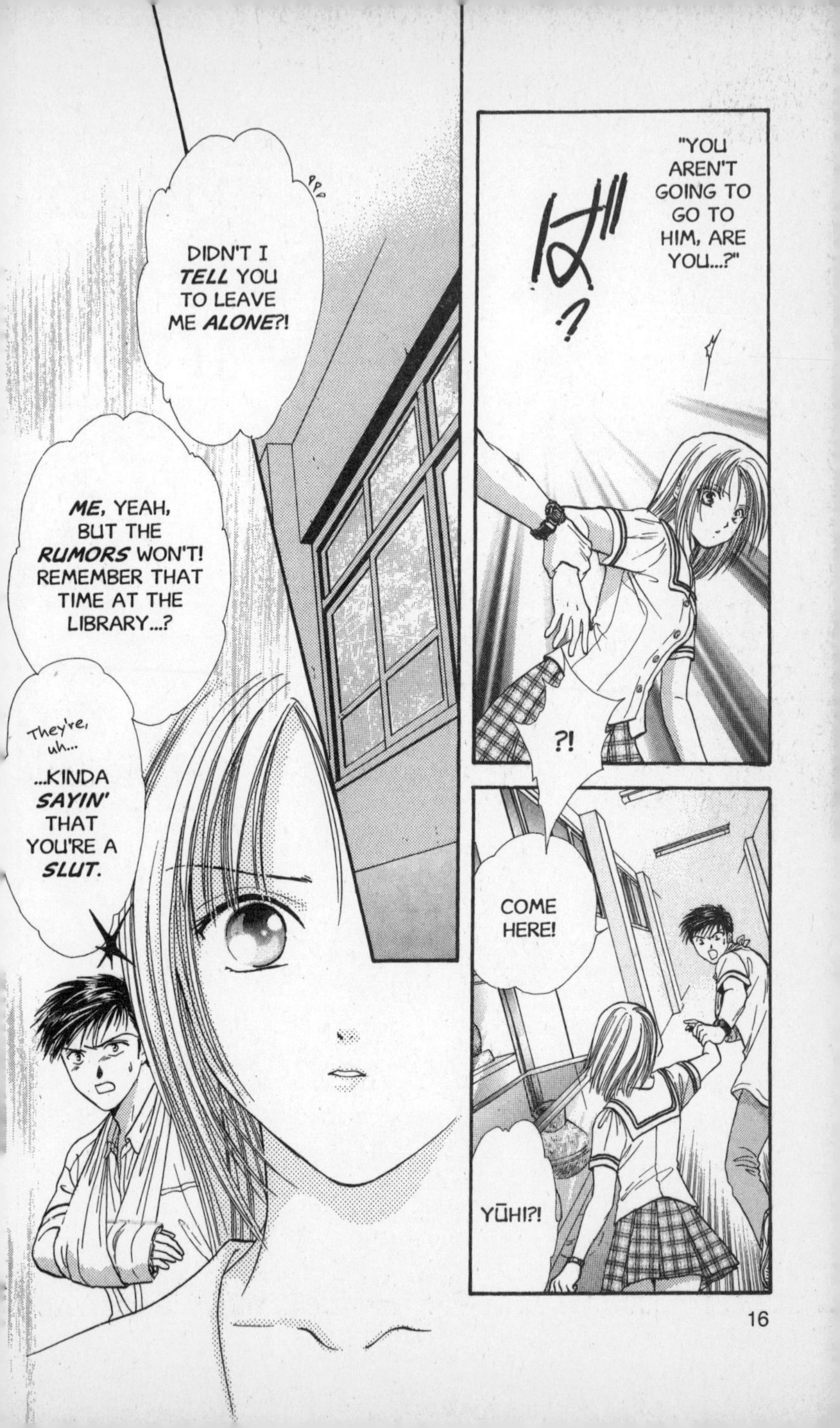
"YOU AREN'T GOING TO GO TO HIM, ARE YOU...?"
ば
?
?!
COME HERE!
YŪHI?!
DIDN'T I *TELL* YOU TO LEAVE ME *ALONE*?!
ME, YEAH, BUT THE *RUMORS* WON'T! REMEMBER THAT TIME AT THE LIBRARY...?
They're, uh...
...KINDA *SAYIN'* THAT YOU'RE A *SLUT*.

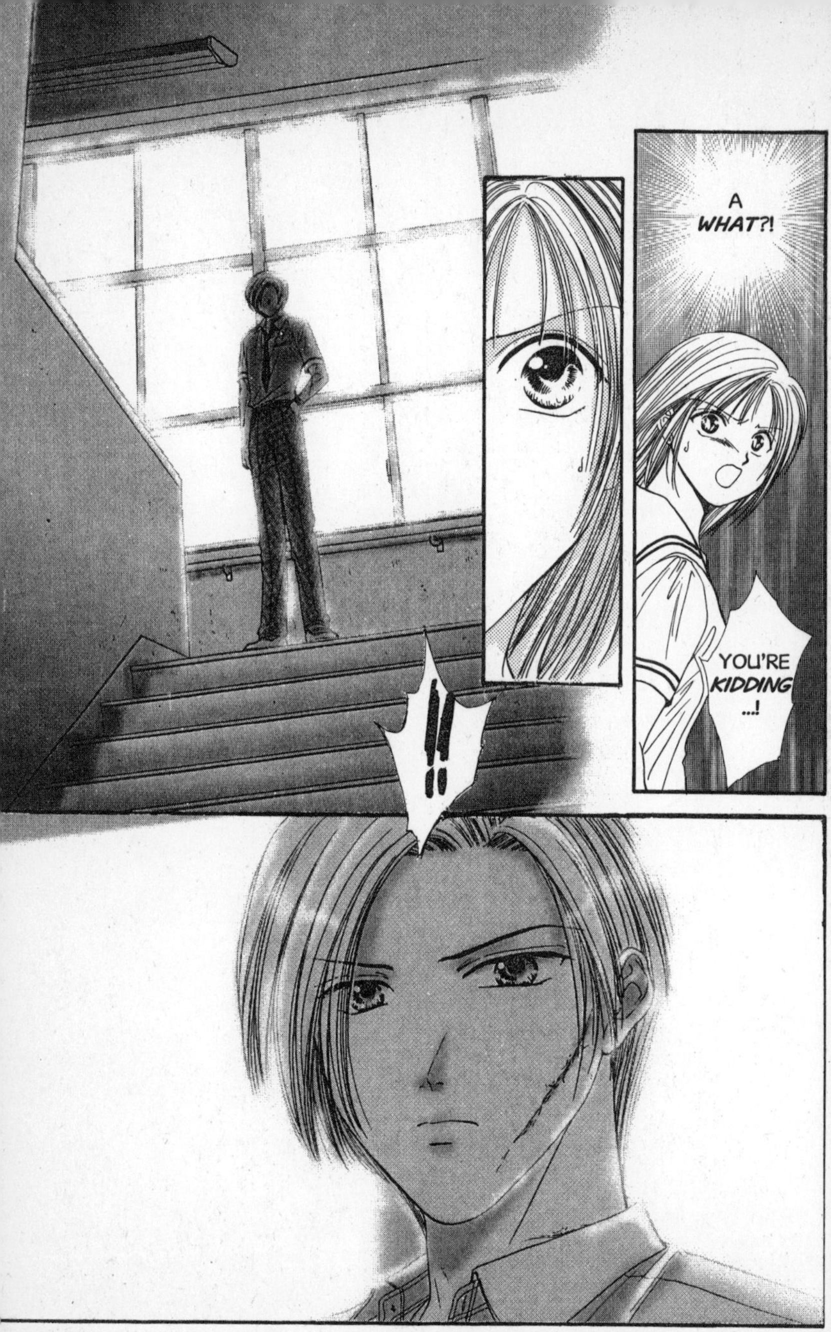
A WHAT?!
YOU'RE KIDDING ...!
!!

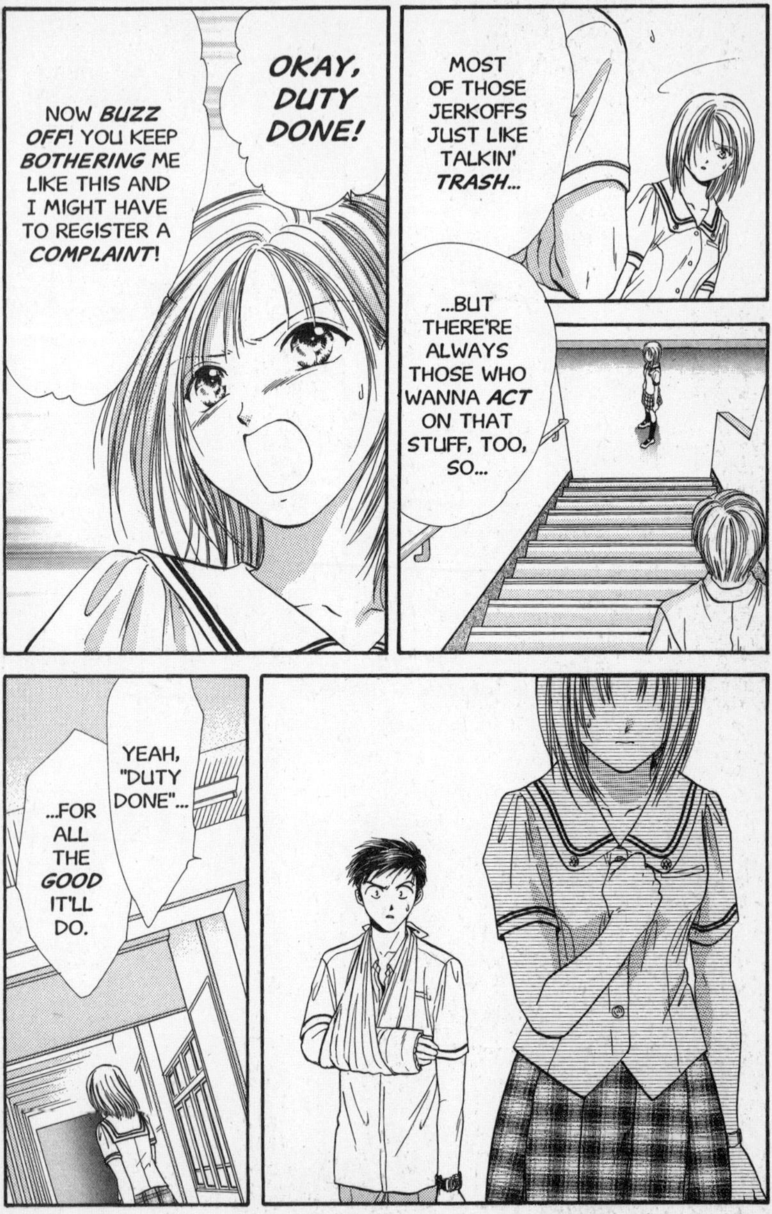
MOST OF THOSE JERKOFFS JUST LIKE TALKIN' TRASH...
...BUT THERE'RE ALWAYS THOSE WHO WANNA ACT ON THAT STUFF, TOO, SO...
OKAY, DUTY DONE!
NOW BUZZ OFF! YOU KEEP BOTHERING ME LIKE THIS AND I MIGHT HAVE TO REGISTER A COMPLAINT!
YEAH, "DUTY DONE"...
...FOR ALL THE GOOD IT'LL DO.

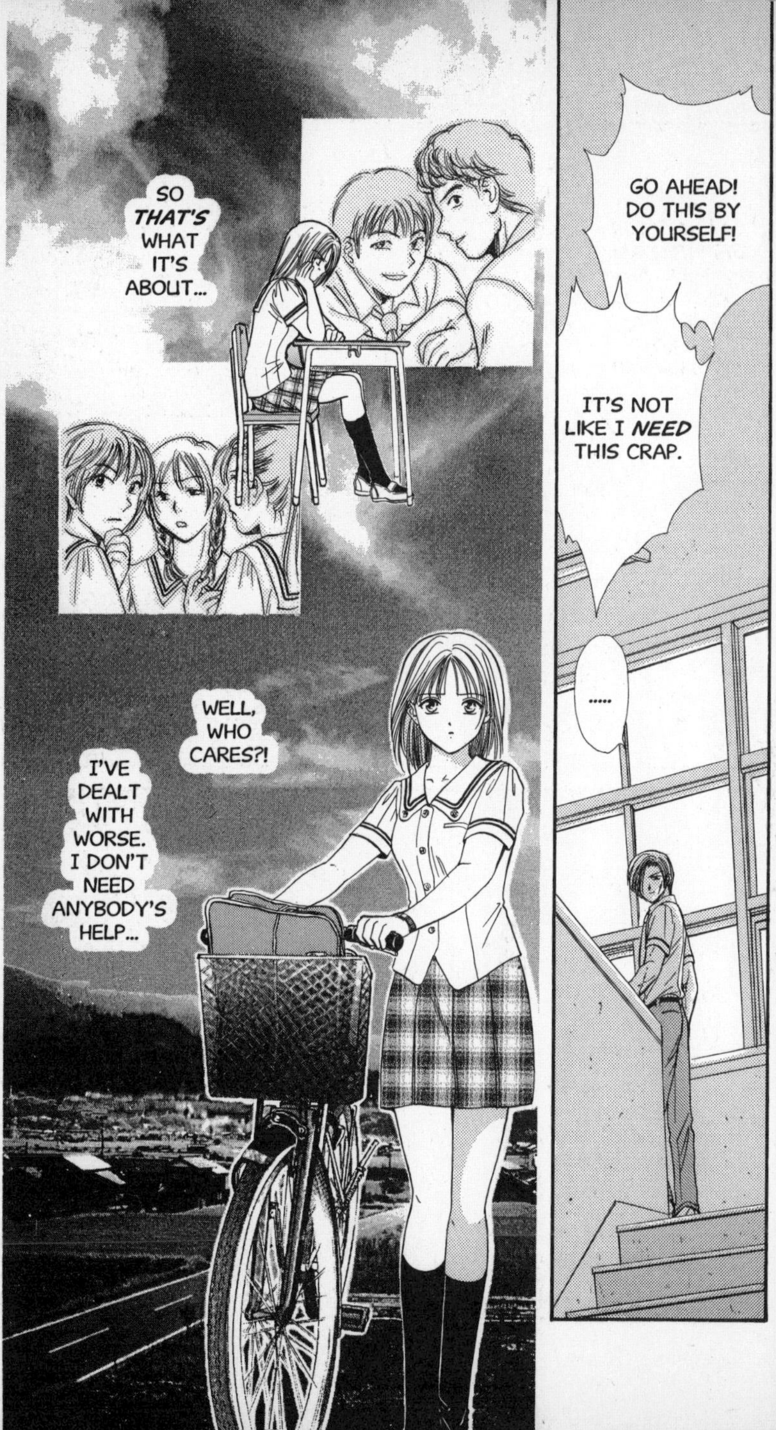
GO AHEAD! DO THIS BY YOURSELF!
IT'S NOT LIKE I *NEED* THIS CRAP.
......
SO *THAT'S* WHAT IT'S ABOUT...
WELL, WHO CARES?!
I'VE DEALT WITH WORSE. I DON'T NEED ANYBODY'S HELP...

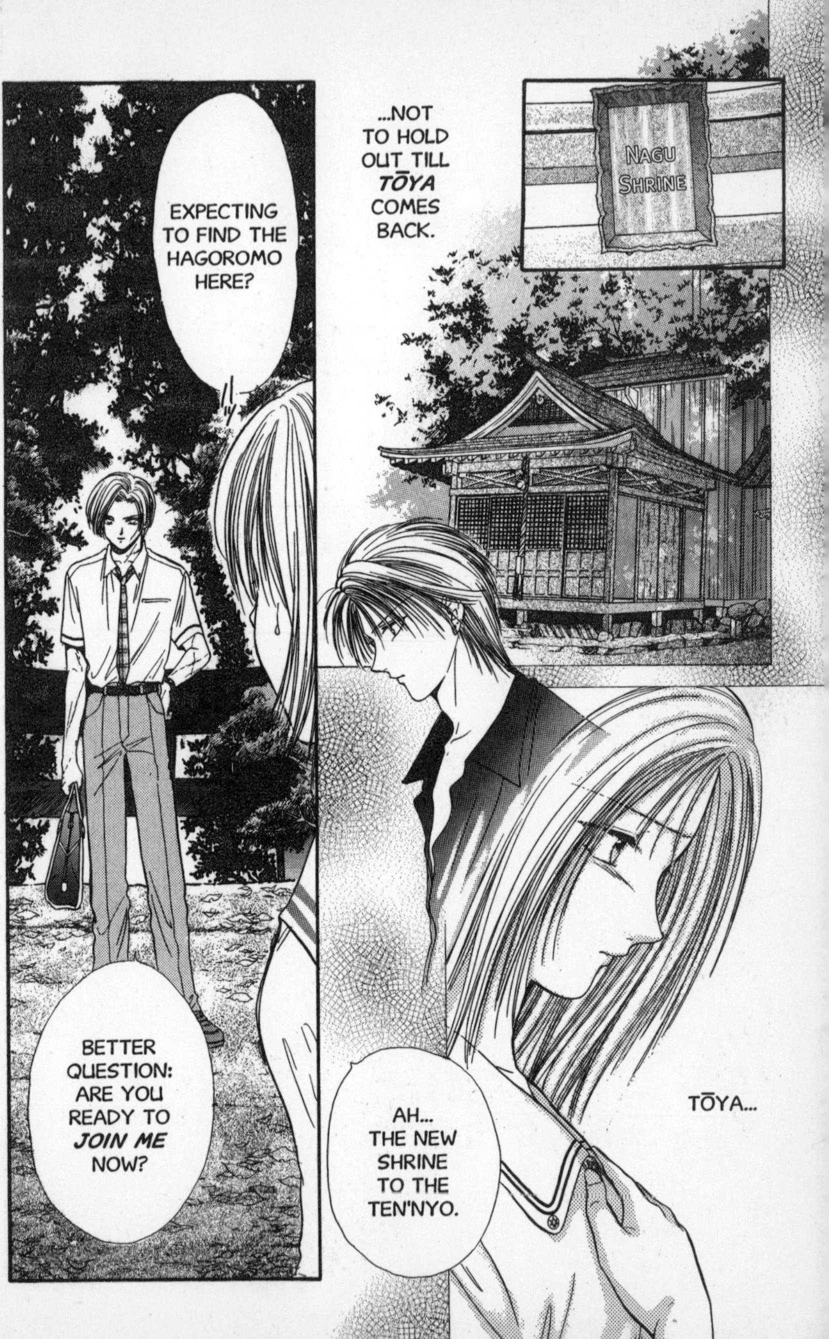
NAGU SHRINE
...NOT TO HOLD OUT TILL *TŌYA* COMES BACK.
TŌYA...
AH... THE NEW SHRINE TO THE TEN'NYO.
EXPECTING TO FIND THE HAGOROMO HERE?
BETTER QUESTION: ARE YOU READY TO *JOIN ME* NOW?

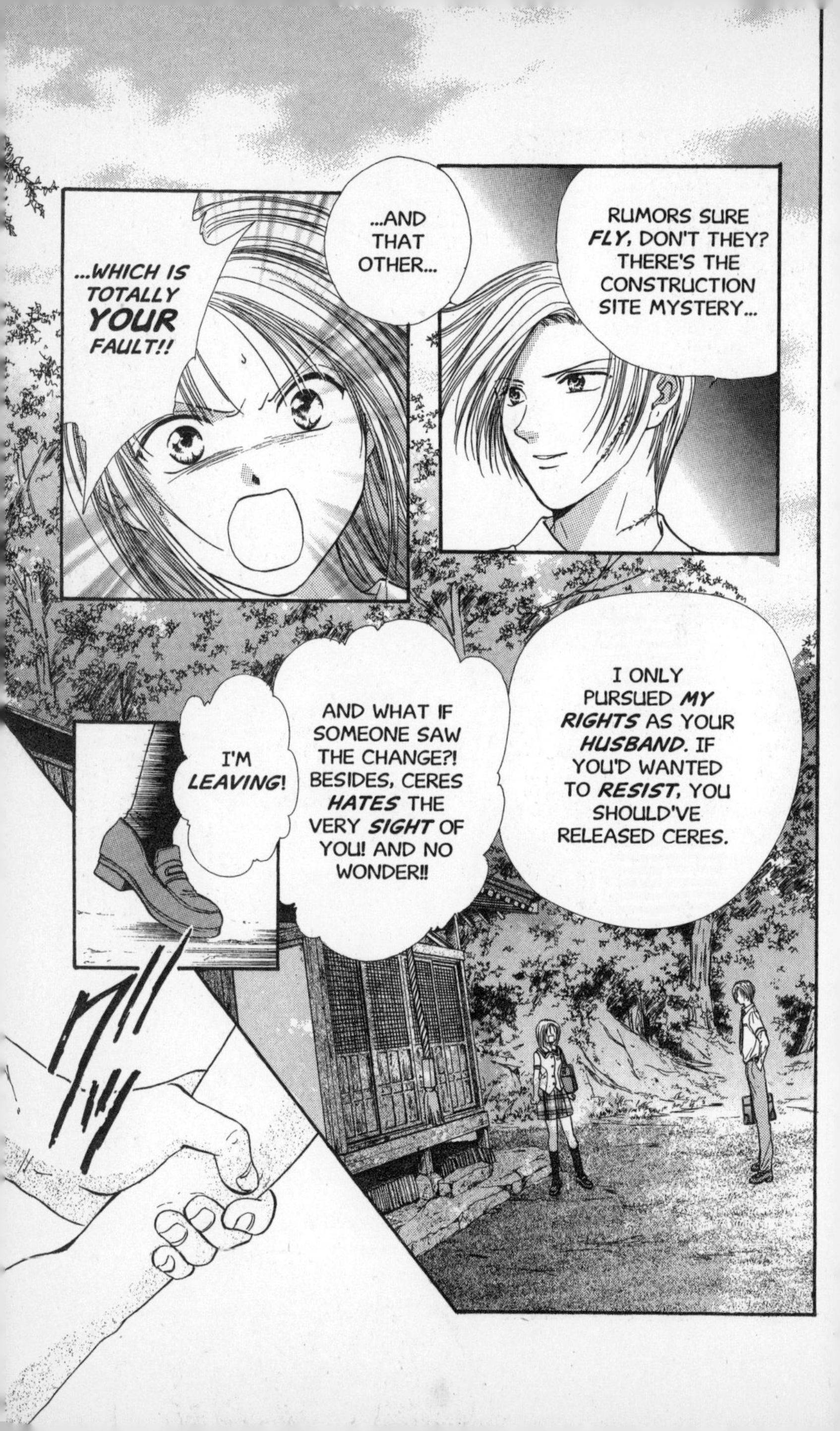
RUMORS SURE FLY, DON'T THEY? THERE'S THE CONSTRUCTION SITE MYSTERY...
...AND THAT OTHER...
...WHICH IS TOTALLY YOUR FAULT!!
I ONLY PURSUED MY RIGHTS AS YOUR HUSBAND. IF YOU'D WANTED TO RESIST, YOU SHOULD'VE RELEASED CERES.
AND WHAT IF SOMEONE SAW THE CHANGE?! BESIDES, CERES HATES THE VERY SIGHT OF YOU! AND NO WONDER!!
I'M LEAVING!

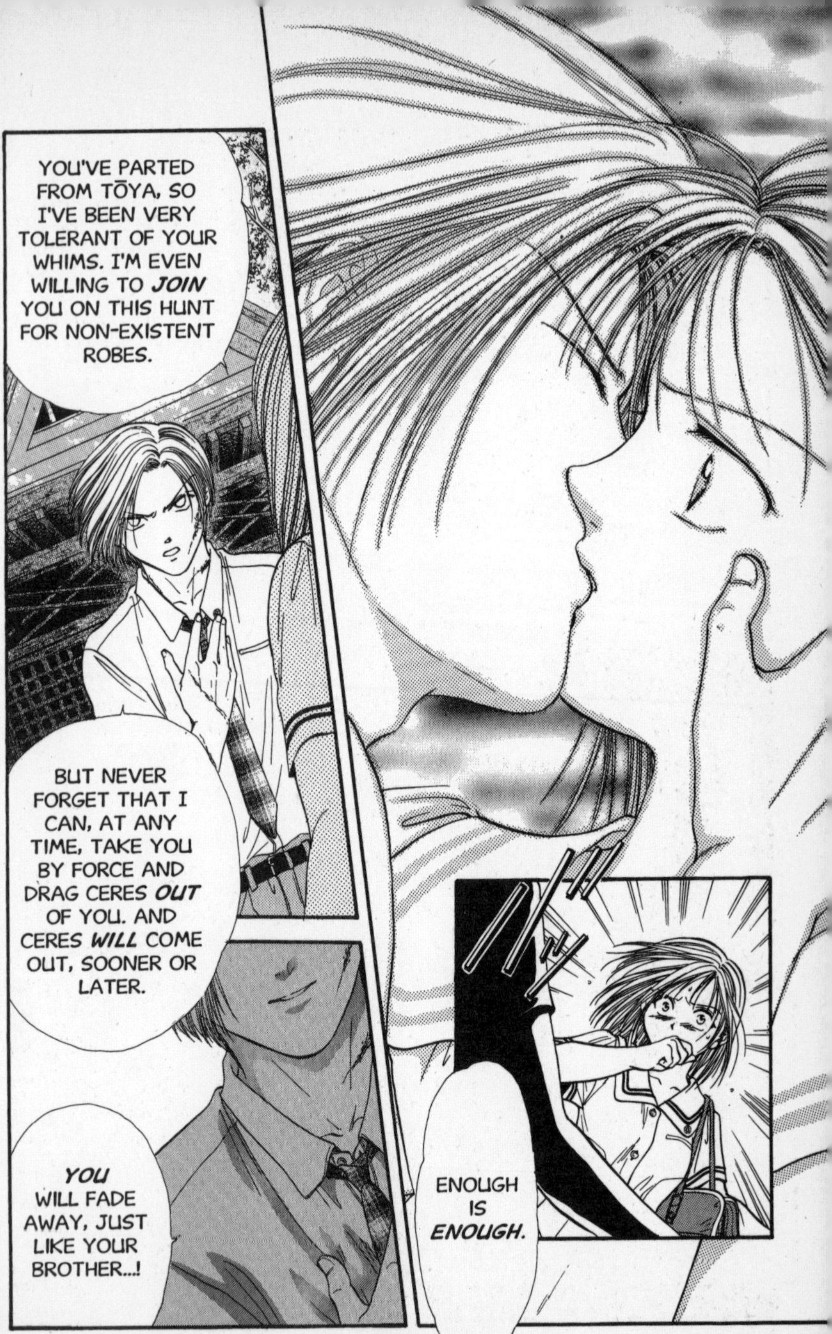
ENOUGH IS ENOUGH.
YOU'VE PARTED FROM TŌYA, SO I'VE BEEN VERY TOLERANT OF YOUR WHIMS. I'M EVEN WILLING TO JOIN YOU ON THIS HUNT FOR NON-EXISTENT ROBES.
BUT NEVER FORGET THAT I CAN, AT ANY TIME, TAKE YOU BY FORCE AND DRAG CERES OUT OF YOU. AND CERES WILL COME OUT, SOONER OR LATER.
YOU WILL FADE AWAY, JUST LIKE YOUR BROTHER...!

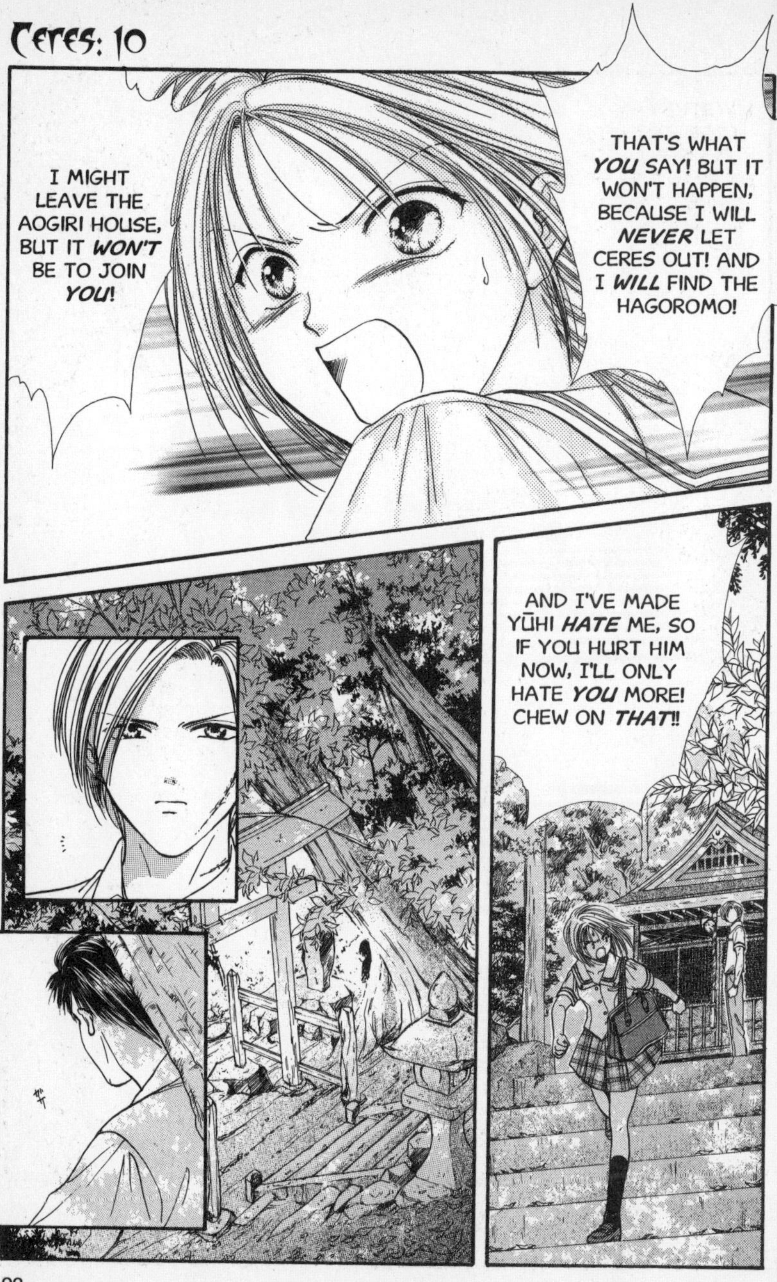
THAT'S WHAT YOU SAY! BUT IT WON'T HAPPEN, BECAUSE I WILL NEVER LET CERES OUT! AND I WILL FIND THE HAGOROMO!
I MIGHT LEAVE THE AOGIRI HOUSE, BUT IT WON'T BE TO JOIN YOU!
AND I'VE MADE YŪHI HATE ME, SO IF YOU HURT HIM NOW, I'LL ONLY HATE YOU MORE! CHEW ON THAT!!

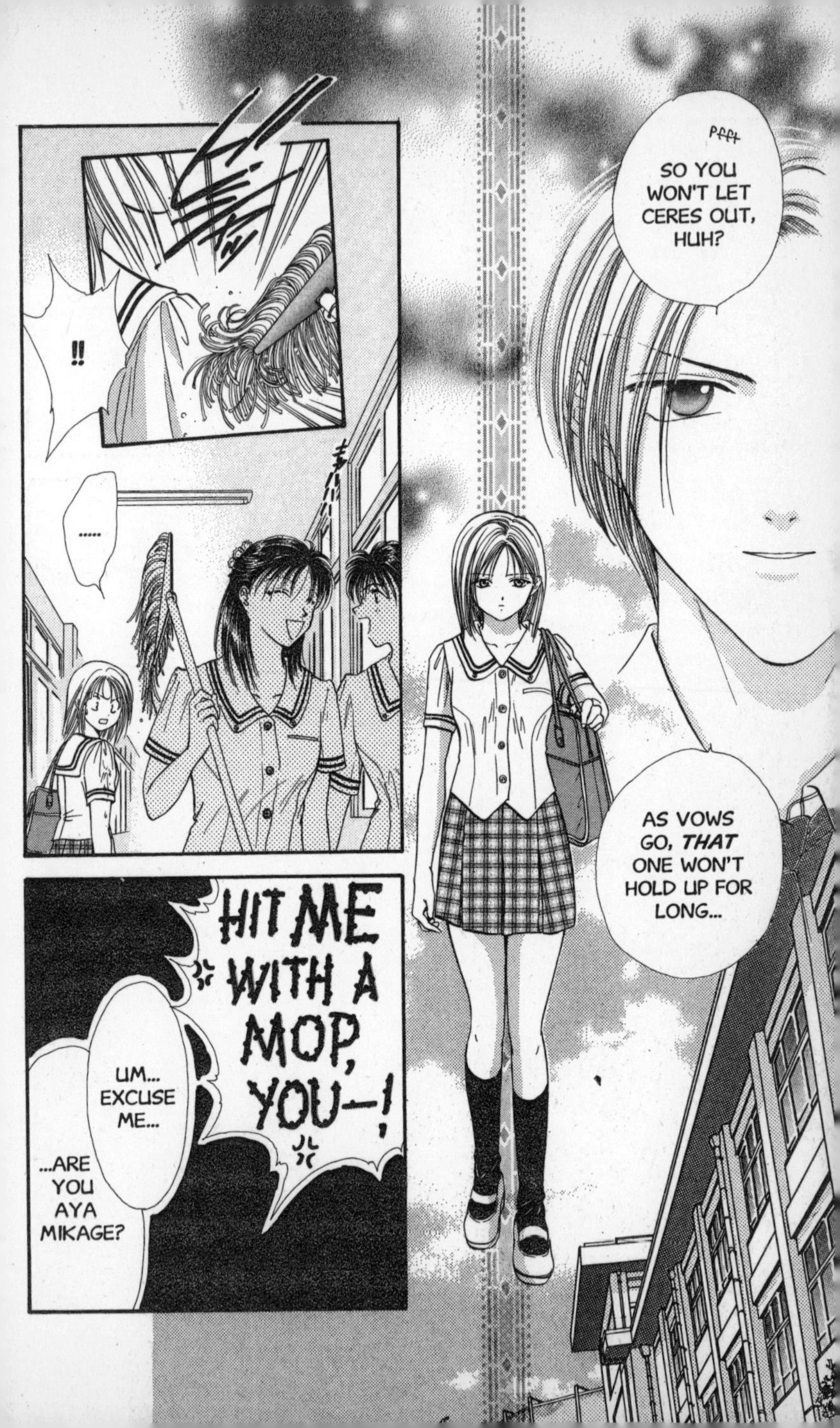
Pfft
SO YOU WON'T LET CERES OUT, HUH?
AS VOWS GO, *THAT* ONE WON'T HOLD UP FOR LONG...
!!
......
HIT ME WITH A MOP, YOU—!
UM... EXCUSE ME...
...ARE YOU AYA MIKAGE?

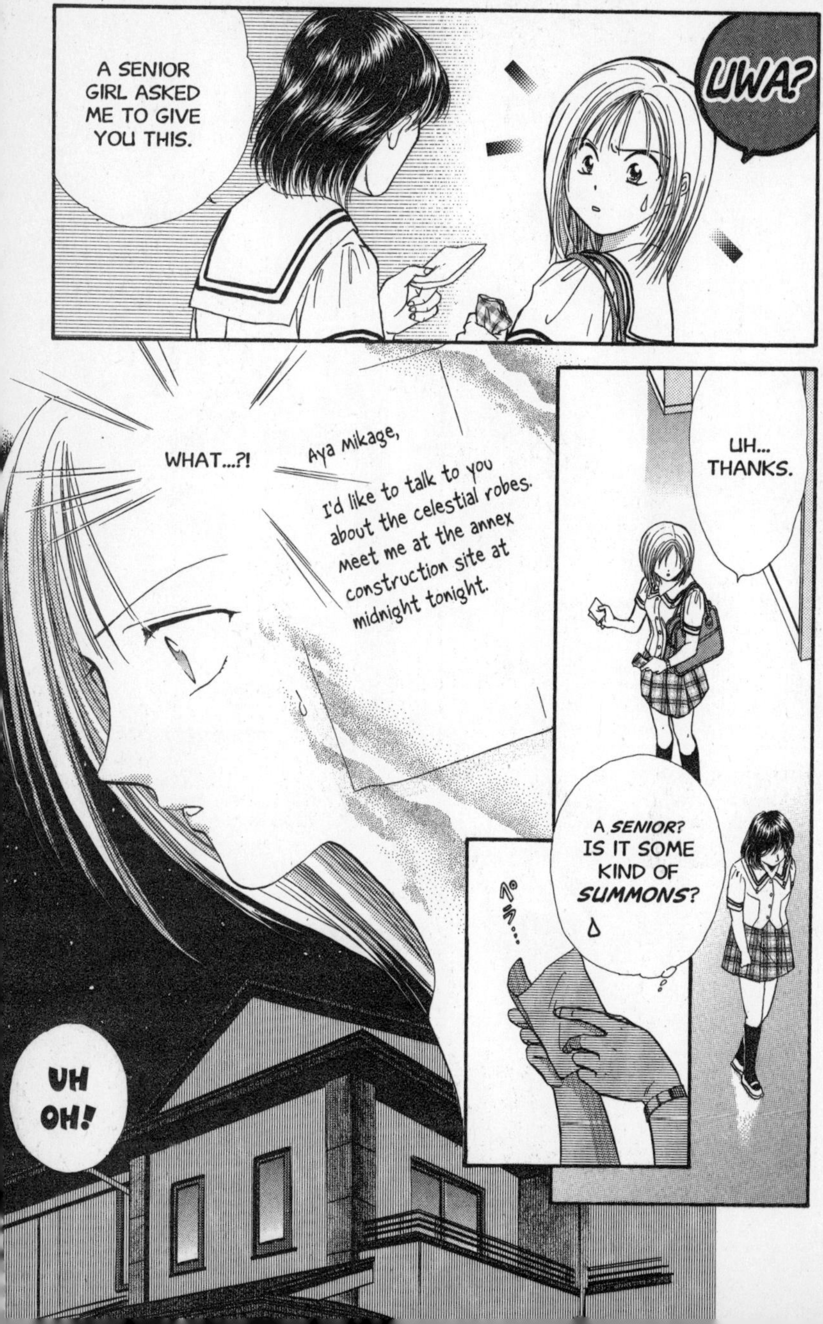
UWA?
A SENIOR GIRL ASKED ME TO GIVE YOU THIS.
UH... THANKS.
A *SENIOR*? IS IT SOME KIND OF *SUMMONS*?
ぺら...
WHAT...?!
Aya Mikage,
I'd like to talk to you about the celestial robes. Meet me at the annex construction site at midnight tonight.
UH OH!

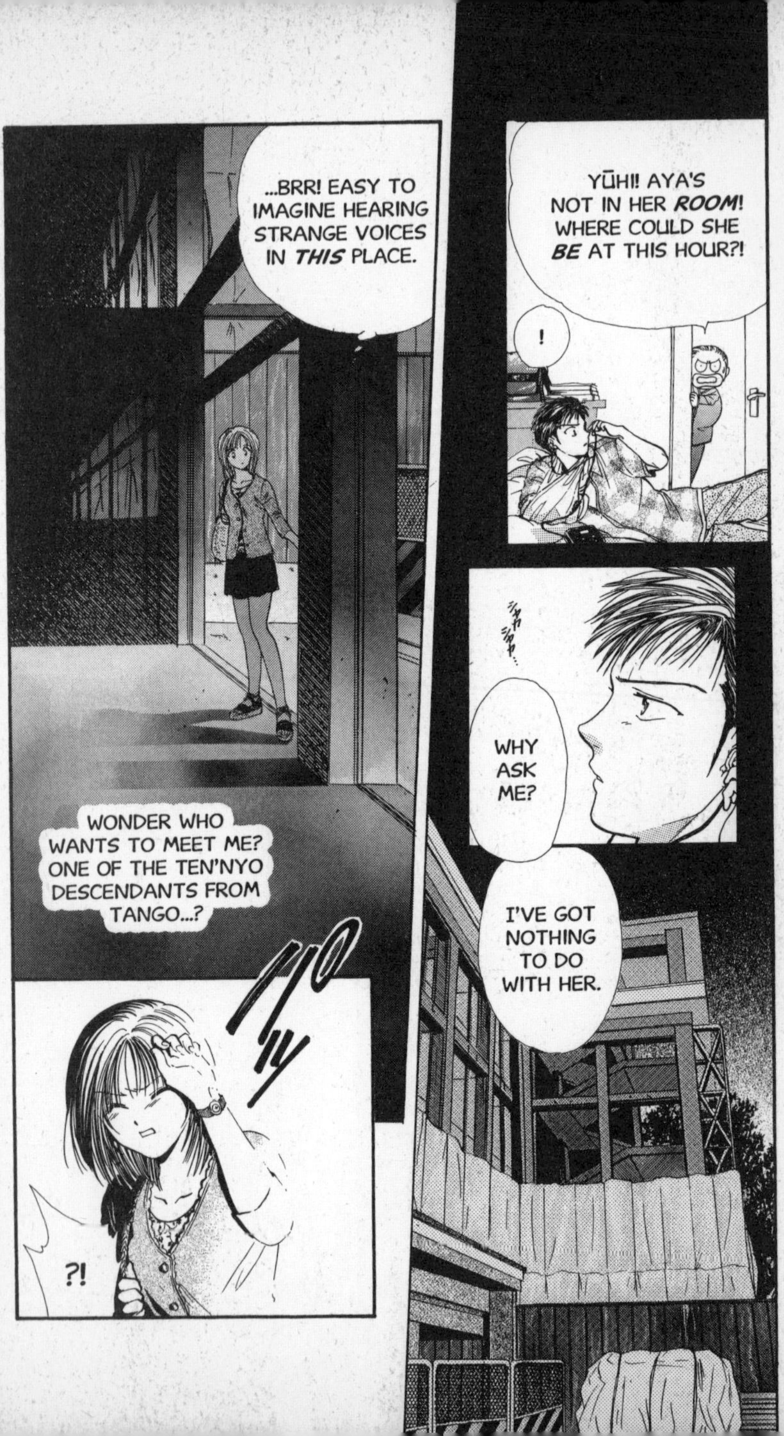
YŪHI! AYA'S NOT IN HER *ROOM*! WHERE COULD SHE *BE* AT THIS HOUR?!
!
WHY ASK ME?
I'VE GOT NOTHING TO DO WITH HER.
...BRR! EASY TO IMAGINE HEARING STRANGE VOICES IN *THIS* PLACE.
WONDER WHO WANTS TO MEET ME? ONE OF THE TEN'NYO DESCENDANTS FROM TANGO...?
?!

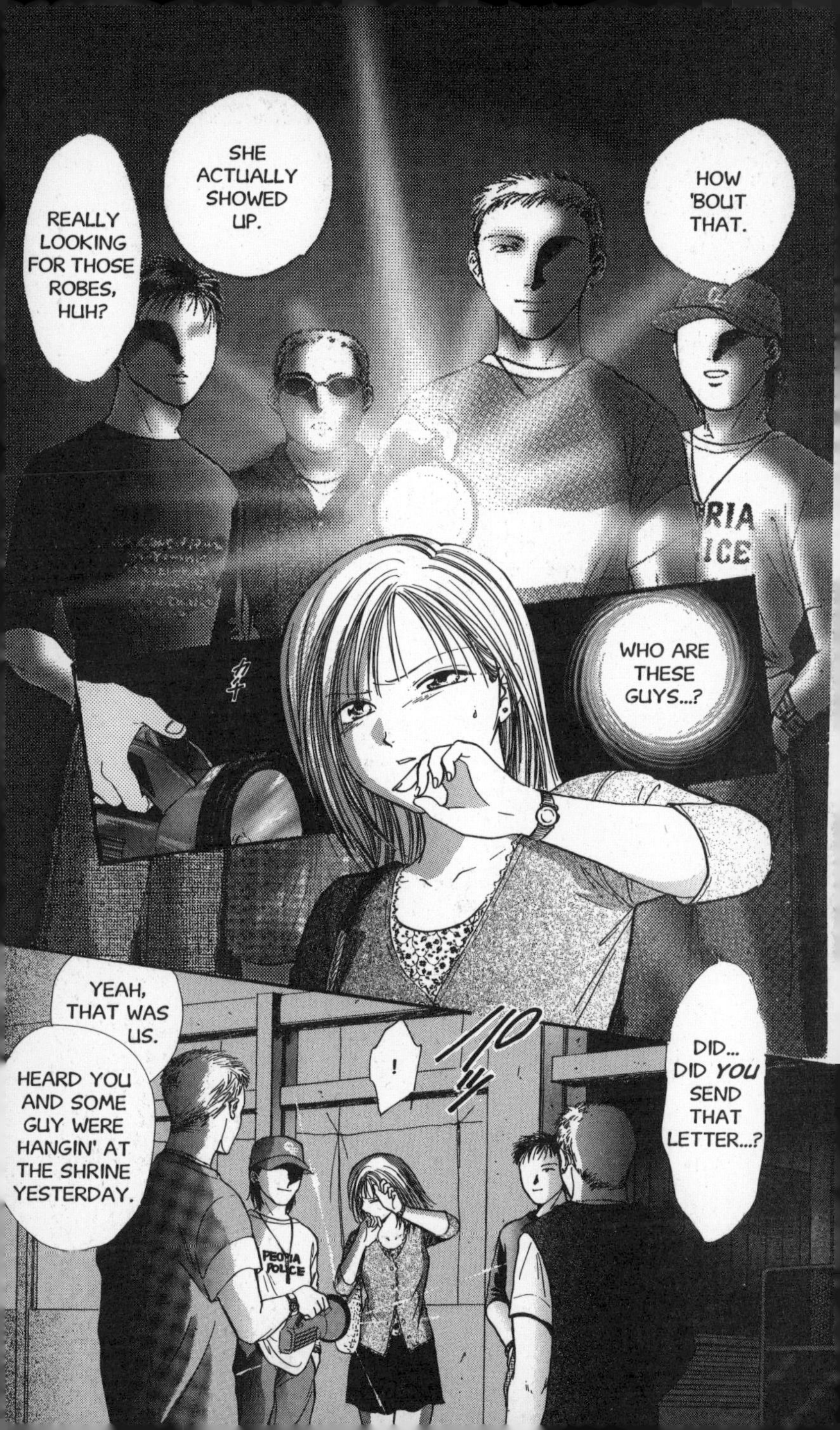
HOW 'BOUT THAT.
SHE ACTUALLY SHOWED UP.
REALLY LOOKING FOR THOSE ROBES, HUH?
WHO ARE THESE GUYS...?
DID... DID *YOU* SEND THAT LETTER...?
!
YEAH, THAT WAS US.
HEARD YOU AND SOME GUY WERE HANGIN' AT THE SHRINE YESTERDAY.

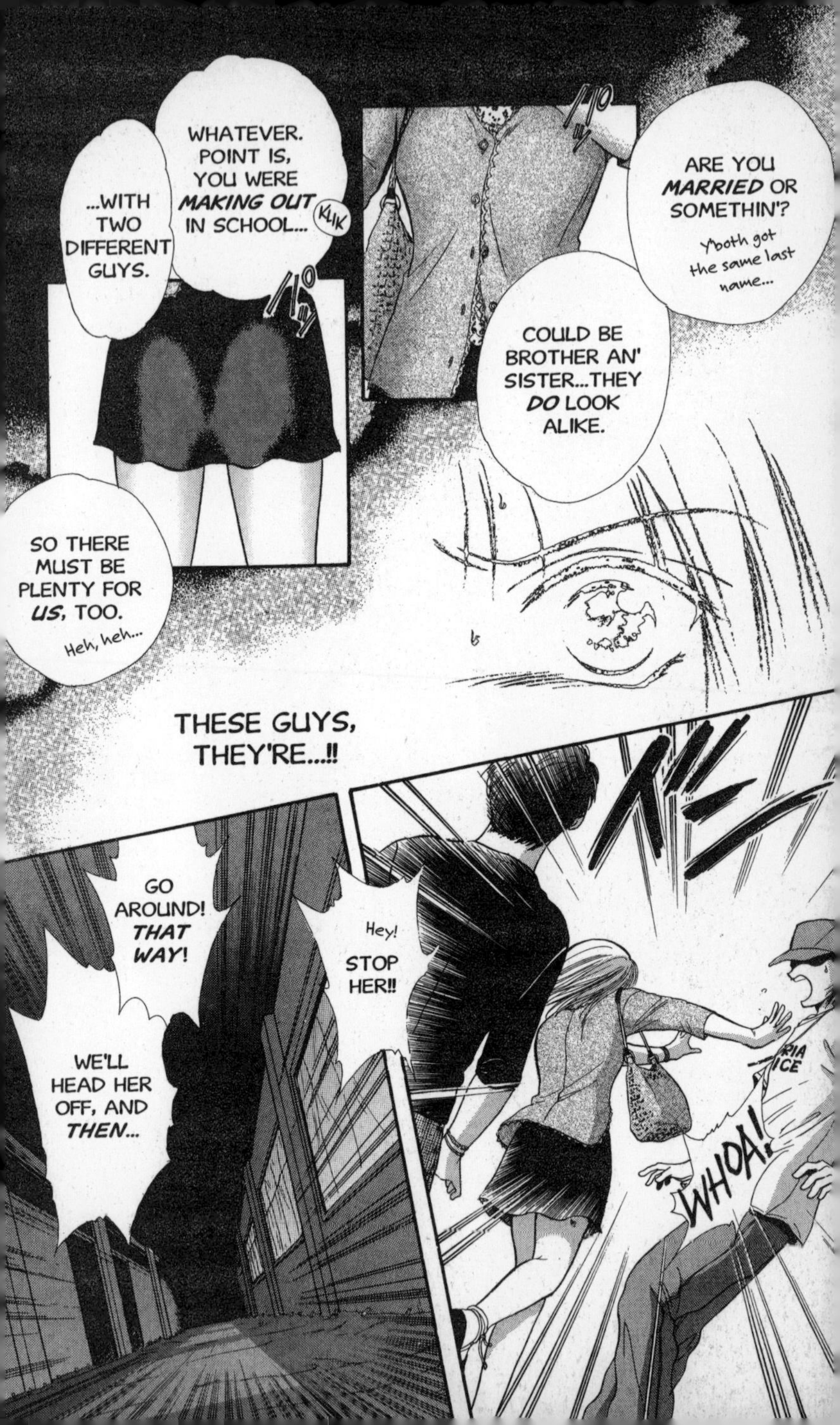
ARE YOU MARRIED OR SOMETHIN'?
Y'both got the same last name...
COULD BE BROTHER AN' SISTER...THEY DO LOOK ALIKE.
WHATEVER. POINT IS, YOU WERE MAKING OUT IN SCHOOL...
KLIK
...WITH TWO DIFFERENT GUYS.
SO THERE MUST BE PLENTY FOR US, TOO.
Heh, heh...
THESE GUYS, THEY'RE...!!
WHOA!
Hey!
STOP HER!!
GO AROUND! THAT WAY!
WE'LL HEAD HER OFF, AND THEN...

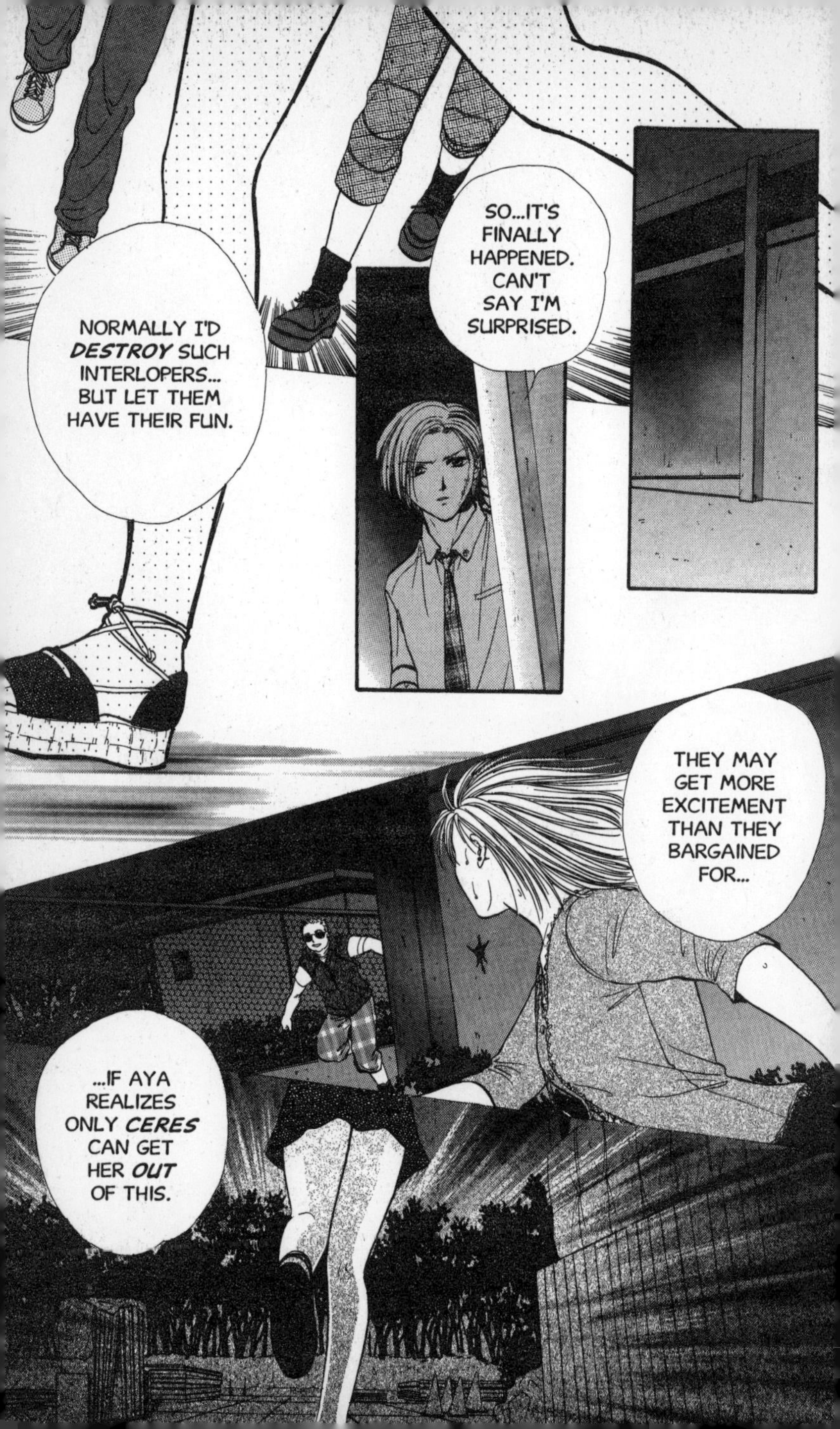
SO...IT'S FINALLY HAPPENED. CAN'T SAY I'M SURPRISED.
NORMALLY I'D *DESTROY* SUCH INTERLOPERS... BUT LET THEM HAVE THEIR FUN.
THEY MAY GET MORE EXCITEMENT THAN THEY BARGAINED FOR...
...IF AYA REALIZES ONLY *CERES* CAN GET HER *OUT* OF THIS.

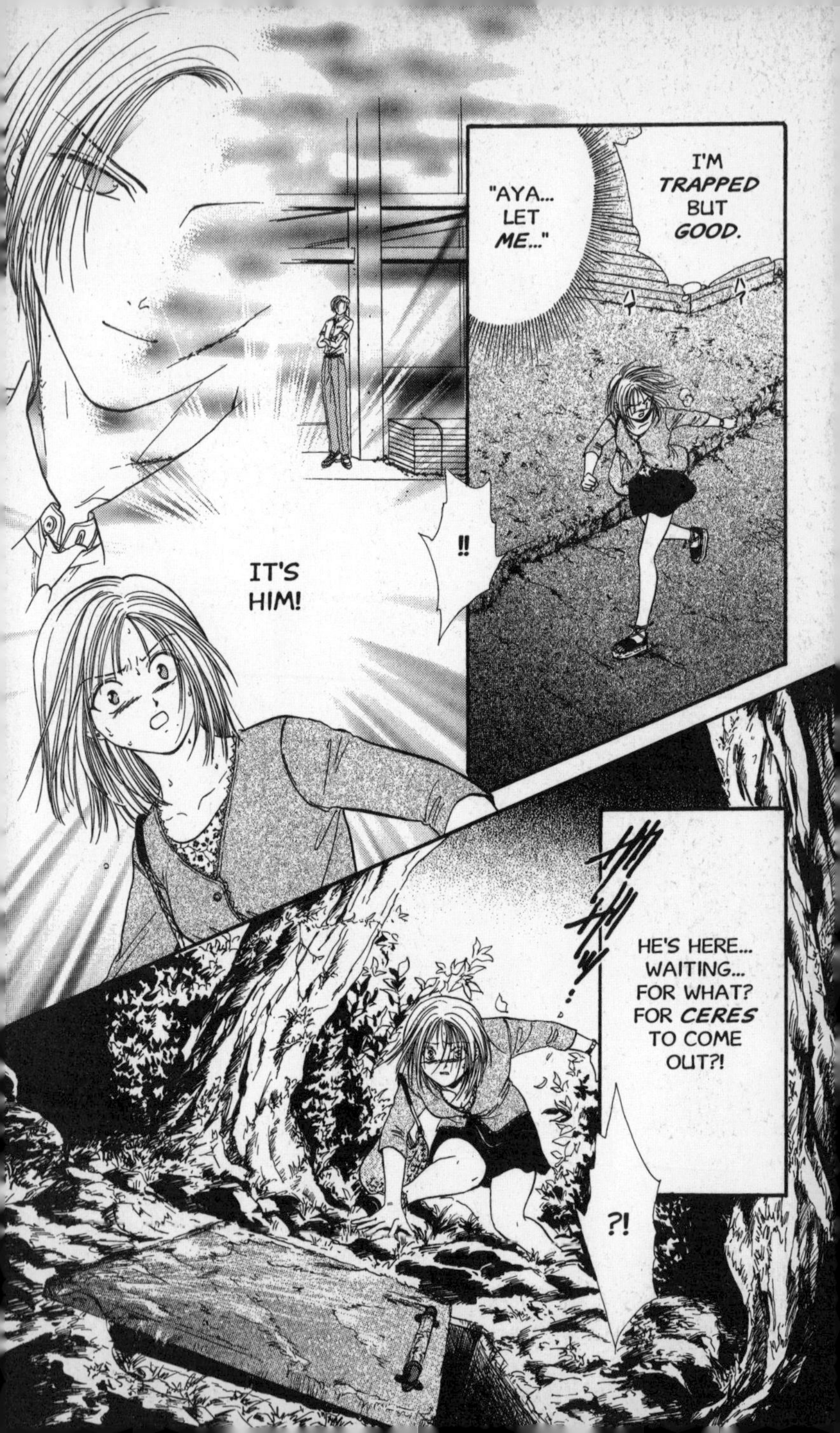
I'M TRAPPED BUT GOOD.
"AYA... LET ME..."
!!
IT'S HIM!
HE'S HERE... WAITING... FOR WHAT? FOR CERES TO COME OUT?!
?!

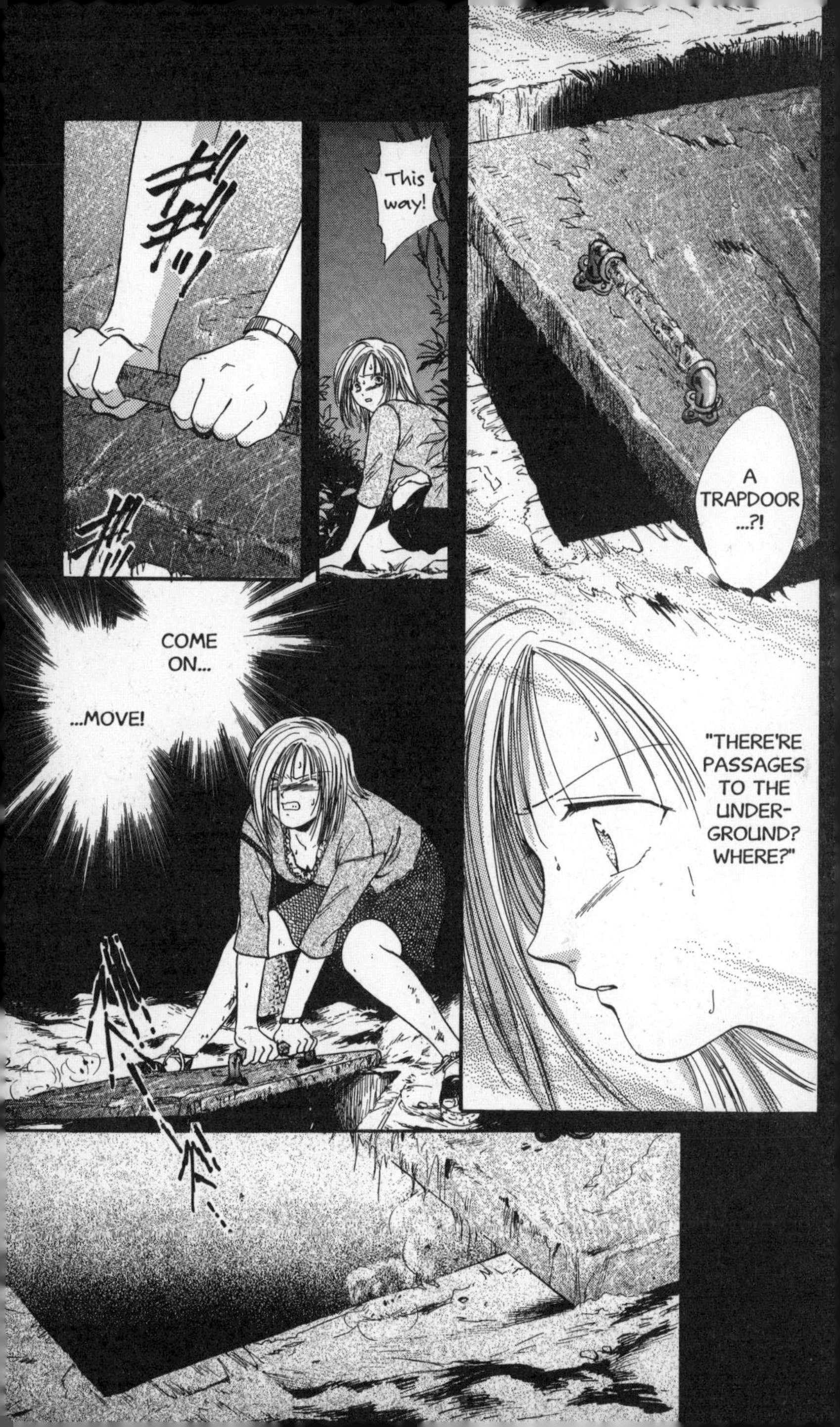
A TRAPDOOR ...?!
This way!
"THERE'RE PASSAGES TO THE UNDER-GROUND? WHERE?"
COME ON...
...MOVE!

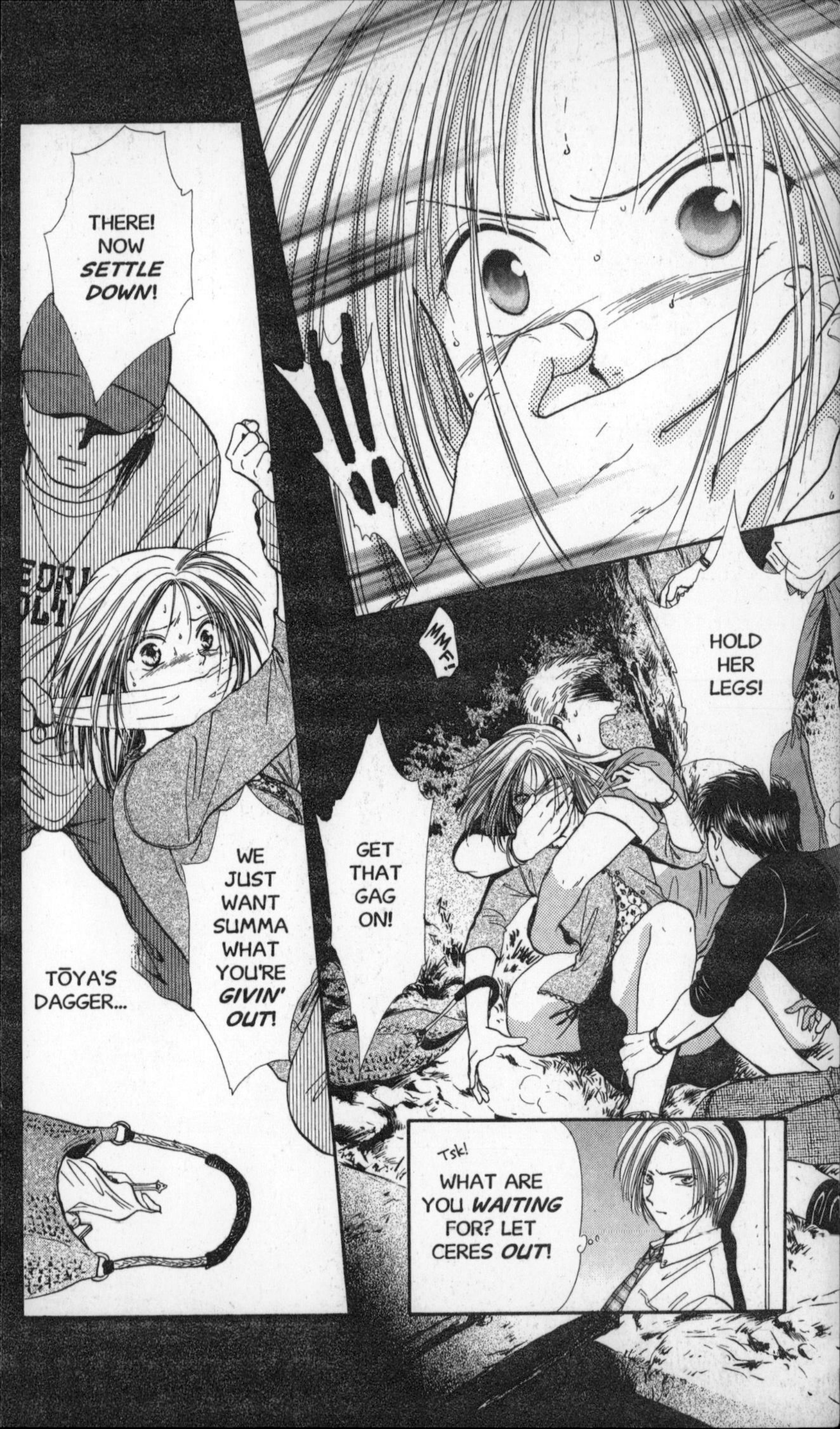
HOLD HER LEGS!
MMF!
GET THAT GAG ON!
Tsk!
WHAT ARE YOU WAITING FOR? LET CERES OUT!
THERE! NOW SETTLE DOWN!
WE JUST WANT SUMMA WHAT YOU'RE GIVIN' OUT!
TŌYA'S DAGGER...

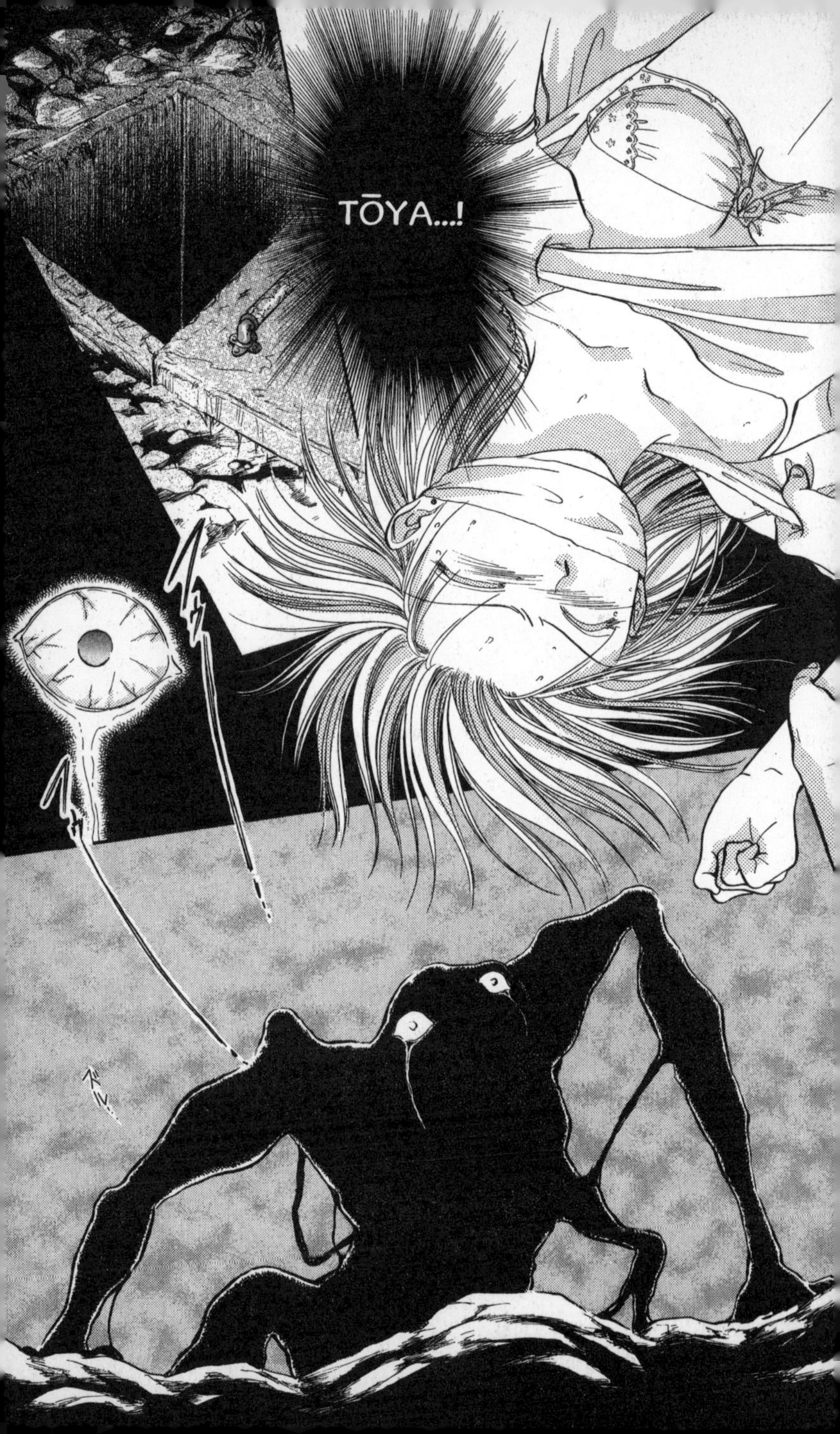
TŌYA...!

BIRTHDAY 7/25 (Leo)

BLOOD TYPE A

HEIGHT: 5'7"   WAIST: 22"
CHEST: 31"   HIPS: 32"

HOBBIES Composing, Karate, Guitar

SPECIALTIES Scuba Diving, Doing
Stuff with my Voice

SHURO TSUKASA

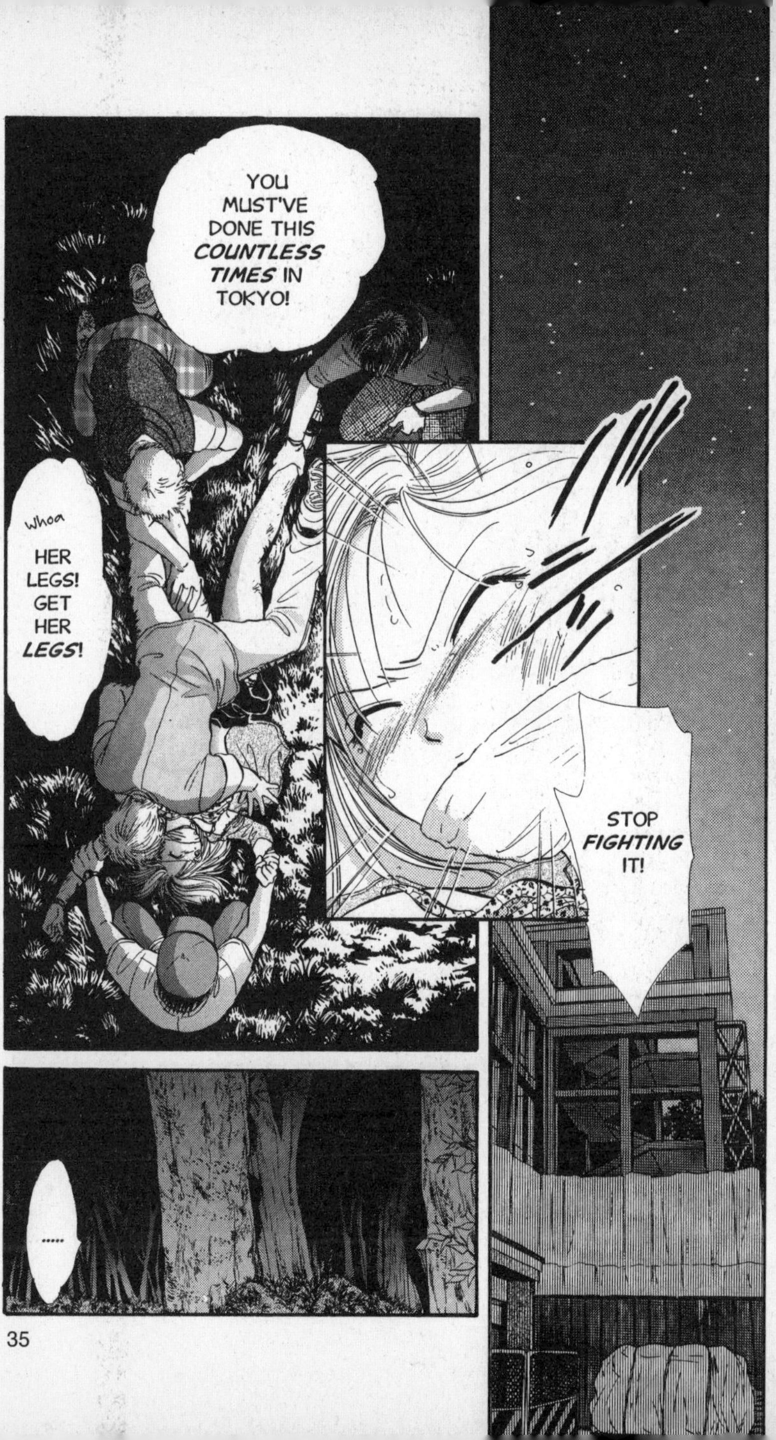
STOP *FIGHTING* IT!
YOU MUST'VE DONE THIS ***COUNTLESS TIMES*** IN TOKYO!
Whoa
HER LEGS! GET HER ***LEGS***!
......

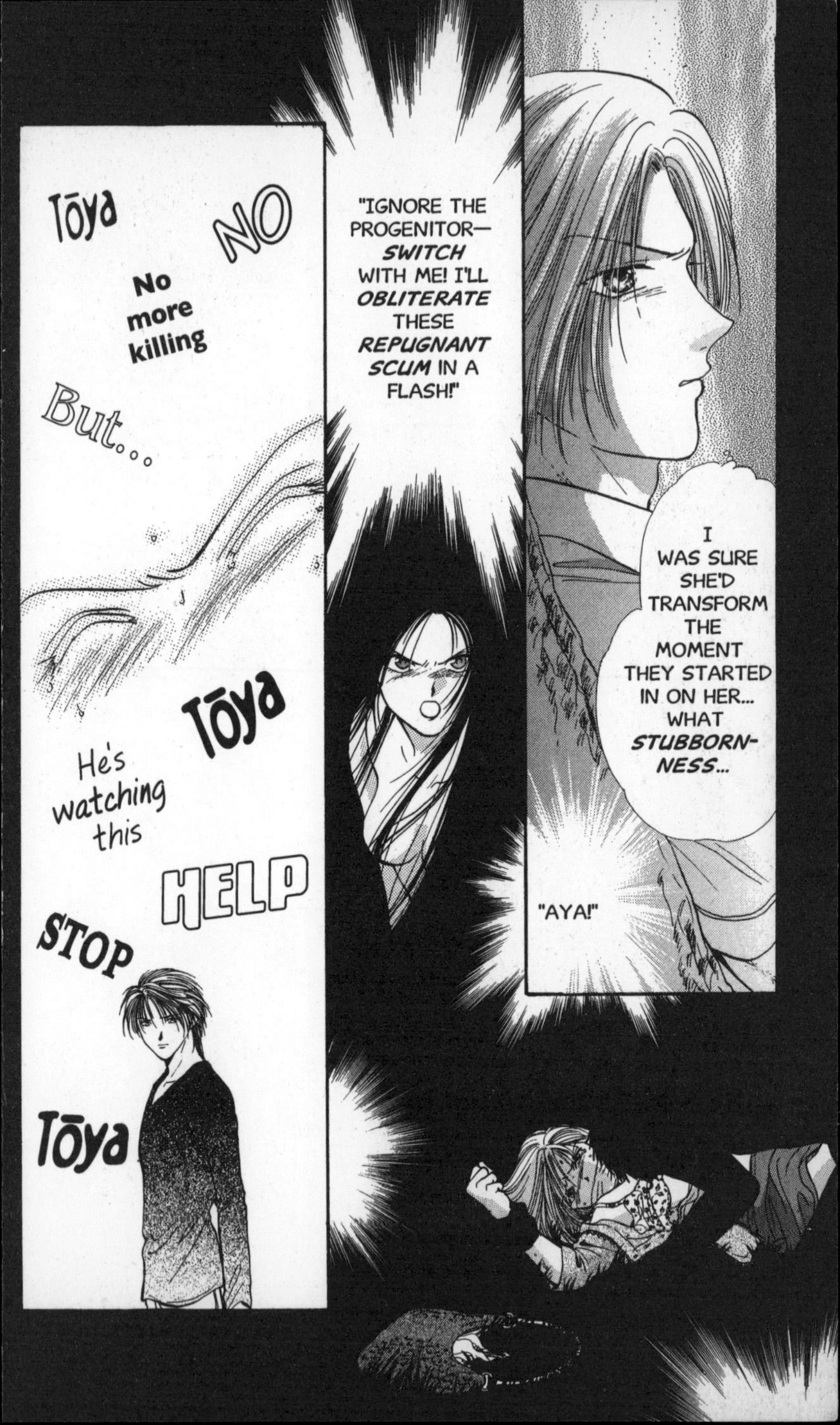
I WAS SURE SHE'D TRANSFORM THE MOMENT THEY STARTED IN ON HER... WHAT STUBBORN-NESS...
"AYA!"
"IGNORE THE PROGENITOR—SWITCH WITH ME! I'LL OBLITERATE THESE REPUGNANT SCUM IN A FLASH!"
NO
Tōya
No more killing
But...
Tōya
He's watching this
HELP
STOP
Tōya

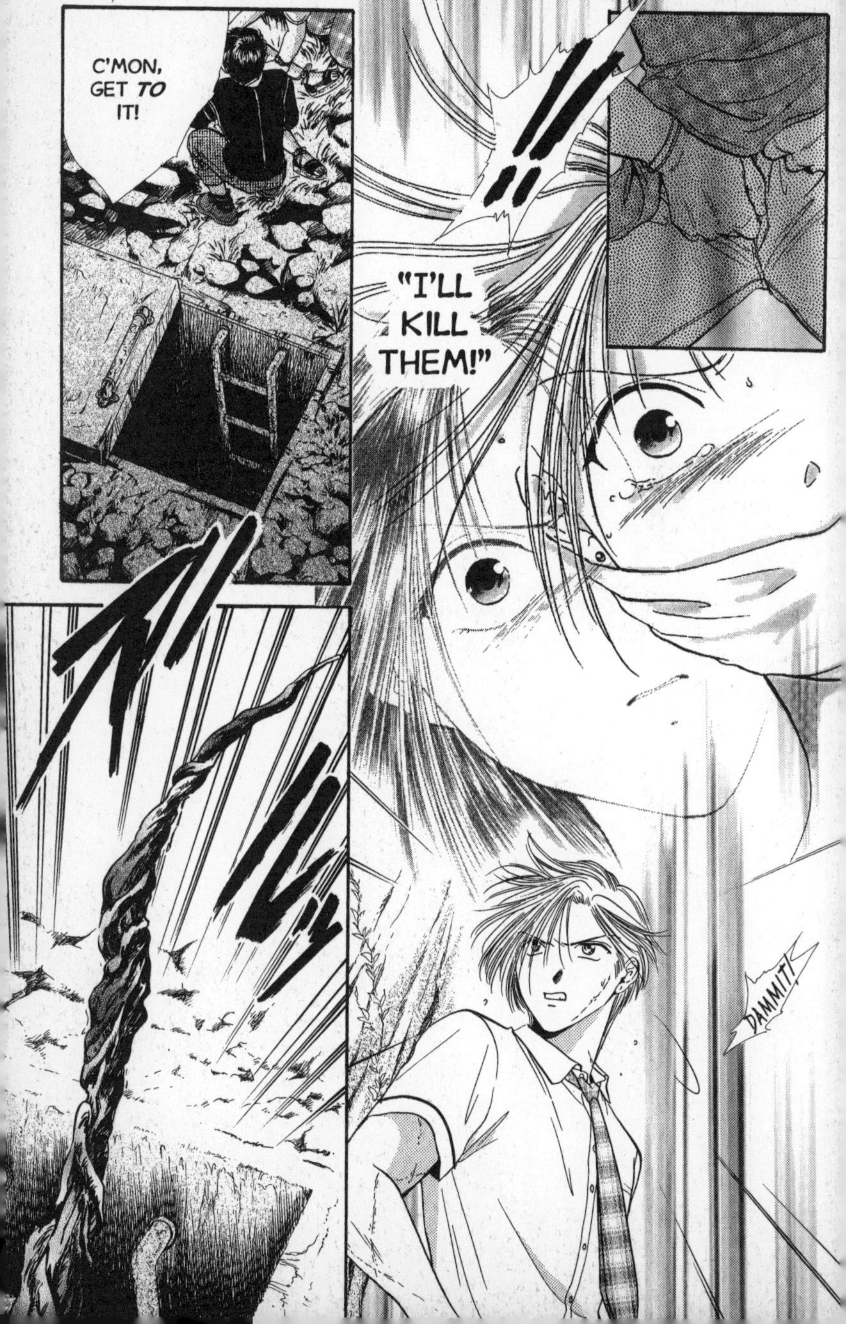
"I'LL KILL THEM!"
C'MON, GET *TO* IT!
DAMMIT!

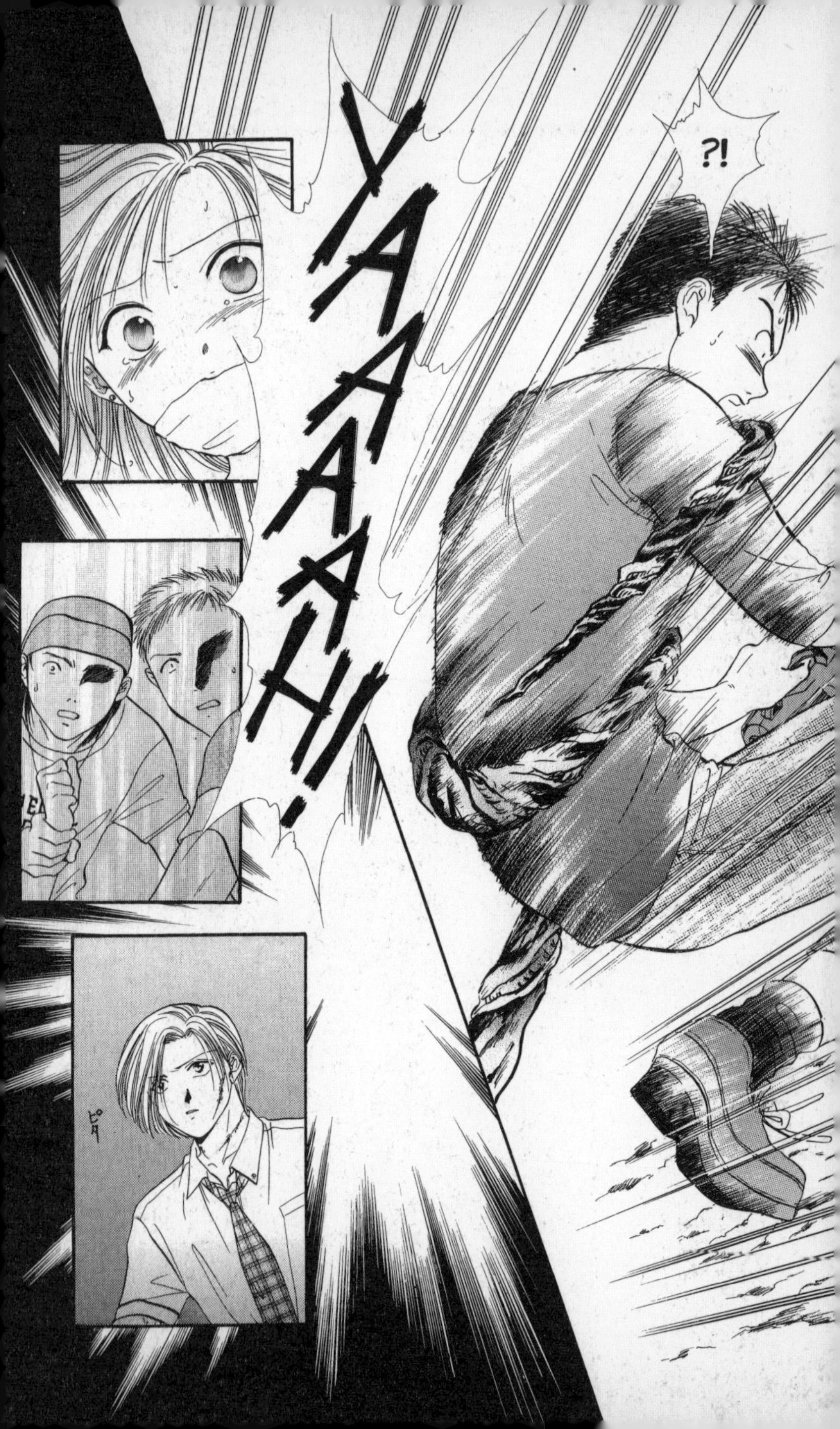
?!
YAAAAH!!

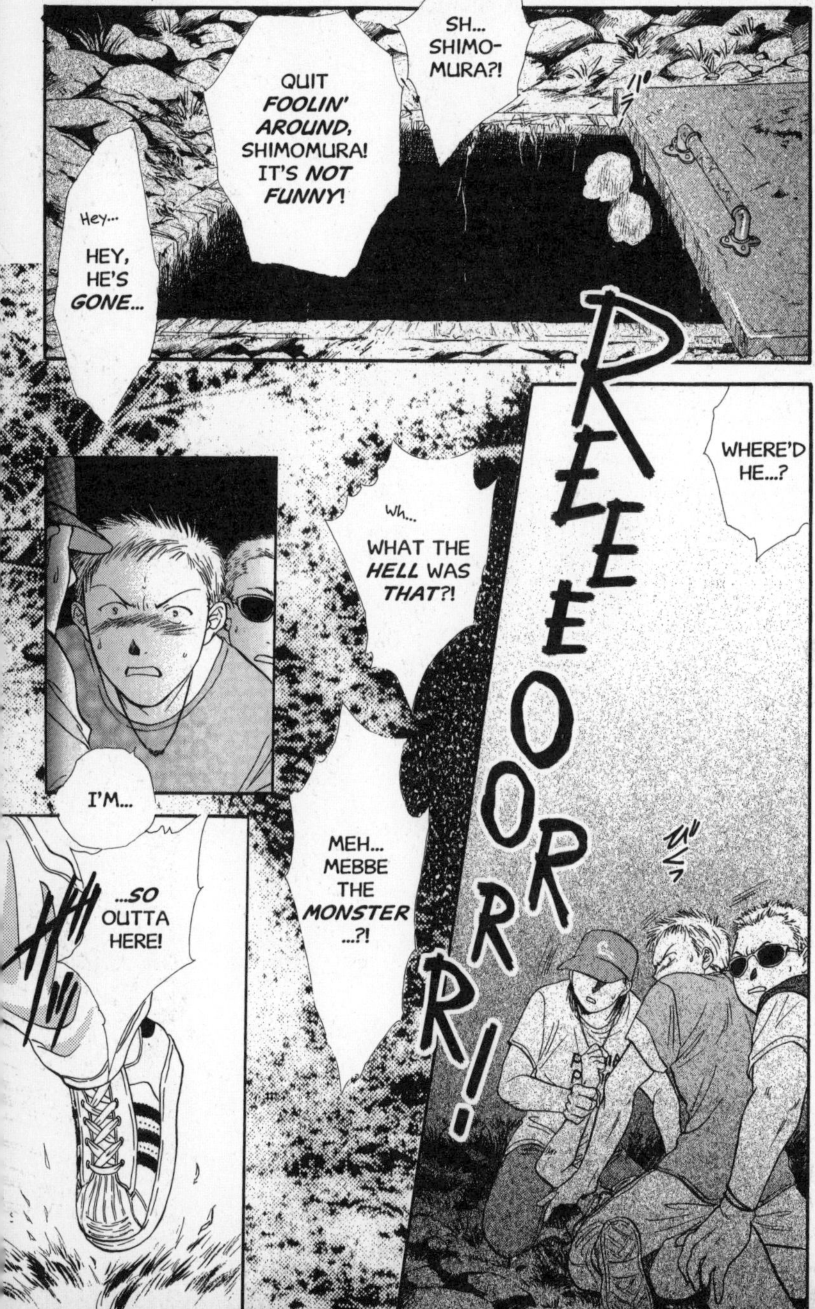
SH... SHIMOMURA?!
QUIT FOOLIN' AROUND, SHIMOMURA! IT'S NOT FUNNY!
Hey...
HEY, HE'S GONE...
WHERE'D HE...?
REEEOORRRI!
Wh...
WHAT THE HELL WAS THAT?!
MEH... MEBBE THE MONSTER...?!
I'M...
...SO OUTTA HERE!

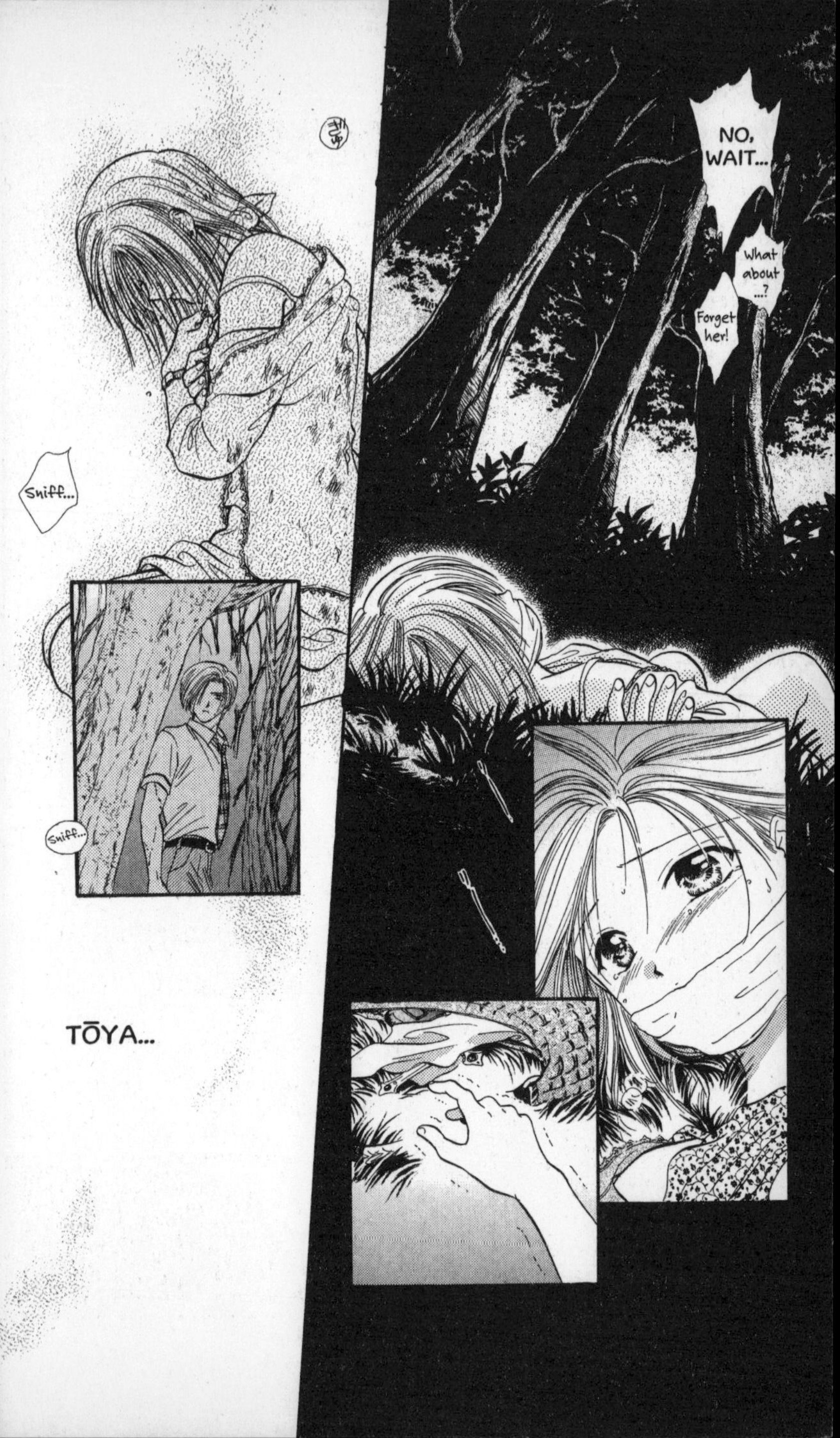
NO, WAIT...
What about ...?
Forget her!
Sniff...
Sniff...
TŌYA...

♦ Monster ♦

Well then, let's talk a bit about Aki. He kept getting weaker until he finally vanished, but he really is a cheerful, kind person. Never a teacher's pet, when he was himself, he was an all-around, nice kind of guy. Probably he would've been popular with the girls, but he never found a girlfriend. ...Hmm. I think maybe the "Progenitor" side of him was unconsciously distracted by Aya (but not in a weird way). Assistant "J," who adores Aki, brought over a hand-made felt doll the other day. Um, okay. She liked "Amiboshi" in *FY*—she's predictable that way. (I drew a tiny picture of Aki cosplaying as Amiboshi on a fax I sent her.) One of my friends, who's also an Aki fan, wondered if people would ever get to see what the Progenitor **really** looked like. You will, sooner or later. Stay tuned! The fans are gonna get mad at me if he turns out to be some middle-aged guy....

His popularity's really shot up since he became the Progenitor. I guess people like how aggressive he is...but isn't he still a jerk?! Doesn't matter, you say? This "Tango" story arc is...well, everything bad about men's been put forward in it, so there've been a lot of upset readers. They feel bad for Aya, that she's "suffering every nightmare a woman can experience." Yes, all women should feel anger in reading this arc. While drawing it, I had a pretty angry brow, myself. I hope I was able to express my personal revulsion. One person wrote, "Sex without love is a crime. Is Ceres' body the only thing the Progenitor wants? That's not what being husband and wife is about. He has no right to call her his wife. I hate him for not thinking of women as human beings." Another wrote, "How dare he do this to Aya?! Coercion won't get you someone's heart!" The assistants were pissed at the male students: "All the guys at this school are idiots!"

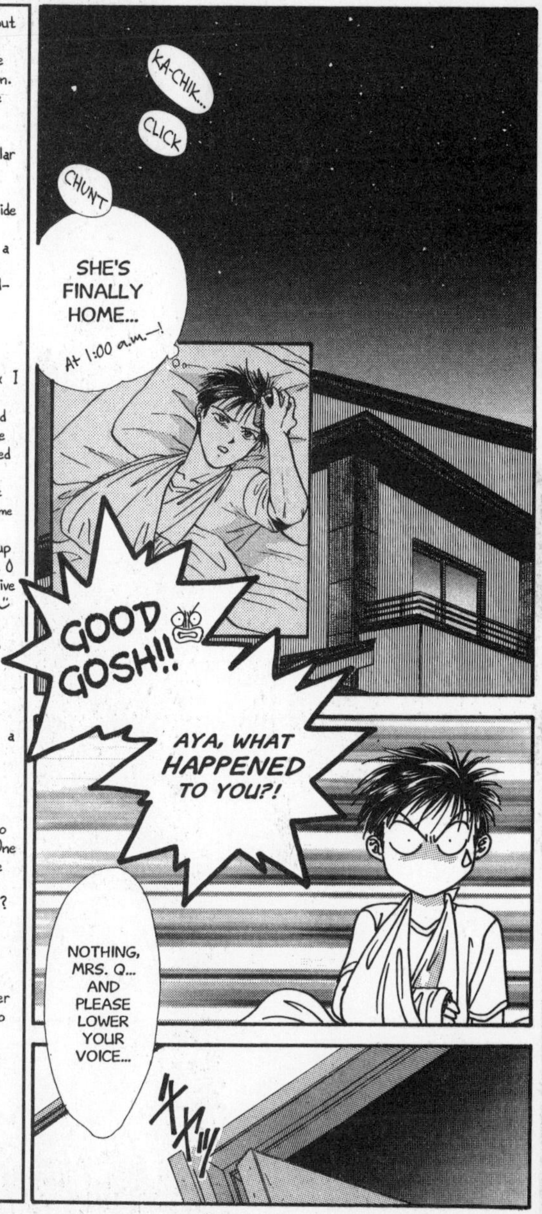
KA-CHIK...
CLICK
CHUNT
SHE'S FINALLY HOME...
At 1:00 a.m.—!
GOOD GOSH!!
AYA, WHAT HAPPENED TO YOU?!
NOTHING, MRS. Q... AND PLEASE LOWER YOUR VOICE...

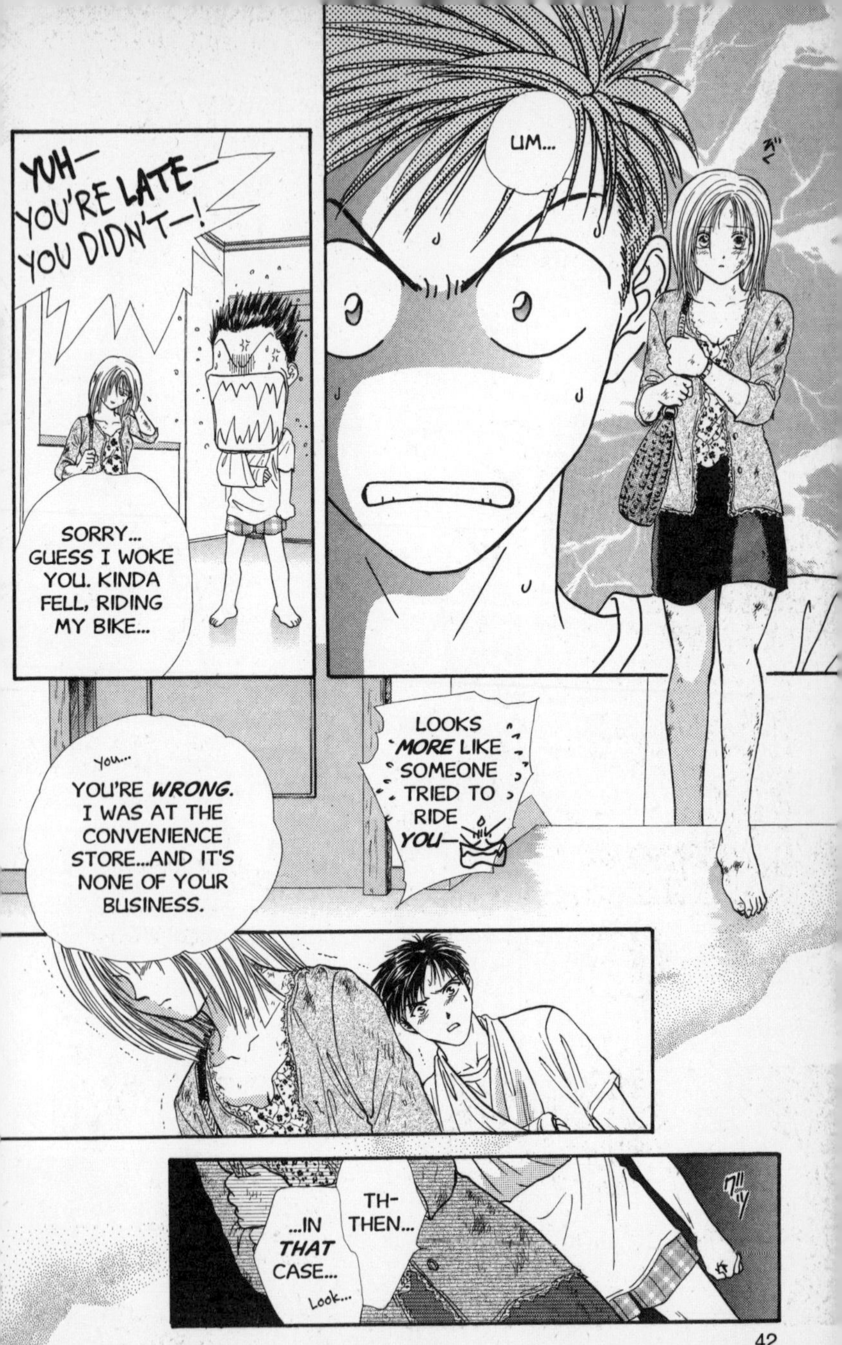
UM...
YUH— YOU'RE LATE— YOU DIDN'T—!
SORRY... GUESS I WOKE YOU. KINDA FELL, RIDING MY BIKE...
LOOKS MORE LIKE SOMEONE TRIED TO RIDE YOU—
you... YOU'RE WRONG. I WAS AT THE CONVENIENCE STORE...AND IT'S NONE OF YOUR BUSINESS.
TH- THEN...
...IN THAT CASE...
Look...

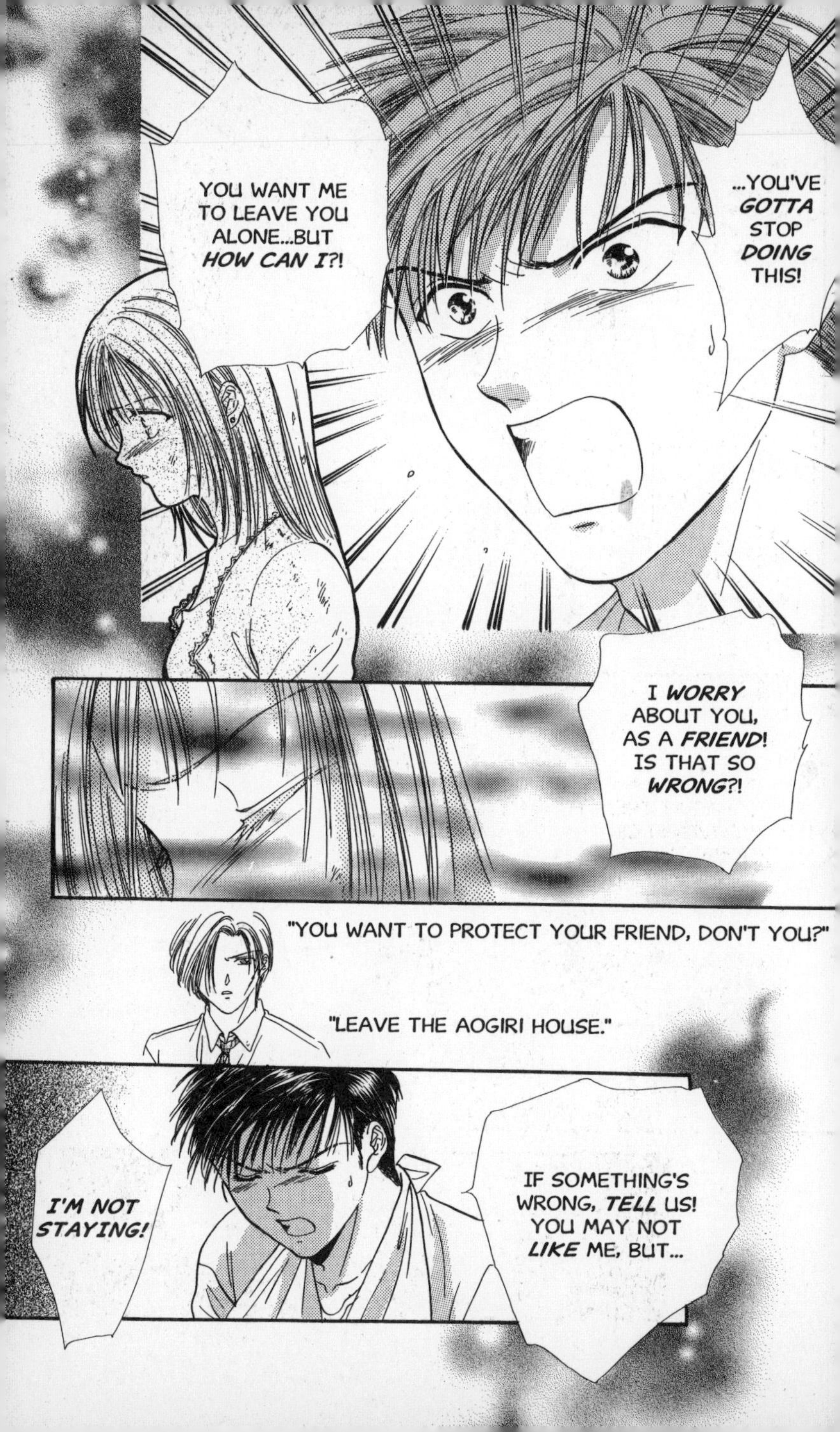
...YOU'VE GOTTA STOP DOING THIS!
YOU WANT ME TO LEAVE YOU ALONE...BUT HOW CAN I?!
I WORRY ABOUT YOU, AS A FRIEND! IS THAT SO WRONG?!
"YOU WANT TO PROTECT YOUR FRIEND, DON'T YOU?"
"LEAVE THE AOGIRI HOUSE."
IF SOMETHING'S WRONG, TELL US! YOU MAY NOT LIKE ME, BUT...
I'M NOT STAYING!

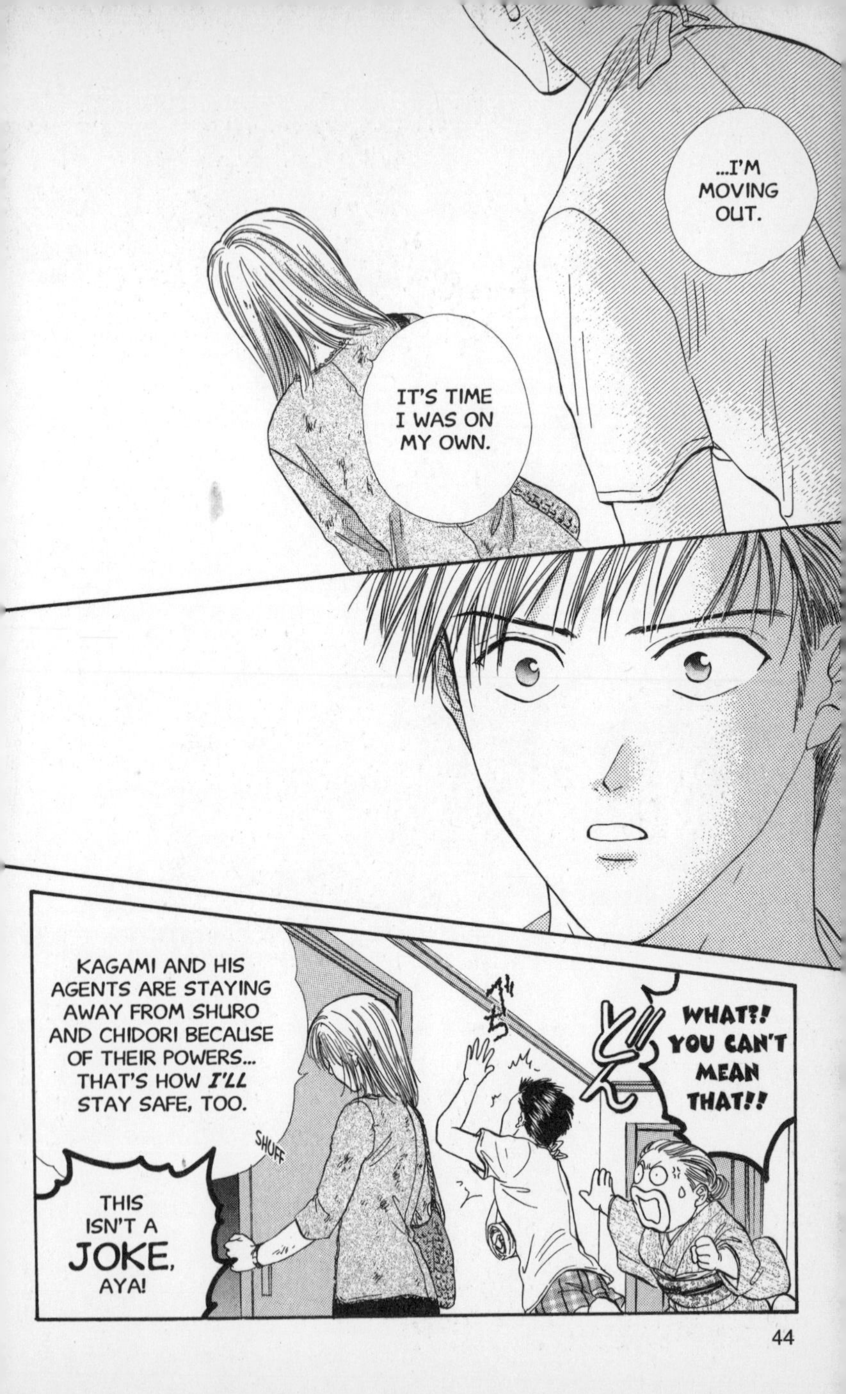
...I'M MOVING OUT.
IT'S TIME I WAS ON MY OWN.
WHAT?! YOU CAN'T MEAN THAT!!
KAGAMI AND HIS AGENTS ARE STAYING AWAY FROM SHURO AND CHIDORI BECAUSE OF THEIR POWERS... THAT'S HOW *I'LL* STAY SAFE, TOO.
SHUFF
THIS ISN'T A JOKE, AYA!

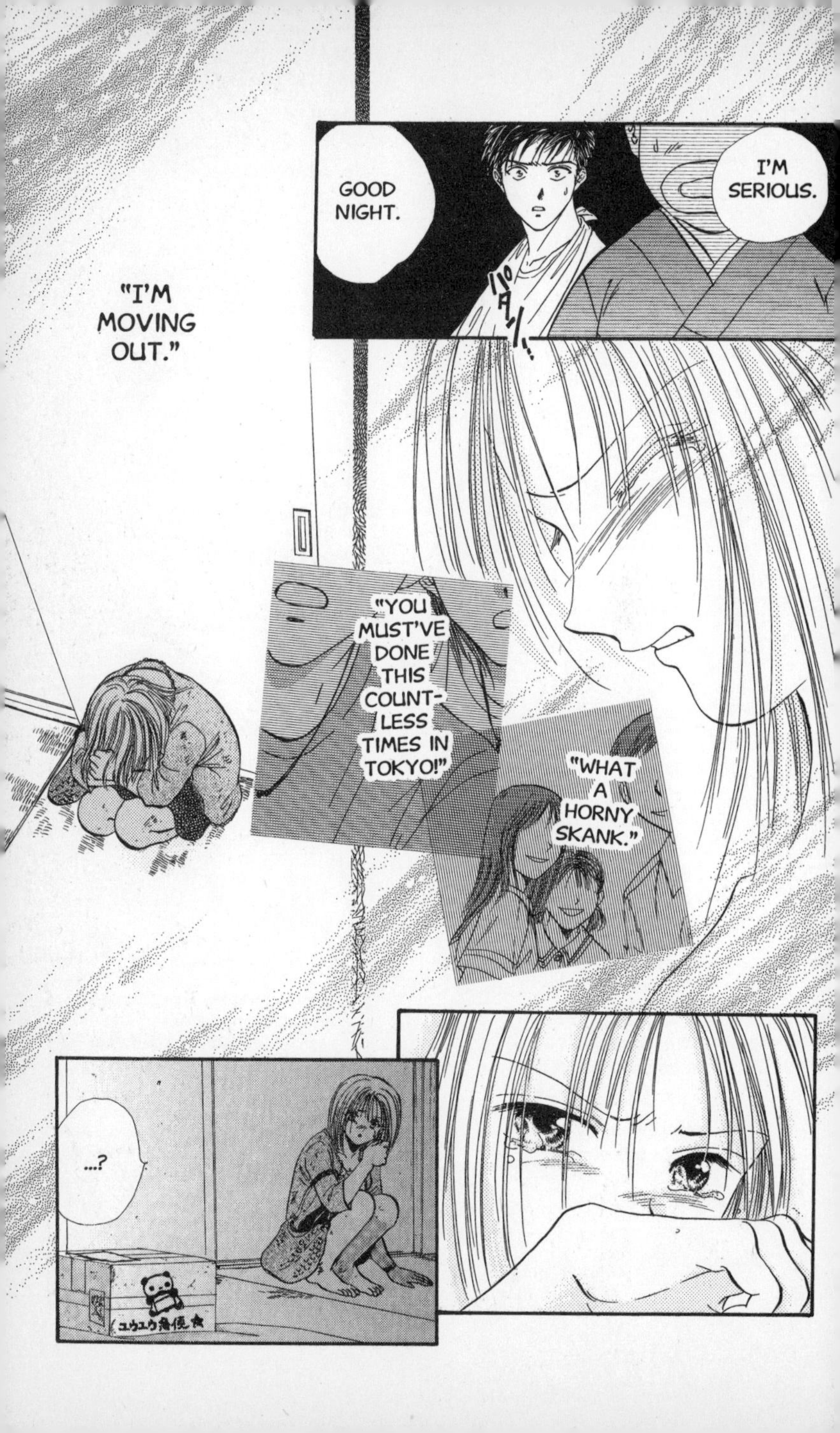
I'M SERIOUS.
GOOD NIGHT.
"I'M MOVING OUT."
"YOU MUST'VE DONE THIS COUNTLESS TIMES IN TOKYO!"
"WHAT A HORNY SKANK."
...?

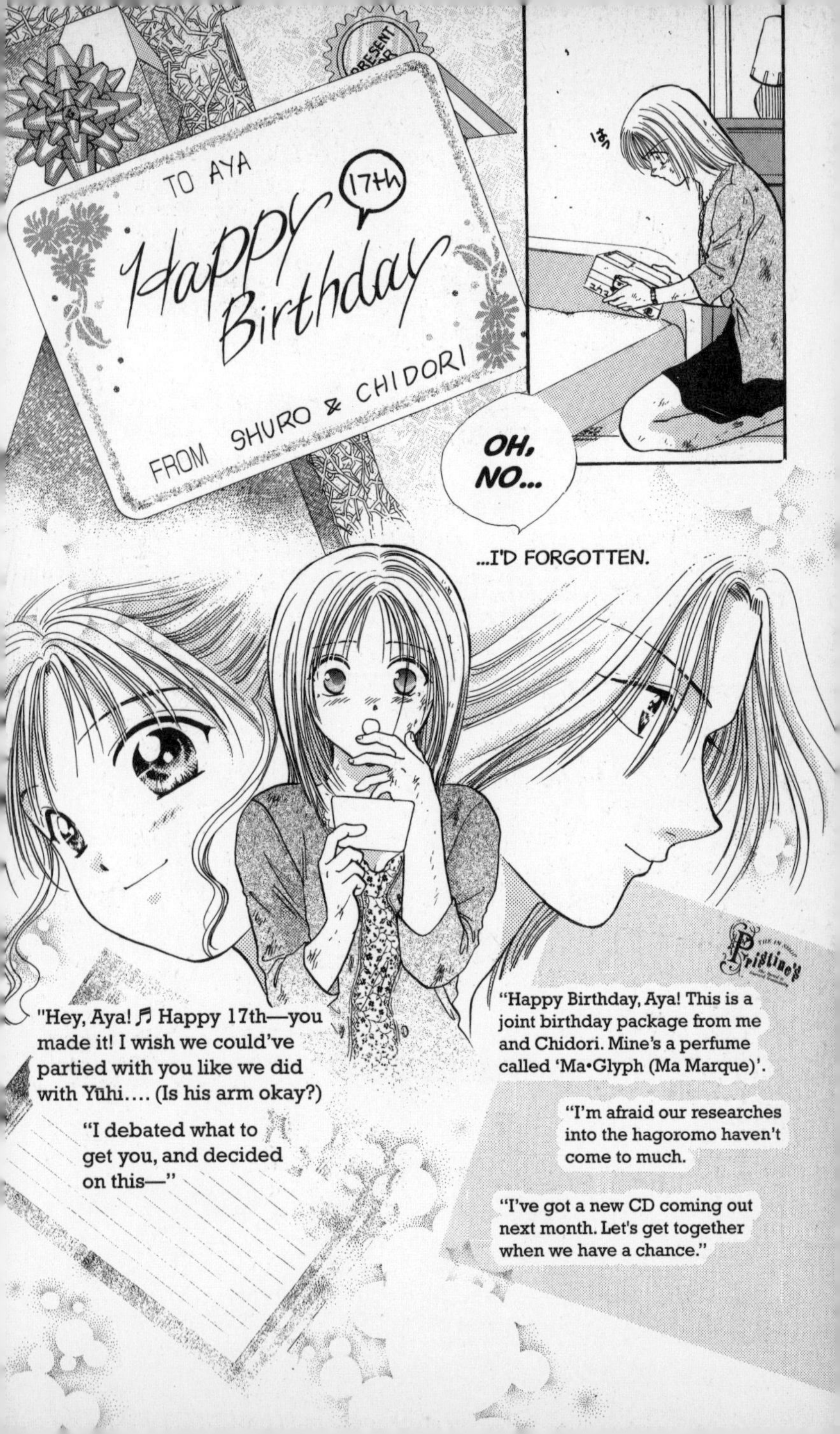

OH, NO...
TO AYA
Happy Birthday
17th
FROM SHURO & CHIDORI
...I'D FORGOTTEN.
"Happy Birthday, Aya! This is a joint birthday package from me and Chidori. Mine's a perfume called 'Ma•Glyph (Ma Marque)'.
"I'm afraid our researches into the hagoromo haven't come to much.
"I've got a new CD coming out next month. Let's get together when we have a chance."
"Hey, Aya! ♬ Happy 17th—you made it! I wish we could've partied with you like we did with Yūhi.... (Is his arm okay?)
"I debated what to get you, and decided on this—"

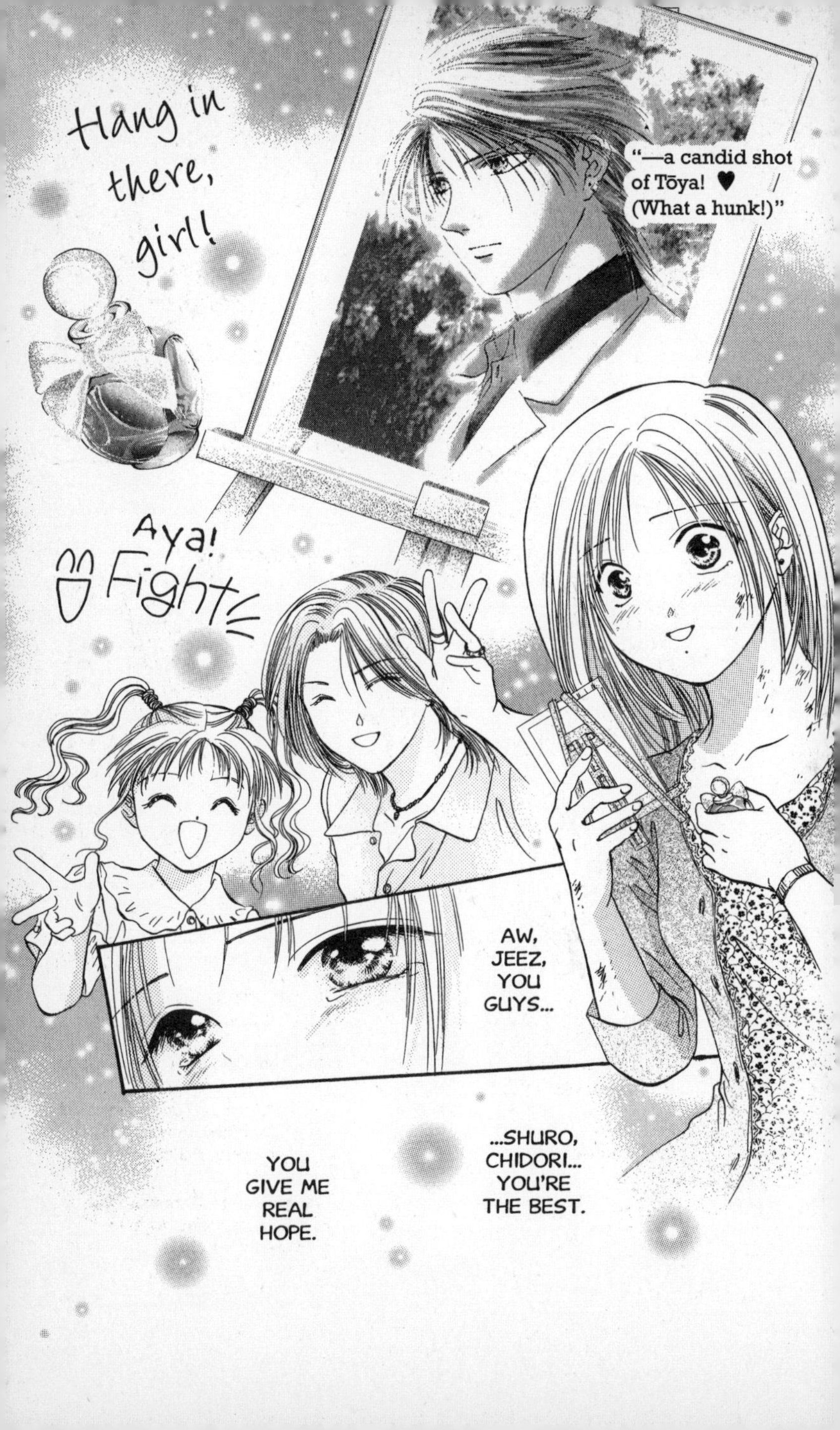
"—a candid shot of Tōya! ♥ (What a hunk!)"
Hang in there, girl!
Aya! Fight
AW, JEEZ, YOU GUYS...
...SHURO, CHIDORI... YOU'RE THE BEST.
YOU GIVE ME REAL HOPE.

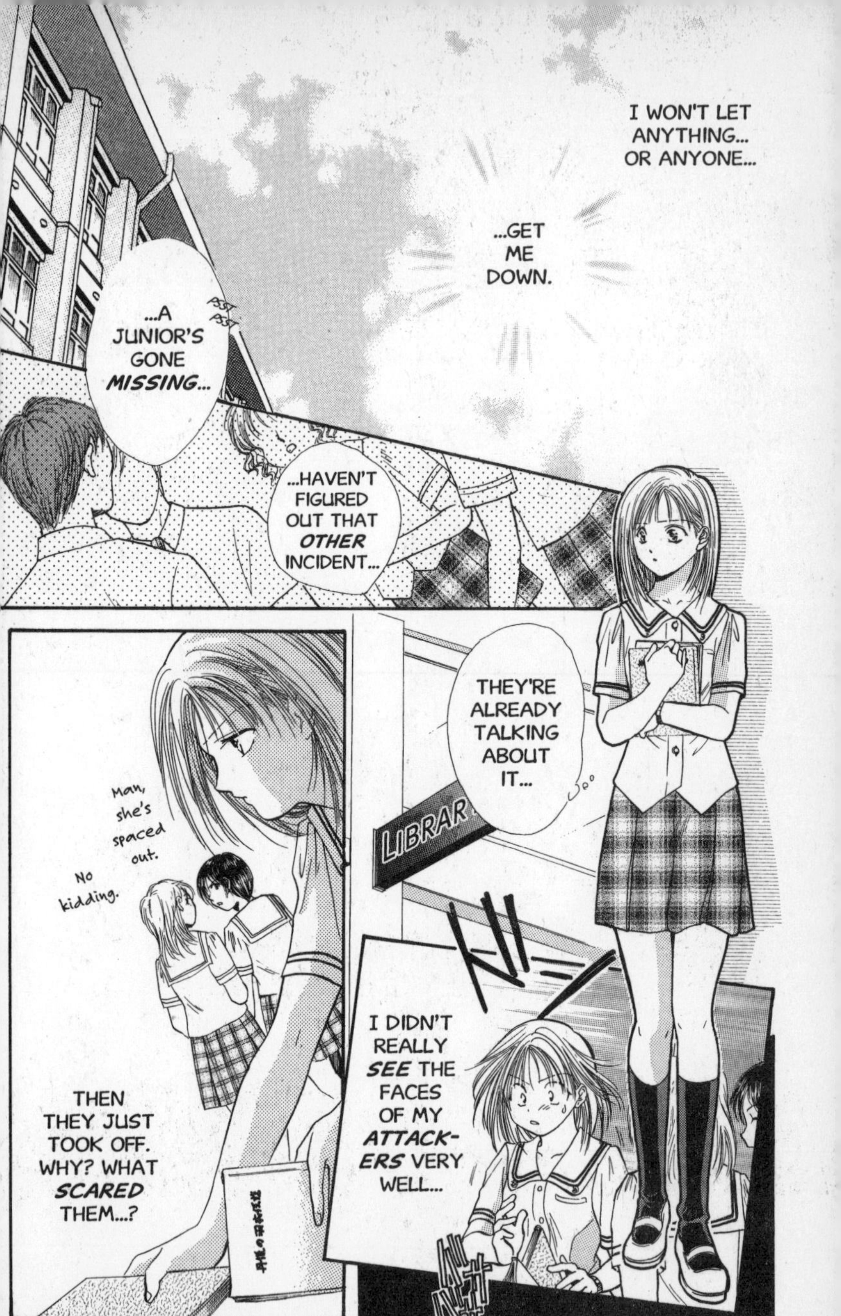
I WON'T LET ANYTHING... OR ANYONE...
...GET ME DOWN.
PSST PSST
...A JUNIOR'S GONE MISSING...
...HAVEN'T FIGURED OUT THAT OTHER INCIDENT...
THEY'RE ALREADY TALKING ABOUT IT...
LIBRAR
I DIDN'T REALLY SEE THE FACES OF MY ATTACKERS VERY WELL...
Man, she's spaced out.
No kidding.
THEN THEY JUST TOOK OFF. WHY? WHAT SCARED THEM...?

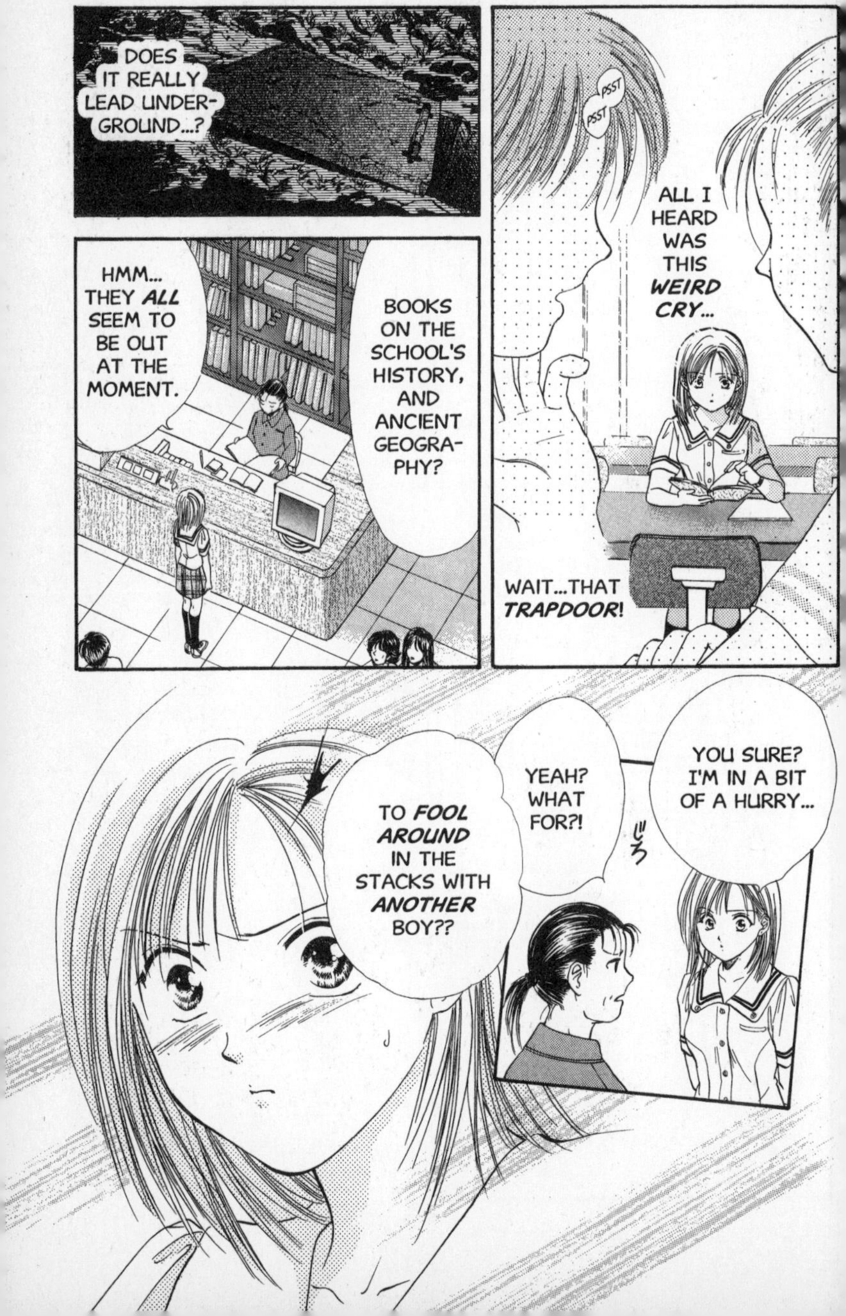
PSST
PSST
ALL I HEARD WAS THIS *WEIRD CRY*...
WAIT...THAT *TRAPDOOR*!
DOES IT REALLY LEAD UNDER-GROUND...?
BOOKS ON THE SCHOOL'S HISTORY, AND ANCIENT GEOGRA-PHY?
HMM... THEY *ALL* SEEM TO BE OUT AT THE MOMENT.
YOU SURE? I'M IN A BIT OF A HURRY...
YEAH? WHAT FOR?!
じろ
TO *FOOL AROUND* IN THE STACKS WITH *ANOTHER* BOY??

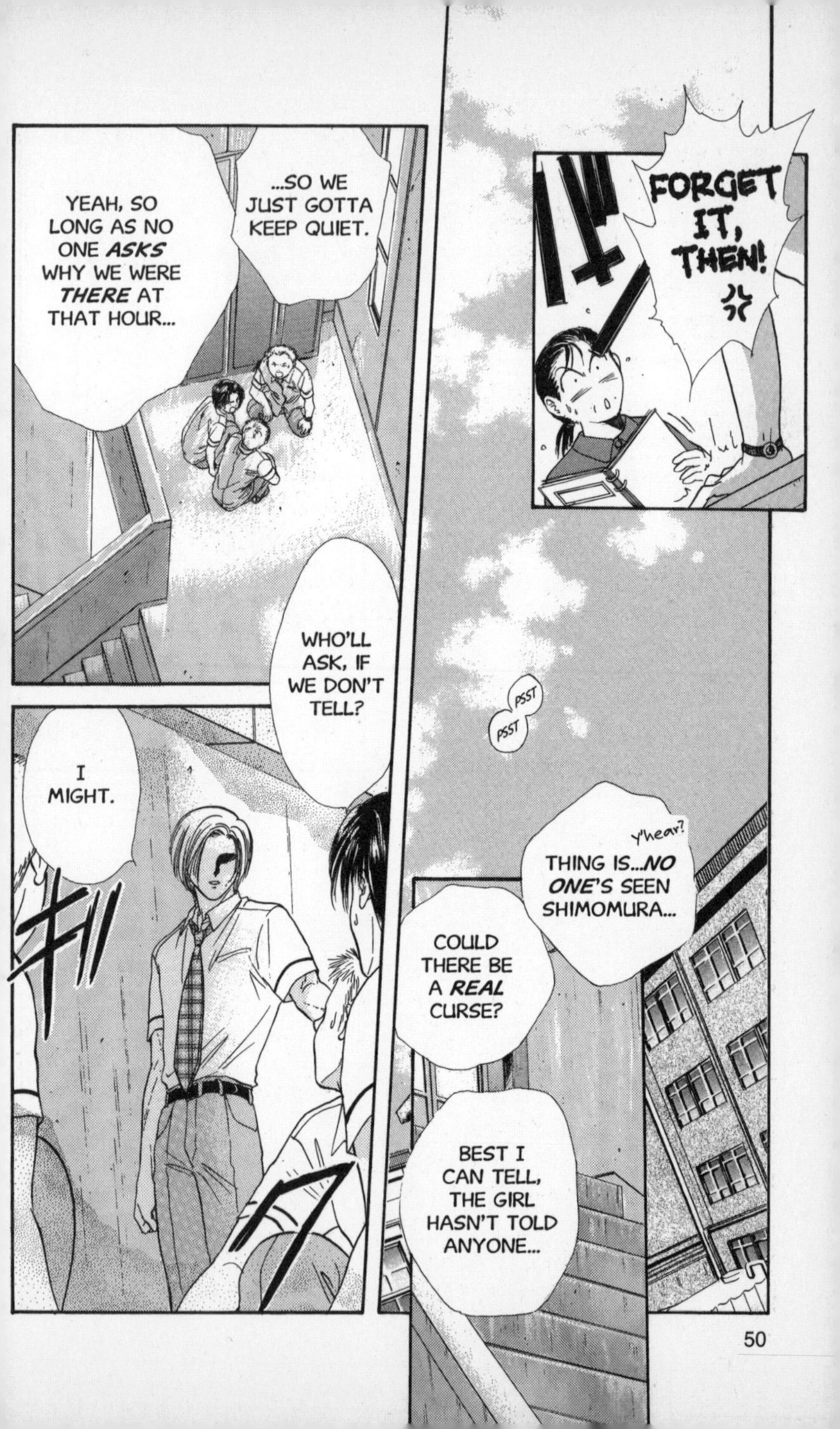
FORGET IT, THEN!
PSST PSST
Y'hear?
THING IS...NO ONE'S SEEN SHIMOMURA...
COULD THERE BE A REAL CURSE?
BEST I CAN TELL, THE GIRL HASN'T TOLD ANYONE...
YEAH, SO LONG AS NO ONE ASKS WHY WE WERE THERE AT THAT HOUR...
...SO WE JUST GOTTA KEEP QUIET.
WHO'LL ASK, IF WE DON'T TELL?
I MIGHT.

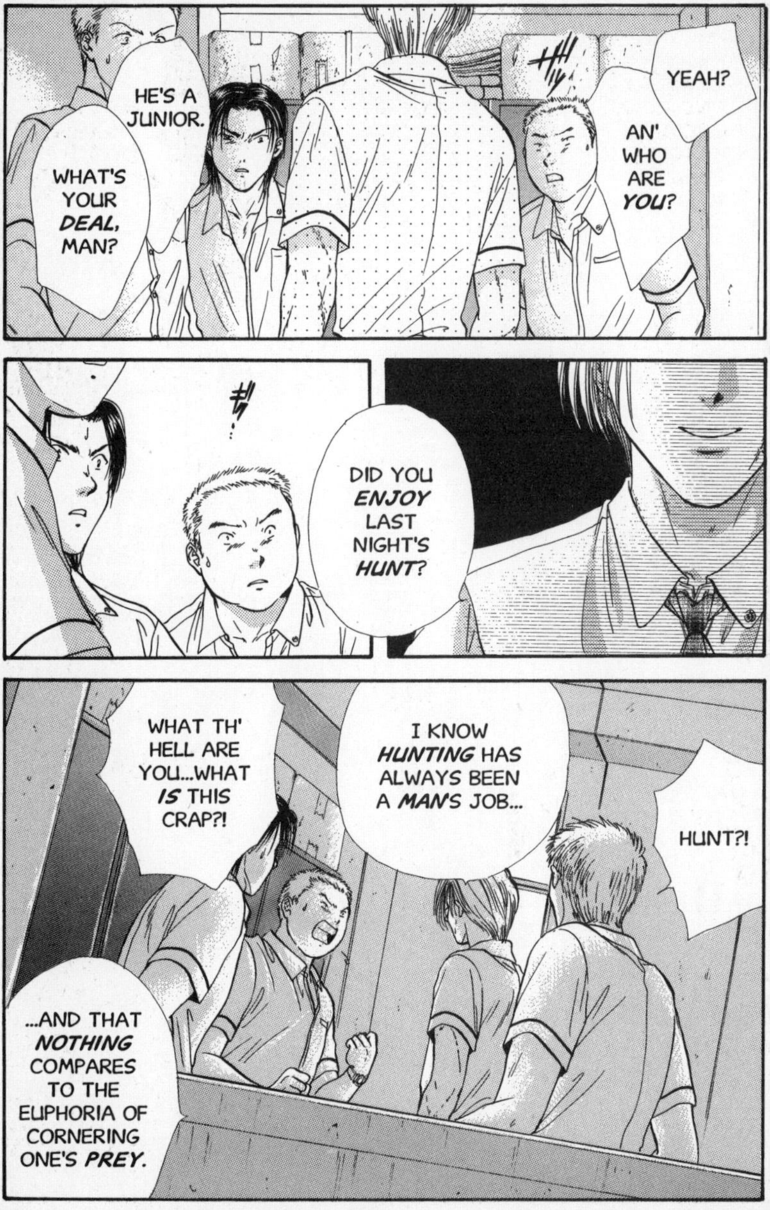
YEAH?
AN' WHO ARE *YOU*?
HE'S A JUNIOR.
WHAT'S YOUR *DEAL*, MAN?
DID YOU *ENJOY* LAST NIGHT'S *HUNT*?
HUNT?!
WHAT TH' HELL ARE YOU...WHAT *IS* THIS CRAP?!
I KNOW *HUNTING* HAS ALWAYS BEEN A *MAN*'S JOB...
...AND THAT *NOTHING* COMPARES TO THE EUPHORIA OF CORNERING ONE'S *PREY*.

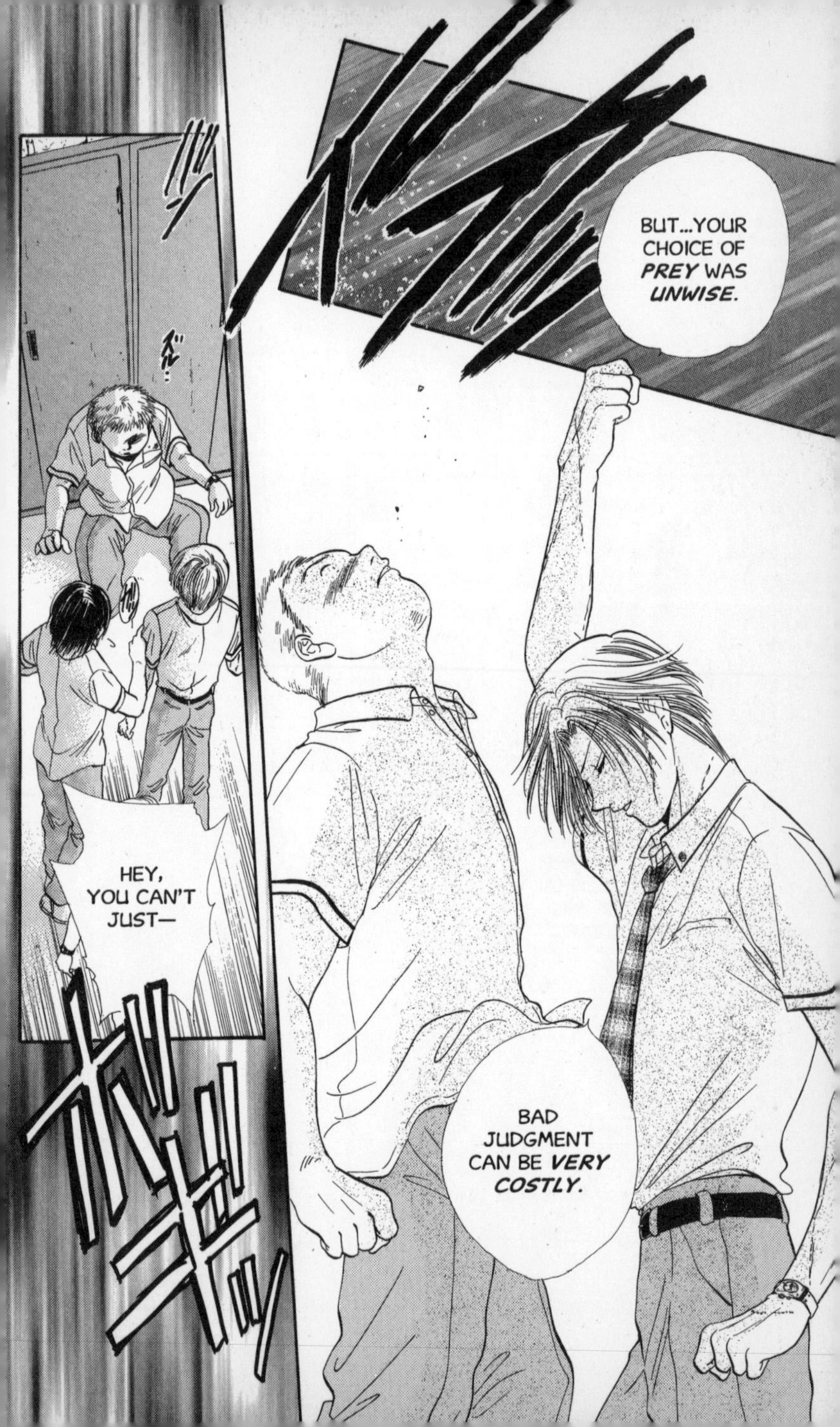
BUT...YOUR CHOICE OF *PREY* WAS *UNWISE.*
BAD JUDGMENT CAN BE *VERY COSTLY.*
HEY, YOU CAN'T JUST—

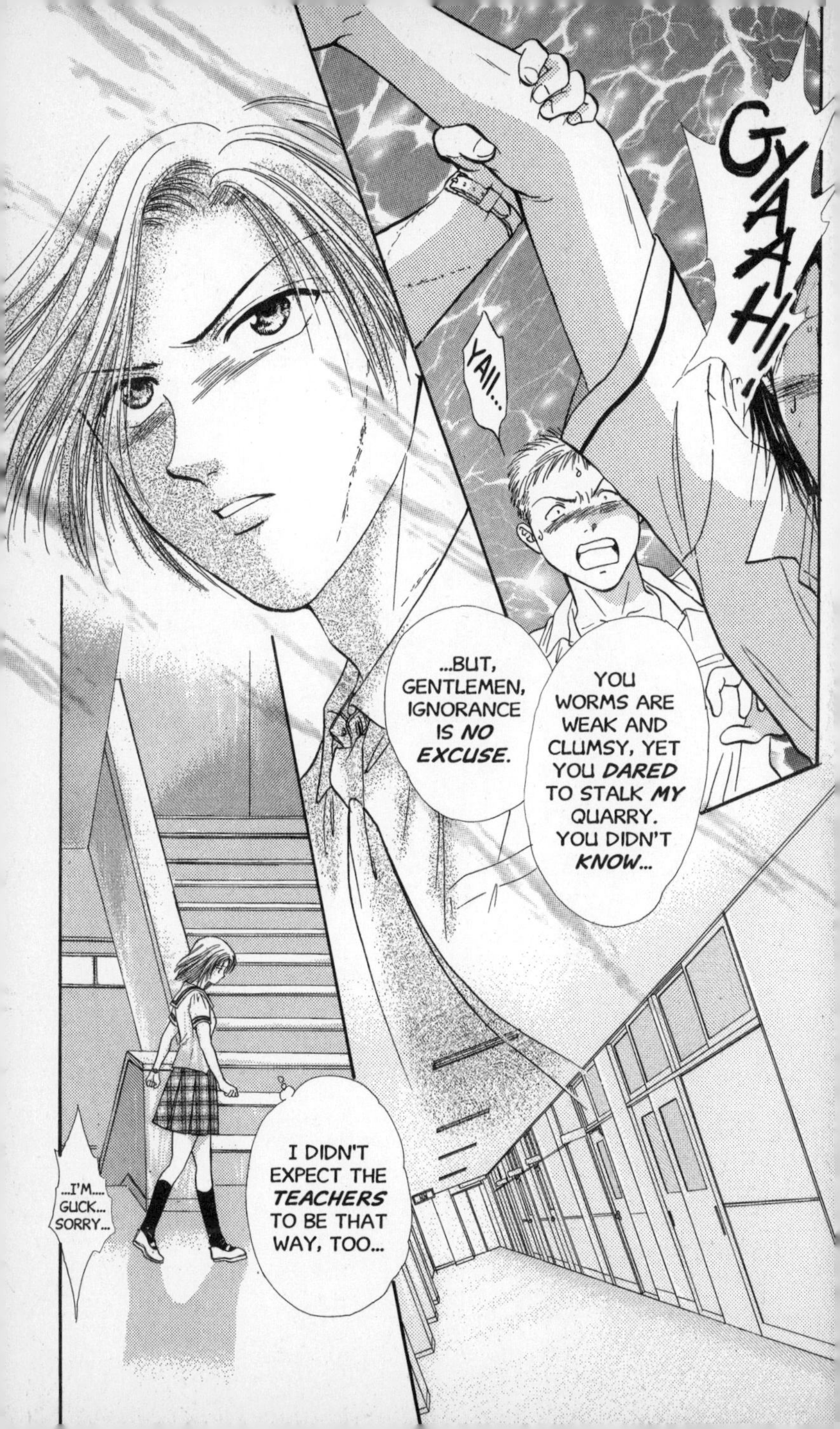
GYAAAH!!
YAII...
YOU WORMS ARE WEAK AND CLUMSY, YET YOU *DARED* TO STALK *MY* QUARRY. YOU DIDN'T *KNOW*...
...BUT, GENTLEMEN, IGNORANCE IS *NO EXCUSE*.
I DIDN'T EXPECT THE *TEACHERS* TO BE THAT WAY, TOO...
...I'M... GUCK... SORRY...

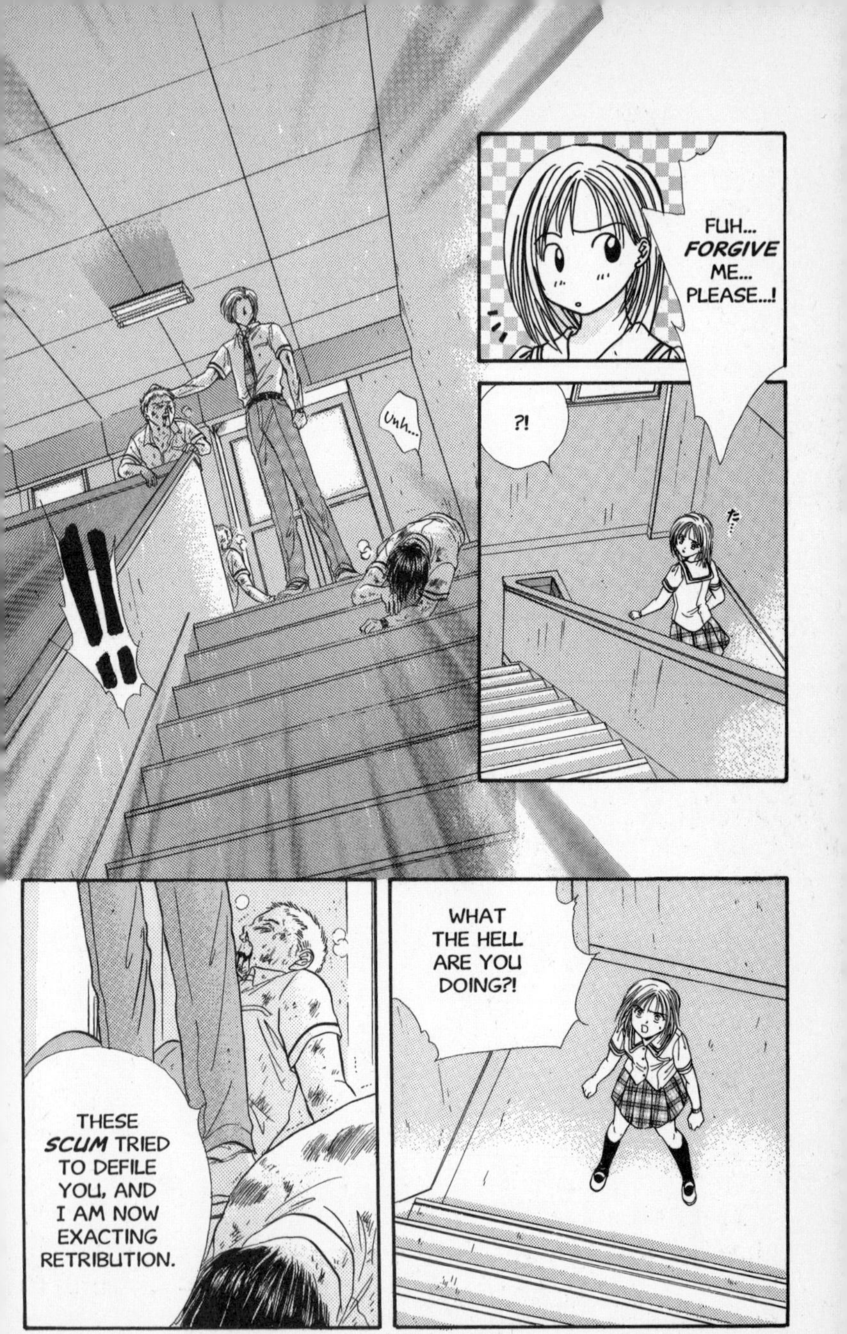
FUH... FORGIVE ME... PLEASE...!
?!
Unh...
!!
WHAT THE HELL ARE YOU DOING?!
THESE SCUM TRIED TO DEFILE YOU, AND I AM NOW EXACTING RETRIBUTION.

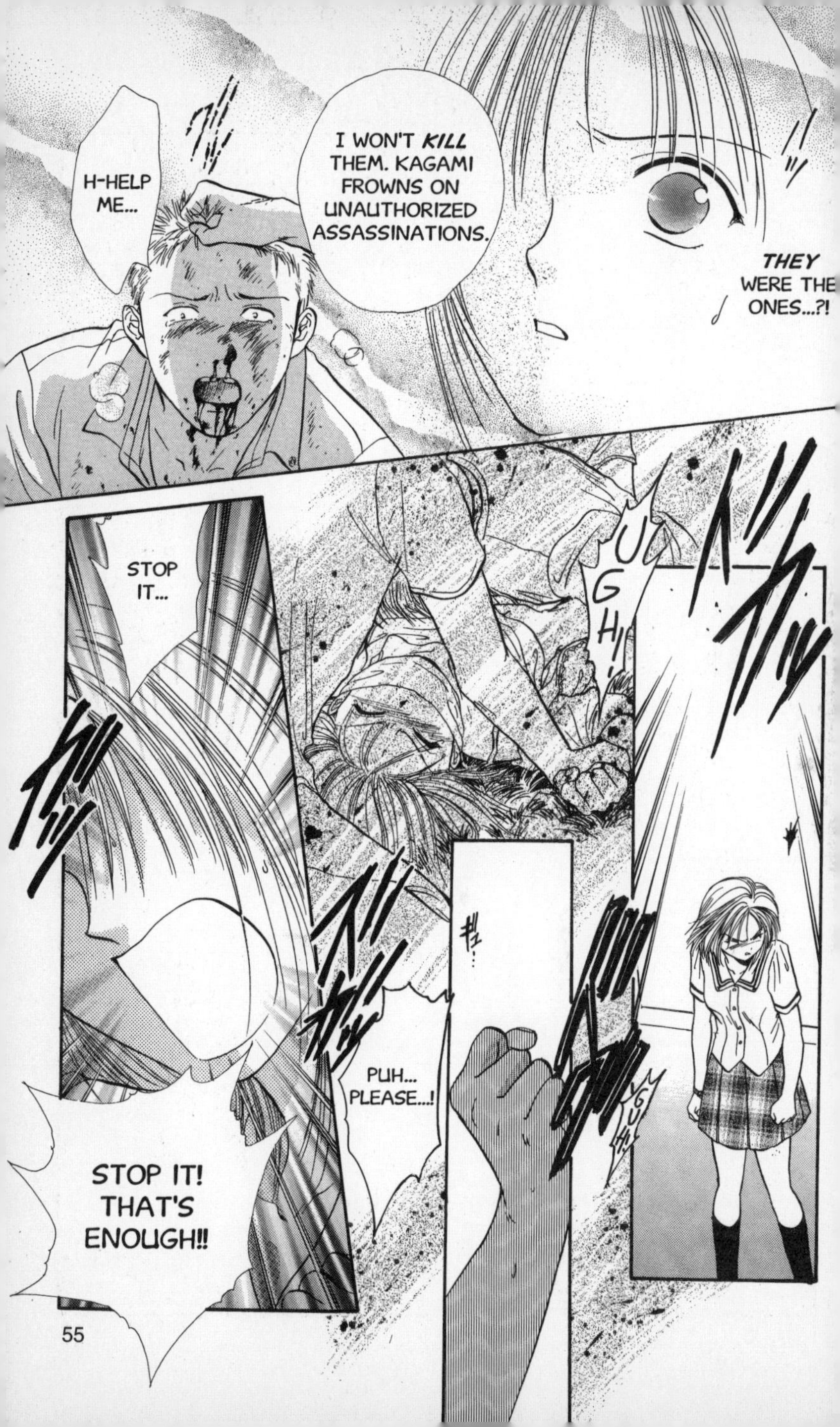

THEY WERE THE ONES...?!
I WON'T KILL THEM. KAGAMI FROWNS ON UNAUTHORIZED ASSASSINATIONS.
H-HELP ME...
UGH!
STOP IT...
YGUH!
PUH... PLEASE...!
STOP IT! THAT'S ENOUGH!!

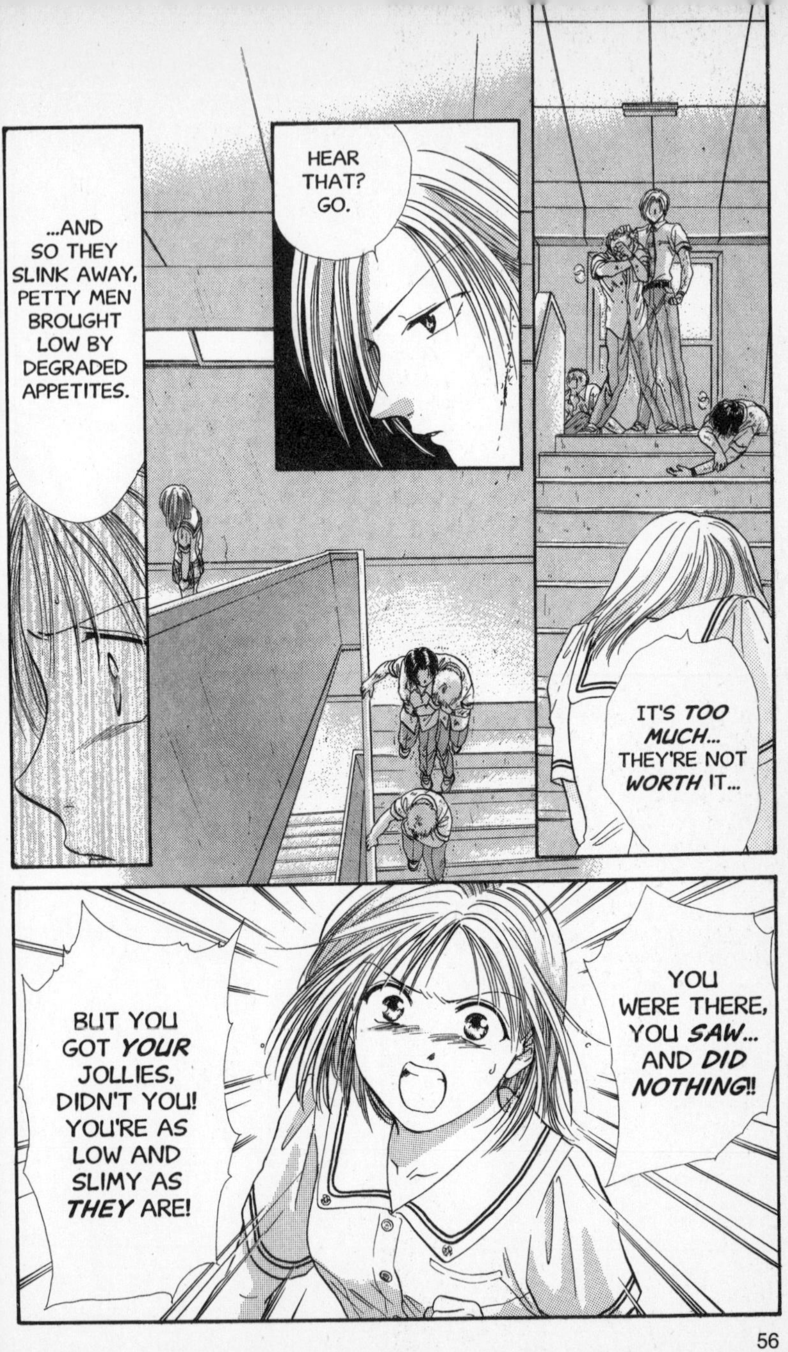
HEAR THAT? GO.
...AND SO THEY SLINK AWAY, PETTY MEN BROUGHT LOW BY DEGRADED APPETITES.
IT'S *TOO MUCH*... THEY'RE NOT *WORTH* IT...
YOU WERE THERE, YOU *SAW*... AND *DID NOTHING*!!
BUT YOU GOT *YOUR* JOLLIES, DIDN'T YOU! YOU'RE AS LOW AND SLIMY AS *THEY* ARE!

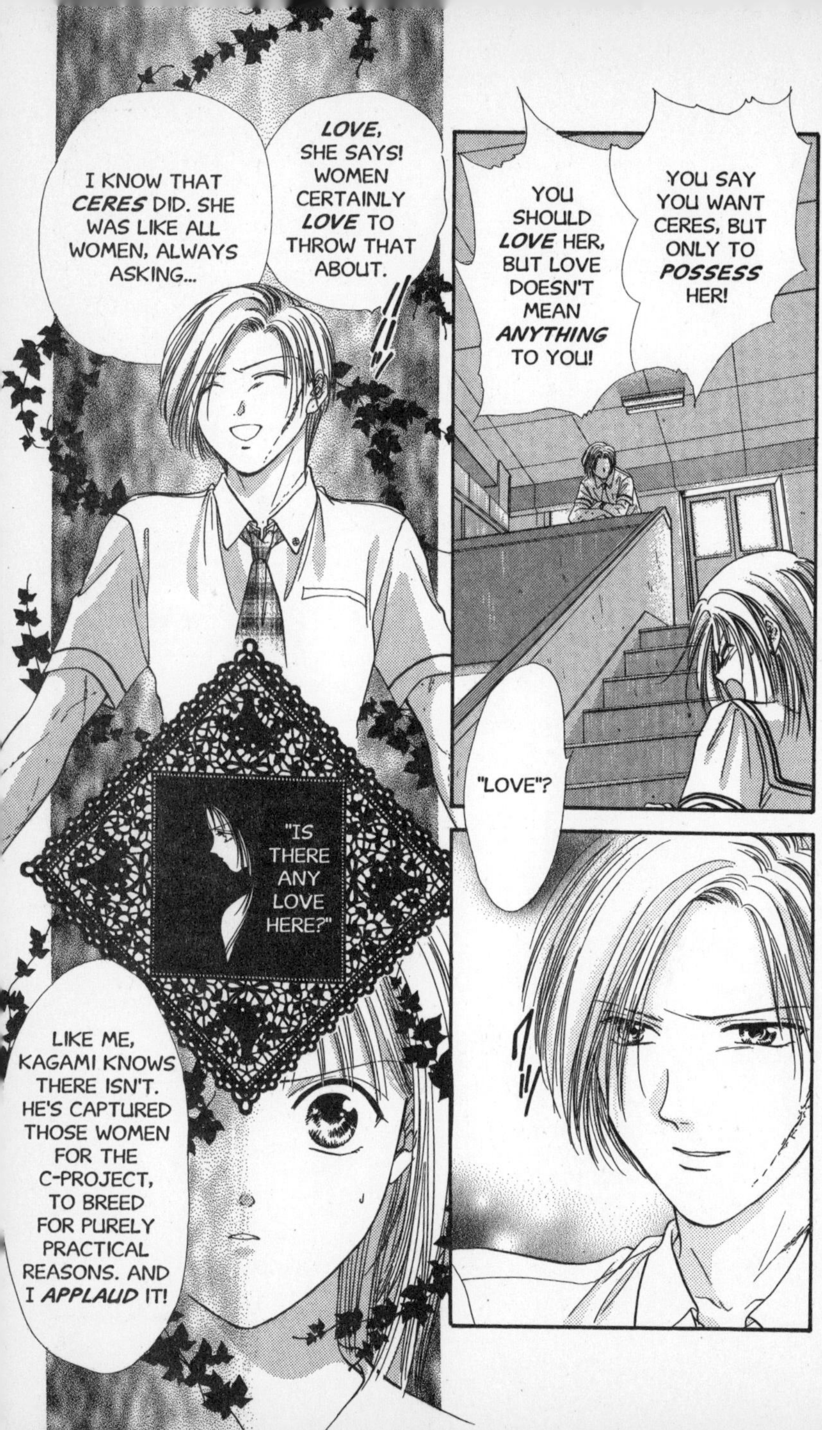
YOU SAY YOU WANT CERES, BUT ONLY TO POSSESS HER!
YOU SHOULD LOVE HER, BUT LOVE DOESN'T MEAN ANYTHING TO YOU!
"LOVE"?
LOVE, SHE SAYS! WOMEN CERTAINLY LOVE TO THROW THAT ABOUT.
I KNOW THAT CERES DID. SHE WAS LIKE ALL WOMEN, ALWAYS ASKING...
"IS THERE ANY LOVE HERE?"
LIKE ME, KAGAMI KNOWS THERE ISN'T. HE'S CAPTURED THOSE WOMEN FOR THE C-PROJECT, TO BREED FOR PURELY PRACTICAL REASONS. AND I APPLAUD IT!

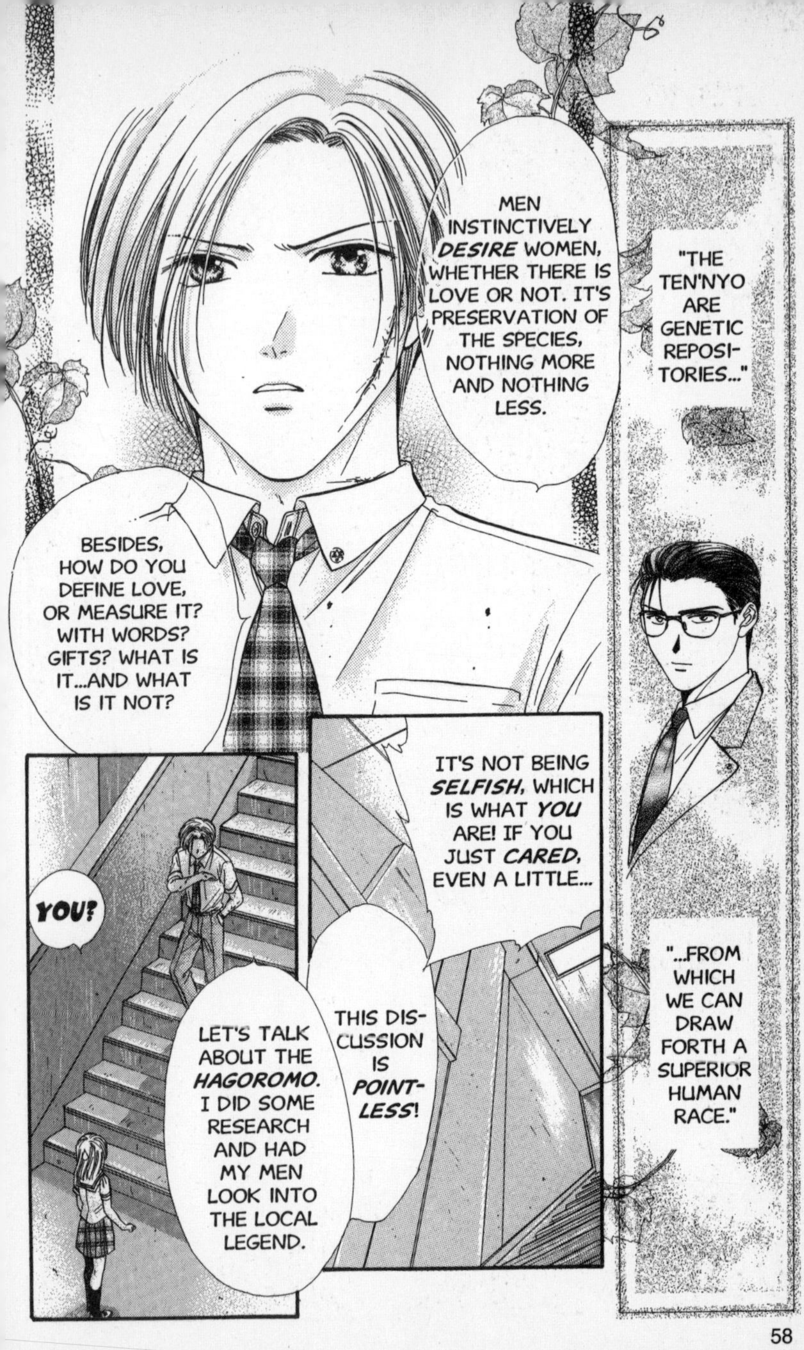
"THE TEN'NYO ARE GENETIC REPOSI- TORIES..."
"...FROM WHICH WE CAN DRAW FORTH A SUPERIOR HUMAN RACE."
MEN INSTINCTIVELY *DESIRE* WOMEN, WHETHER THERE IS LOVE OR NOT. IT'S PRESERVATION OF THE SPECIES, NOTHING MORE AND NOTHING LESS.
BESIDES, HOW DO YOU DEFINE LOVE, OR MEASURE IT? WITH WORDS? GIFTS? WHAT IS IT...AND WHAT IS IT NOT?
IT'S NOT BEING *SELFISH*, WHICH IS WHAT *YOU* ARE! IF YOU JUST *CARED*, EVEN A LITTLE...
THIS DIS- CUSSION IS *POINT- LESS*!
YOU?
LET'S TALK ABOUT THE *HAGOROMO*. I DID SOME RESEARCH AND HAD MY MEN LOOK INTO THE LOCAL LEGEND.

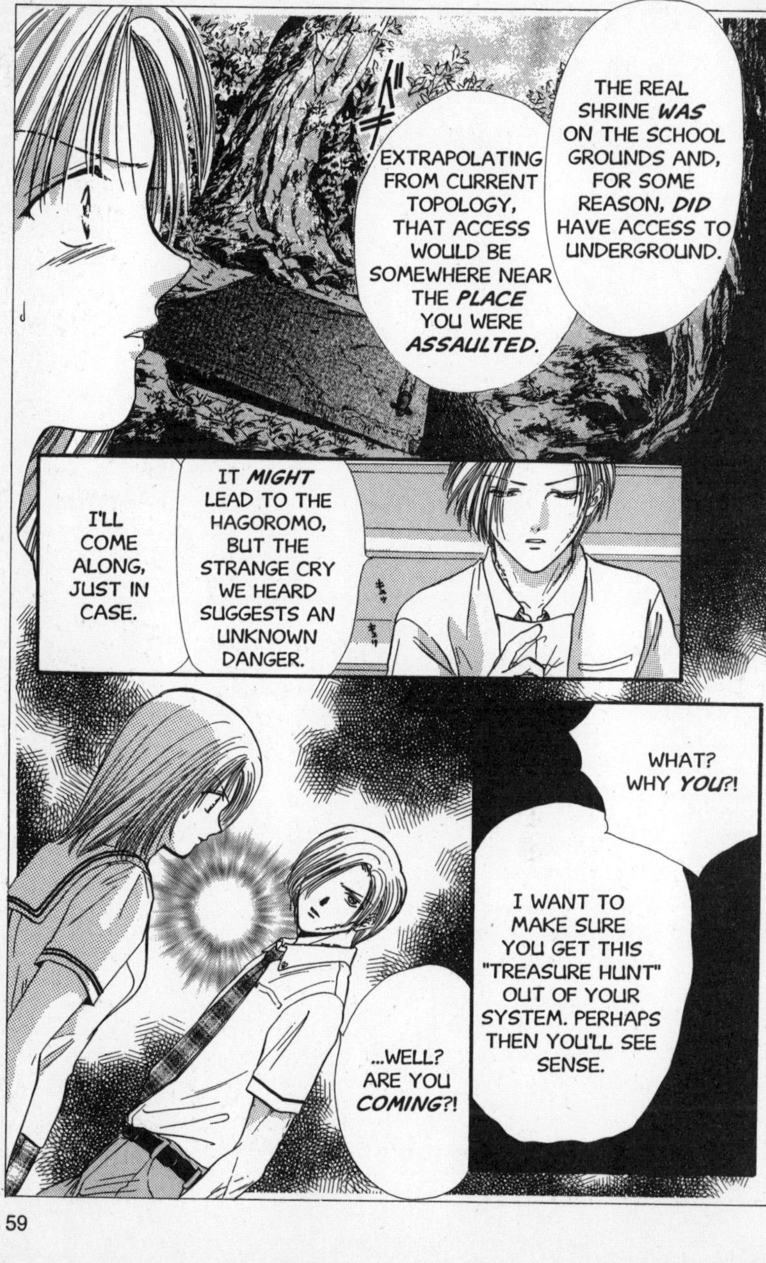
THE REAL SHRINE *WAS* ON THE SCHOOL GROUNDS AND, FOR SOME REASON, *DID* HAVE ACCESS TO UNDERGROUND.
EXTRAPOLATING FROM CURRENT TOPOLOGY, THAT ACCESS WOULD BE SOMEWHERE NEAR THE *PLACE* YOU WERE *ASSAULTED*.
IT *MIGHT* LEAD TO THE HAGOROMO, BUT THE STRANGE CRY WE HEARD SUGGESTS AN UNKNOWN DANGER.
I'LL COME ALONG, JUST IN CASE.
WHAT? WHY *YOU*?!
I WANT TO MAKE SURE YOU GET THIS "TREASURE HUNT" OUT OF YOUR SYSTEM. PERHAPS THEN YOU'LL SEE SENSE.
...WELL? ARE YOU *COMING*?!

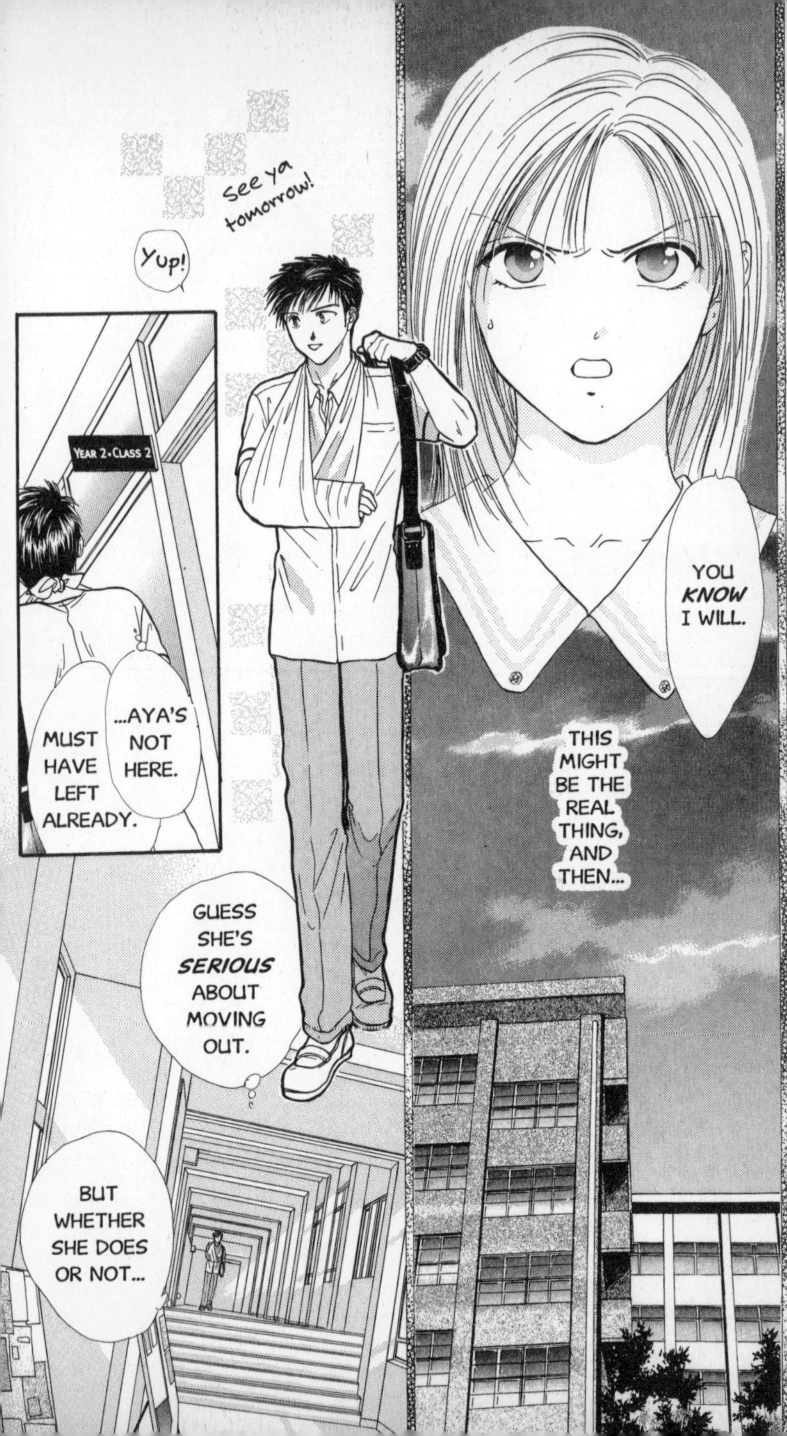
YOU *KNOW* I WILL.
THIS MIGHT BE THE REAL THING, AND THEN...
See ya tomorrow!
Yup!
YEAR 2 • CLASS 2
...AYA'S NOT HERE.
MUST HAVE LEFT ALREADY.
GUESS SHE'S *SERIOUS* ABOUT MOVING OUT.
BUT WHETHER SHE DOES OR NOT...

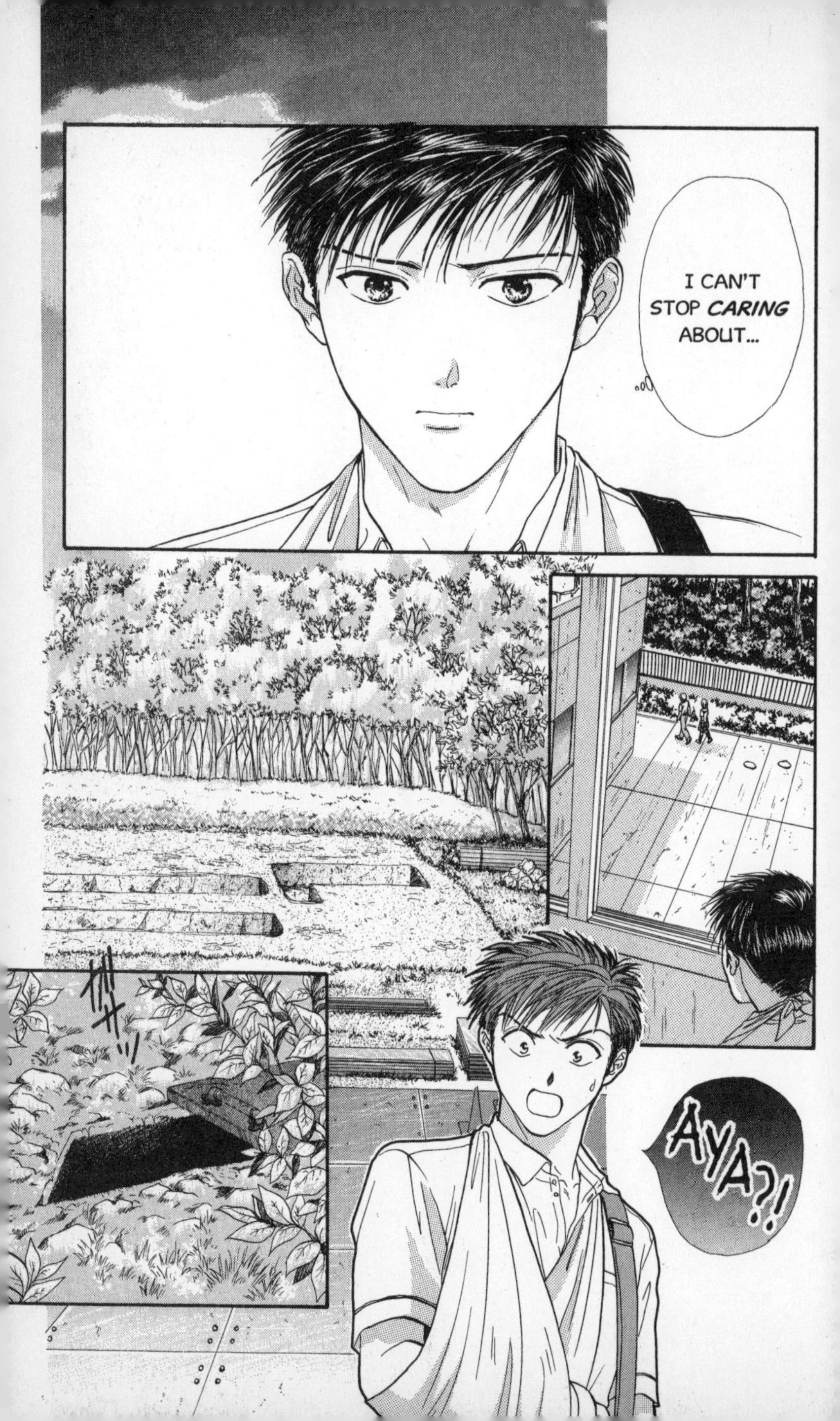
I CAN'T STOP CARING ABOUT...
AYA?!

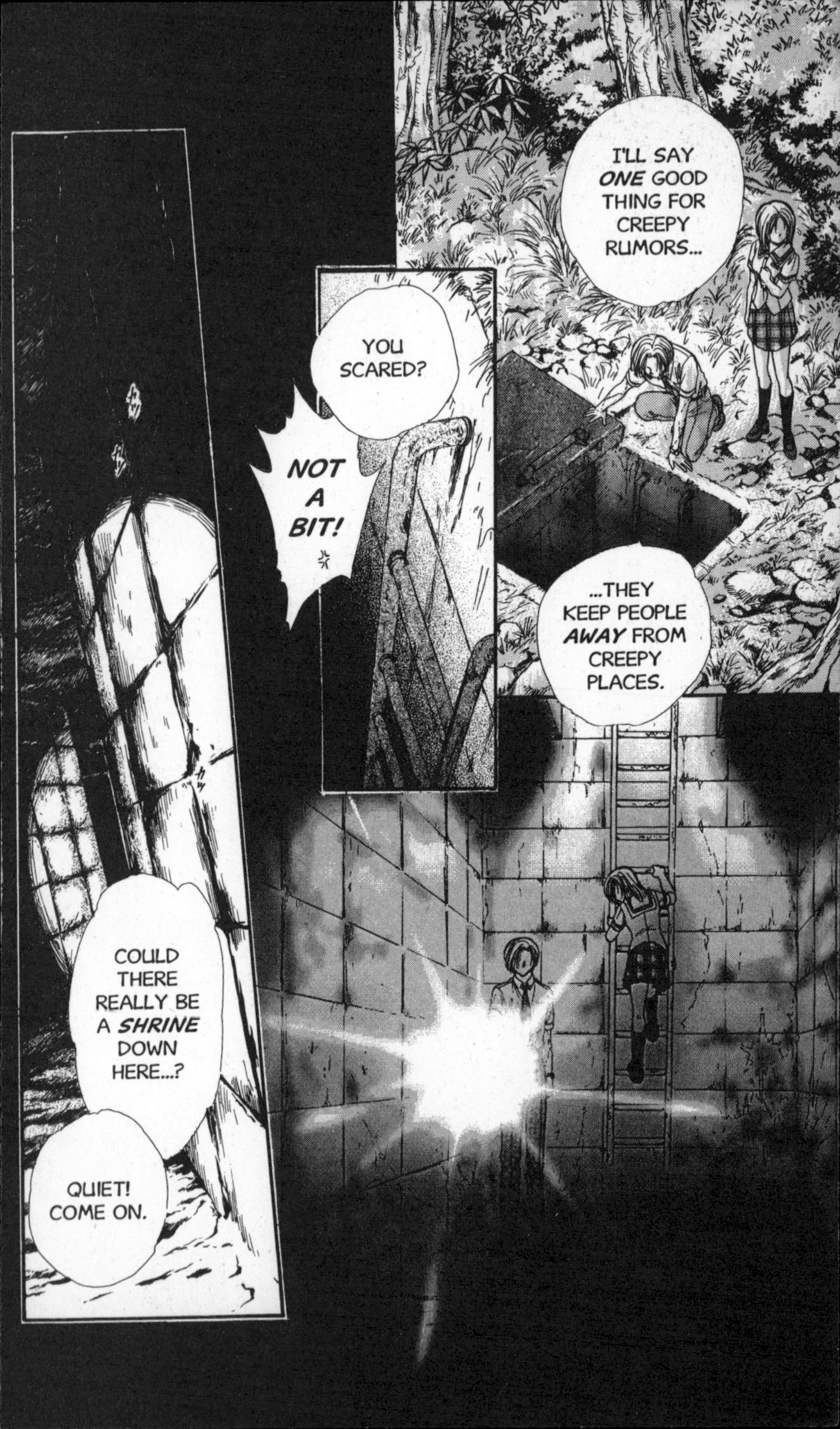
I'LL SAY ONE GOOD THING FOR CREEPY RUMORS...
...THEY KEEP PEOPLE AWAY FROM CREEPY PLACES.
YOU SCARED?
NOT A BIT!
COULD THERE REALLY BE A SHRINE DOWN HERE...?
QUIET! COME ON.

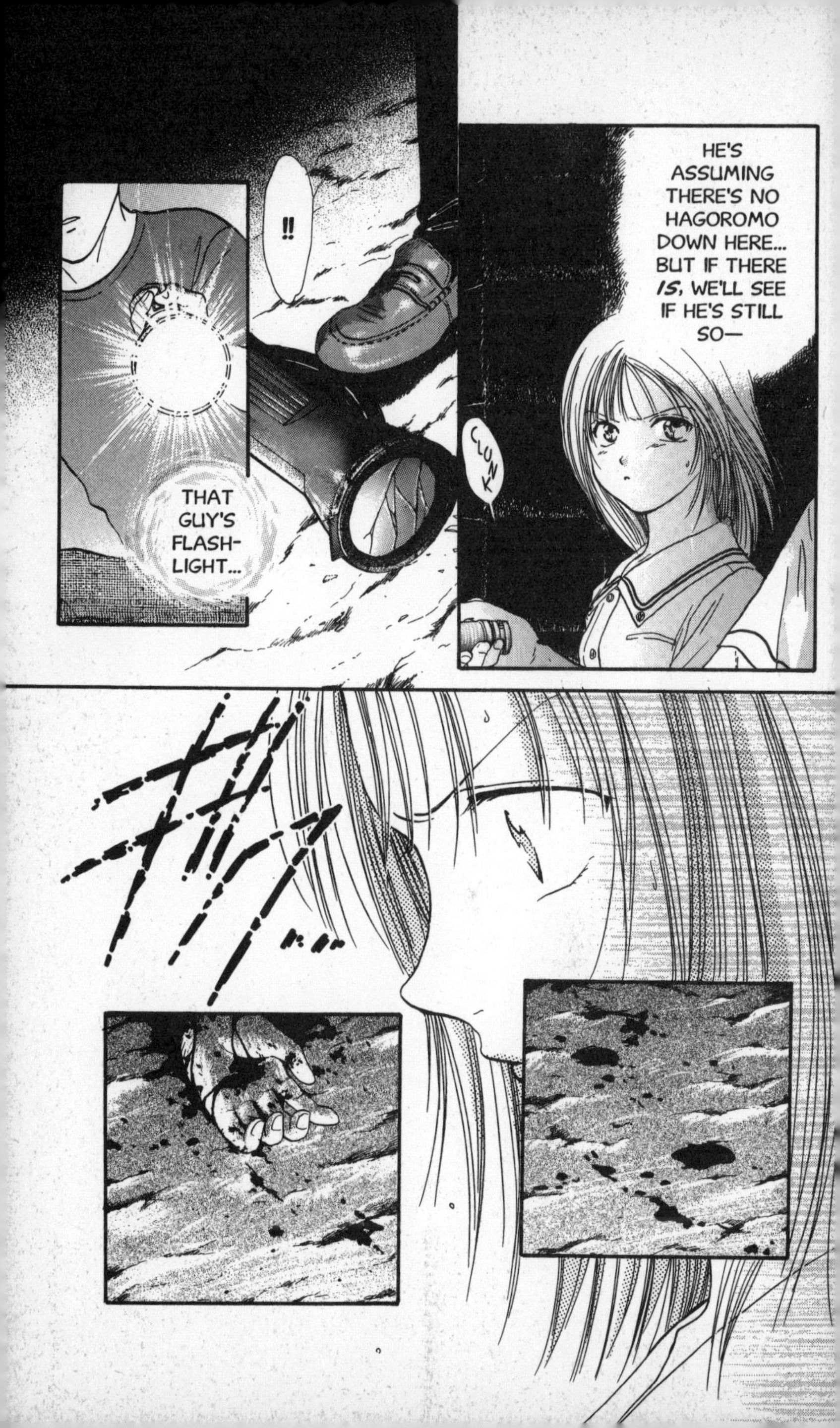
HE'S ASSUMING THERE'S NO HAGOROMO DOWN HERE... BUT IF THERE *IS*, WE'LL SEE IF HE'S STILL SO—
CLUNK
!!
THAT GUY'S FLASH-LIGHT...

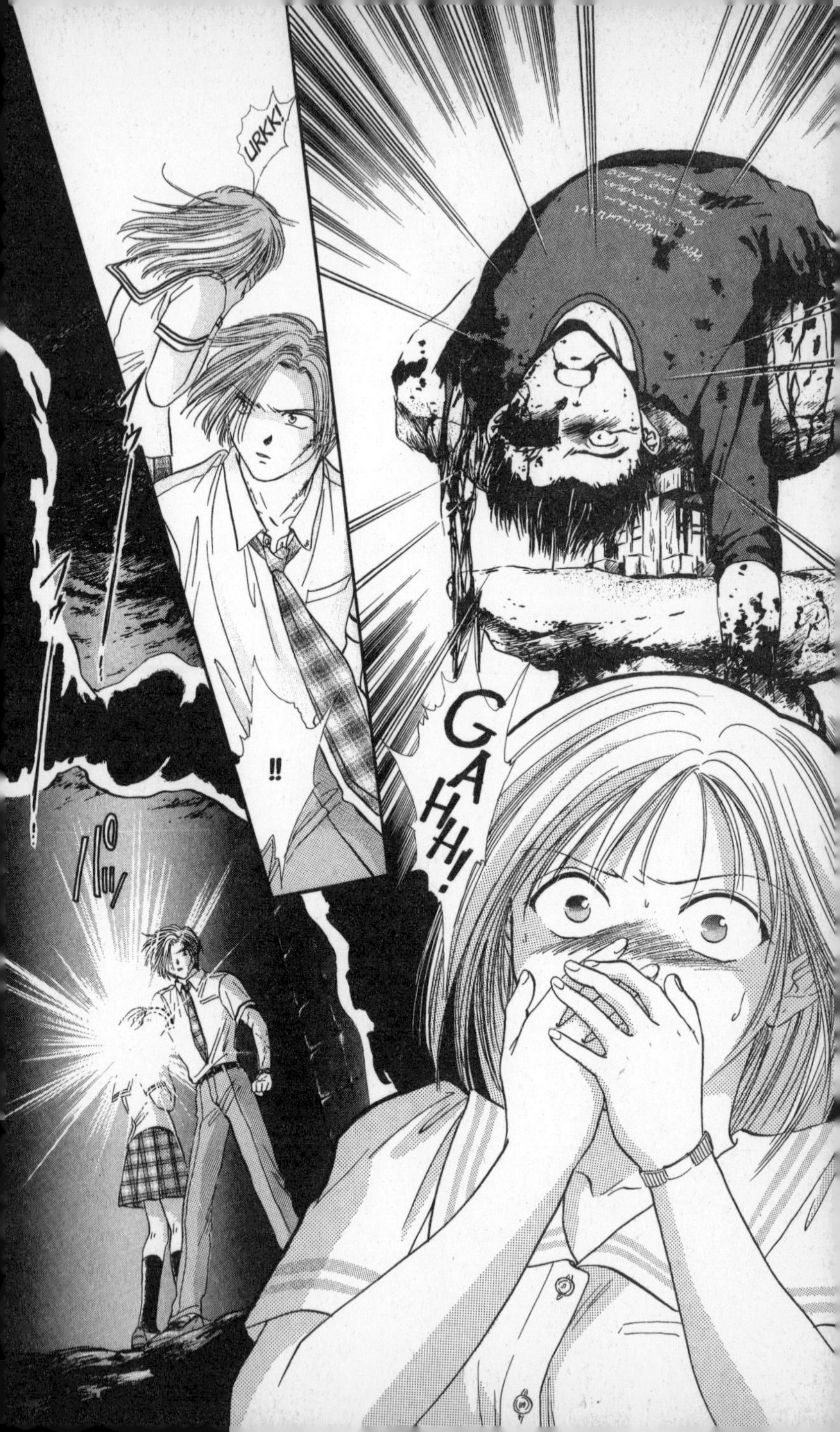
GAHHH!
URKK!
!!

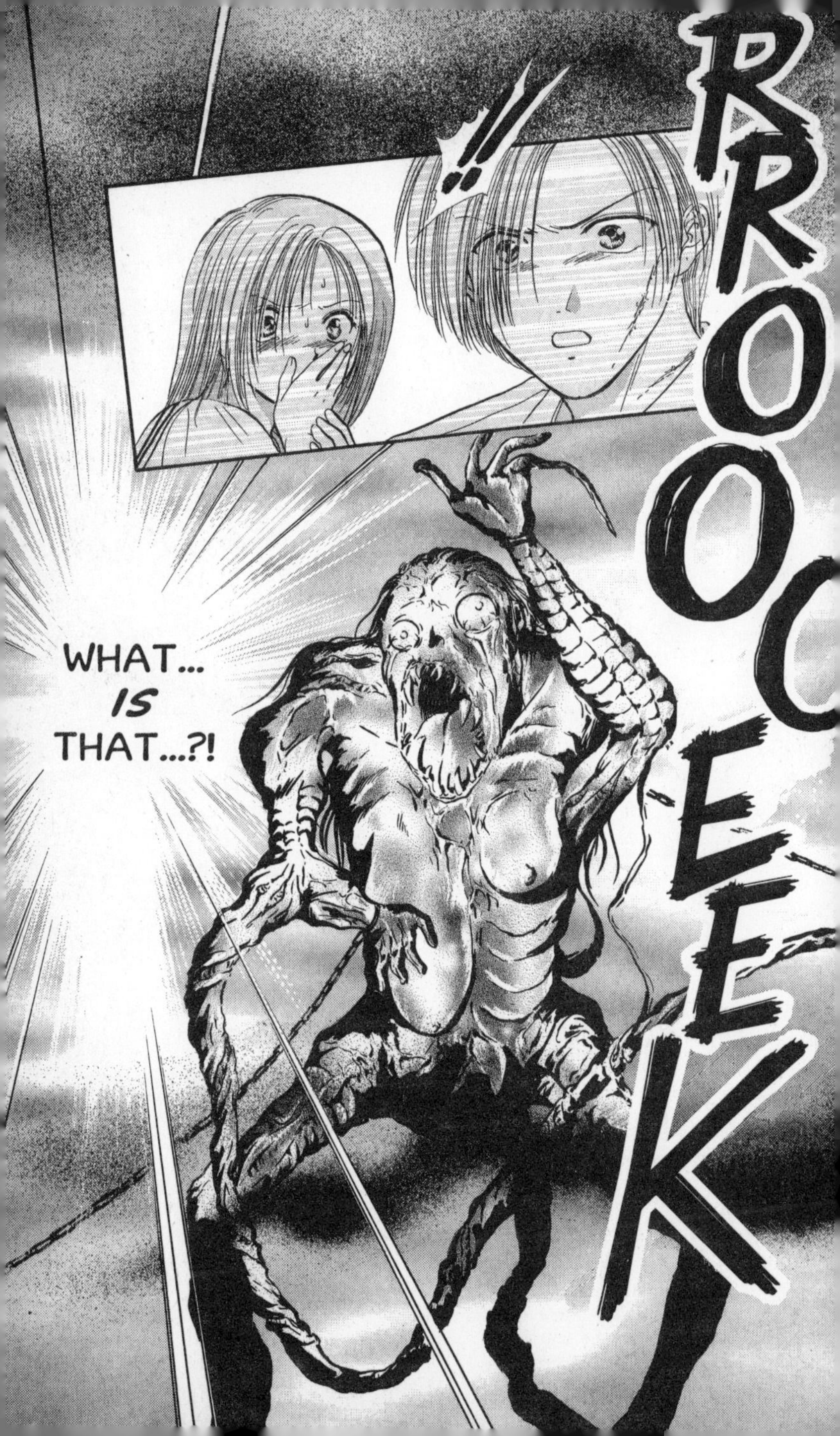
!!
RROOOEEEK
WHAT... *IS* THAT...?!

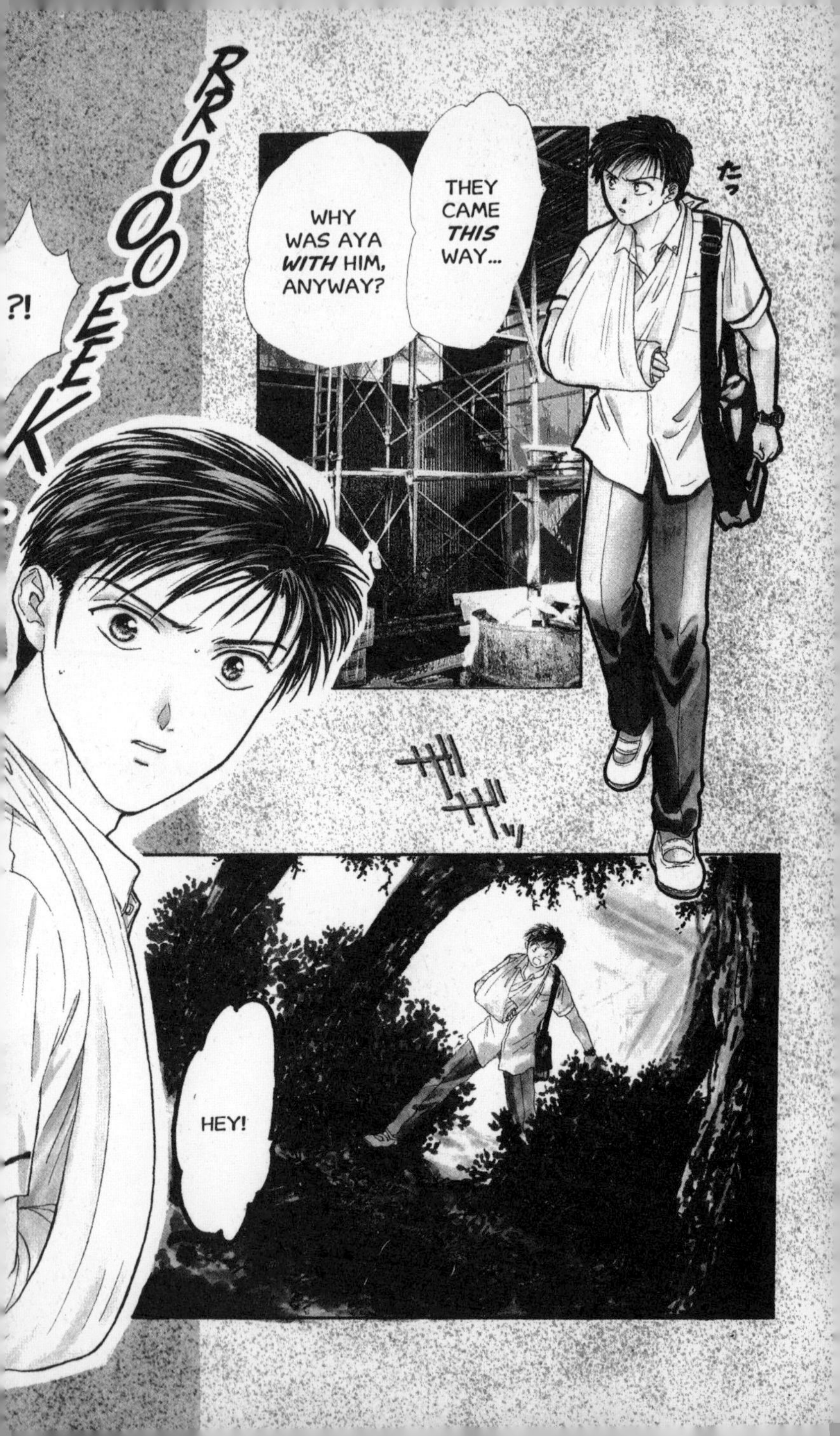
THEY CAME *THIS* WAY...
WHY WAS AYA *WITH* HIM, ANYWAY?
HEY!
RROOOEEEK
?!

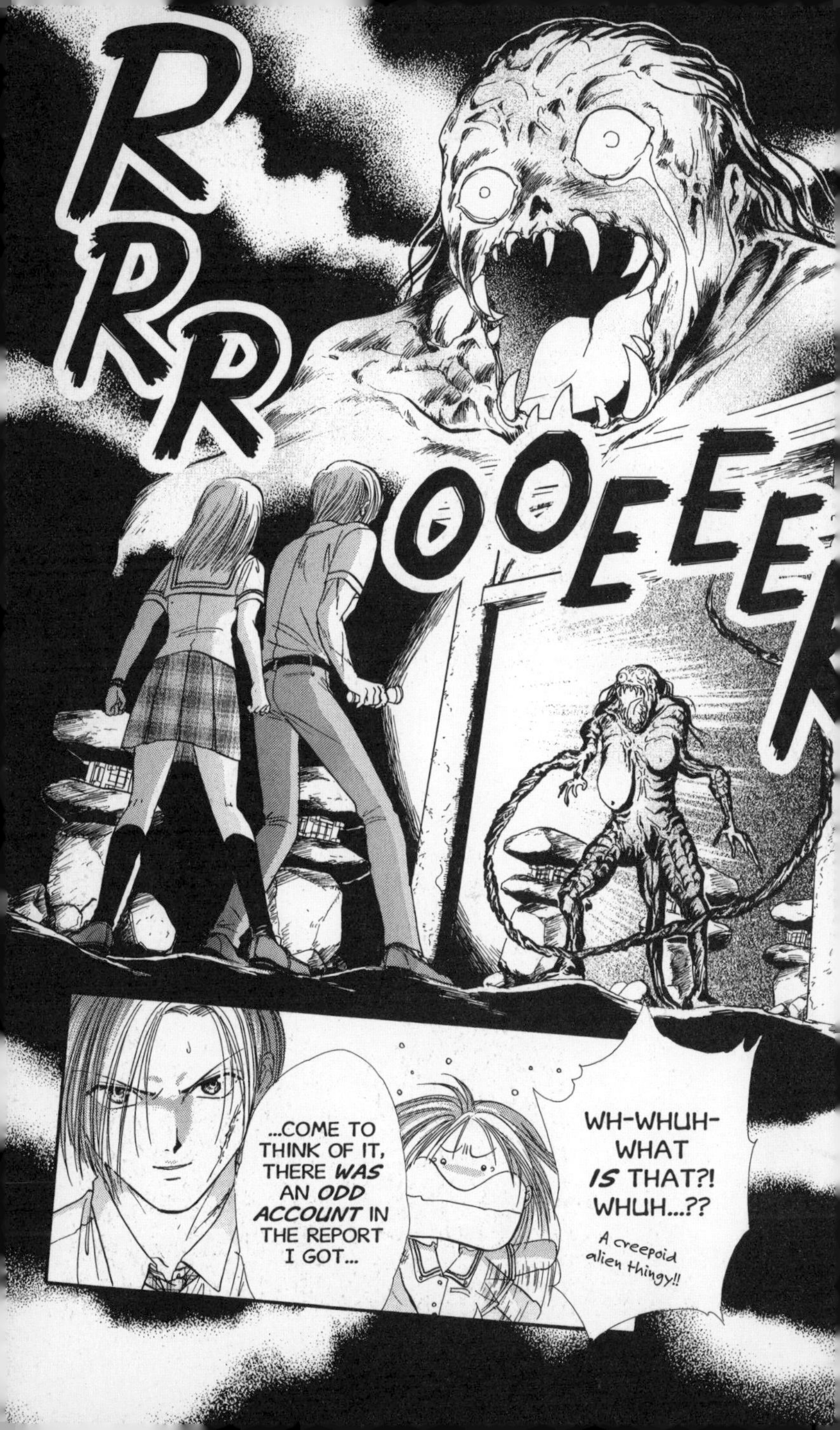
RRROOEEE
WH-WHUH-WHAT *IS* THAT?! WHUH...??
A creepoid alien thingy!!
...COME TO THINK OF IT, THERE *WAS* AN *ODD ACCOUNT* IN THE REPORT I GOT...

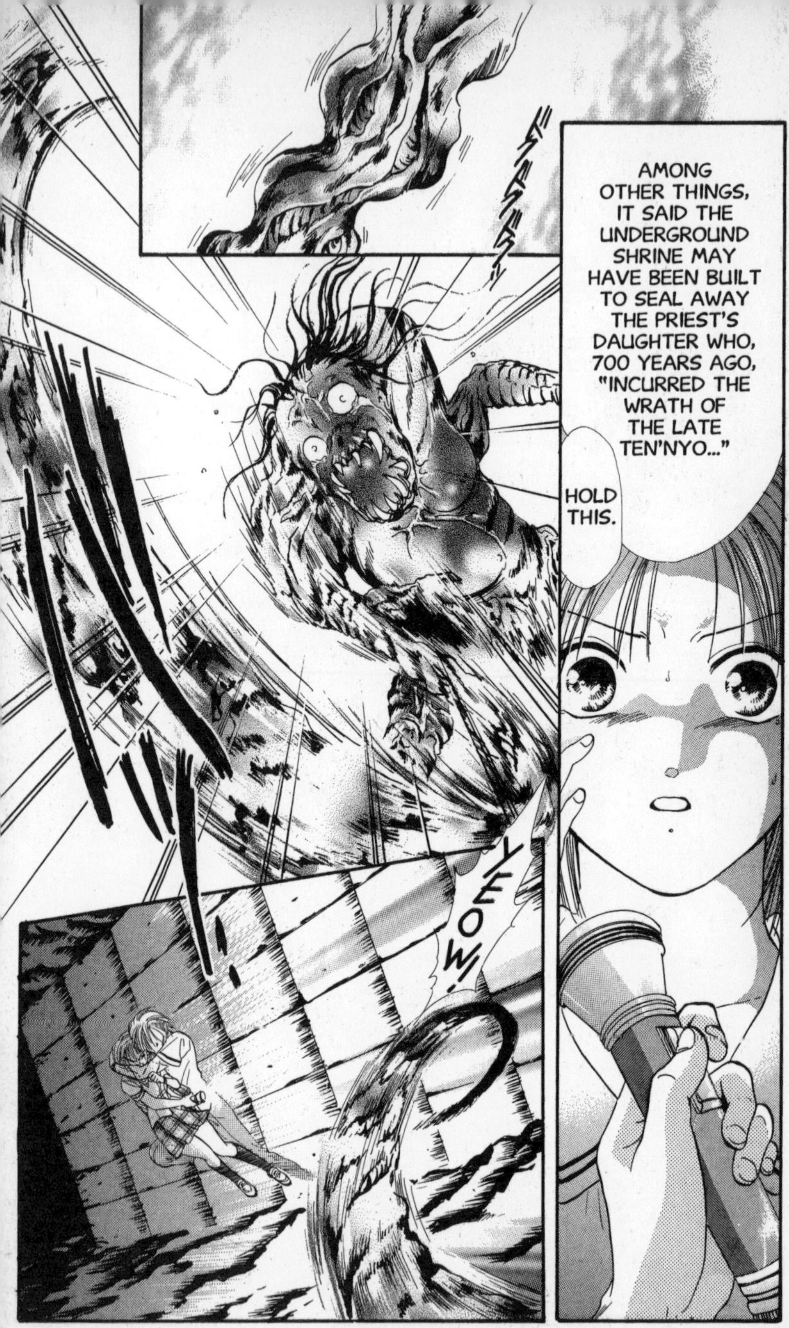
AMONG OTHER THINGS, IT SAID THE UNDERGROUND SHRINE MAY HAVE BEEN BUILT TO SEAL AWAY THE PRIEST'S DAUGHTER WHO, 700 YEARS AGO, "INCURRED THE WRATH OF THE LATE TEN'NYO..."
HOLD THIS.
YEEOW!

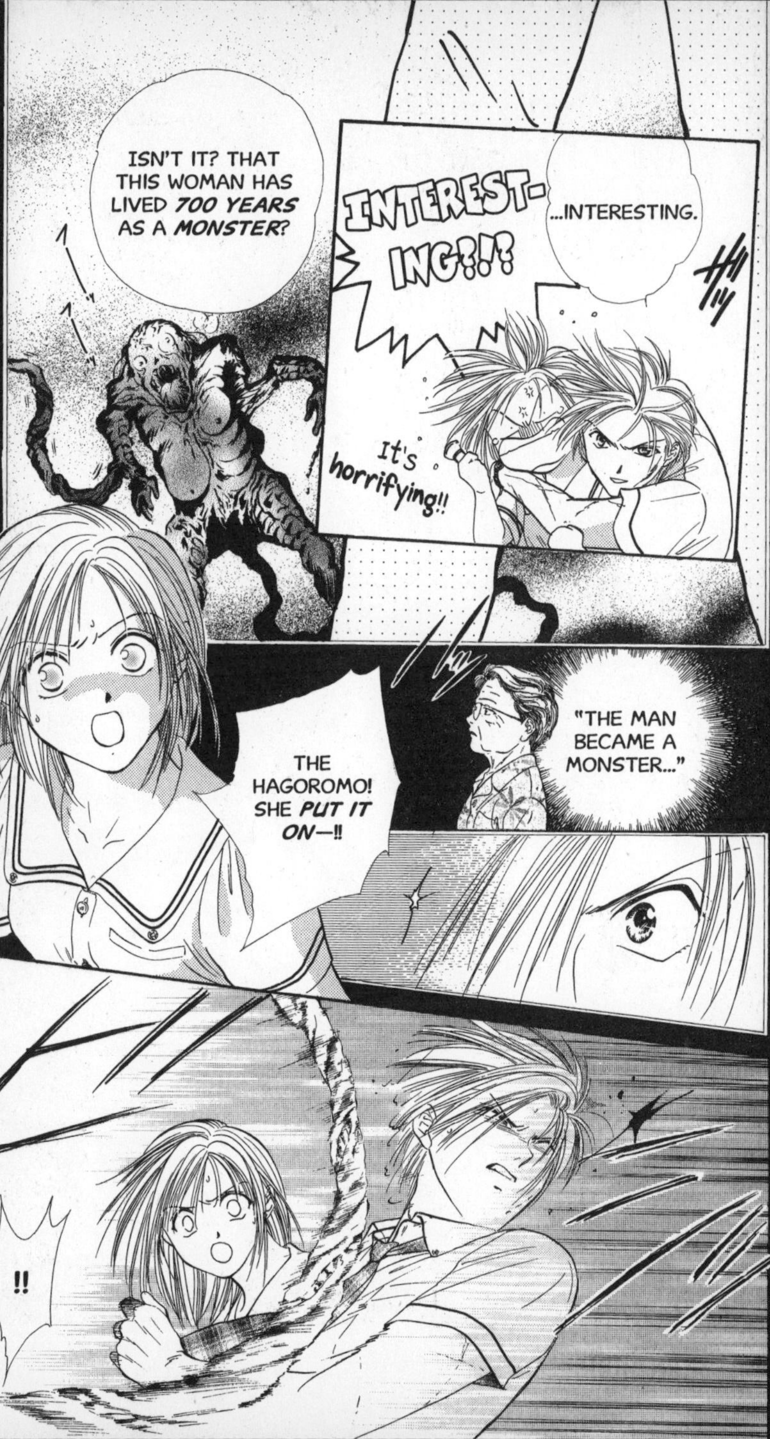
...INTERESTING.
INTEREST-ING?!?
It's horrifying!!
ISN'T IT? THAT THIS WOMAN HAS LIVED *700 YEARS* AS A *MONSTER*?
"THE MAN BECAME A MONSTER..."
THE HAGOROMO! SHE *PUT IT ON*—!!
!!

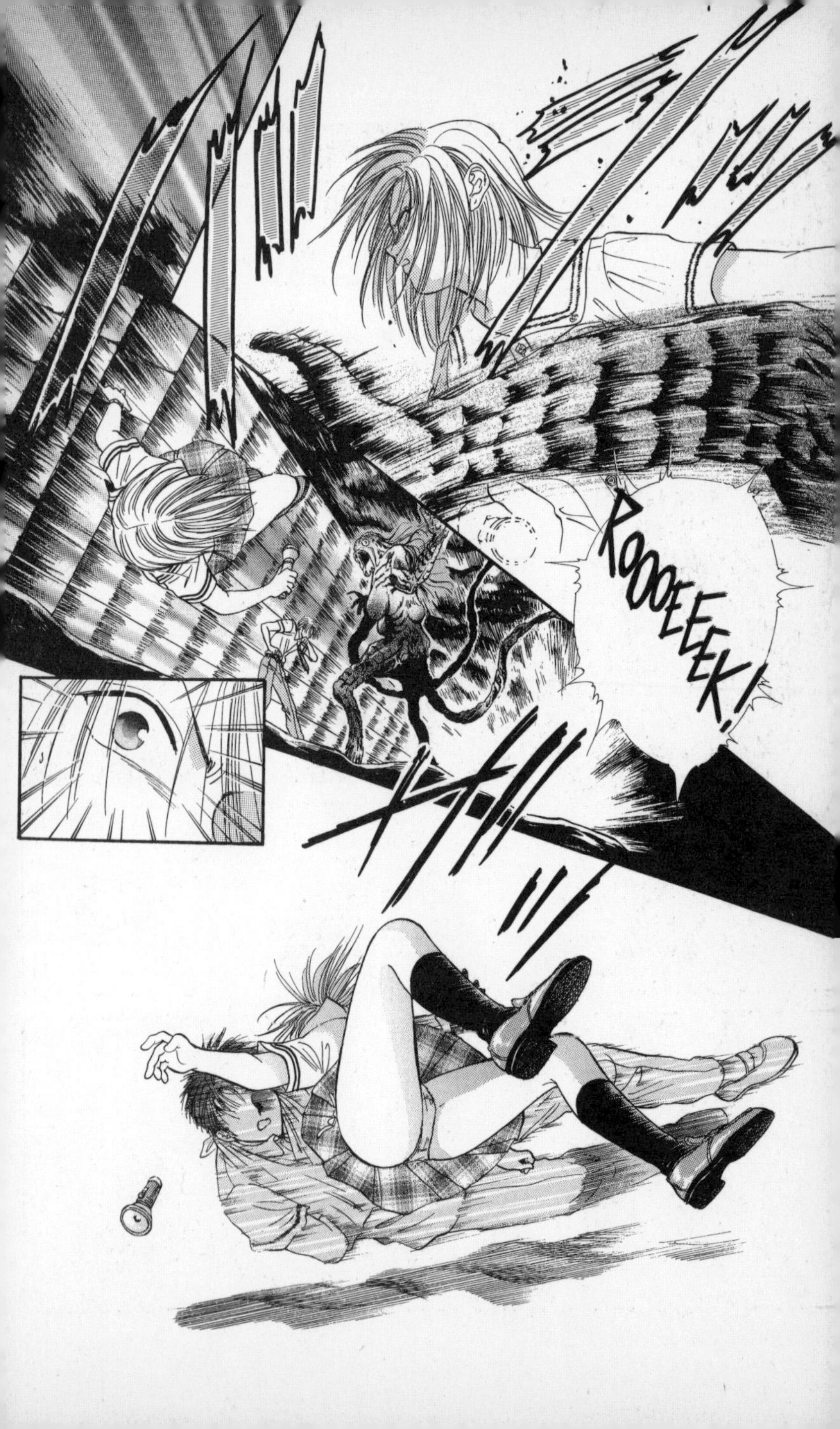
ROOOEEEEK!

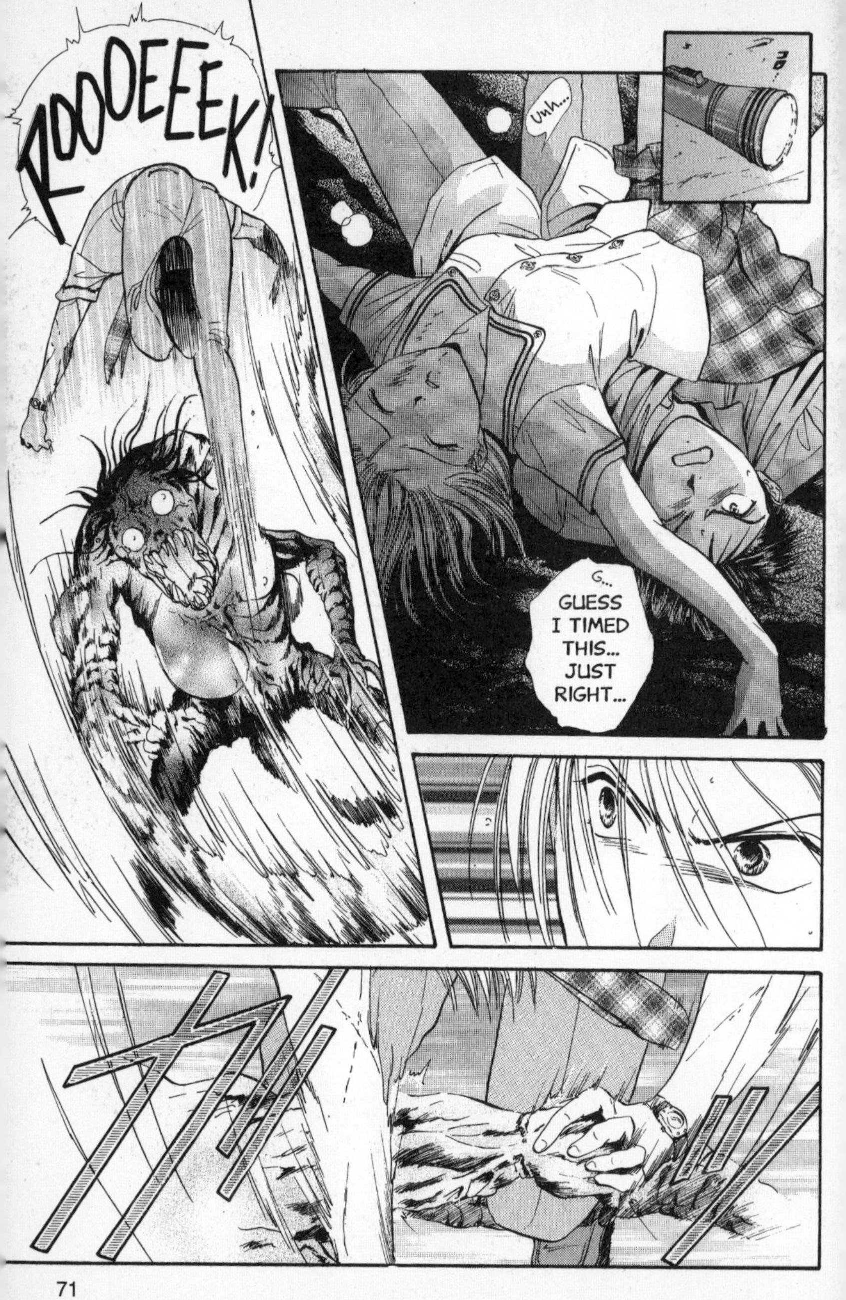

Unh...
G... GUESS I TIMED THIS... JUST RIGHT...
ROOOEEEK!

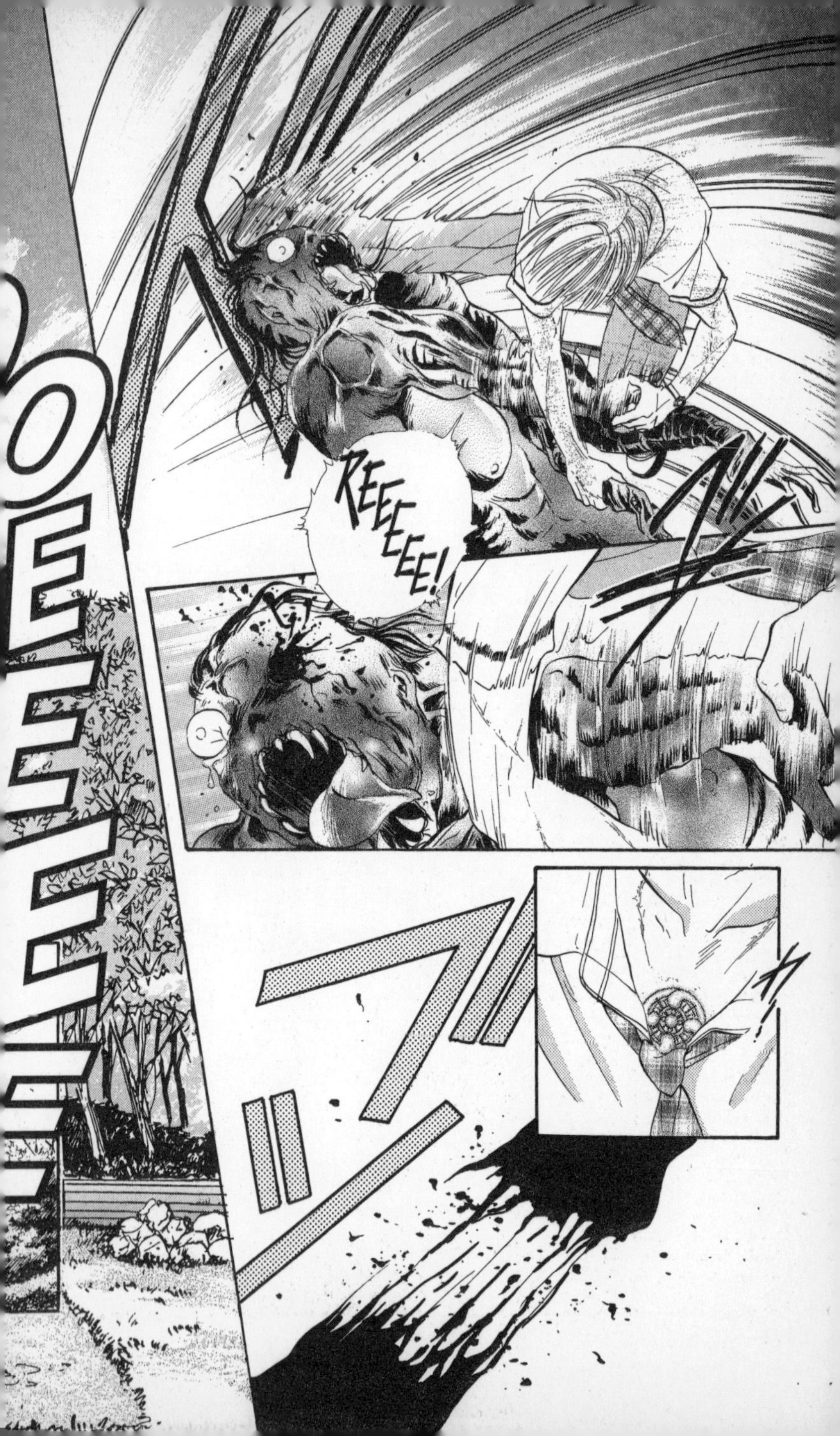
REEEEEE!

♦ Monster ♦

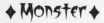

Fact is, men sometimes have this "rape fantasy." When asked what they'd do if the world were going to end, girls generally reply, "Stay home." Guys, though, generally answer " 'Do it' as much as possible." What a charming way to put it, huh? I'm sure not **all** guys think like that; maybe **you** think it's "sick," or "smutty," but it does come from a survival instinct of the species to leave offspring. We'd better hope for peace on Earth. A manga artist (♂) who came over to help me out shared some opinions from his perspective: "During their teen years, boys don't understand if it's 'love' or 'lust' that they feel." This is why there are sad tales of boyfriends suddenly "losing interest" once they've had sex—I guess maybe they wanted to "just do it." Boys can't even tell the difference themselves—bad news to girls who break down and agree to do whatever the boy wants so he'll still "like" her! Girls, be strong in your resolve! A writer I greatly respect wrote, "Women have the right to protect themselves, and if the man doesn't understand, they're not worth spending time on. A satisfying, fulfilling relationship can only exist between two mature, faithful, and independent individuals.... Ingratiation within a relationship evokes only pathos. It is neither compassion nor love. Real love is mutual dependence. Shallow people are capable only of shallow love." Making yourself into a better person is the **important** thing. "A relationship that sacrifices one's own growth or potential will not lead to happiness.... Teenagers can be shortsighted, unsure of the way to make the most of themselves. They may think falling in love is the greatest thing in the world, but it isn't the only thing in life.... Friendships and love will create stronger bonds the more people nurture their own characters." Pretty deep, huh?

...To be continued.

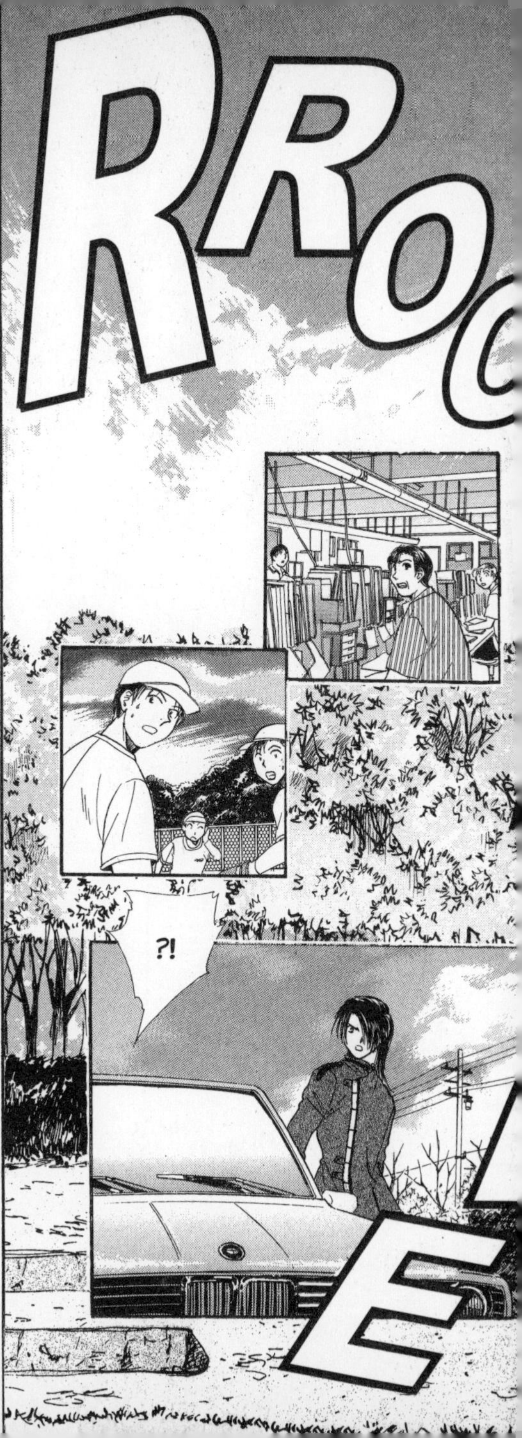
RRO
?!

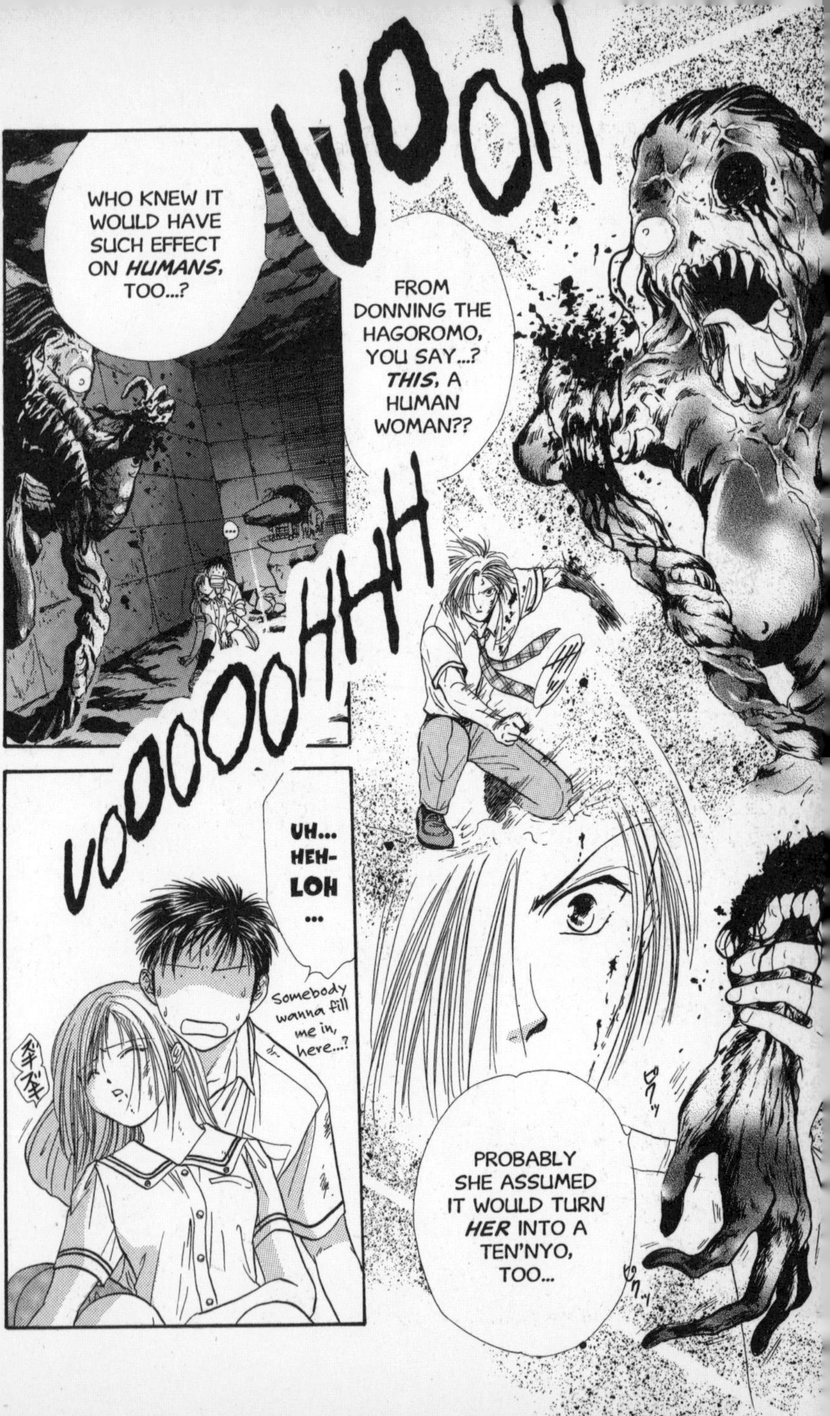
WOOH
FROM DONNING THE HAGOROMO, YOU SAY...? THIS, A HUMAN WOMAN??
VOOOOOHHH
PROBABLY SHE ASSUMED IT WOULD TURN HER INTO A TEN'NYO, TOO...
WHO KNEW IT WOULD HAVE SUCH EFFECT ON HUMANS, TOO...?
...
UH... HEH-LOH...
Somebody wanna fill me in, here...?

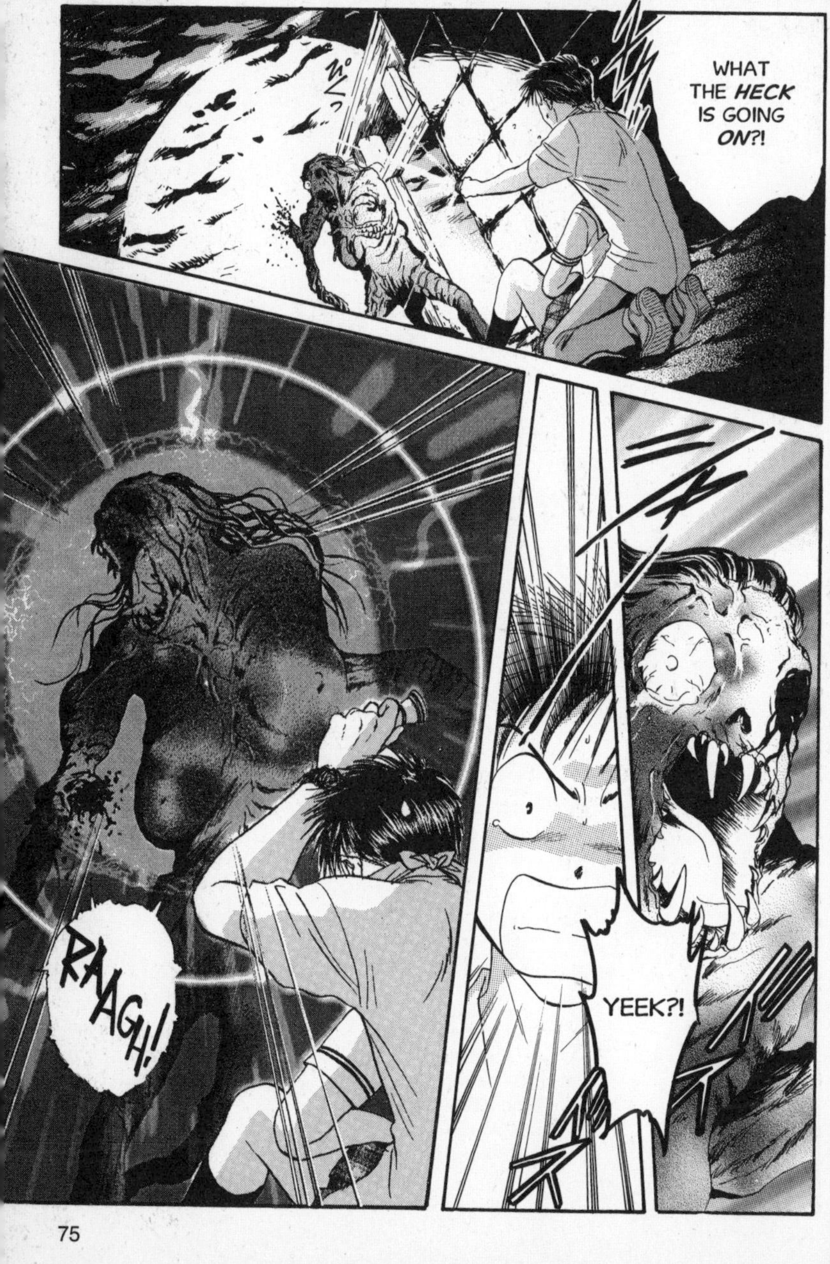
WHAT THE *HECK* IS GOING *ON*?!
YEEK?!
RAAGH!

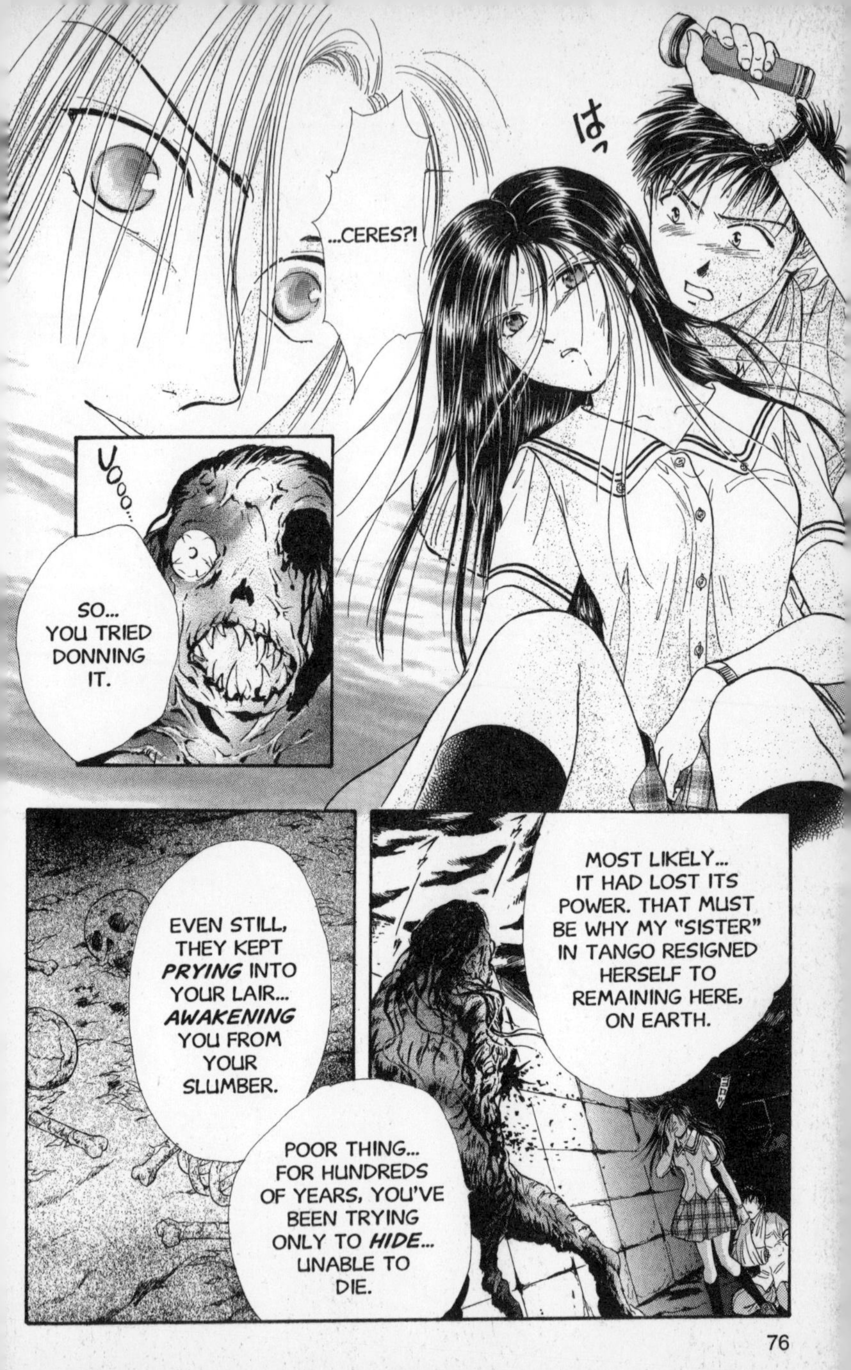
はっ
...CERES?!
VOOO...
SO... YOU TRIED DONNING IT.
MOST LIKELY... IT HAD LOST ITS POWER. THAT MUST BE WHY MY "SISTER" IN TANGO RESIGNED HERSELF TO REMAINING HERE, ON EARTH.
EVEN STILL, THEY KEPT *PRYING* INTO YOUR LAIR... *AWAKENING* YOU FROM YOUR SLUMBER.
POOR THING... FOR HUNDREDS OF YEARS, YOU'VE BEEN TRYING ONLY TO *HIDE*... UNABLE TO DIE.

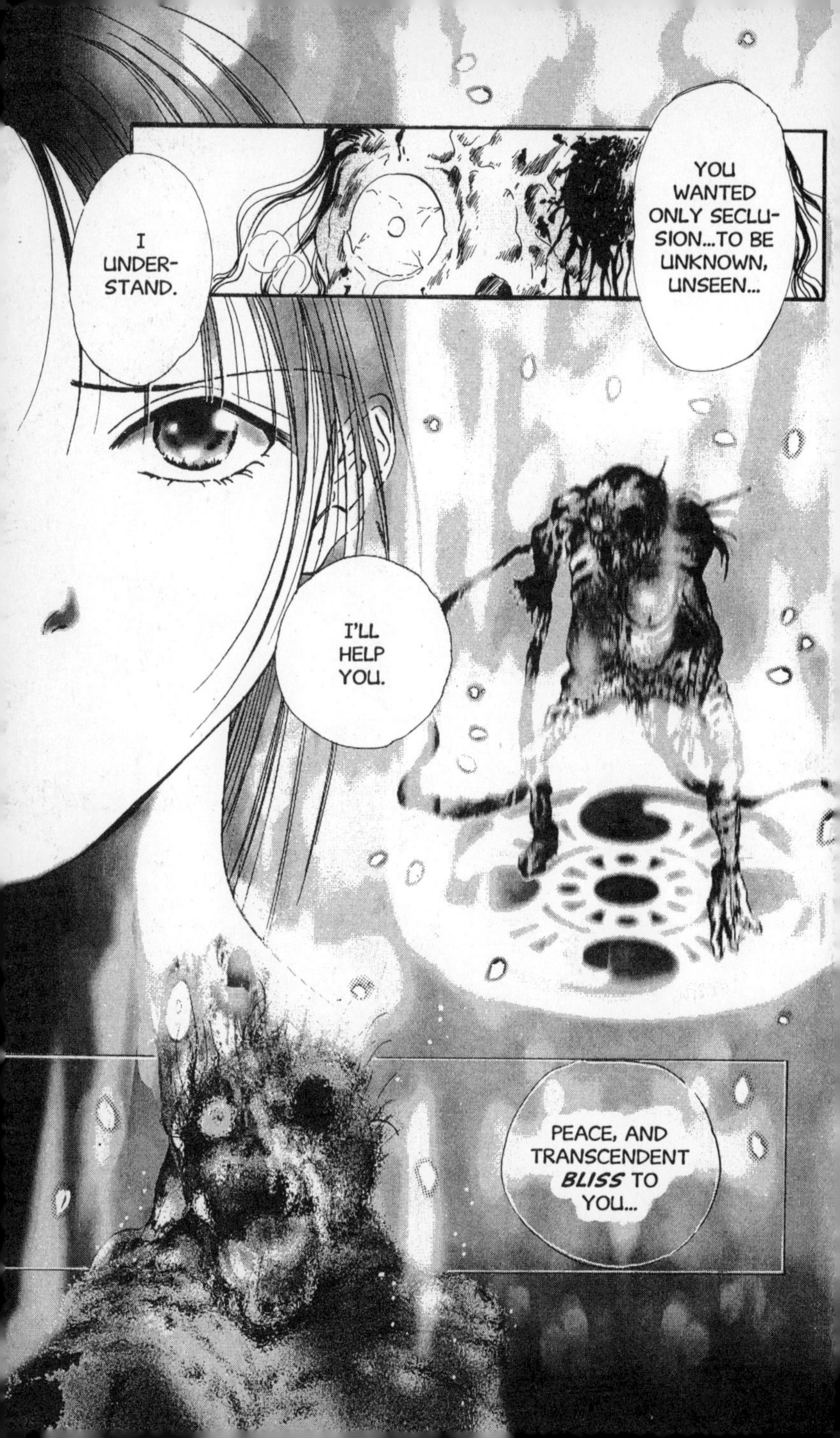
YOU WANTED ONLY SECLUSION...TO BE UNKNOWN, UNSEEN...
I UNDERSTAND.
I'LL HELP YOU.
PEACE, AND TRANSCENDENT *BLISS* TO YOU...

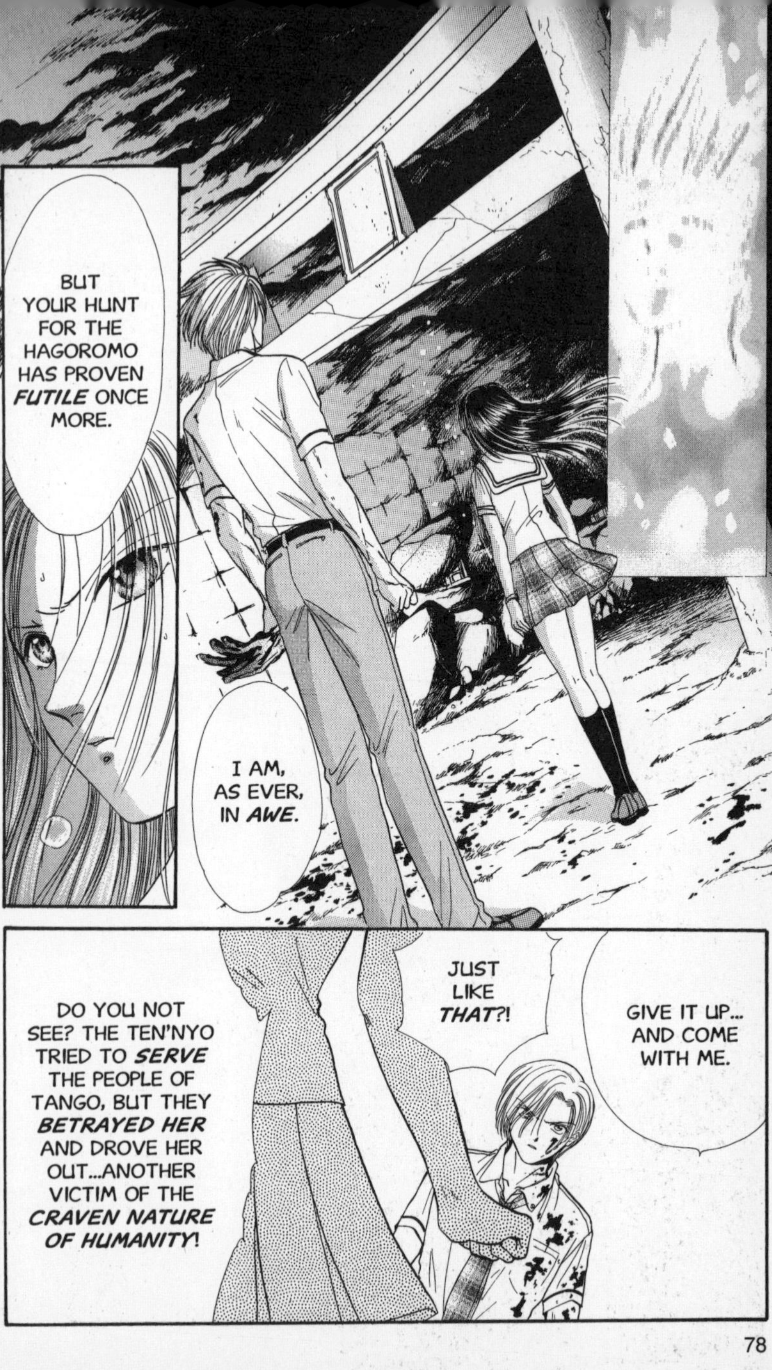
I AM, AS EVER, IN *AWE.*
BUT YOUR HUNT FOR THE HAGOROMO HAS PROVEN *FUTILE* ONCE MORE.
GIVE IT UP... AND COME WITH ME.
JUST LIKE *THAT*?!
DO YOU NOT SEE? THE TEN'NYO TRIED TO *SERVE* THE PEOPLE OF TANGO, BUT THEY *BETRAYED HER* AND DROVE HER OUT...ANOTHER VICTIM OF THE *CRAVEN NATURE OF HUMANITY*!

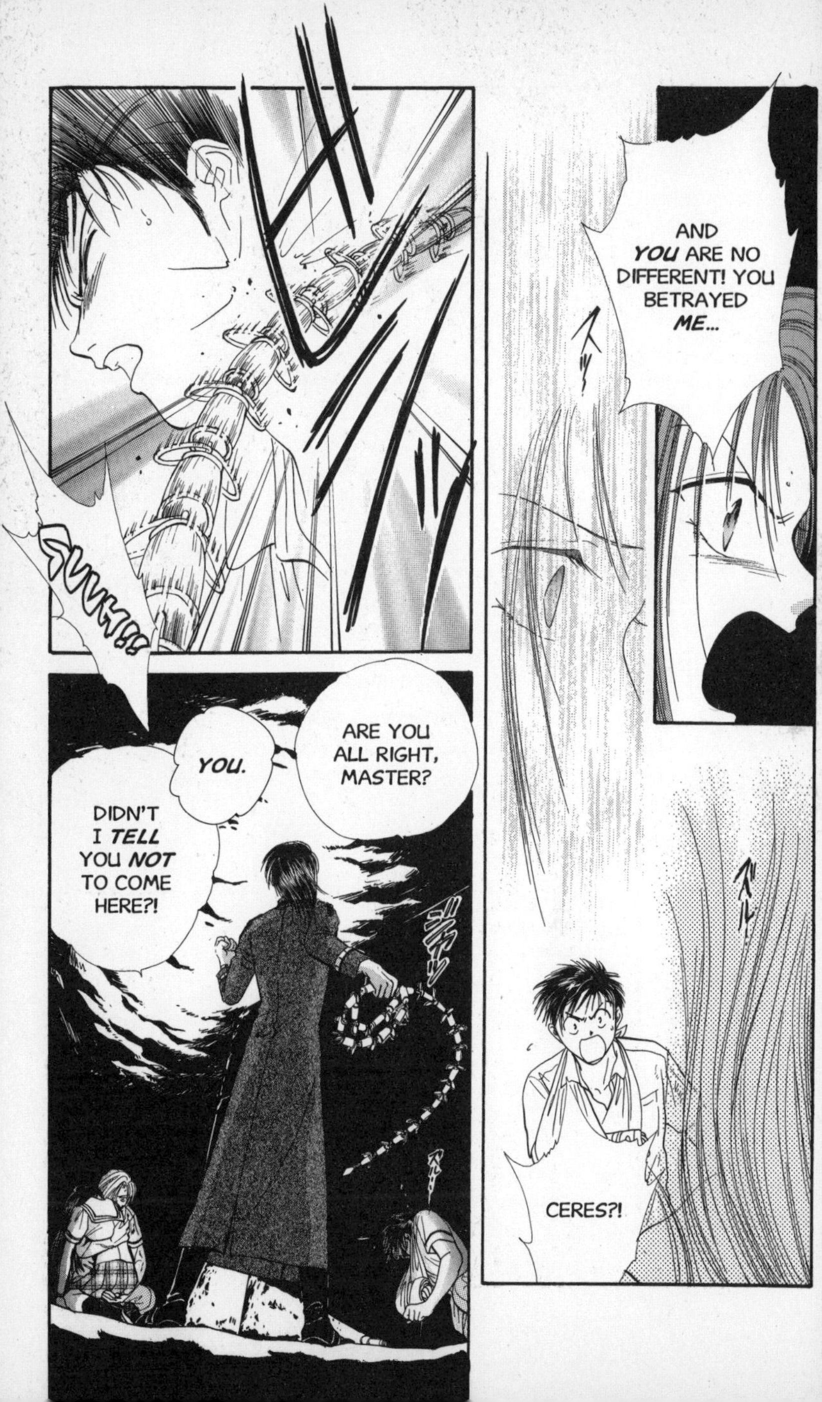
AND *YOU* ARE NO DIFFERENT! YOU BETRAYED *ME*...
CERES?!
ARE YOU ALL RIGHT, MASTER?
YOU.
DIDN'T I *TELL* YOU *NOT* TO COME HERE?!

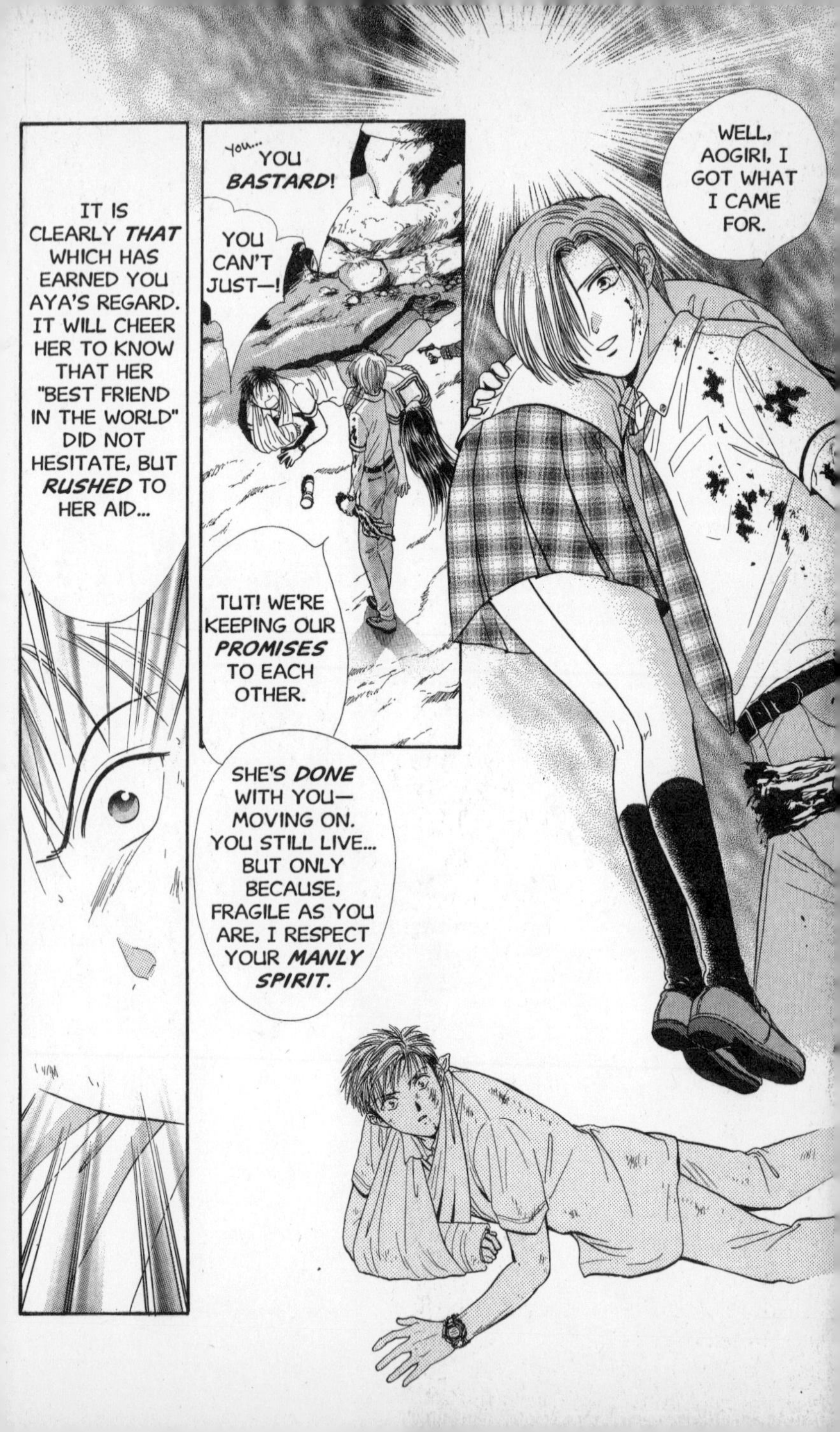
WELL, AOGIRI, I GOT WHAT I CAME FOR.
You... YOU *BASTARD*!
YOU CAN'T JUST—!
TUT! WE'RE KEEPING OUR *PROMISES* TO EACH OTHER.
SHE'S *DONE* WITH YOU— MOVING ON. YOU STILL LIVE... BUT ONLY BECAUSE, FRAGILE AS YOU ARE, I RESPECT YOUR *MANLY SPIRIT*.
IT IS CLEARLY *THAT* WHICH HAS EARNED YOU AYA'S REGARD. IT WILL CHEER HER TO KNOW THAT HER "BEST FRIEND IN THE WORLD" DID NOT HESITATE, BUT *RUSHED* TO HER AID...

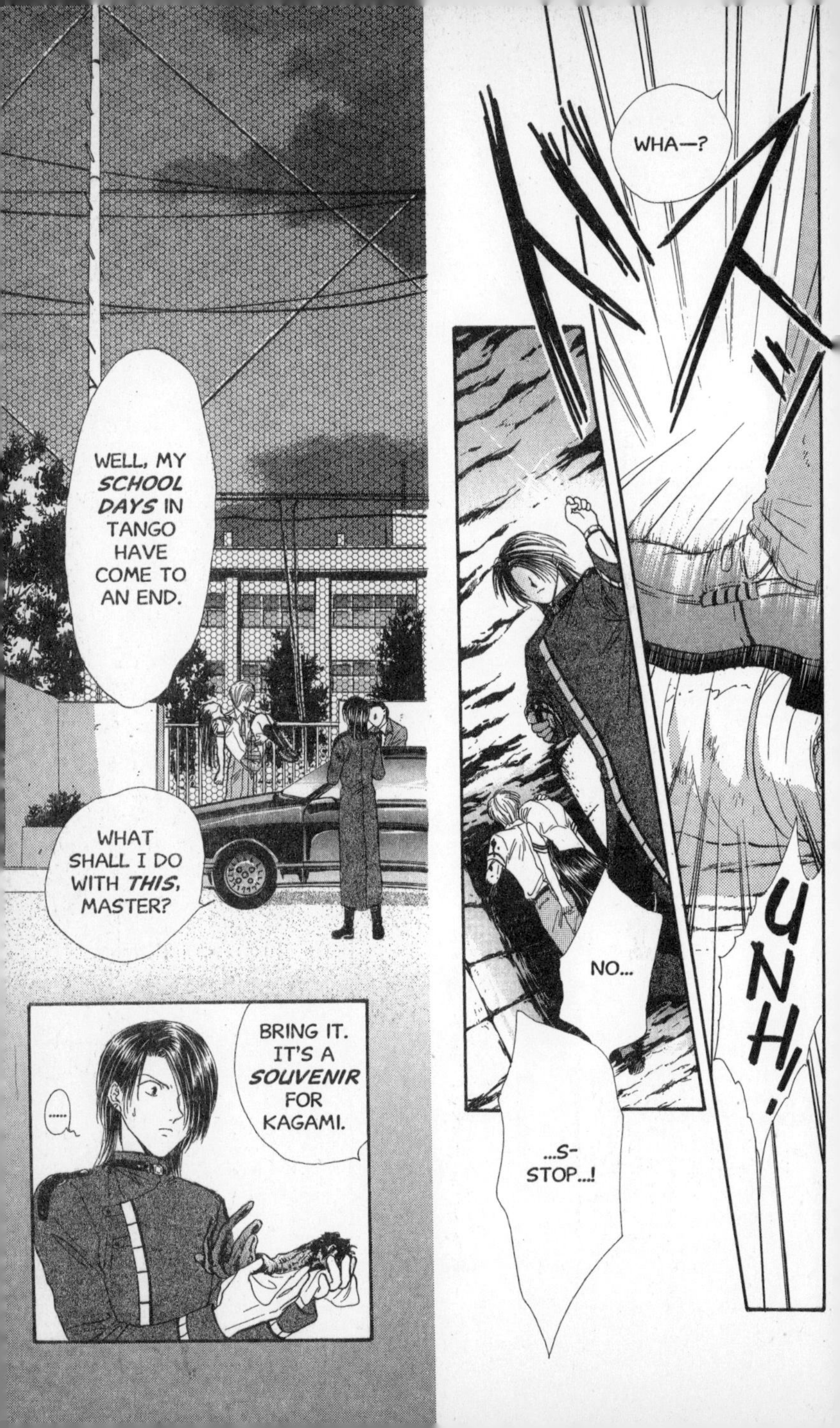
WHA—?
UNH!!
NO...
...S-STOP...!
WELL, MY SCHOOL DAYS IN TANGO HAVE COME TO AN END.
WHAT SHALL I DO WITH THIS, MASTER?
BRING IT. IT'S A SOUVENIR FOR KAGAMI.
......

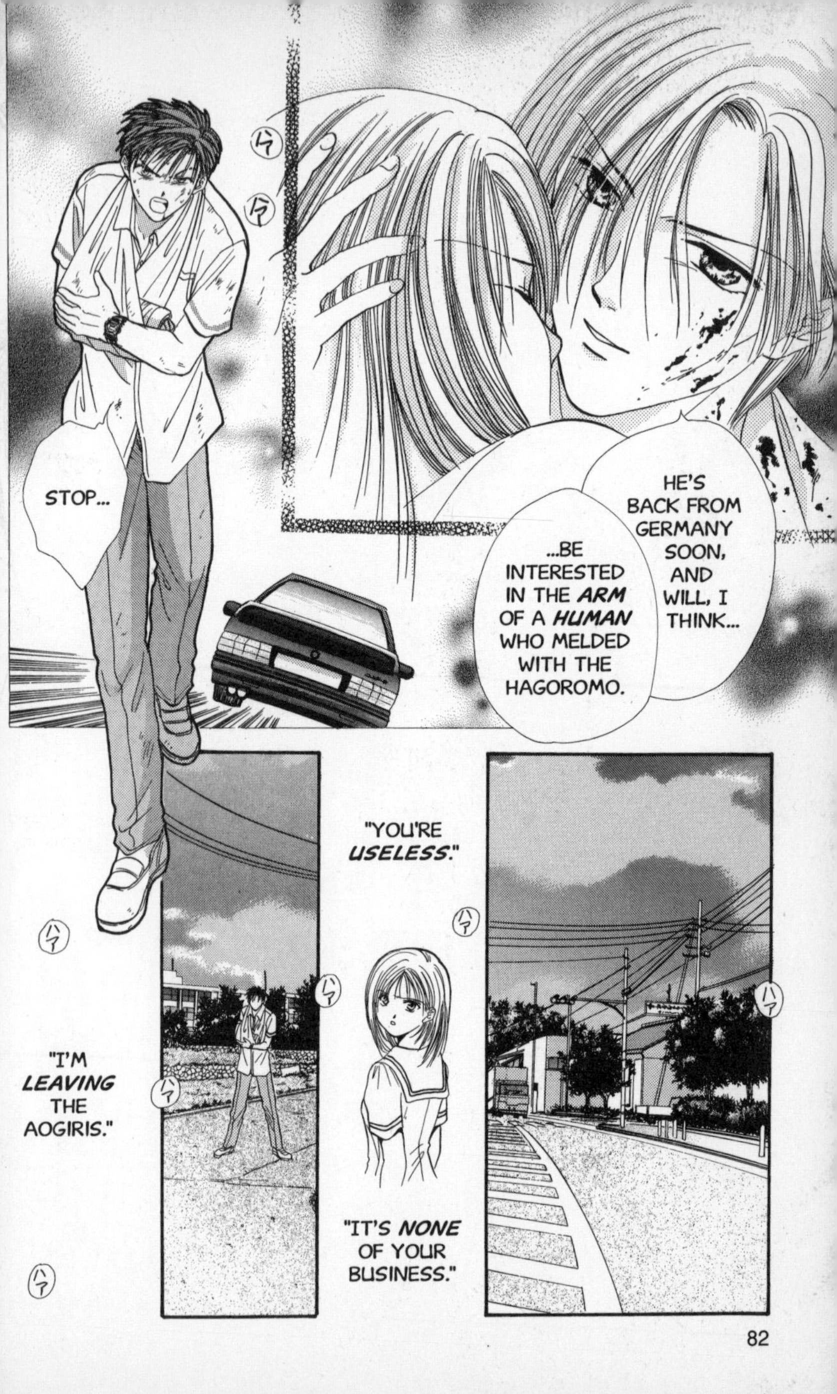
HE'S BACK FROM GERMANY SOON, AND WILL, I THINK...
...BE INTERESTED IN THE ARM OF A HUMAN WHO MELDED WITH THE HAGOROMO.
ハァ
ハァ
STOP...
ハァ
ハァ
"YOU'RE USELESS."
"IT'S NONE OF YOUR BUSINESS."
ハァ
ハァ
"I'M LEAVING THE AOGIRIS."
ハァ
ハァ

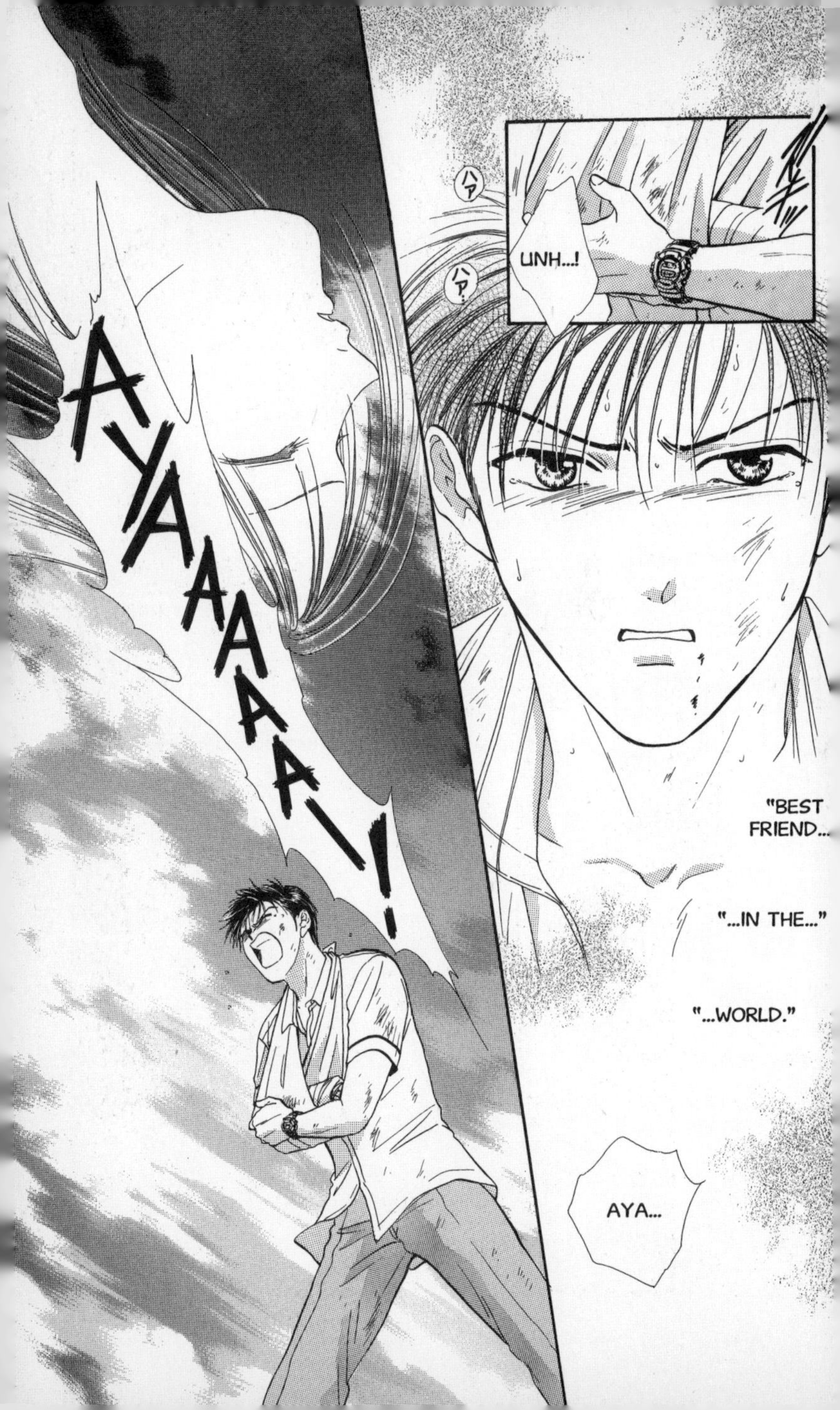
ハア
UNH...!
ハア...
"BEST FRIEND...
"...IN THE..."
"...WORLD."
AYA...
AYAAAAAAI!!

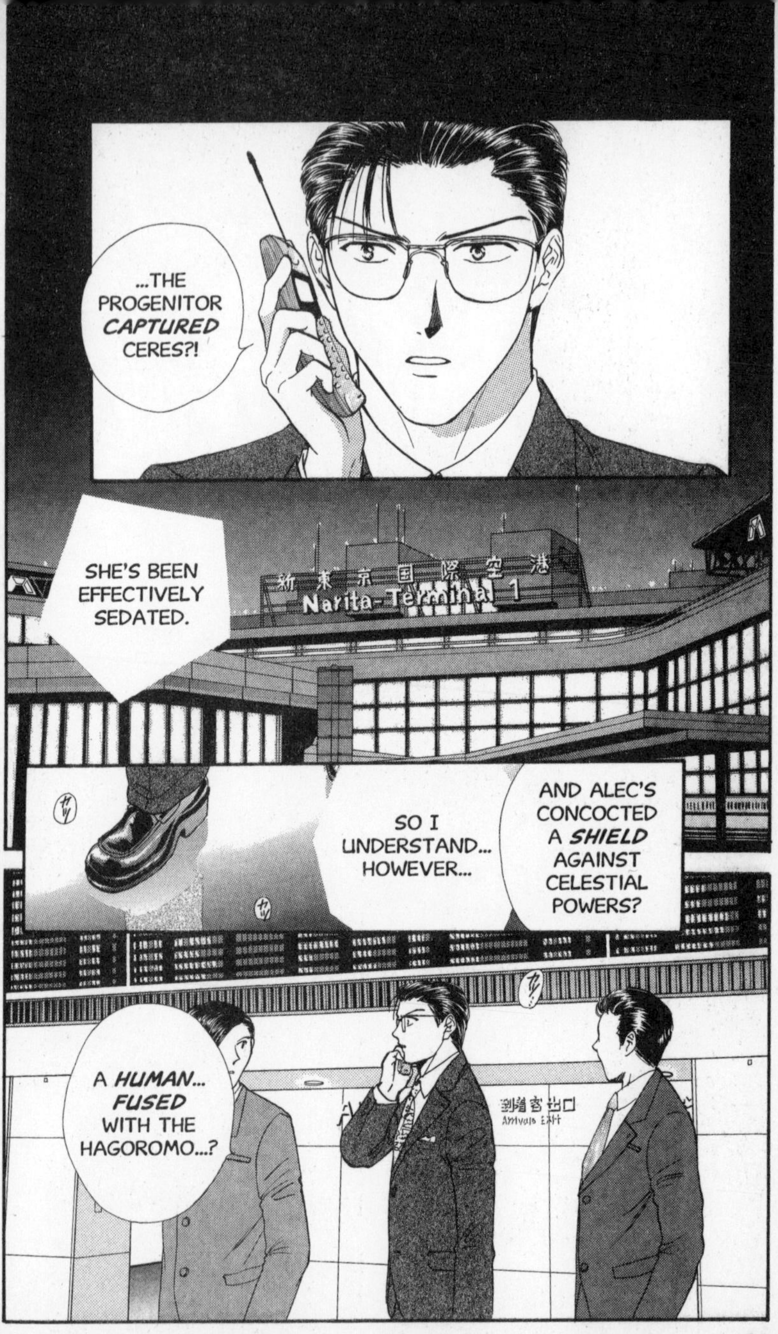
...THE PROGENITOR *CAPTURED* CERES?!
SHE'S BEEN EFFECTIVELY SEDATED.
新東京国際空港
Narita-Terminal 1
AND ALEC'S CONCOCTED A *SHIELD* AGAINST CELESTIAL POWERS?
SO I UNDERSTAND... HOWEVER...
到着客出口
Arrivals Exit
A *HUMAN*... *FUSED* WITH THE HAGOROMO...?

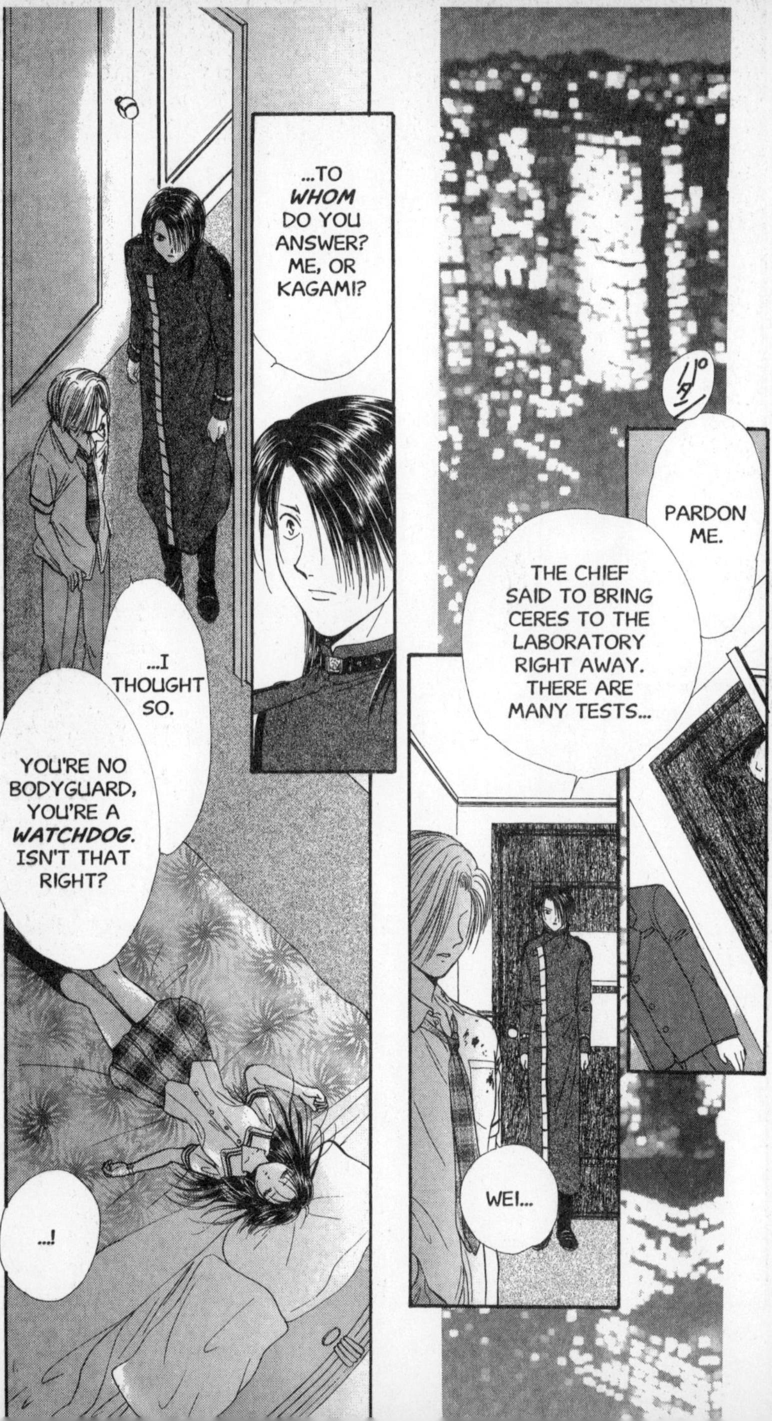
PARDON ME.
THE CHIEF SAID TO BRING CERES TO THE LABORATORY RIGHT AWAY. THERE ARE MANY TESTS...
WEI...
...TO *WHOM* DO YOU ANSWER? ME, OR KAGAMI!?
...I THOUGHT SO.
YOU'RE NO BODYGUARD, YOU'RE A ***WATCHDOG***. ISN'T THAT RIGHT?
...!

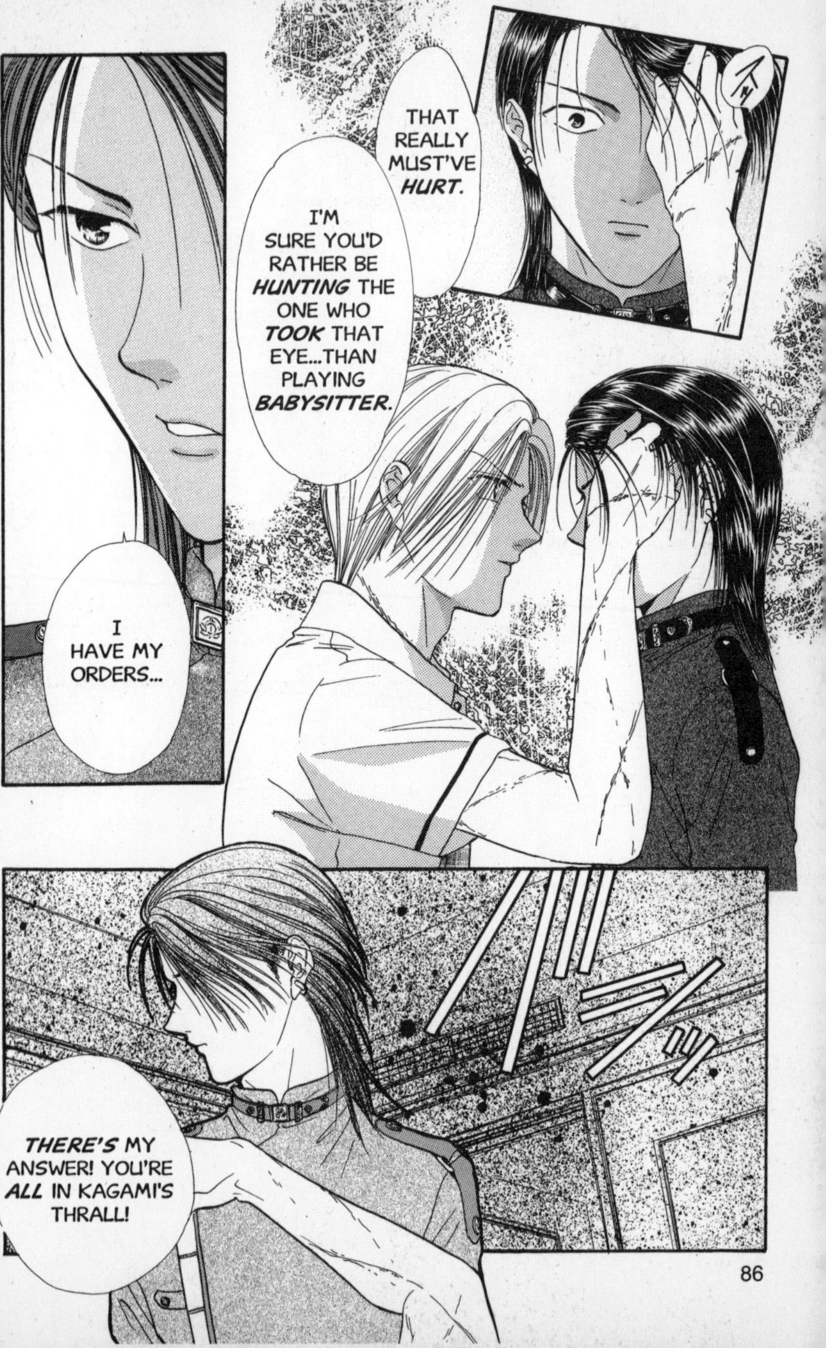
THAT REALLY MUST'VE *HURT*.
I'M SURE YOU'D RATHER BE *HUNTING* THE ONE WHO *TOOK* THAT EYE...THAN PLAYING *BABYSITTER*.
I HAVE MY ORDERS...
THERE'S MY ANSWER! YOU'RE *ALL* IN KAGAMI'S THRALL!

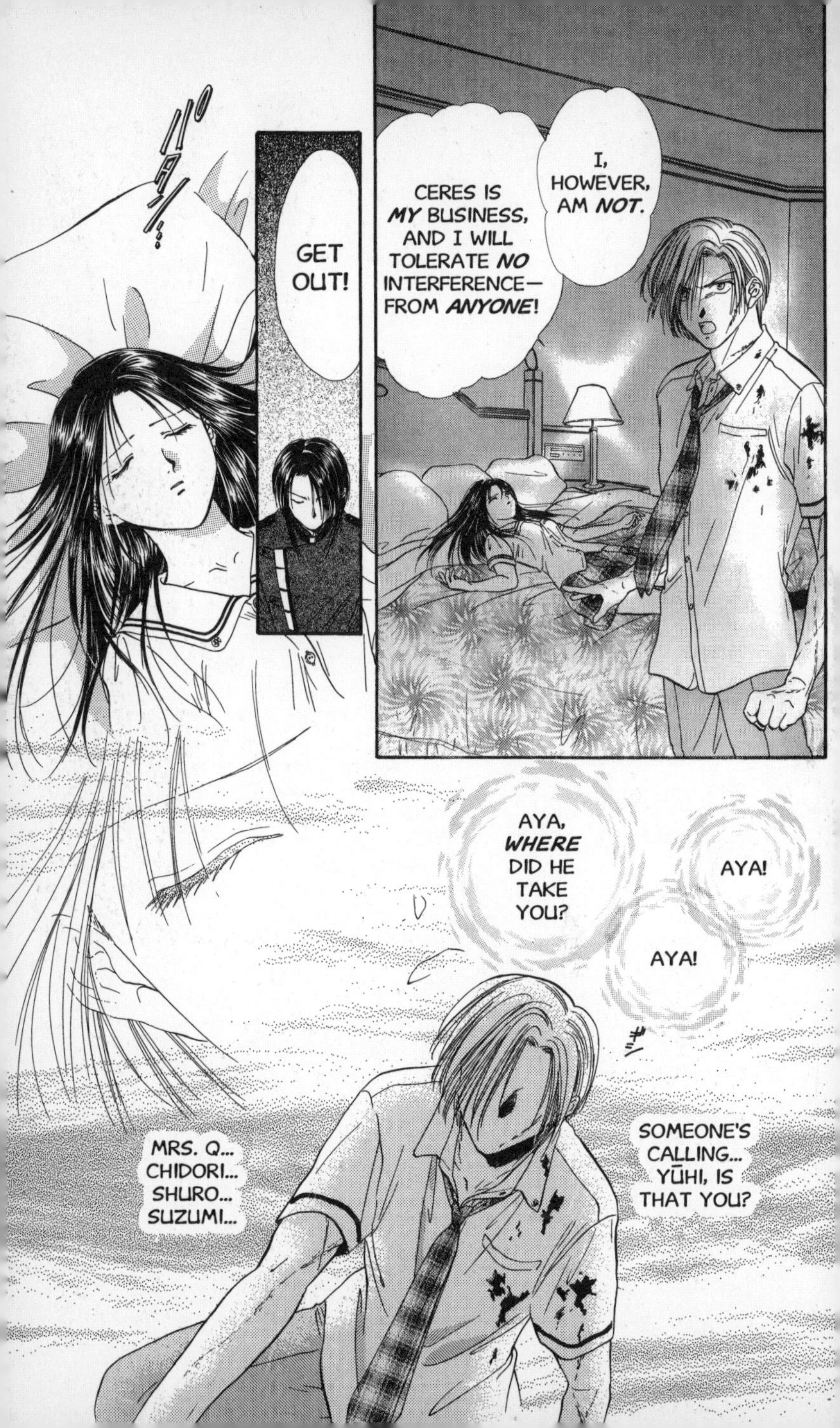

I, HOWEVER, AM *NOT*.
CERES IS *MY* BUSINESS, AND I WILL TOLERATE *NO* INTERFERENCE—FROM *ANYONE*!
GET OUT!
AYA!
AYA, *WHERE* DID HE TAKE YOU?
AYA!
SOMEONE'S CALLING... YŪHI, IS THAT YOU?
MRS. Q... CHIDORI... SHURO... SUZUMI...

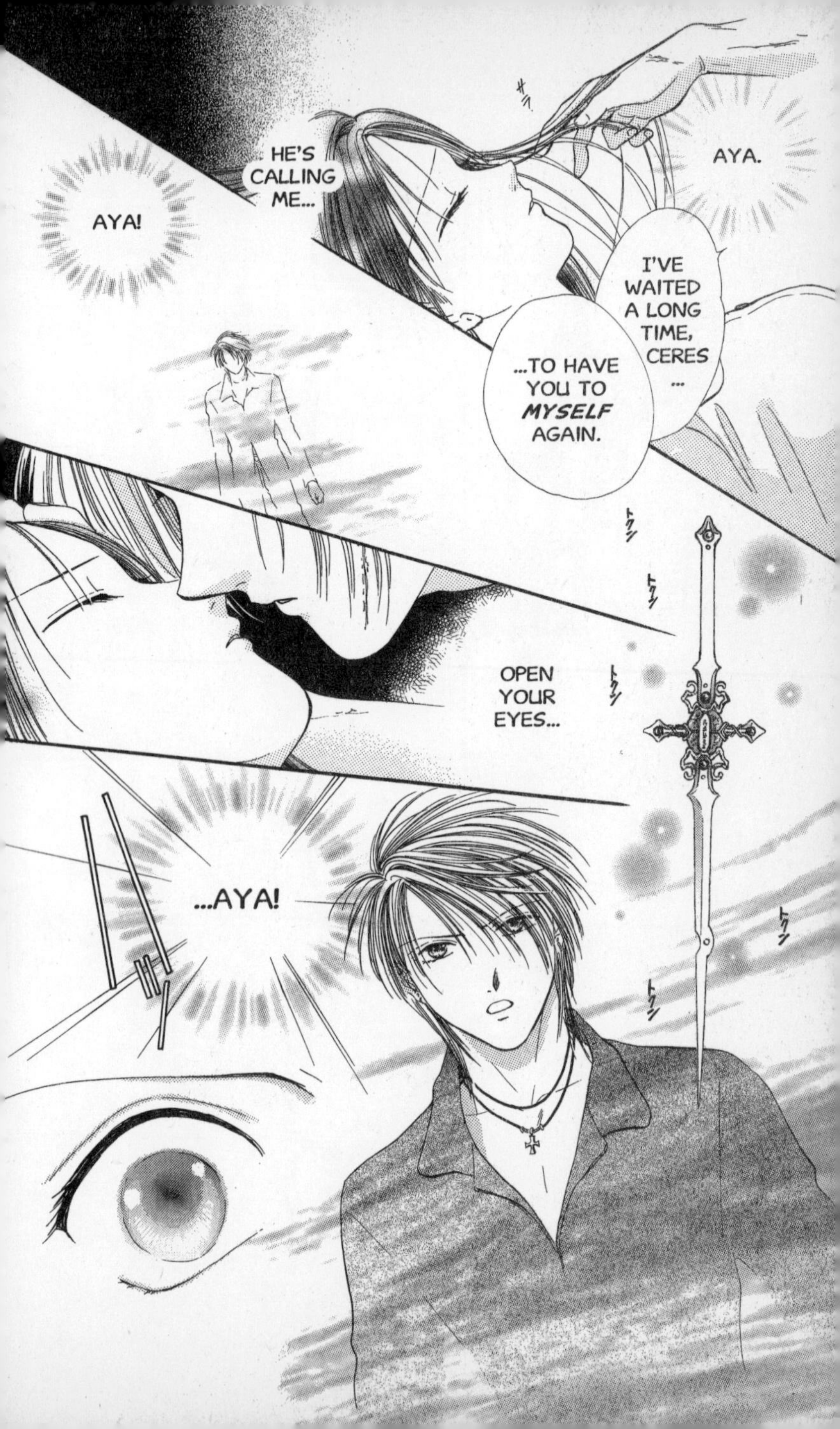
AYA.
HE'S CALLING ME...
AYA!
I'VE WAITED A LONG TIME, CERES ...
...TO HAVE YOU TO *MYSELF* AGAIN.
OPEN YOUR EYES...
...AYA!

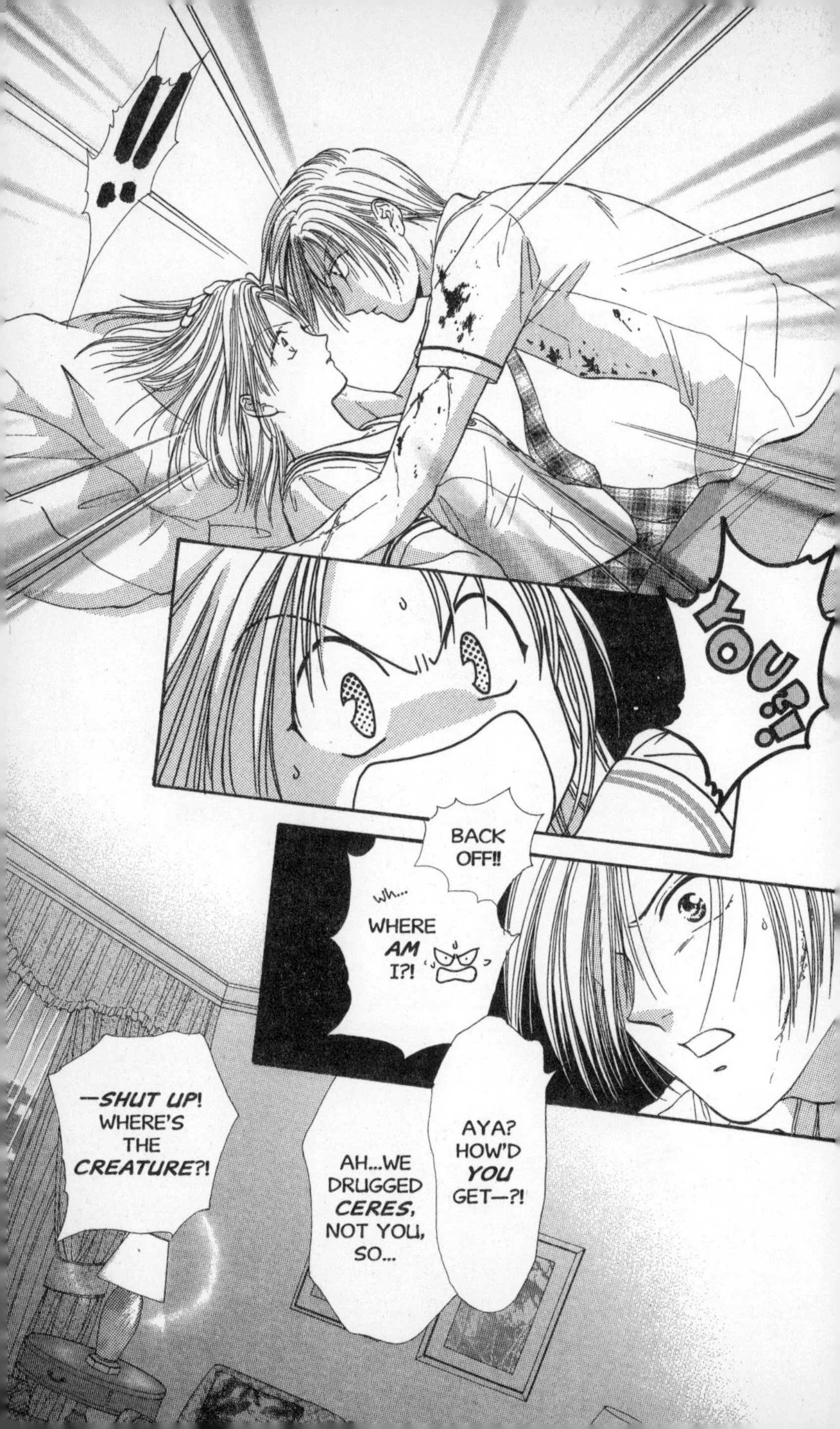
!!
YOU?!!
BACK OFF!!
wh...
WHERE *AM* I?!
AYA? HOW'D *YOU* GET—?!
AH...WE DRUGGED *CERES*, NOT YOU, SO...
—*SHUT UP*! WHERE'S THE *CREATURE*?!

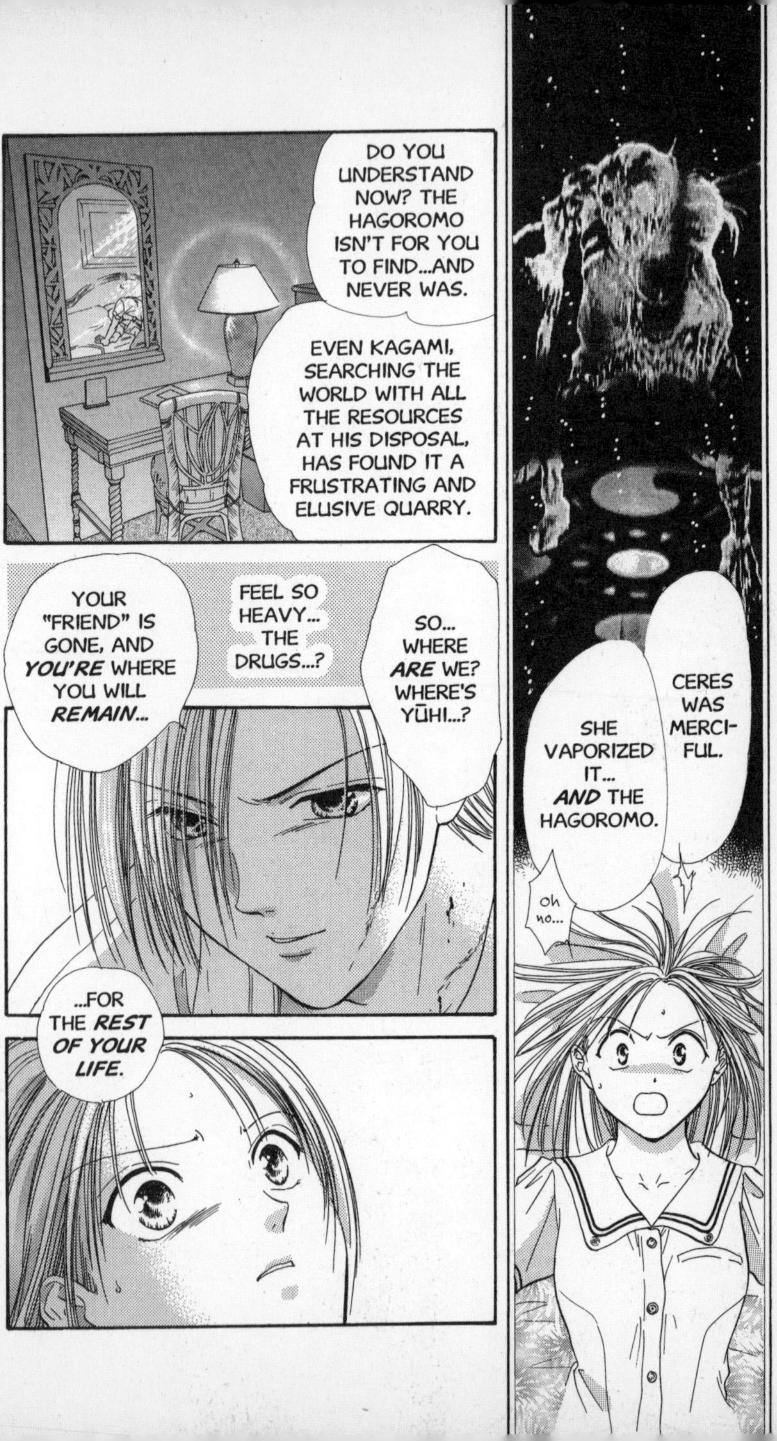
CERES WAS MERCIFUL.
SHE VAPORIZED IT... AND THE HAGOROMO.
oh no...
DO YOU UNDERSTAND NOW? THE HAGOROMO ISN'T FOR YOU TO FIND...AND NEVER WAS.
EVEN KAGAMI, SEARCHING THE WORLD WITH ALL THE RESOURCES AT HIS DISPOSAL, HAS FOUND IT A FRUSTRATING AND ELUSIVE QUARRY.
SO... WHERE ARE WE? WHERE'S YŪHI...?
FEEL SO HEAVY... THE DRUGS...?
YOUR "FRIEND" IS GONE, AND YOU'RE WHERE YOU WILL REMAIN...
...FOR THE REST OF YOUR LIFE.

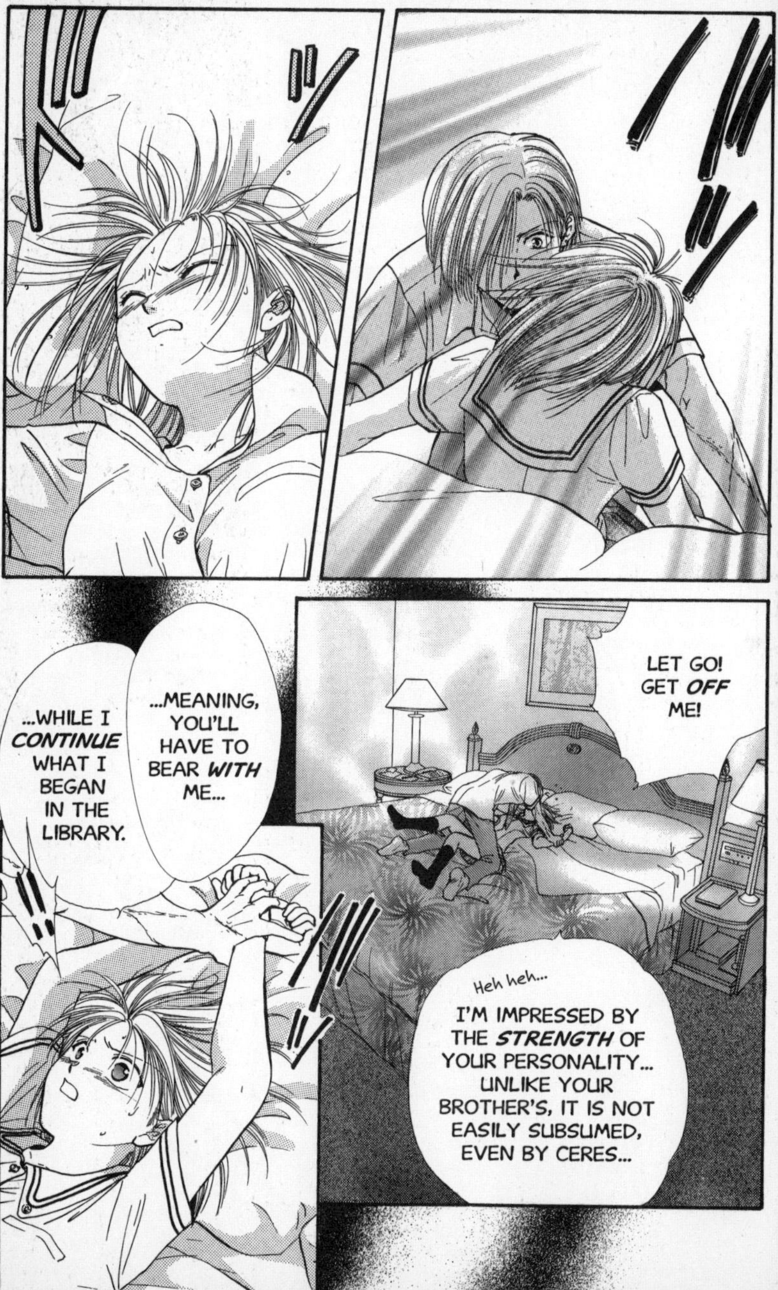
LET GO! GET *OFF* ME!
Heh heh...
I'M IMPRESSED BY THE *STRENGTH* OF YOUR PERSONALITY... UNLIKE YOUR BROTHER'S, IT IS NOT EASILY SUBSUMED, EVEN BY CERES...
...MEANING, YOU'LL HAVE TO BEAR *WITH* ME...
...WHILE I *CONTINUE* WHAT I BEGAN IN THE LIBRARY.

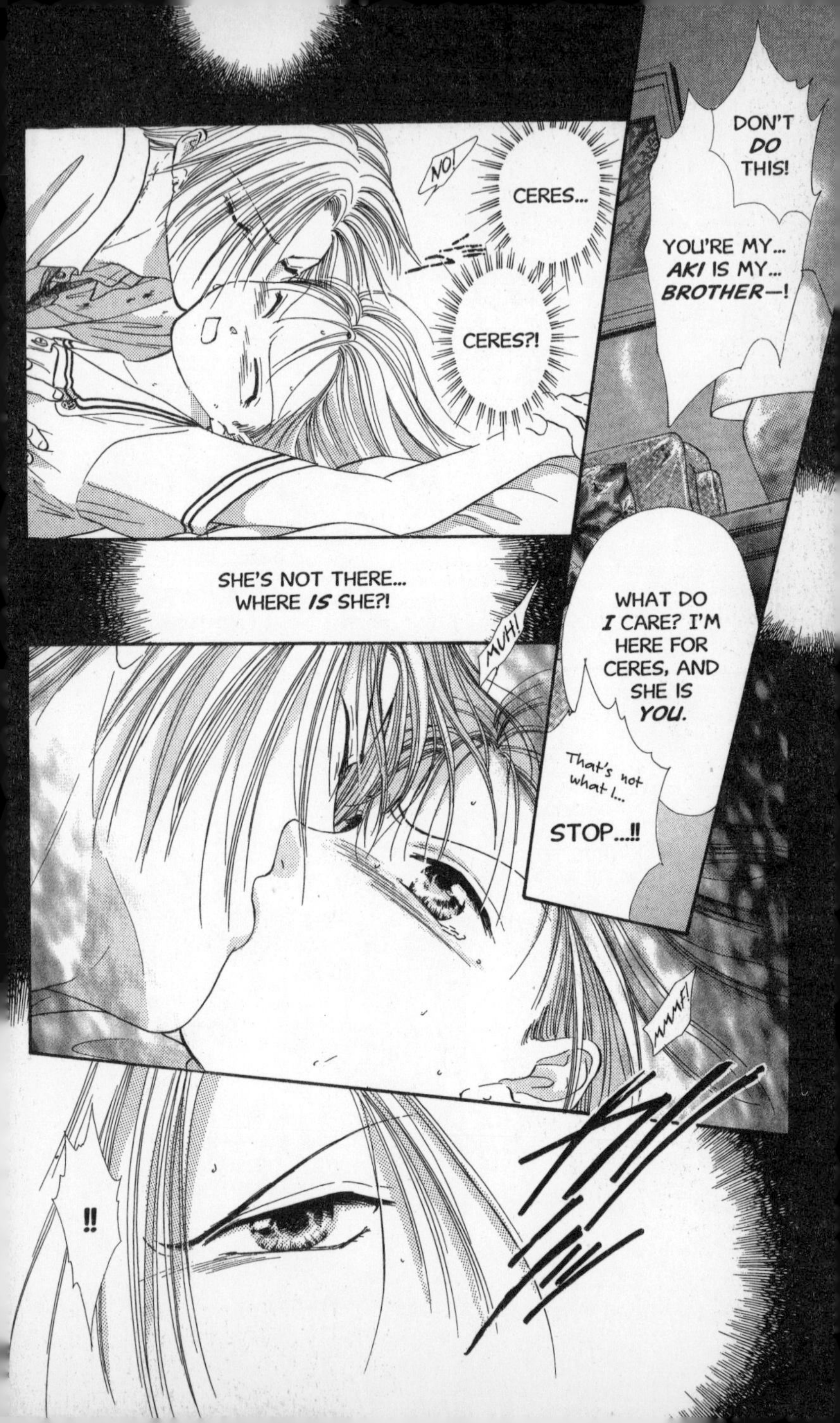
DON'T *DO* THIS!
YOU'RE MY... *AKI* IS MY... *BROTHER*—!
WHAT DO *I* CARE? I'M HERE FOR CERES, AND SHE IS *YOU*.
That's not what I...
STOP...!!
NO!
CERES...
CERES?!
SHE'S NOT THERE... WHERE *IS* SHE?!
MUH!
MMMF!
!!

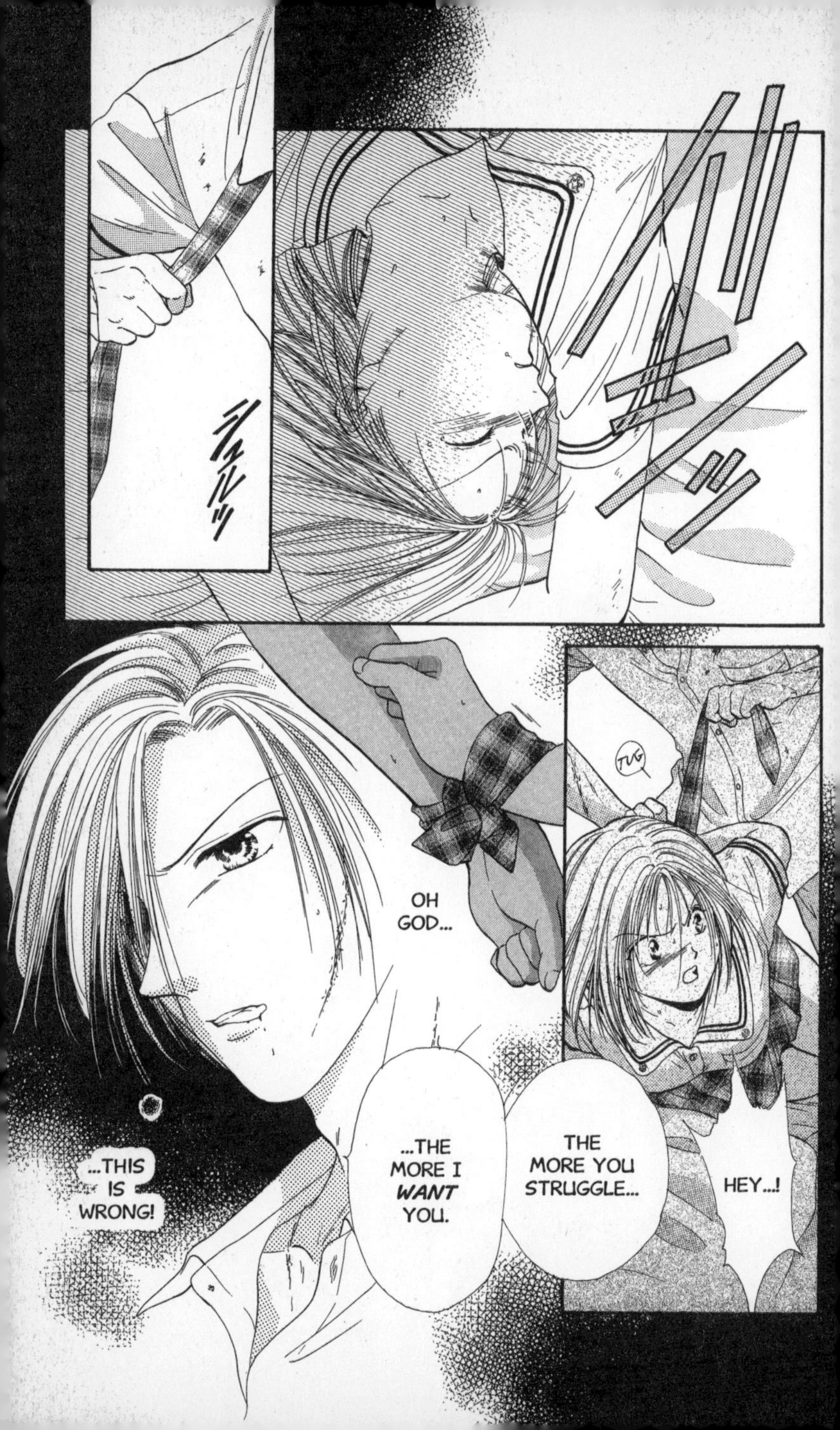
シュルッ
TUG
HEY...!
THE MORE YOU STRUGGLE...
...THE MORE I *WANT* YOU.
OH GOD...
...THIS IS WRONG!

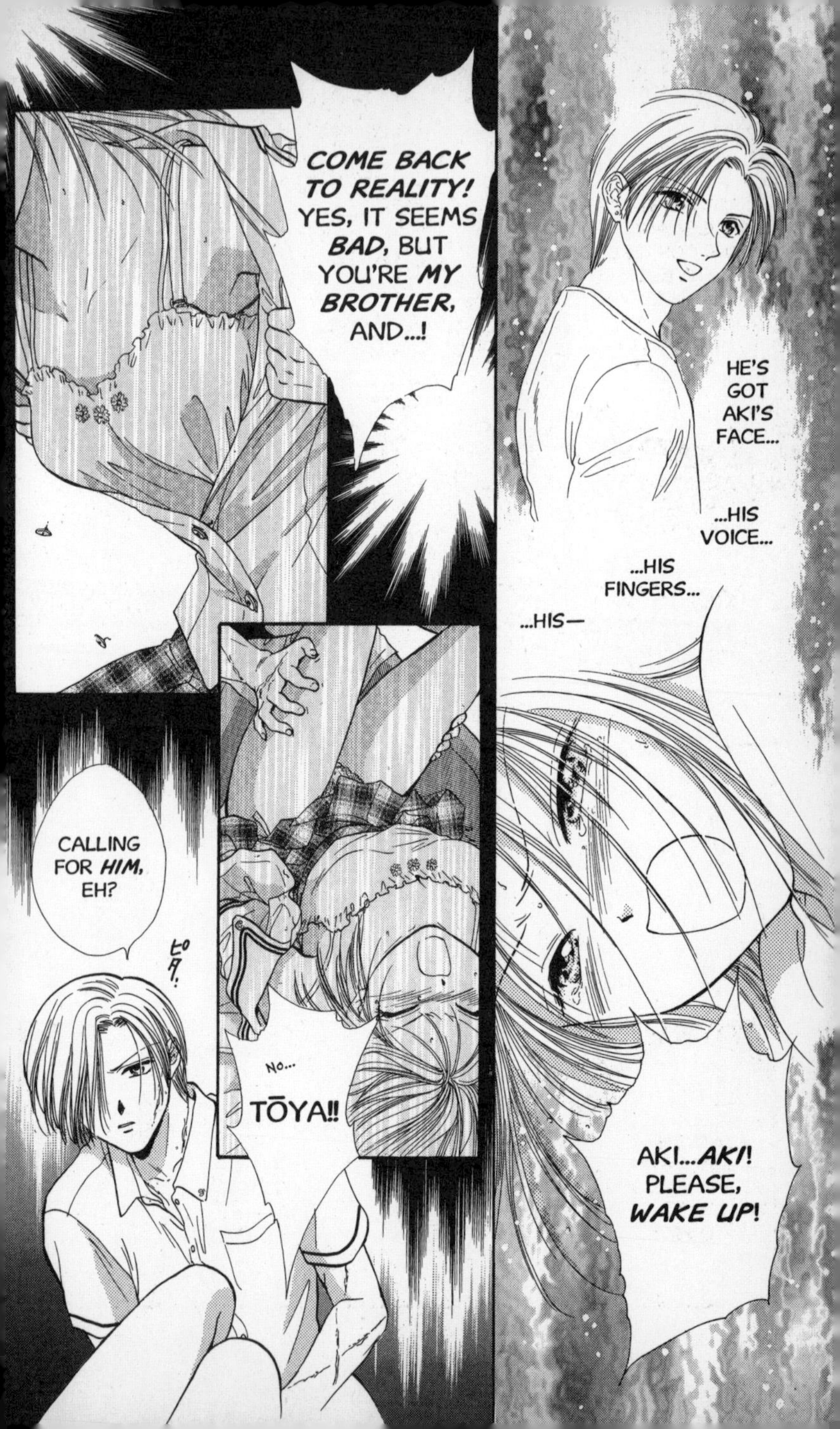
HE'S GOT AKI'S FACE...
...HIS VOICE...
...HIS FINGERS...
...HIS—
AKI...*AKI*! PLEASE, *WAKE UP*!
COME BACK TO REALITY! YES, IT SEEMS *BAD*, BUT YOU'RE *MY BROTHER*, AND...!
NO...
TŌYA!!
CALLING FOR *HIM*, EH?

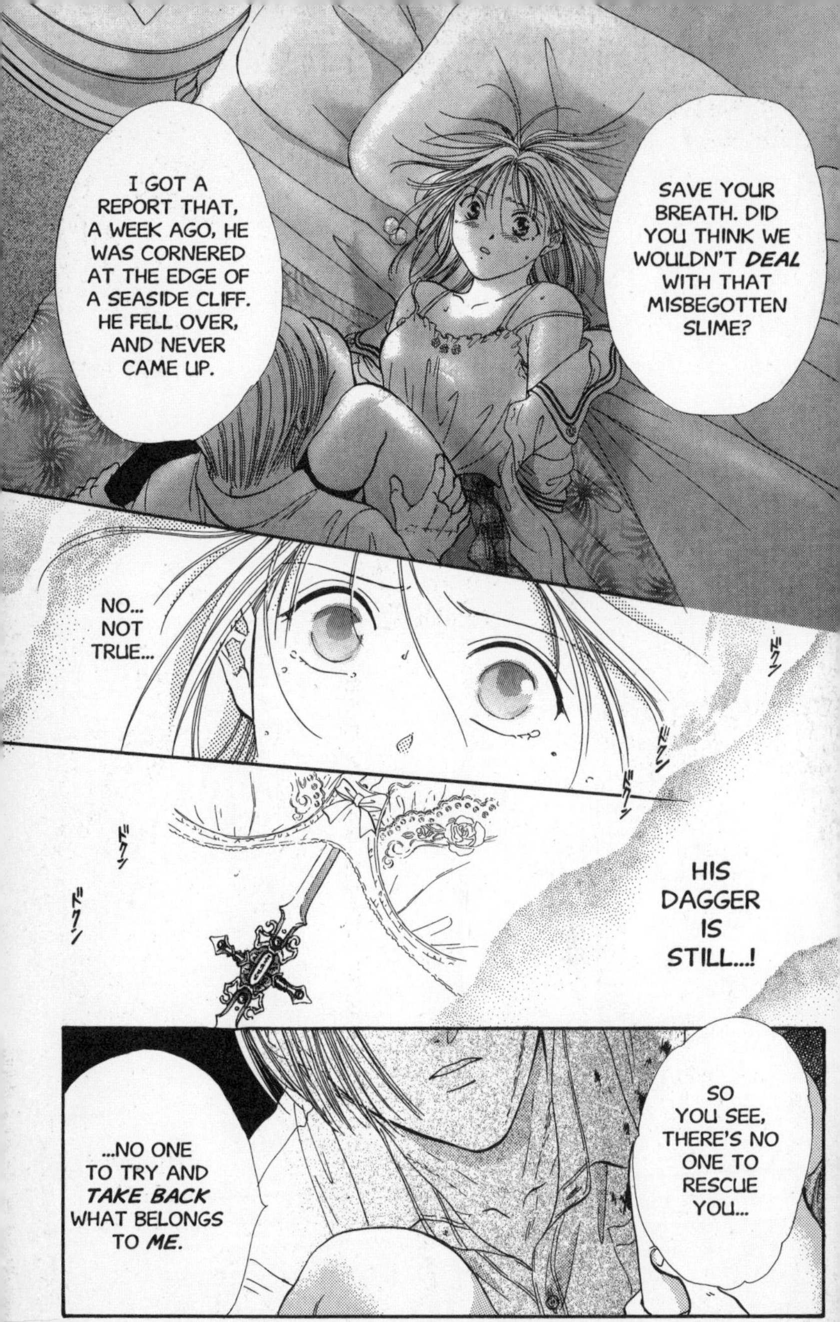
SAVE YOUR BREATH. DID YOU THINK WE WOULDN'T *DEAL* WITH THAT MISBEGOTTEN SLIME?
I GOT A REPORT THAT, A WEEK AGO, HE WAS CORNERED AT THE EDGE OF A SEASIDE CLIFF. HE FELL OVER, AND NEVER CAME UP.
NO... NOT TRUE...
HIS DAGGER IS STILL...!
SO YOU SEE, THERE'S NO ONE TO RESCUE YOU...
...NO ONE TO TRY AND *TAKE BACK* WHAT BELONGS TO *ME*.

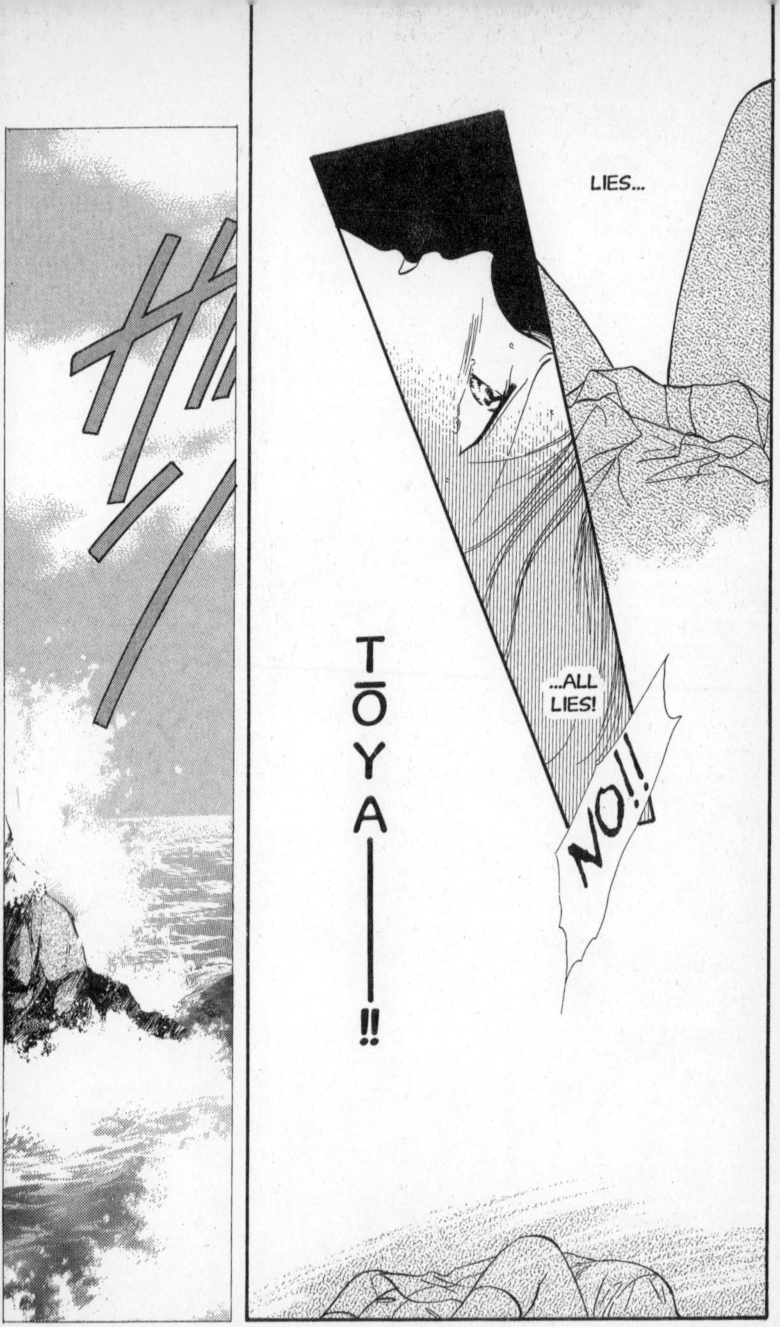
LIES...
...ALL LIES!
NO!!
TŌYA——!!

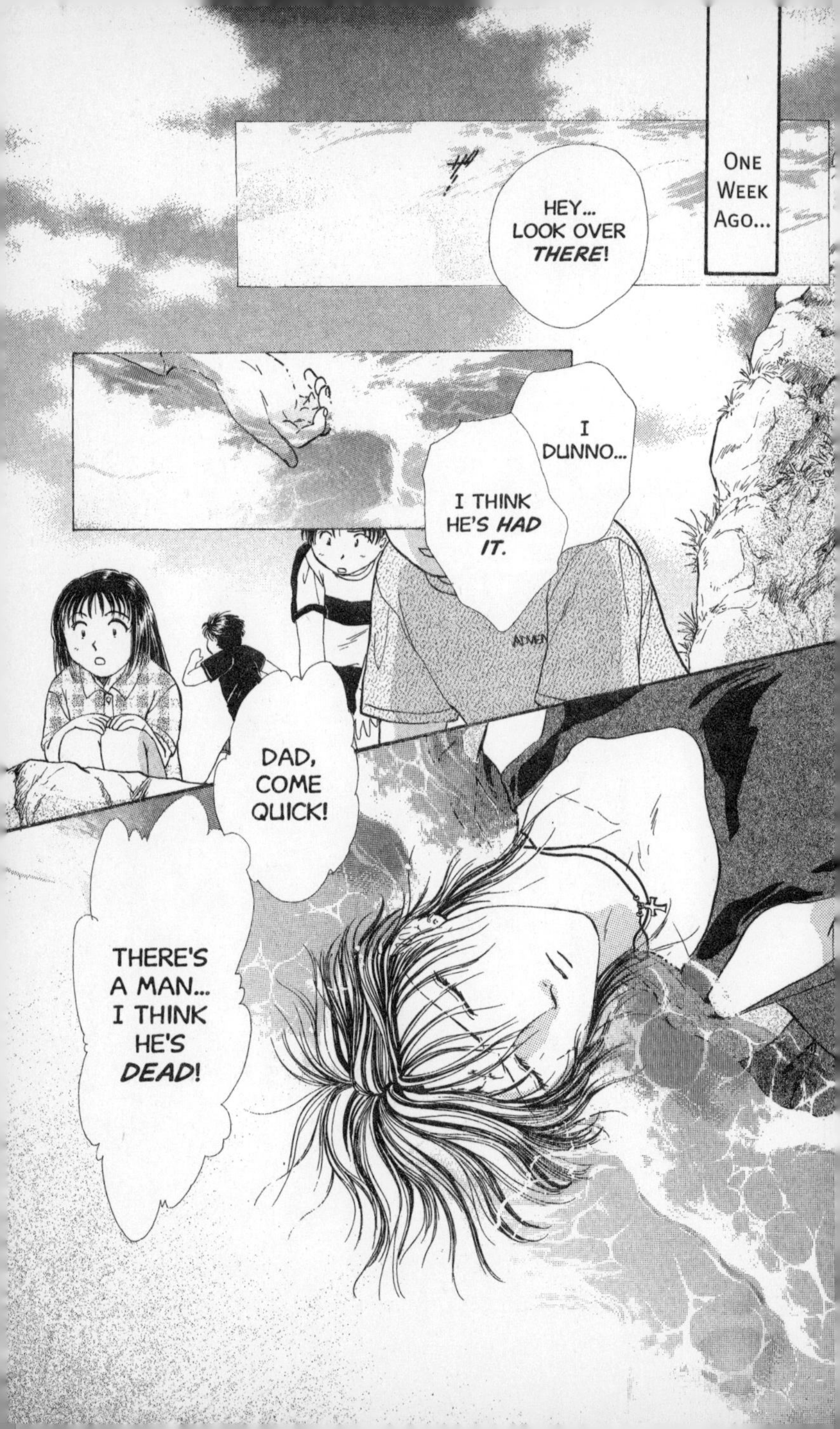
ONE WEEK AGO...
HEY... LOOK OVER THERE!
I DUNNO...
I THINK HE'S HAD IT.
DAD, COME QUICK!
THERE'S A MAN... I THINK HE'S DEAD!

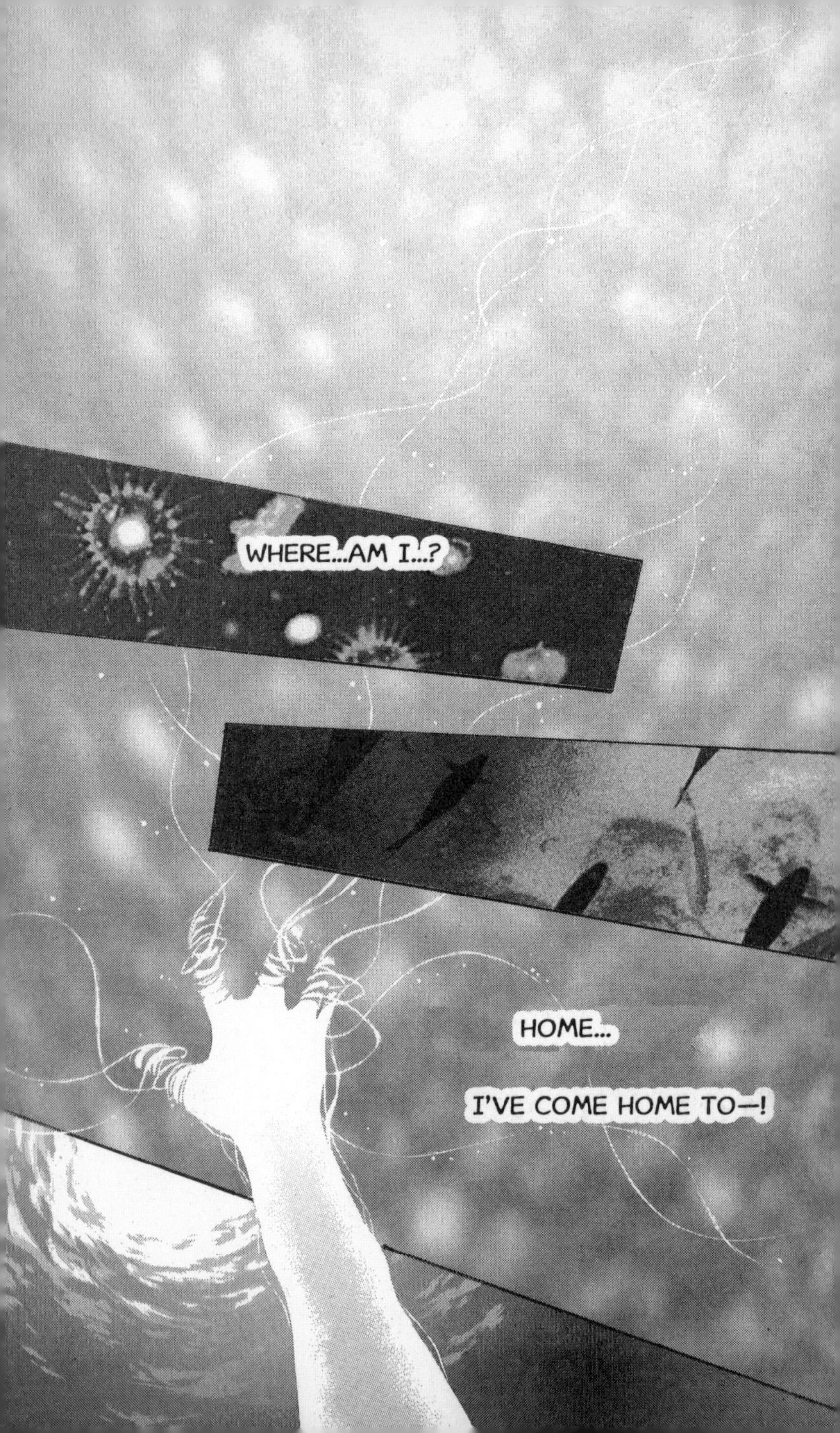
WHERE...AM I...?
HOME...
I'VE COME HOME TO—!

CERES: 10

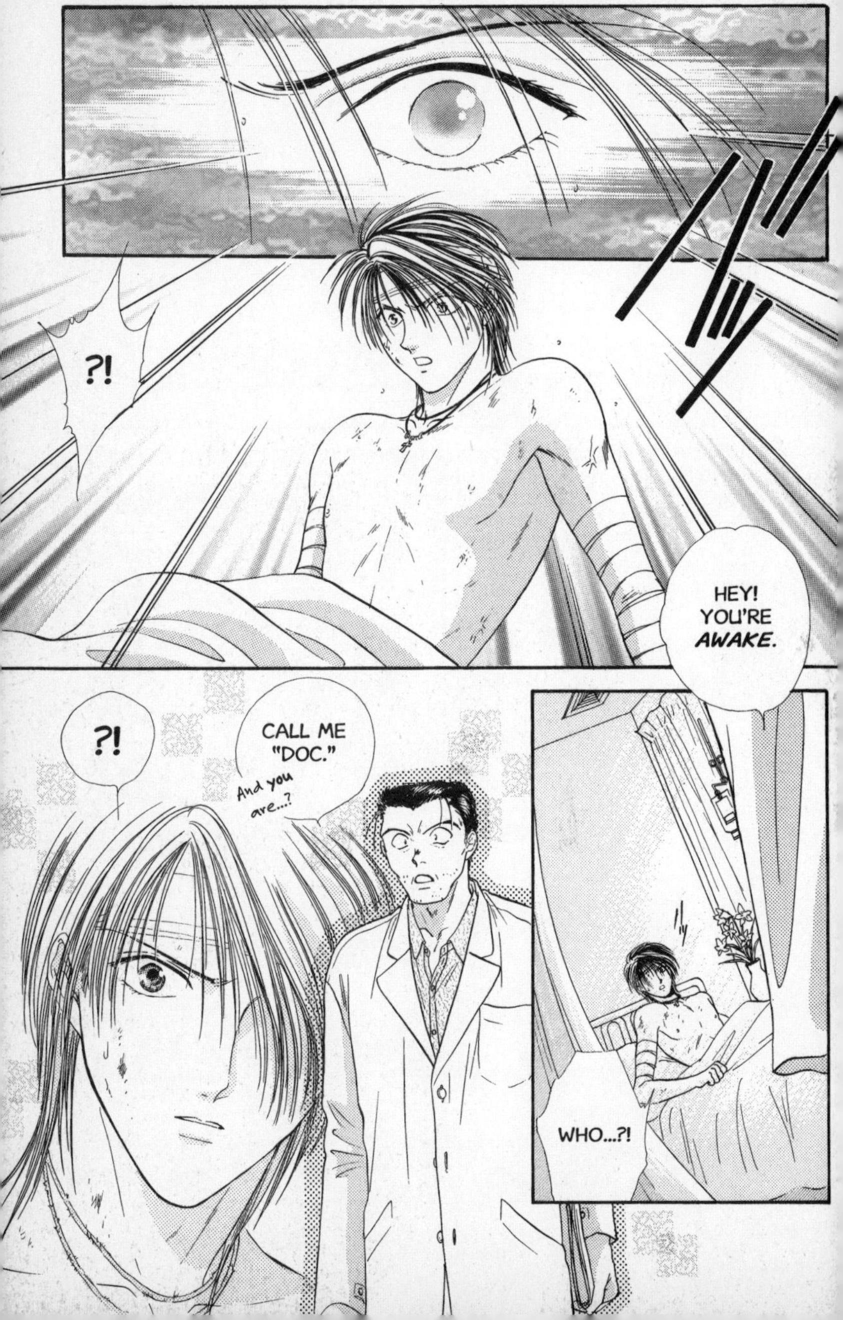
?!
HEY! YOU'RE AWAKE.
WHO...?!
CALL ME "DOC."
And you are...?
?!

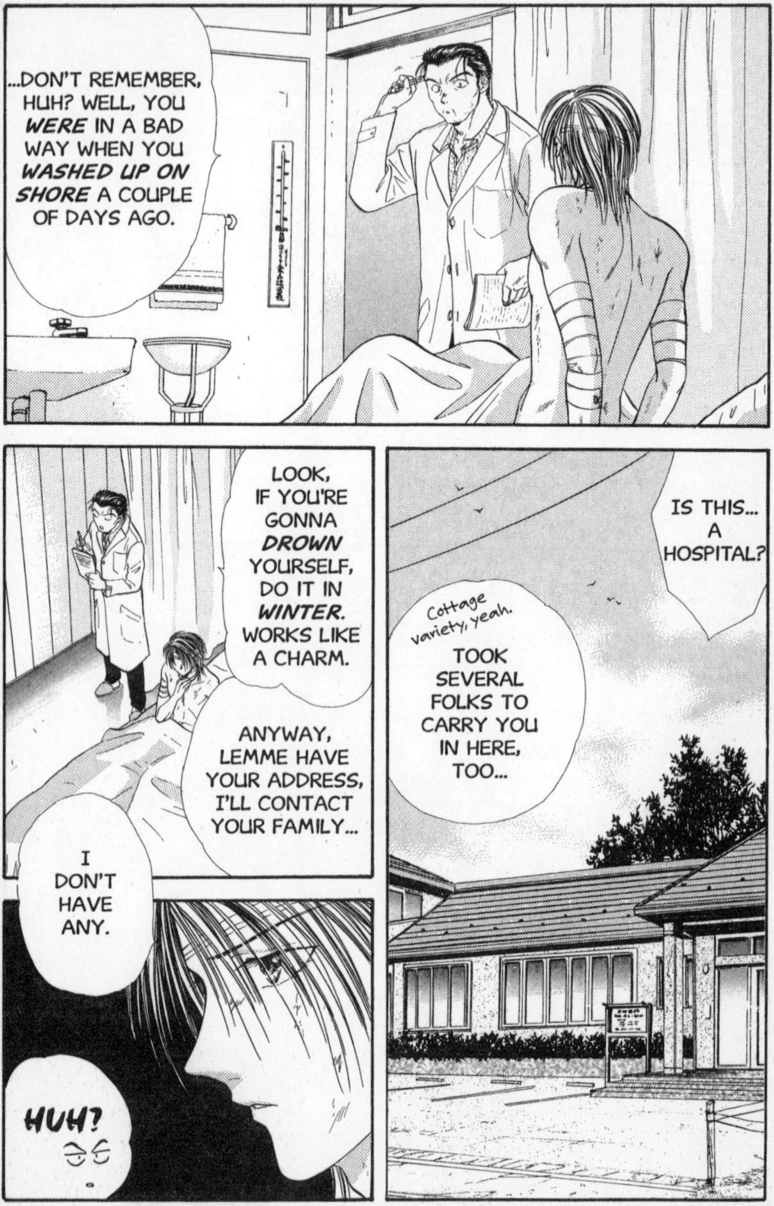
...DON'T REMEMBER, HUH? WELL, YOU *WERE* IN A BAD WAY WHEN YOU *WASHED UP ON SHORE* A COUPLE OF DAYS AGO.
IS THIS... A HOSPITAL?
Cottage variety, yeah.
TOOK SEVERAL FOLKS TO CARRY YOU IN HERE, TOO...
LOOK, IF YOU'RE GONNA *DROWN* YOURSELF, DO IT IN *WINTER*. WORKS LIKE A CHARM.
ANYWAY, LEMME HAVE YOUR ADDRESS, I'LL CONTACT YOUR FAMILY...
I DON'T HAVE ANY.
HUH?

♦ Monster ♦

Get this, this is deep. "Men can be considered independent only when they can respect and honor a woman as a human being." ...So, you don't have to rush into love. You have to grow and mature as an individual first. People degrade themselves when they use their bodies purely for entertainment, or to get money. Women with low character attract only men who are equally sleazy. This is absolutely true.

Let's talk about Volume 9. I received a lot of opinions about Miori's death, so here's a sampling. "I was shocked (though I could understand how she felt).... I don't think people are capable of hating someone indefinitely, because hatred isn't a productive emotion. Nothing can come from hatred. I feel a lot of sympathy for her. There might have been other ways, if she'd stayed alive. I hate suicide. No matter what the problem is, ending your life is the worst thing a person can do. Her mother 'died' all over again, at the moment of Miori's own death. Now there will no longer be anyone who remembers or mourns her mother. People don't live in a vacuum." A girl who got accepted into nursing school (congrats!) said, "I think Miori felt very lonely...I was painfully aware of how she must have felt, to have killed herself like that.... On the surface, the suicide was meant to extract revenge upon Aya. If only there were more who'd pause to think what people are going through, we could reach out to kids who are considering suicide. It would be so much better to be able to help them." I also got a postcard that said, "I felt sorry for Tōya, but I felt worse for Miori, as she's the one who made the mistake."

There were many others, but the above were some that stood out (I had to paraphrase a bit). It would make me happy if you guys could keep thinking this over. It's important stuff.

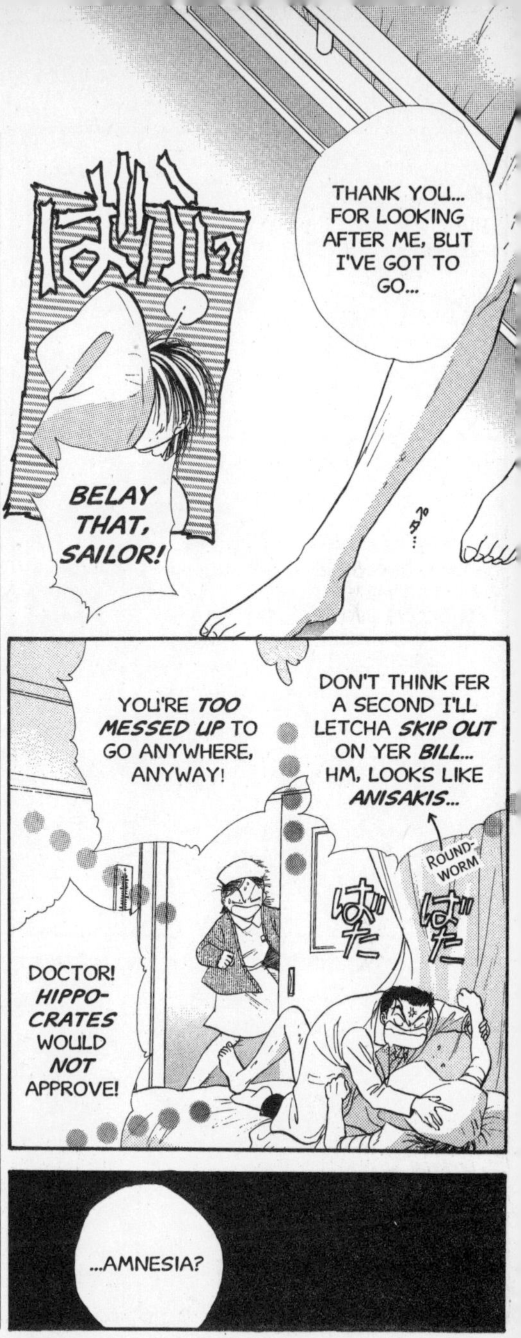
THANK YOU... FOR LOOKING AFTER ME, BUT I'VE GOT TO GO...
BELAY THAT, SAILOR!
DON'T THINK FER A SECOND I'LL LETCHA SKIP OUT ON YER BILL... HM, LOOKS LIKE ANISAKIS...
ROUND-WORM
YOU'RE TOO MESSED UP TO GO ANYWHERE, ANYWAY!
ばた ばた
DOCTOR! HIPPOCRATES WOULD NOT APPROVE!
...AMNESIA?

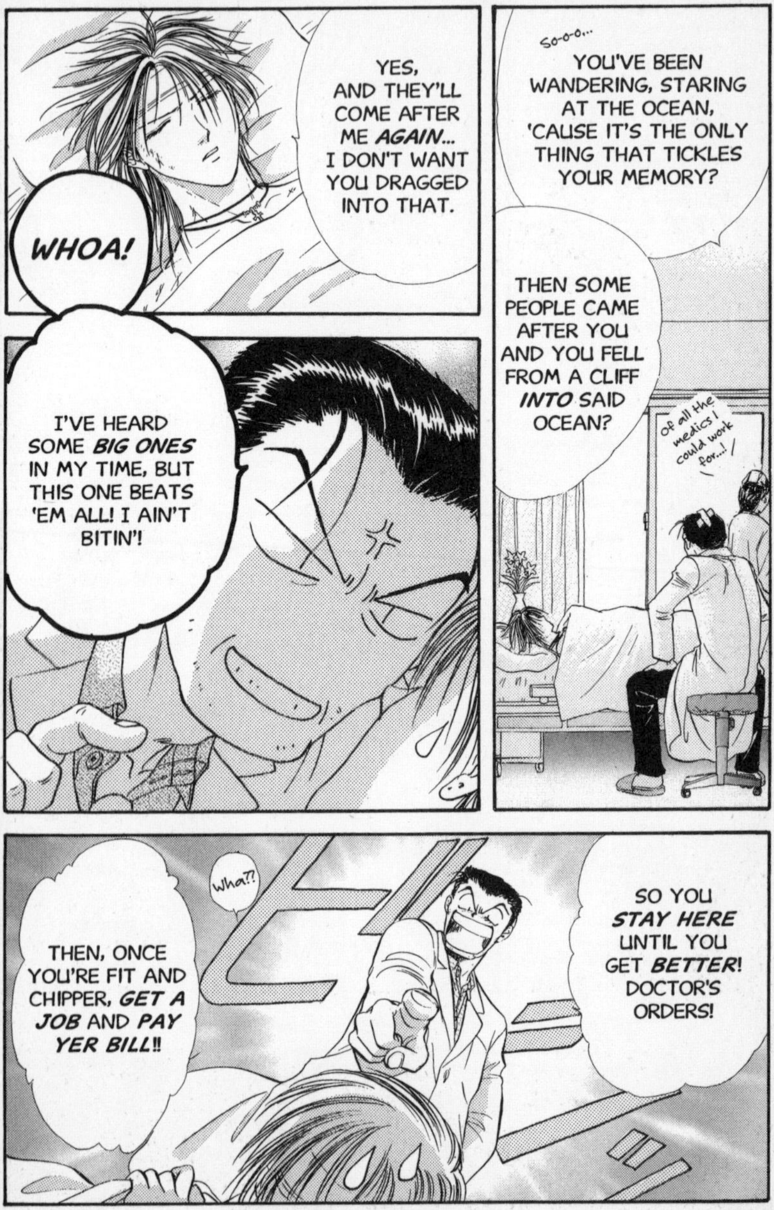
So-o-o...
YOU'VE BEEN WANDERING, STARING AT THE OCEAN, 'CAUSE IT'S THE ONLY THING THAT TICKLES YOUR MEMORY?
THEN SOME PEOPLE CAME AFTER YOU AND YOU FELL FROM A CLIFF *INTO* SAID OCEAN?
of all the medics I could work for...!
YES, AND THEY'LL COME AFTER ME *AGAIN*... I DON'T WANT YOU DRAGGED INTO THAT.
WHOA!
I'VE HEARD SOME *BIG ONES* IN MY TIME, BUT THIS ONE BEATS 'EM ALL! I AIN'T BITIN'!
SO YOU *STAY HERE* UNTIL YOU GET *BETTER*! DOCTOR'S ORDERS!
Wha??
THEN, ONCE YOU'RE FIT AND CHIPPER, *GET A JOB* AND *PAY YER BILL*!!

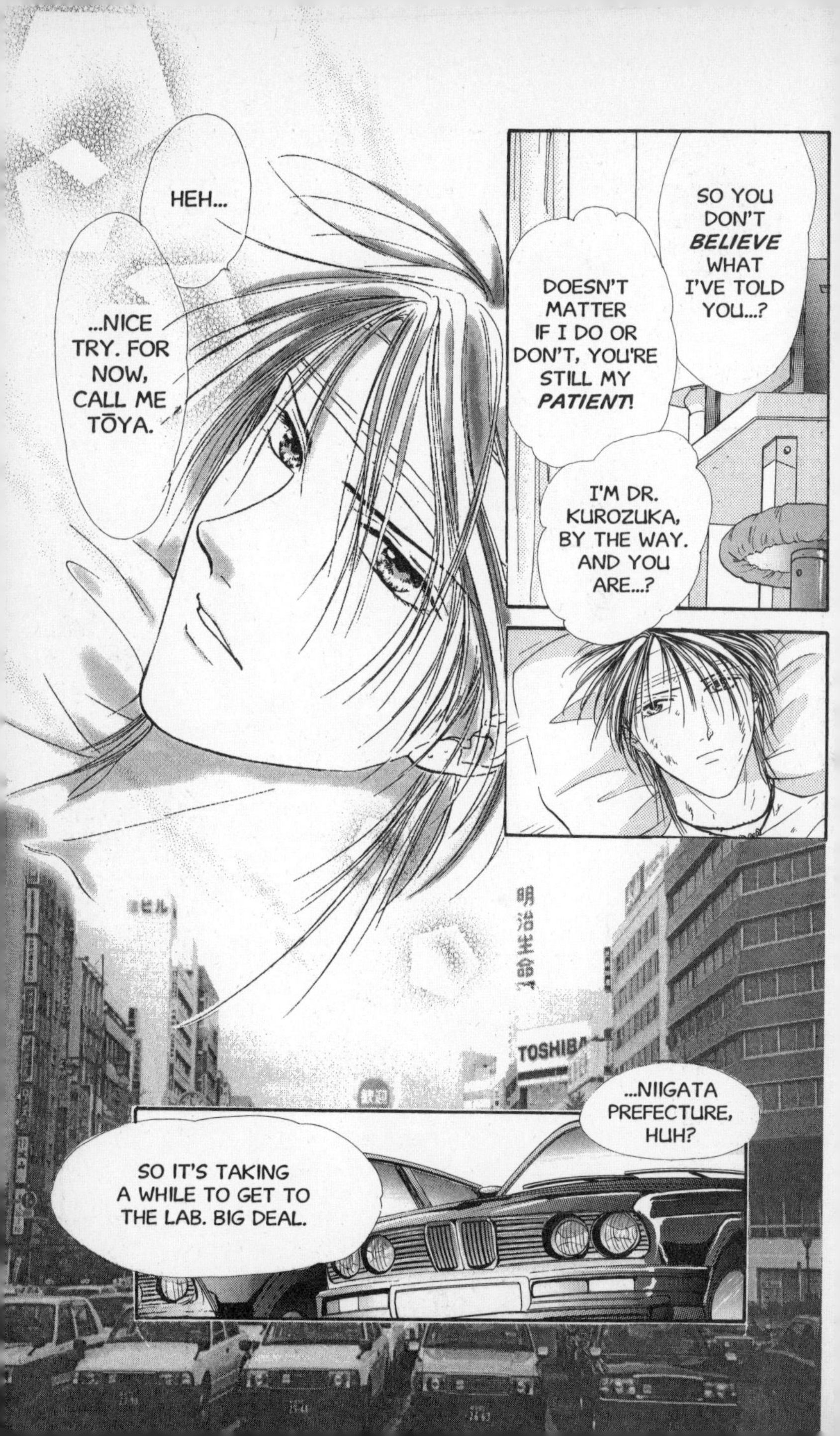
SO YOU DON'T *BELIEVE* WHAT I'VE TOLD YOU...?
DOESN'T MATTER IF I DO OR DON'T, YOU'RE STILL MY *PATIENT*!
I'M DR. KUROZUKA, BY THE WAY. AND YOU ARE...?
HEH...
...NICE TRY. FOR NOW, CALL ME TŌYA.
...NIIGATA PREFECTURE, HUH?
SO IT'S TAKING A WHILE TO GET TO THE LAB. BIG DEAL.

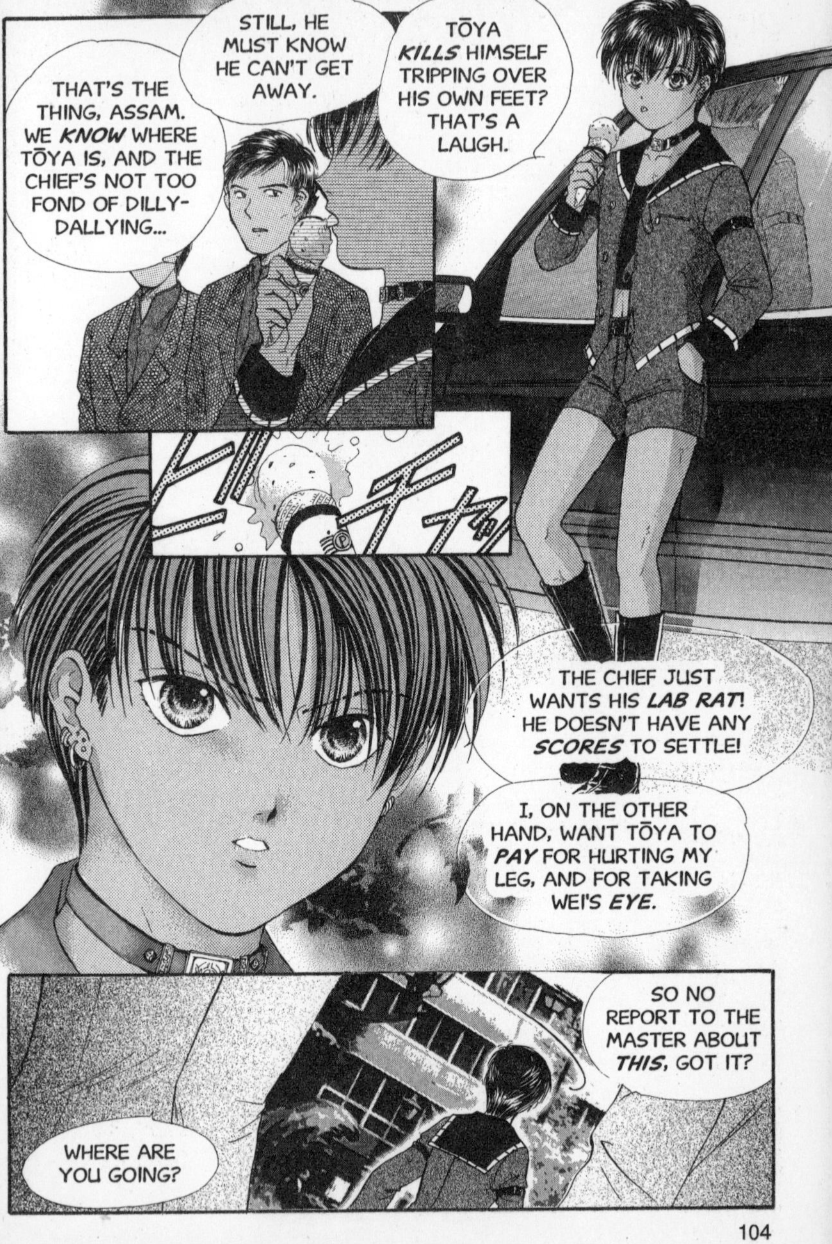
TŌYA *KILLS* HIMSELF TRIPPING OVER HIS OWN FEET? THAT'S A LAUGH.
STILL, HE MUST KNOW HE CAN'T GET AWAY.
THAT'S THE THING, ASSAM. WE *KNOW* WHERE TŌYA IS, AND THE CHIEF'S NOT TOO FOND OF DILLY-DALLYING...
THE CHIEF JUST WANTS HIS *LAB RAT*! HE DOESN'T HAVE ANY *SCORES* TO SETTLE!
I, ON THE OTHER HAND, WANT TŌYA TO *PAY* FOR HURTING MY LEG, AND FOR TAKING WEI'S *EYE*.
SO NO REPORT TO THE MASTER ABOUT *THIS*, GOT IT?
WHERE ARE YOU GOING?

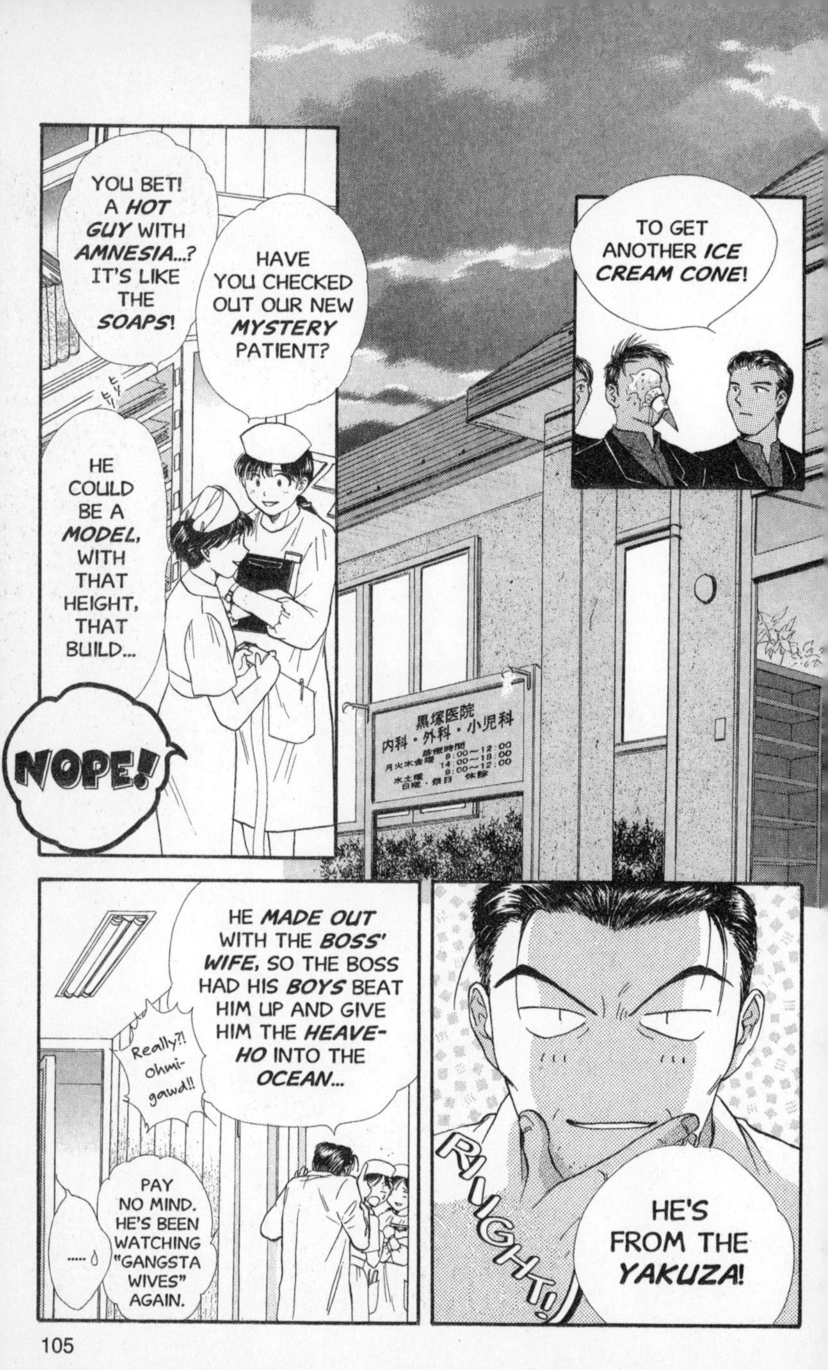
TO GET ANOTHER ICE CREAM CONE!
HAVE YOU CHECKED OUT OUR NEW MYSTERY PATIENT?
YOU BET! A HOT GUY WITH AMNESIA...? IT'S LIKE THE SOAPS!
HE COULD BE A MODEL, WITH THAT HEIGHT, THAT BUILD...
NOPE!
黒塚医院
内科・外科・小児科
RIGHT!
HE'S FROM THE YAKUZA!
HE MADE OUT WITH THE BOSS' WIFE, SO THE BOSS HAD HIS BOYS BEAT HIM UP AND GIVE HIM THE HEAVE-HO INTO THE OCEAN...
Really?! ohmi-gawd!!
PAY NO MIND. HE'S BEEN WATCHING "GANGSTA WIVES" AGAIN.
.....

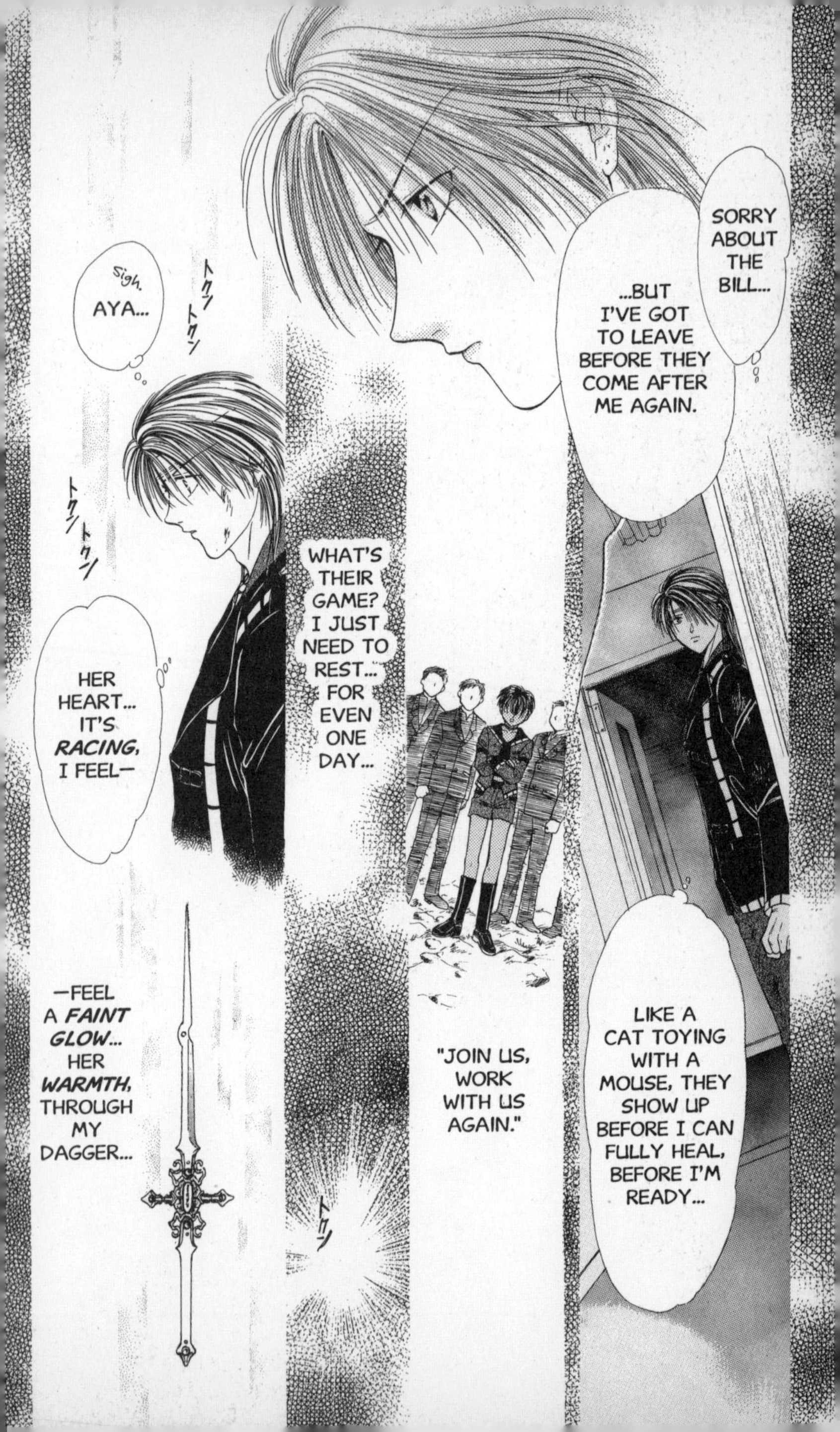
SORRY ABOUT THE BILL...
...BUT I'VE GOT TO LEAVE BEFORE THEY COME AFTER ME AGAIN.
LIKE A CAT TOYING WITH A MOUSE, THEY SHOW UP BEFORE I CAN FULLY HEAL, BEFORE I'M READY...
WHAT'S THEIR GAME? I JUST NEED TO REST... FOR EVEN ONE DAY...
"JOIN US, WORK WITH US AGAIN."
トクン
Sigh. AYA...
トクン トクン
トクン トクン
HER HEART... IT'S *RACING,* I FEEL—
—FEEL A *FAINT GLOW*... HER *WARMTH,* THROUGH MY DAGGER...

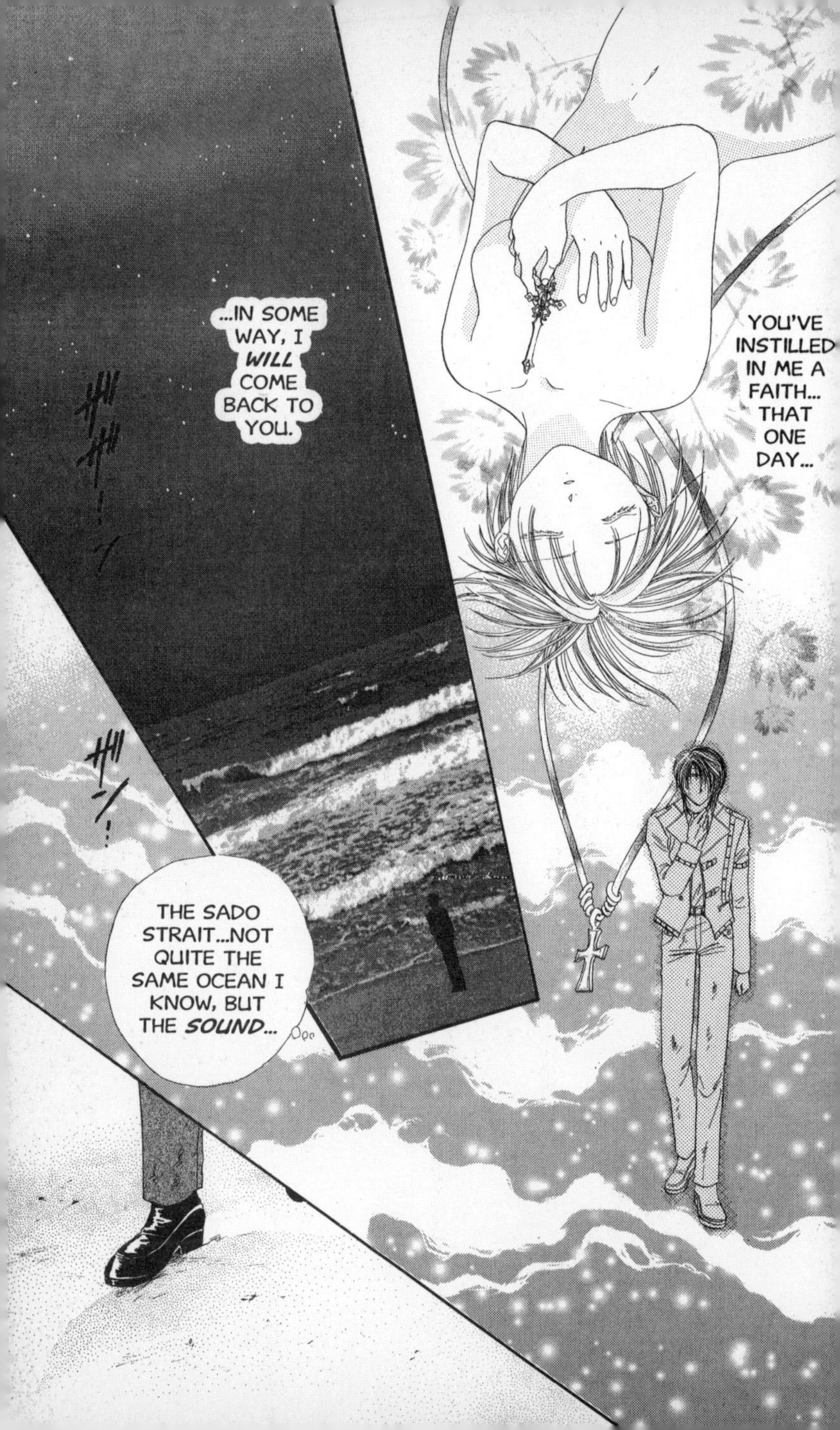
YOU'VE INSTILLED IN ME A FAITH... THAT ONE DAY...
...IN SOME WAY, I *WILL* COME BACK TO YOU.
THE SADO STRAIT...NOT QUITE THE SAME OCEAN I KNOW, BUT THE *SOUND*...

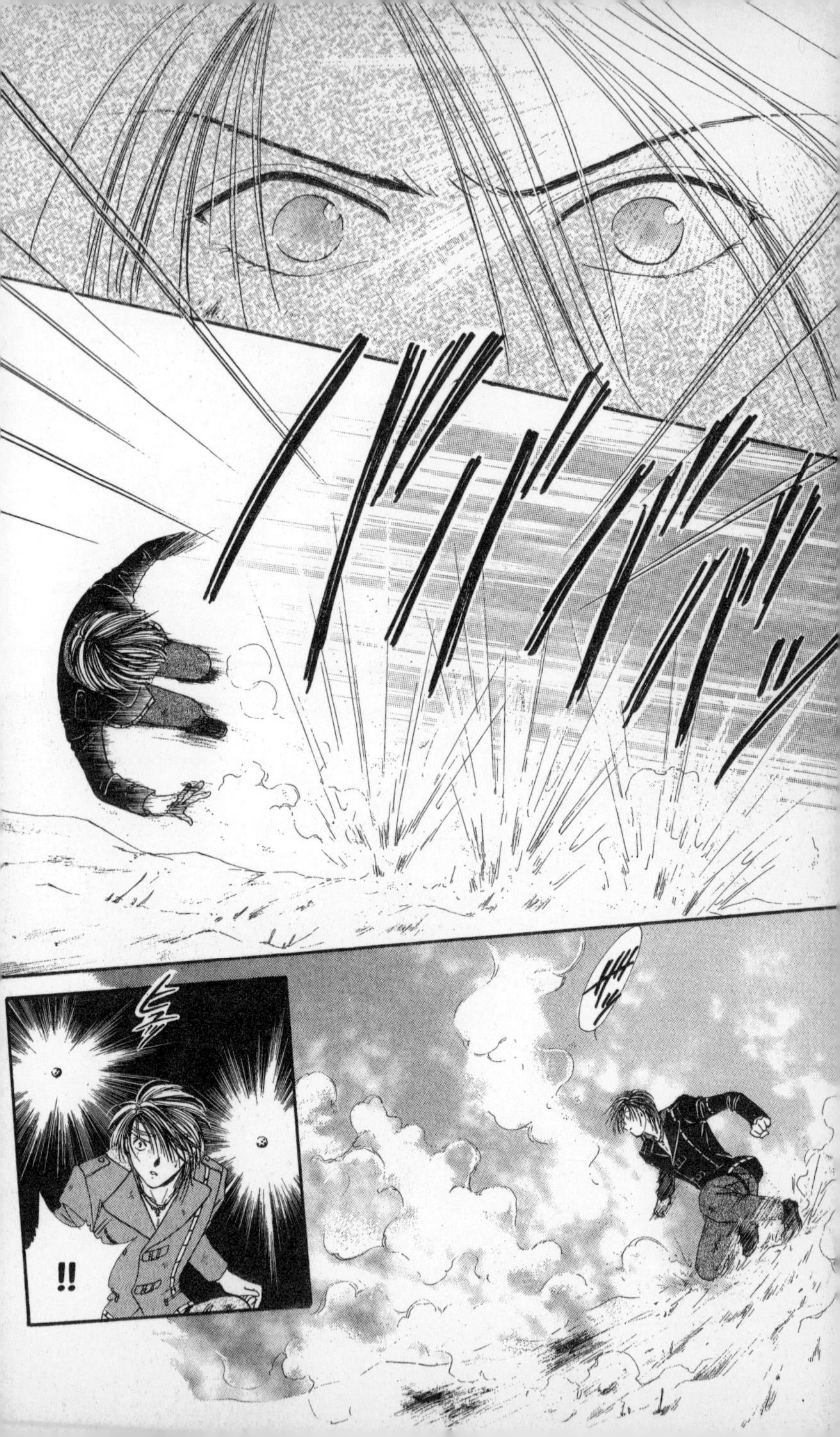
!!

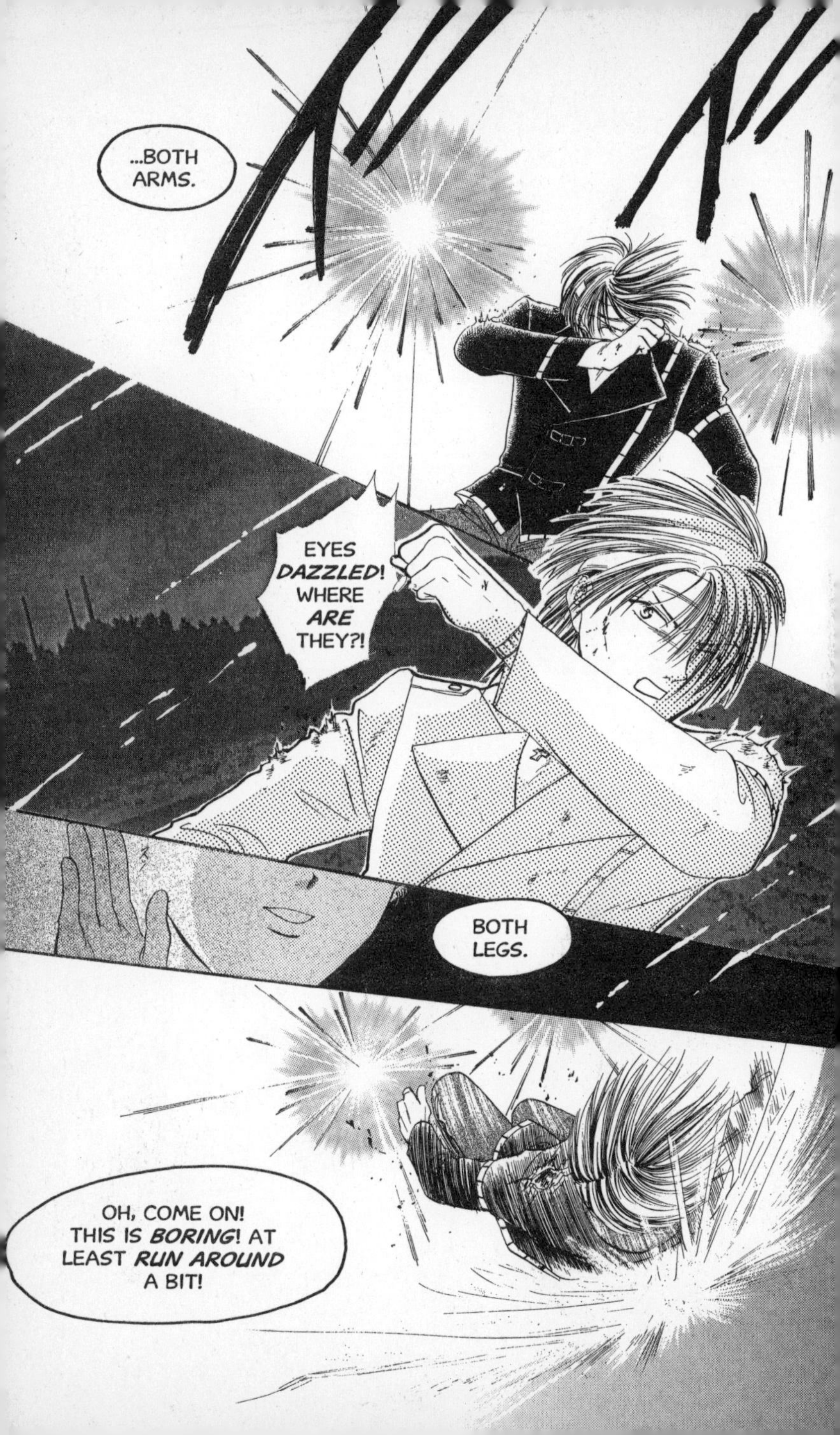
...BOTH ARMS.
EYES DAZZLED! WHERE ARE THEY?!
BOTH LEGS.
OH, COME ON! THIS IS BORING! AT LEAST RUN AROUND A BIT!

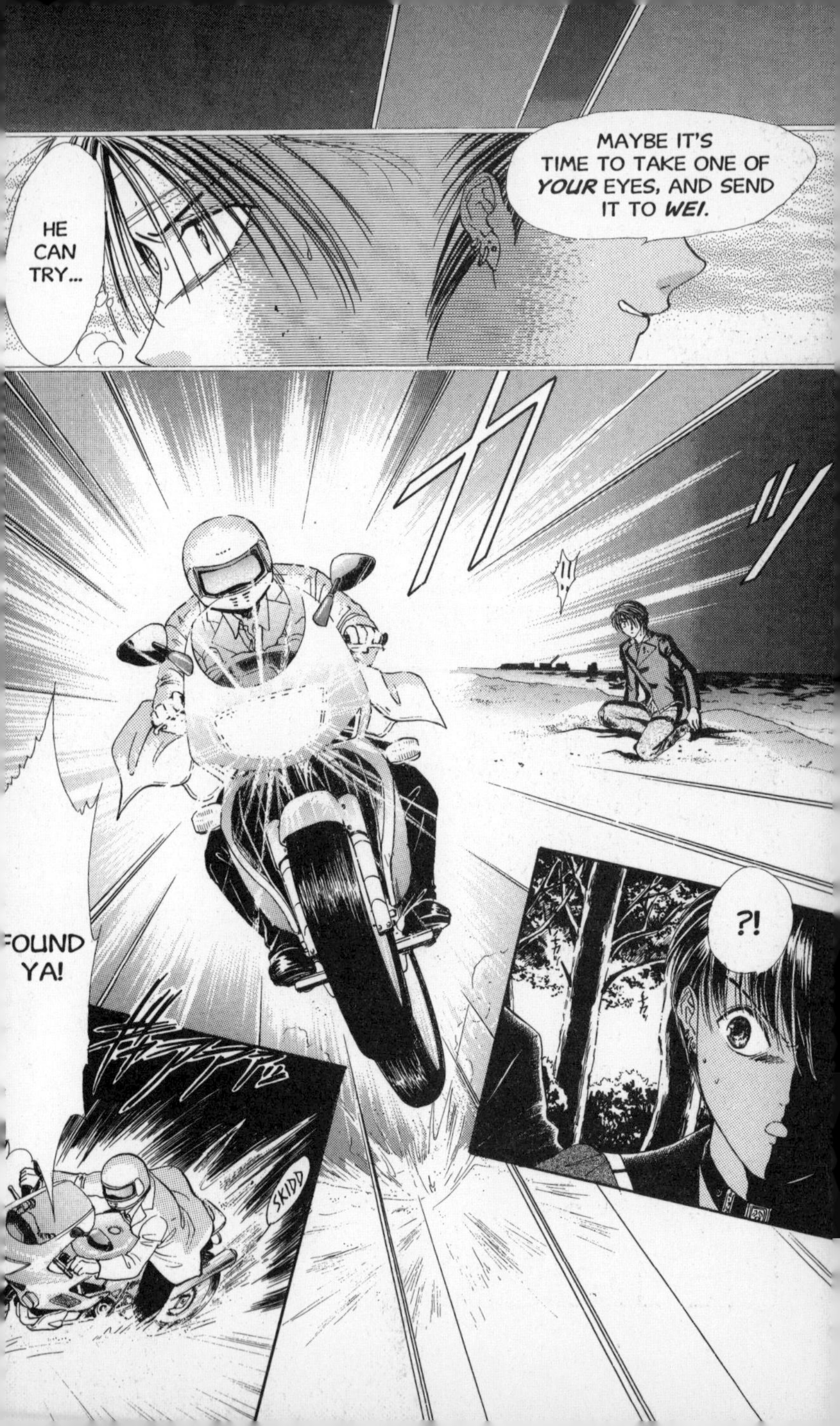

MAYBE IT'S TIME TO TAKE ONE OF *YOUR* EYES, AND SEND IT TO *WEI*.
HE CAN TRY...
!!
?!
FOUND YA!
SKIDD

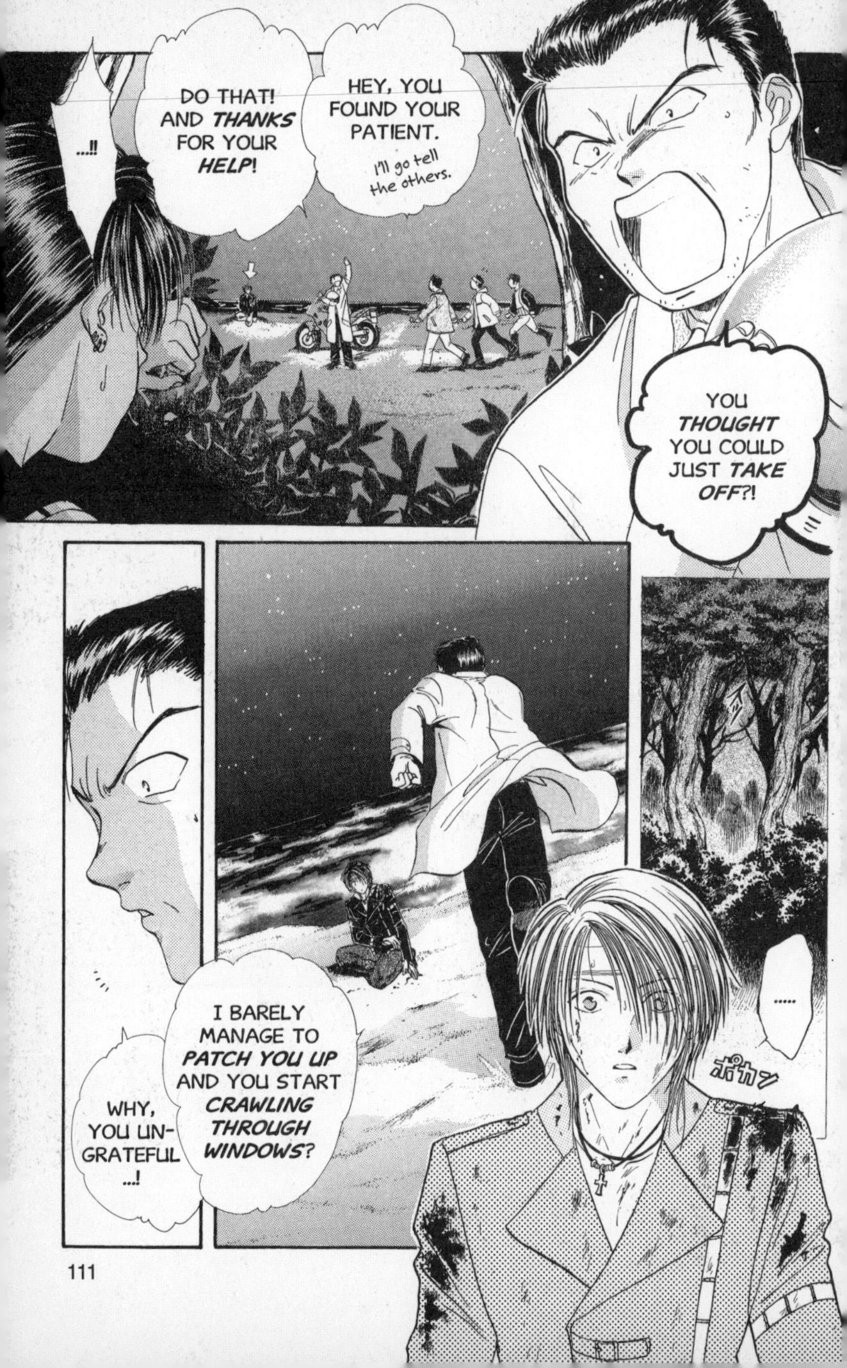
HEY, YOU FOUND YOUR PATIENT.
I'll go tell the others.
DO THAT! AND THANKS FOR YOUR HELP!
...!!
YOU THOUGHT YOU COULD JUST TAKE OFF?!
.....
ポカン
I BARELY MANAGE TO PATCH YOU UP AND YOU START CRAWLING THROUGH WINDOWS?
WHY, YOU UN-GRATEFUL ...!

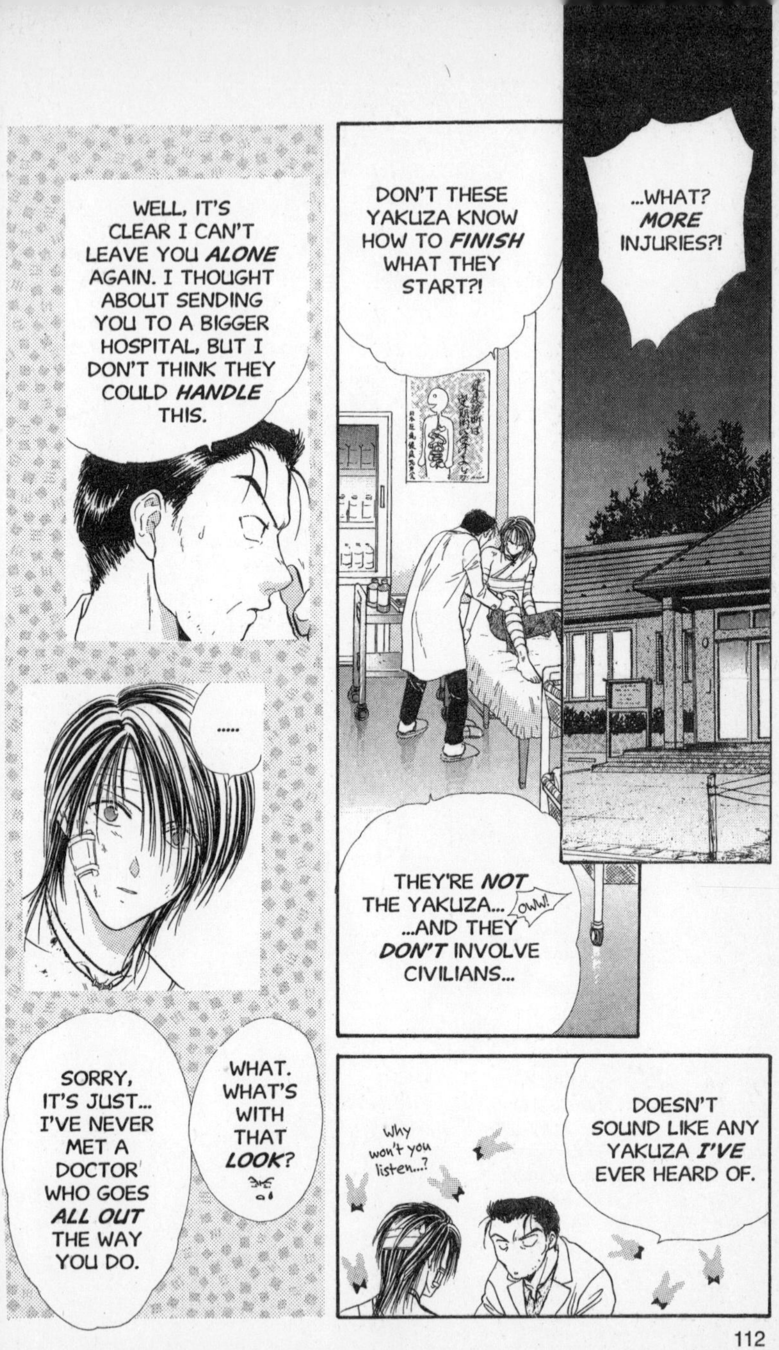
...WHAT? MORE INJURIES?!
DON'T THESE YAKUZA KNOW HOW TO FINISH WHAT THEY START?!
THEY'RE NOT THE YAKUZA... ...AND THEY DON'T INVOLVE CIVILIANS...
OWW!
DOESN'T SOUND LIKE ANY YAKUZA I'VE EVER HEARD OF.
Why won't you listen...?
WELL, IT'S CLEAR I CAN'T LEAVE YOU ALONE AGAIN. I THOUGHT ABOUT SENDING YOU TO A BIGGER HOSPITAL, BUT I DON'T THINK THEY COULD HANDLE THIS.
.....
WHAT. WHAT'S WITH THAT LOOK?
SORRY, IT'S JUST... I'VE NEVER MET A DOCTOR WHO GOES ALL OUT THE WAY YOU DO.

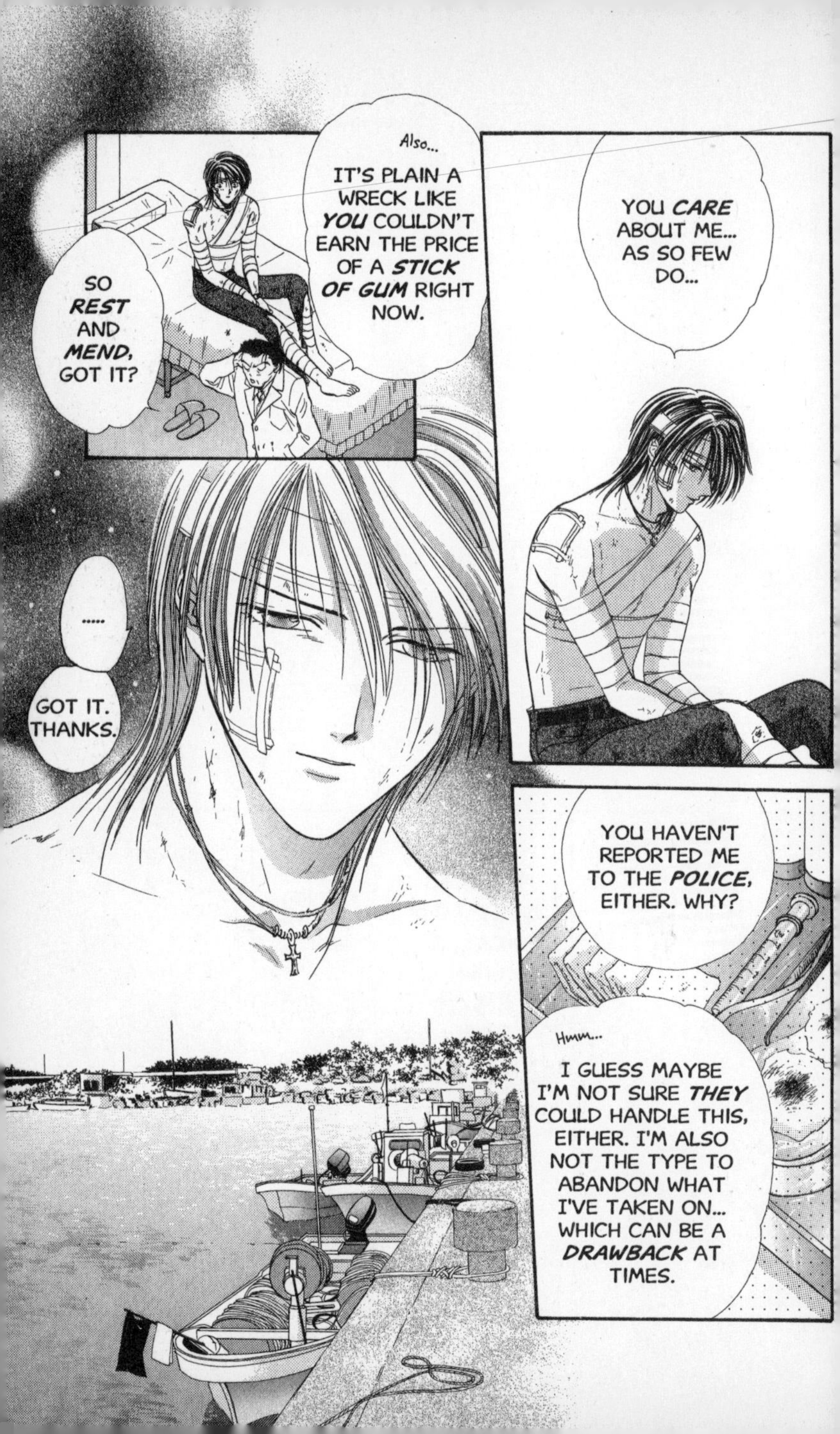
YOU CARE ABOUT ME... AS SO FEW DO...
Also...
IT'S PLAIN A WRECK LIKE YOU COULDN'T EARN THE PRICE OF A STICK OF GUM RIGHT NOW.
SO REST AND MEND, GOT IT?
......
GOT IT. THANKS.
YOU HAVEN'T REPORTED ME TO THE POLICE, EITHER. WHY?
Hmm...
I GUESS MAYBE I'M NOT SURE THEY COULD HANDLE THIS, EITHER. I'M ALSO NOT THE TYPE TO ABANDON WHAT I'VE TAKEN ON... WHICH CAN BE A DRAWBACK AT TIMES.

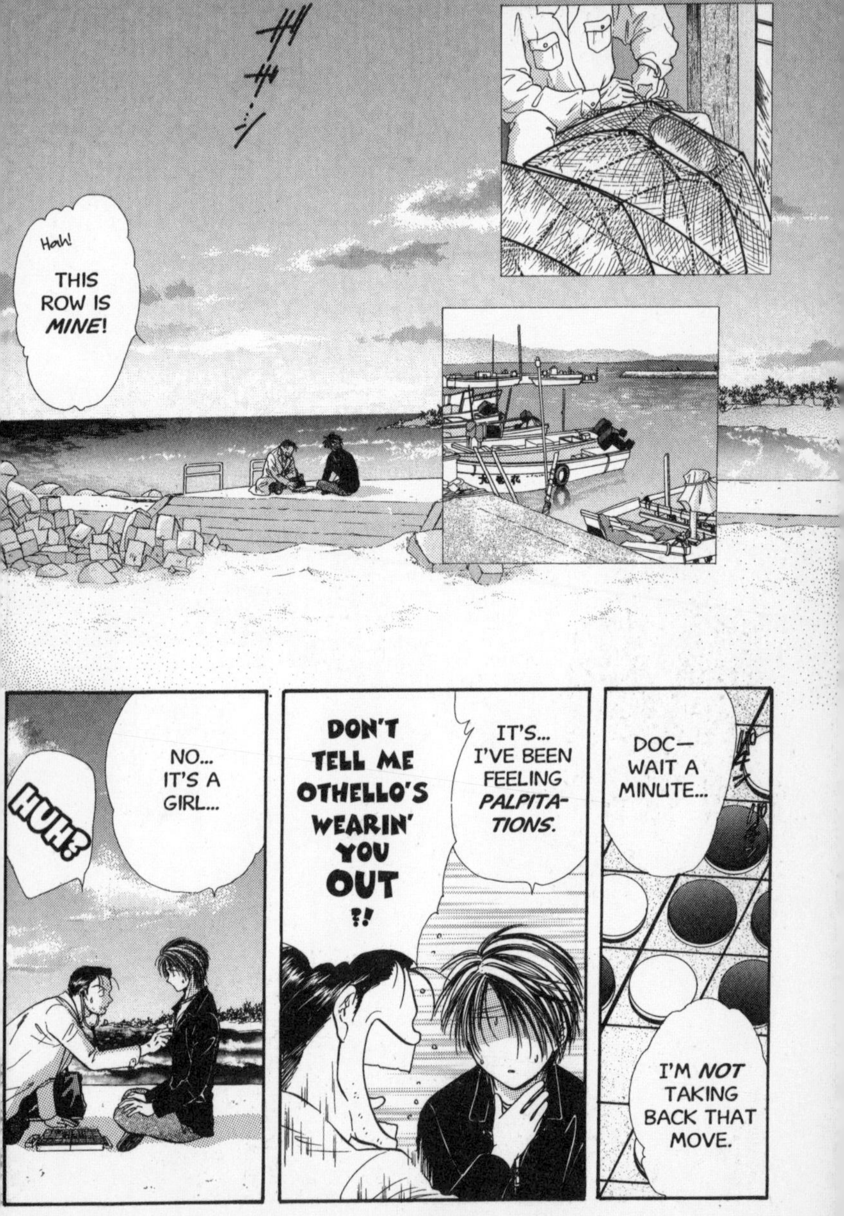
Hah!
THIS ROW IS *MINE*!
DOC— WAIT A MINUTE...
I'M *NOT* TAKING BACK THAT MOVE.
IT'S... I'VE BEEN FEELING *PALPITATIONS*.
DON'T TELL ME OTHELLO'S WEARIN' YOU OUT ?!
NO... IT'S A GIRL...
HUH?

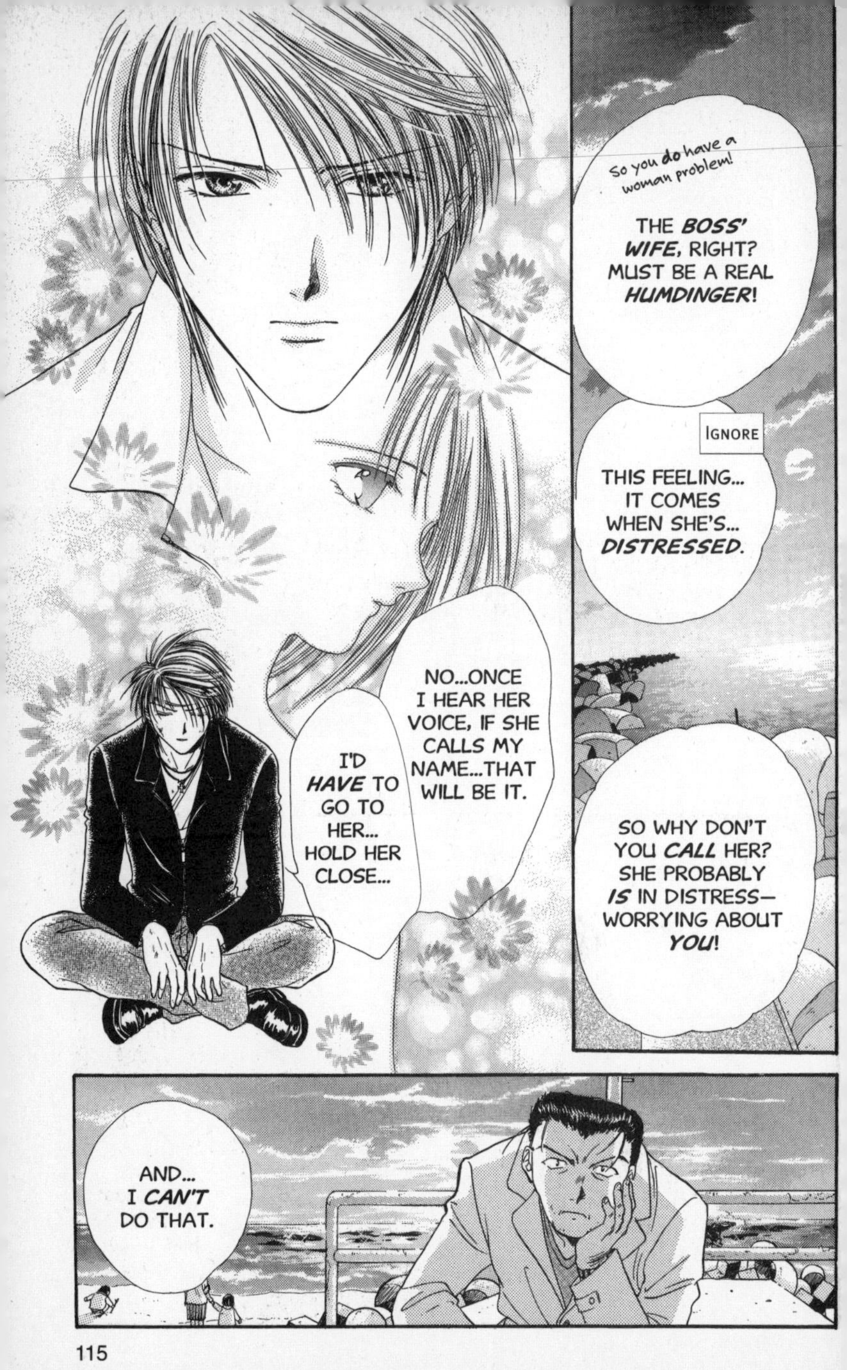
So you do have a woman problem!
THE BOSS' WIFE, RIGHT? MUST BE A REAL HUMDINGER!
IGNORE
THIS FEELING... IT COMES WHEN SHE'S... DISTRESSED.
SO WHY DON'T YOU CALL HER? SHE PROBABLY IS IN DISTRESS— WORRYING ABOUT YOU!
NO...ONCE I HEAR HER VOICE, IF SHE CALLS MY NAME...THAT WILL BE IT.
I'D HAVE TO GO TO HER... HOLD HER CLOSE...
AND... I CAN'T DO THAT.

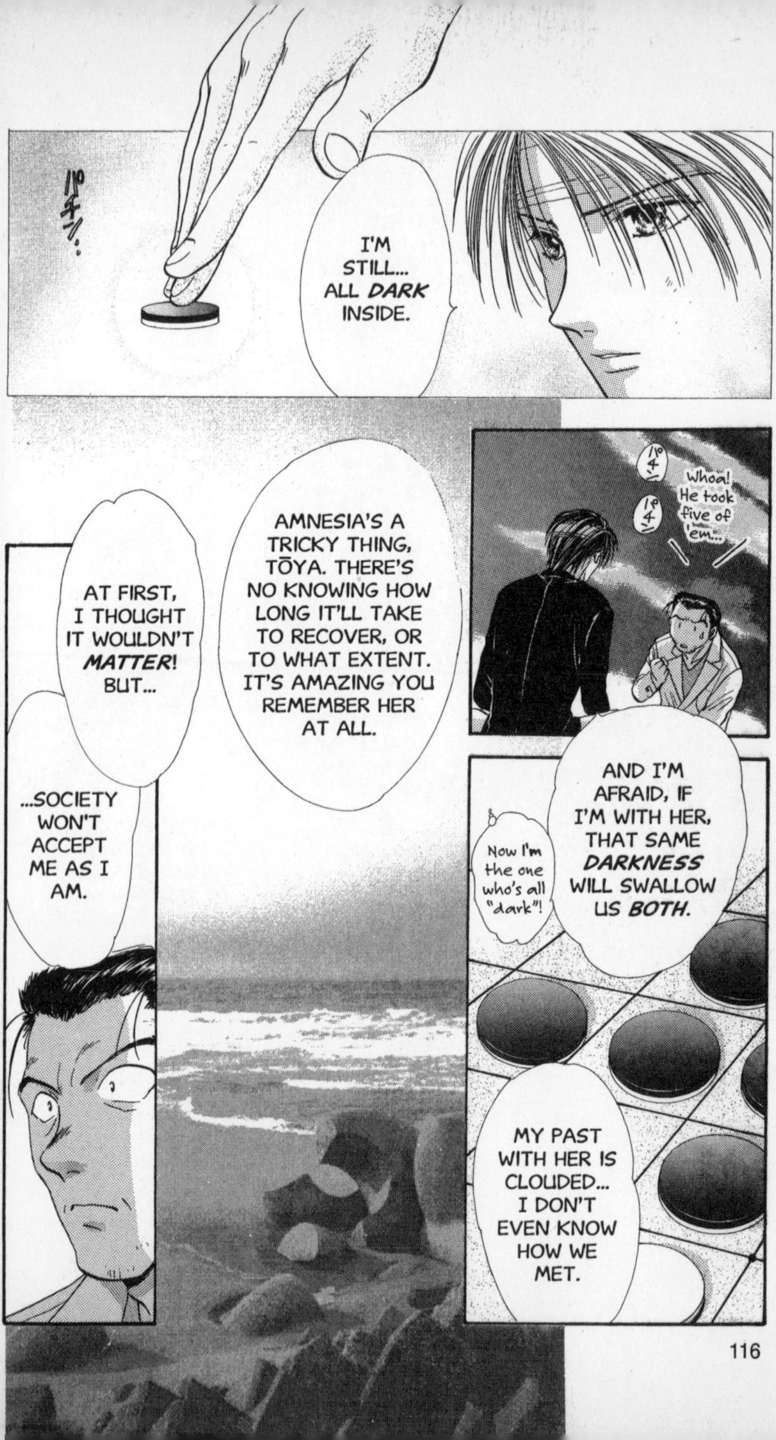
パチン。。
I'M STILL... ALL *DARK* INSIDE.
パ4 パ4
Whoa! He took five of 'em...
AND I'M AFRAID, IF I'M WITH HER, THAT SAME *DARKNESS* WILL SWALLOW US *BOTH*.
Now I'm the one who's all "dark"!
MY PAST WITH HER IS CLOUDED... I DON'T EVEN KNOW HOW WE MET.
AMNESIA'S A TRICKY THING, TŌYA. THERE'S NO KNOWING HOW LONG IT'LL TAKE TO RECOVER, OR TO WHAT EXTENT. IT'S AMAZING YOU REMEMBER HER AT ALL.
AT FIRST, I THOUGHT IT WOULDN'T *MATTER*! BUT...
...SOCIETY WON'T ACCEPT ME AS I AM.

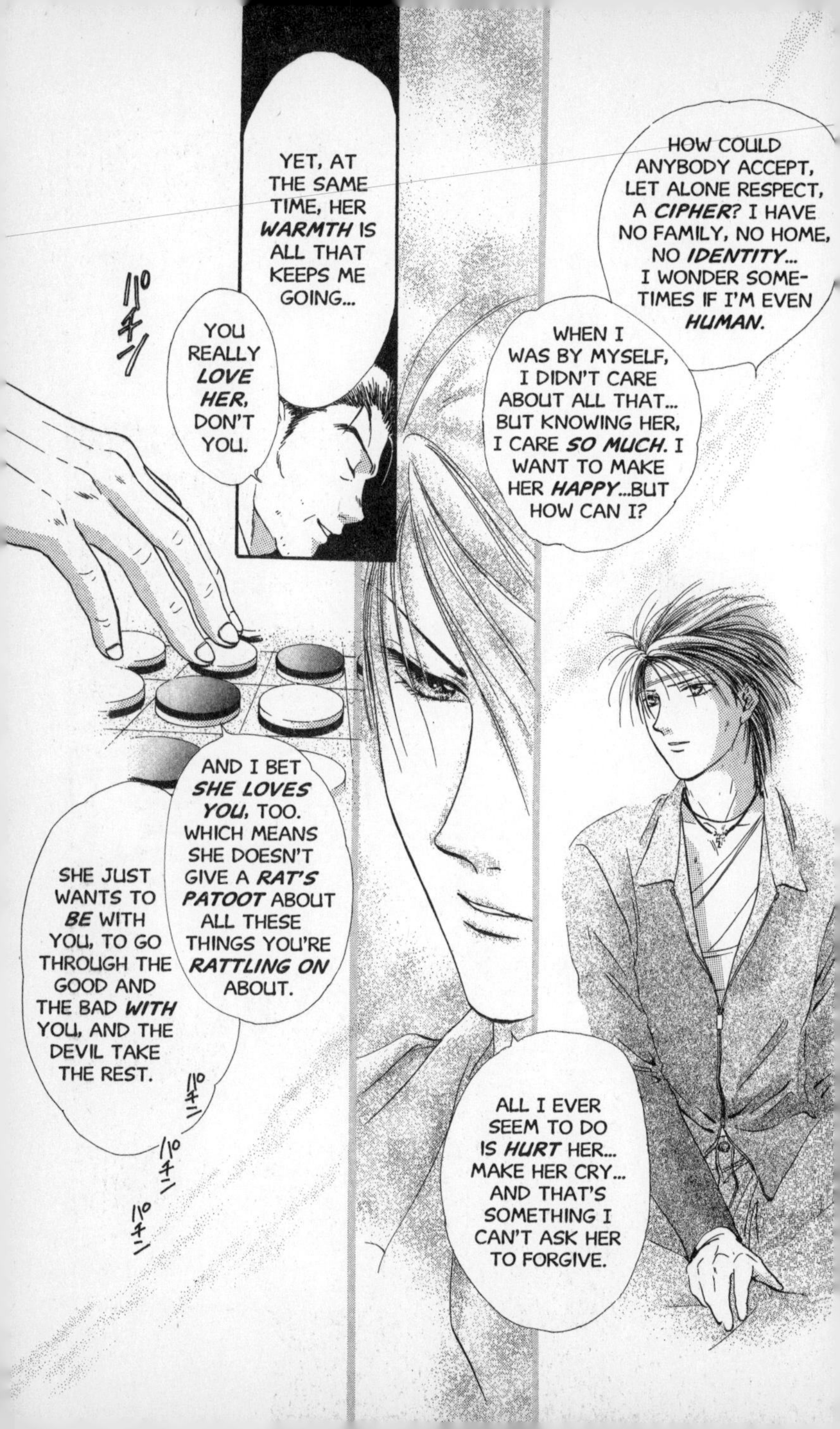
HOW COULD ANYBODY ACCEPT, LET ALONE RESPECT, A *CIPHER*? I HAVE NO FAMILY, NO HOME, NO *IDENTITY*... I WONDER SOMETIMES IF I'M EVEN *HUMAN*.
WHEN I WAS BY MYSELF, I DIDN'T CARE ABOUT ALL THAT... BUT KNOWING HER, I CARE *SO MUCH*. I WANT TO MAKE HER *HAPPY*...BUT HOW CAN I?
ALL I EVER SEEM TO DO IS *HURT* HER... MAKE HER CRY... AND THAT'S SOMETHING I CAN'T ASK HER TO FORGIVE.
YET, AT THE SAME TIME, HER *WARMTH* IS ALL THAT KEEPS ME GOING...
パチン
YOU REALLY *LOVE HER*, DON'T YOU.
AND I BET *SHE LOVES YOU*, TOO. WHICH MEANS SHE DOESN'T GIVE A *RAT'S PATOOT* ABOUT ALL THESE THINGS YOU'RE *RATTLING ON* ABOUT.
SHE JUST WANTS TO *BE* WITH YOU, TO GO THROUGH THE GOOD AND THE BAD *WITH* YOU, AND THE DEVIL TAKE THE REST.
パチン
パチン
パチン

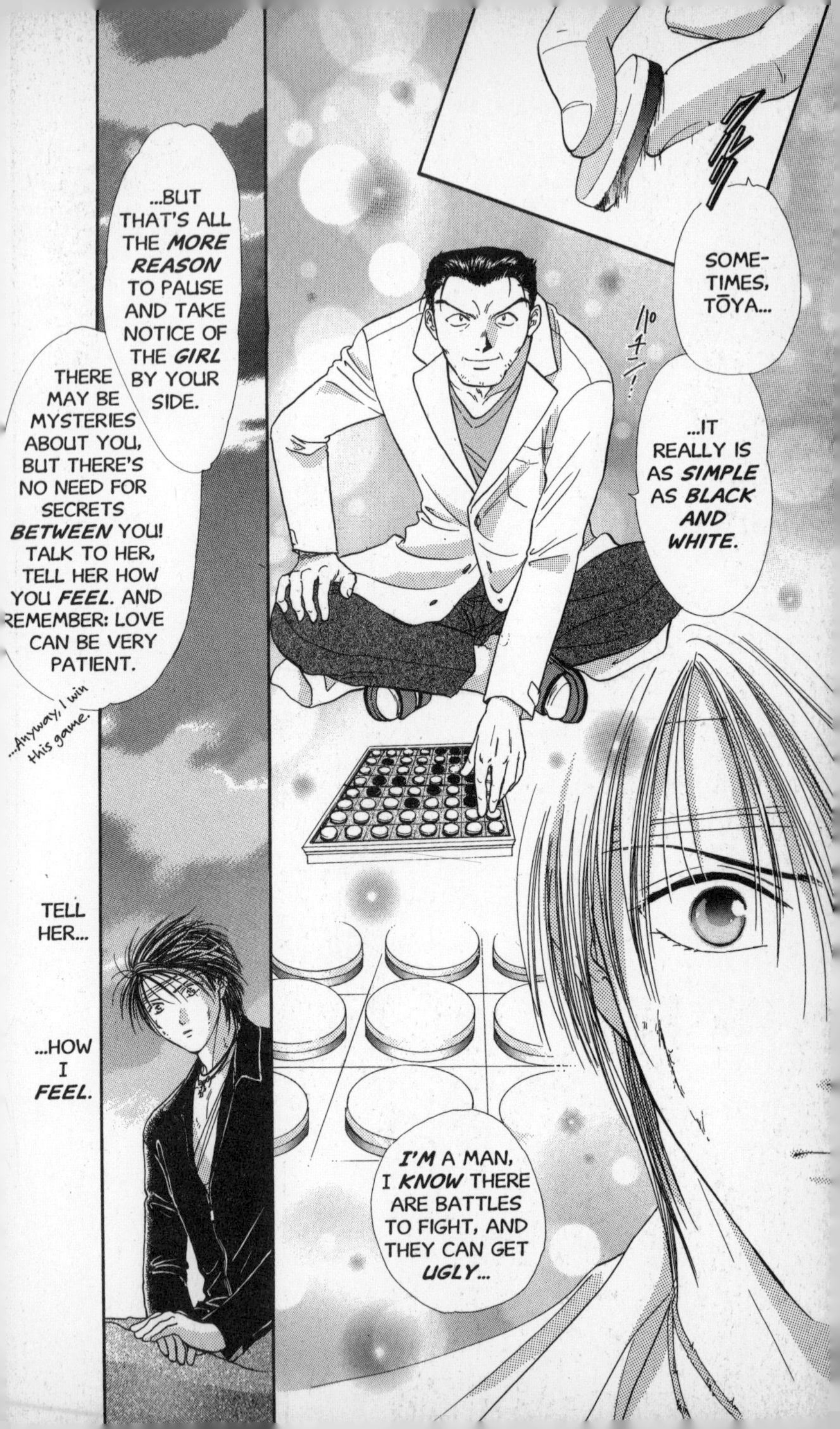

SOME-TIMES, TŌYA...
...IT REALLY IS AS SIMPLE AS BLACK AND WHITE.
I'M A MAN, I KNOW THERE ARE BATTLES TO FIGHT, AND THEY CAN GET UGLY...
...BUT THAT'S ALL THE MORE REASON TO PAUSE AND TAKE NOTICE OF THE GIRL BY YOUR SIDE.
THERE MAY BE MYSTERIES ABOUT YOU, BUT THERE'S NO NEED FOR SECRETS BETWEEN YOU! TALK TO HER, TELL HER HOW YOU FEEL. AND REMEMBER: LOVE CAN BE VERY PATIENT.
...Anyway, I win this game.
TELL HER...
...HOW I FEEL.

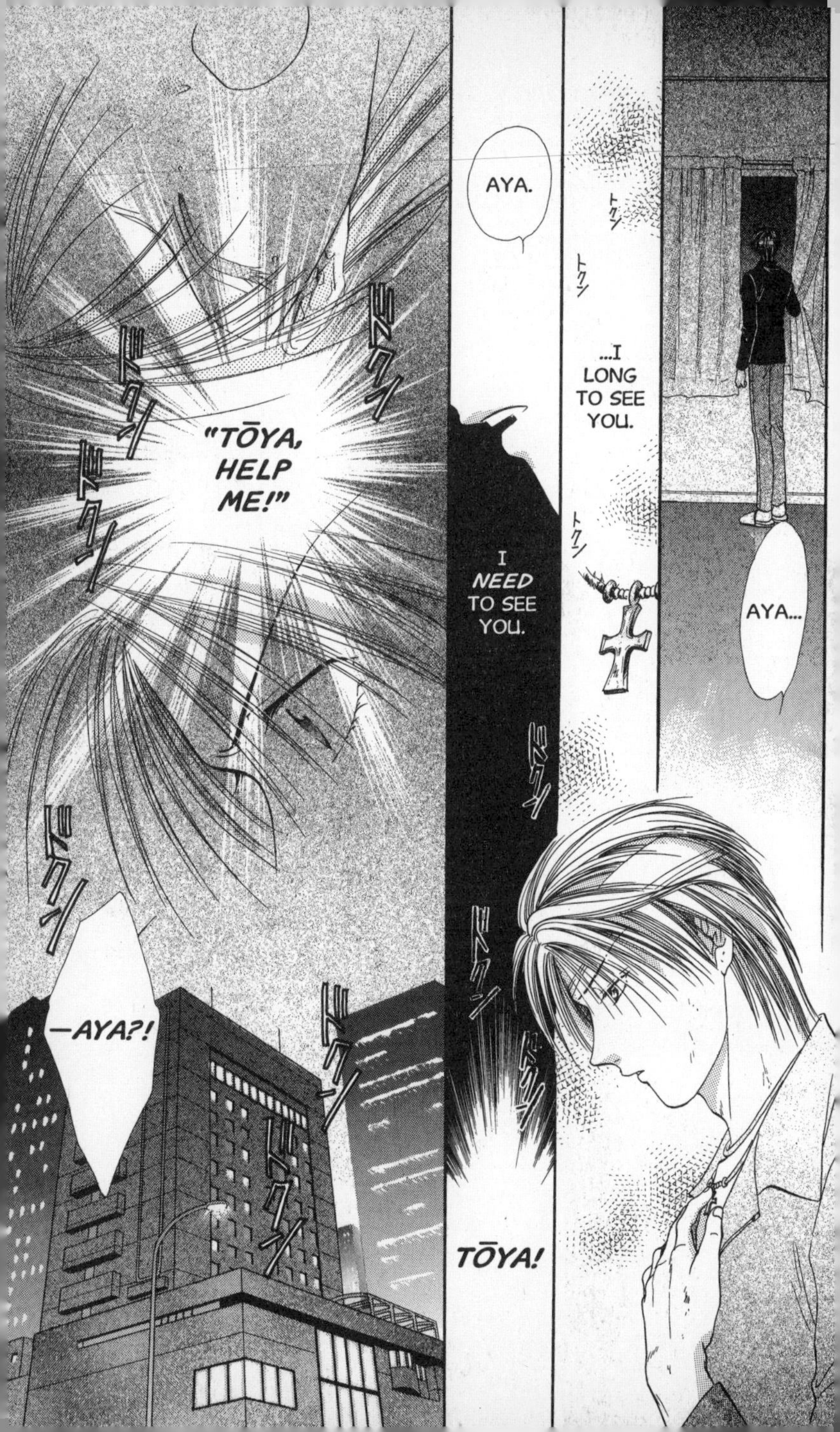
AYA...
トクン
トクン
...I LONG TO SEE YOU.
トクン
AYA.
I NEED TO SEE YOU.
TŌYA!
"TŌYA, HELP ME!"
—AYA?!

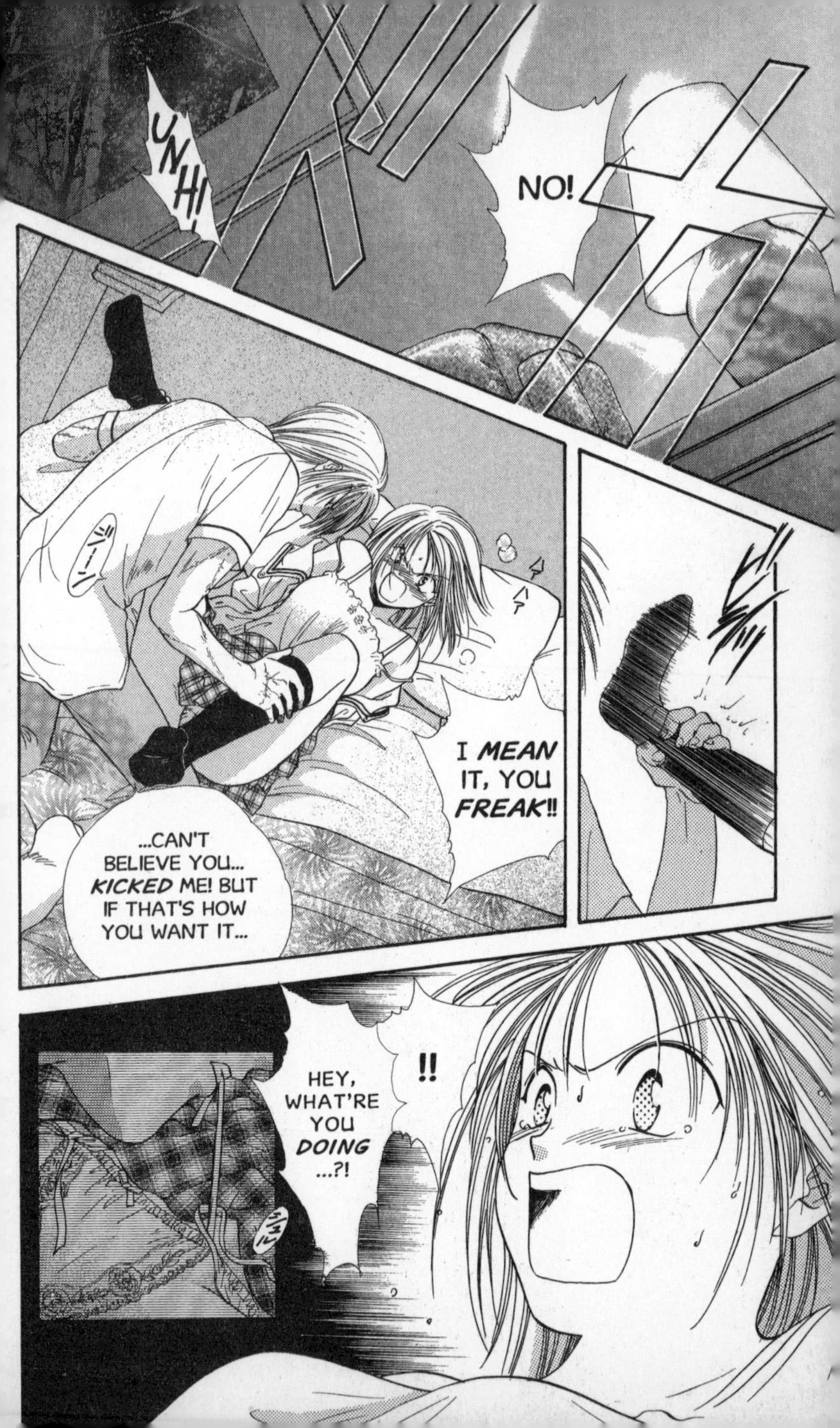
NO!
UNH!
I MEAN IT, YOU FREAK!!
...CAN'T BELIEVE YOU... KICKED ME! BUT IF THAT'S HOW YOU WANT IT...
!!
HEY, WHAT'RE YOU DOING ...?!

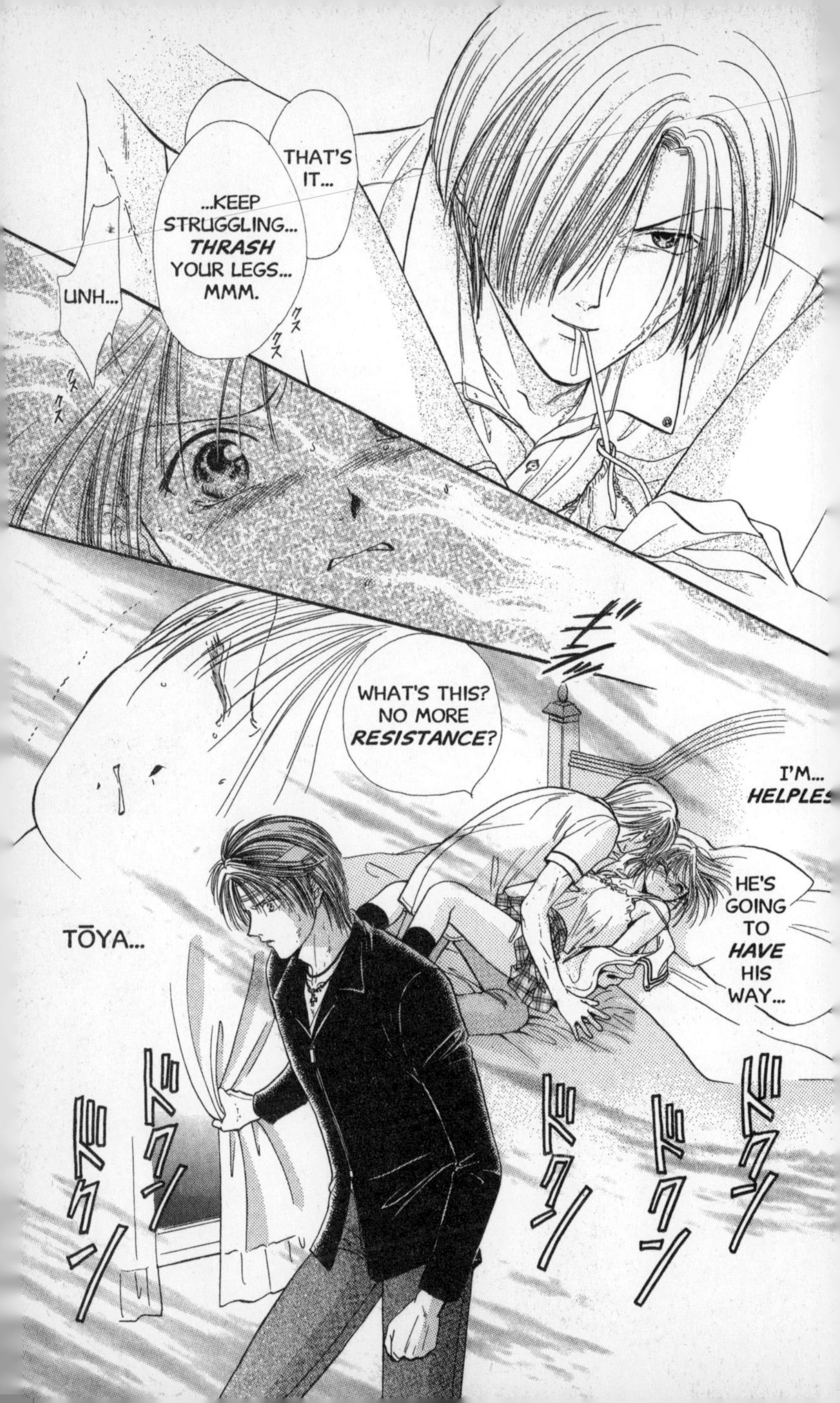
THAT'S IT...
...KEEP STRUGGLING... THRASH YOUR LEGS... MMM.
UNH...
WHAT'S THIS? NO MORE RESISTANCE?
I'M... HELPLES
HE'S GOING TO HAVE HIS WAY...
TŌYA...

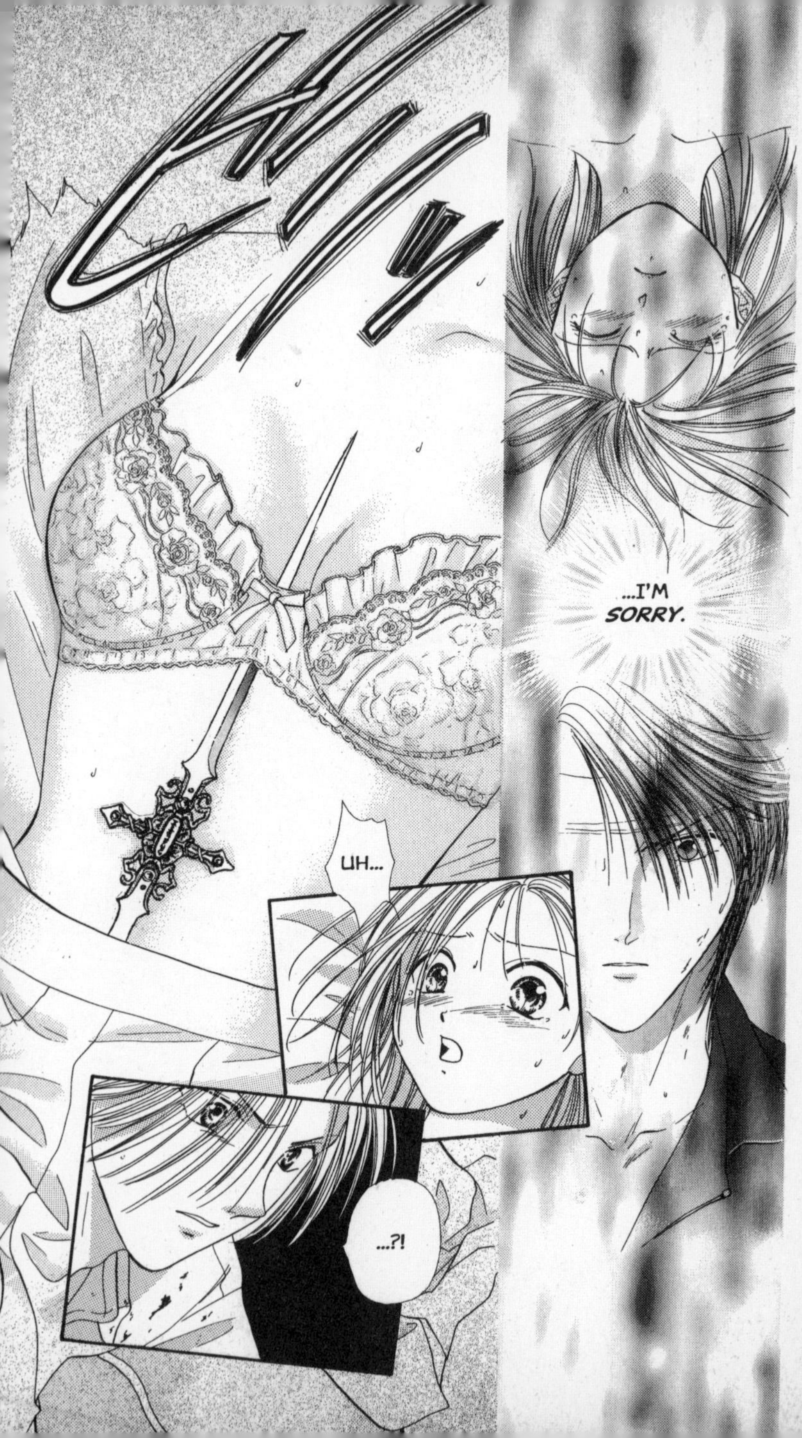
...I'M SORRY.
UH...
...?!

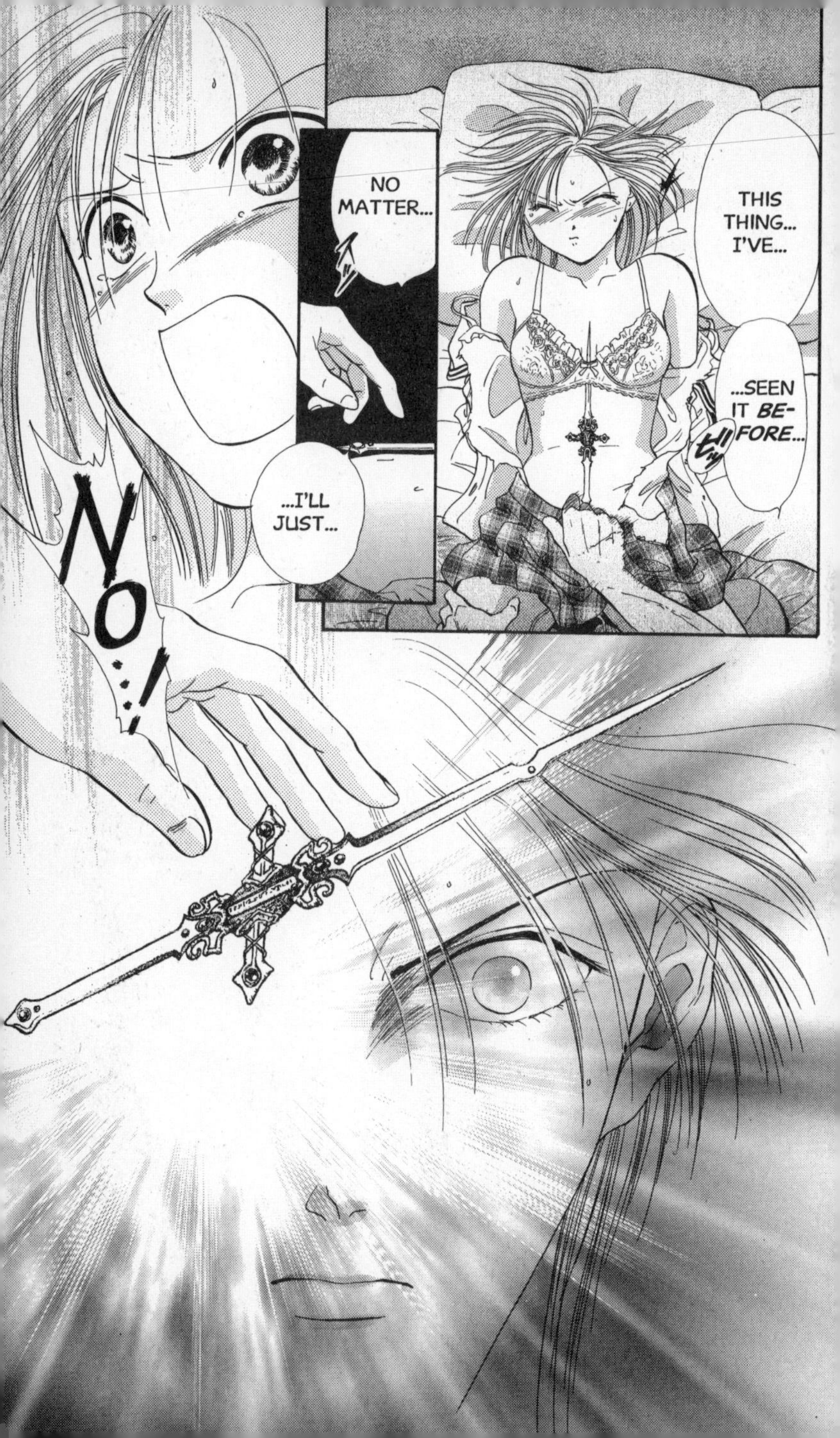
THIS THING... I'VE...
...SEEN IT BE-FORE...
NO MATTER...
...I'LL JUST...
NO...!

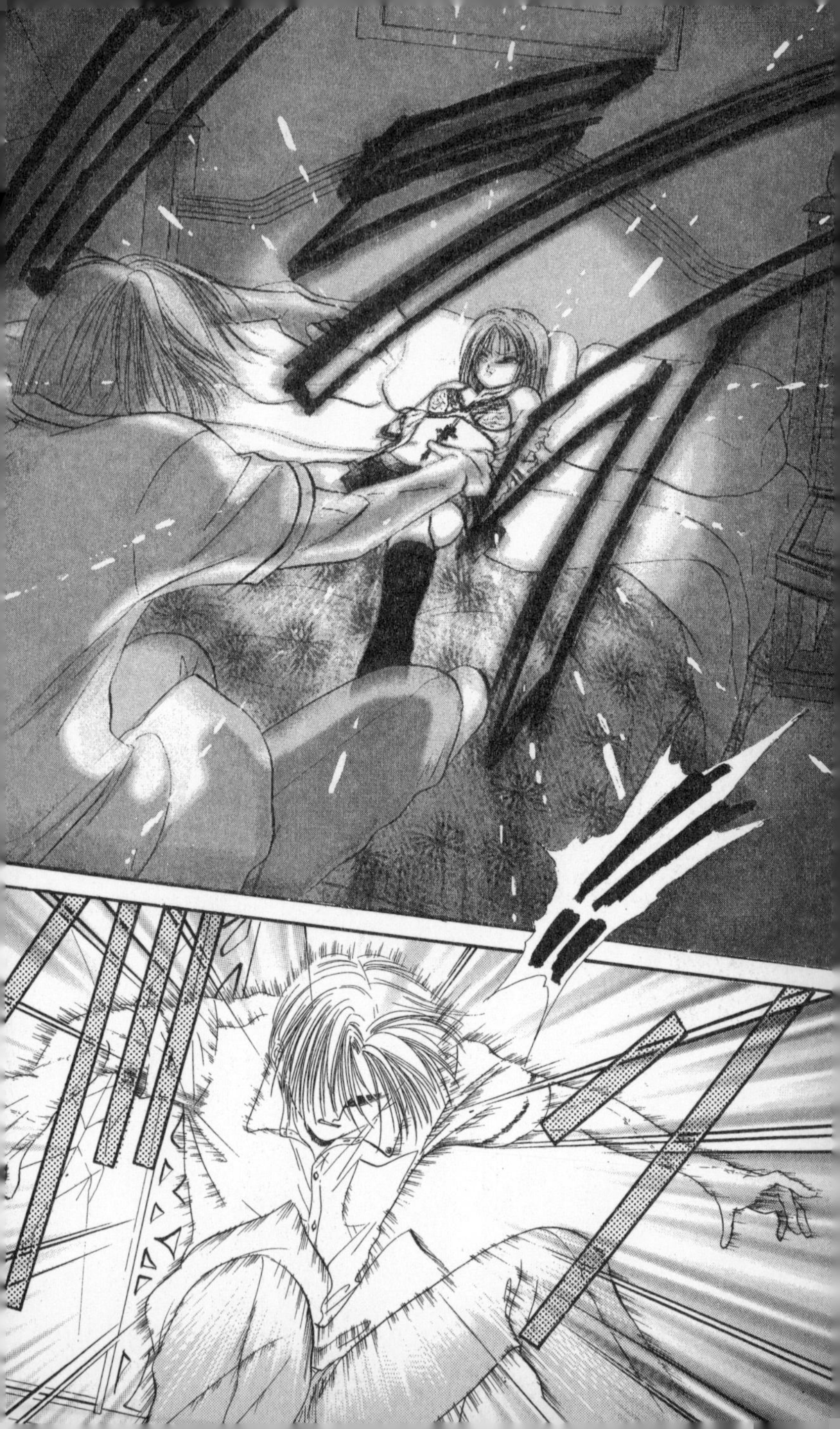

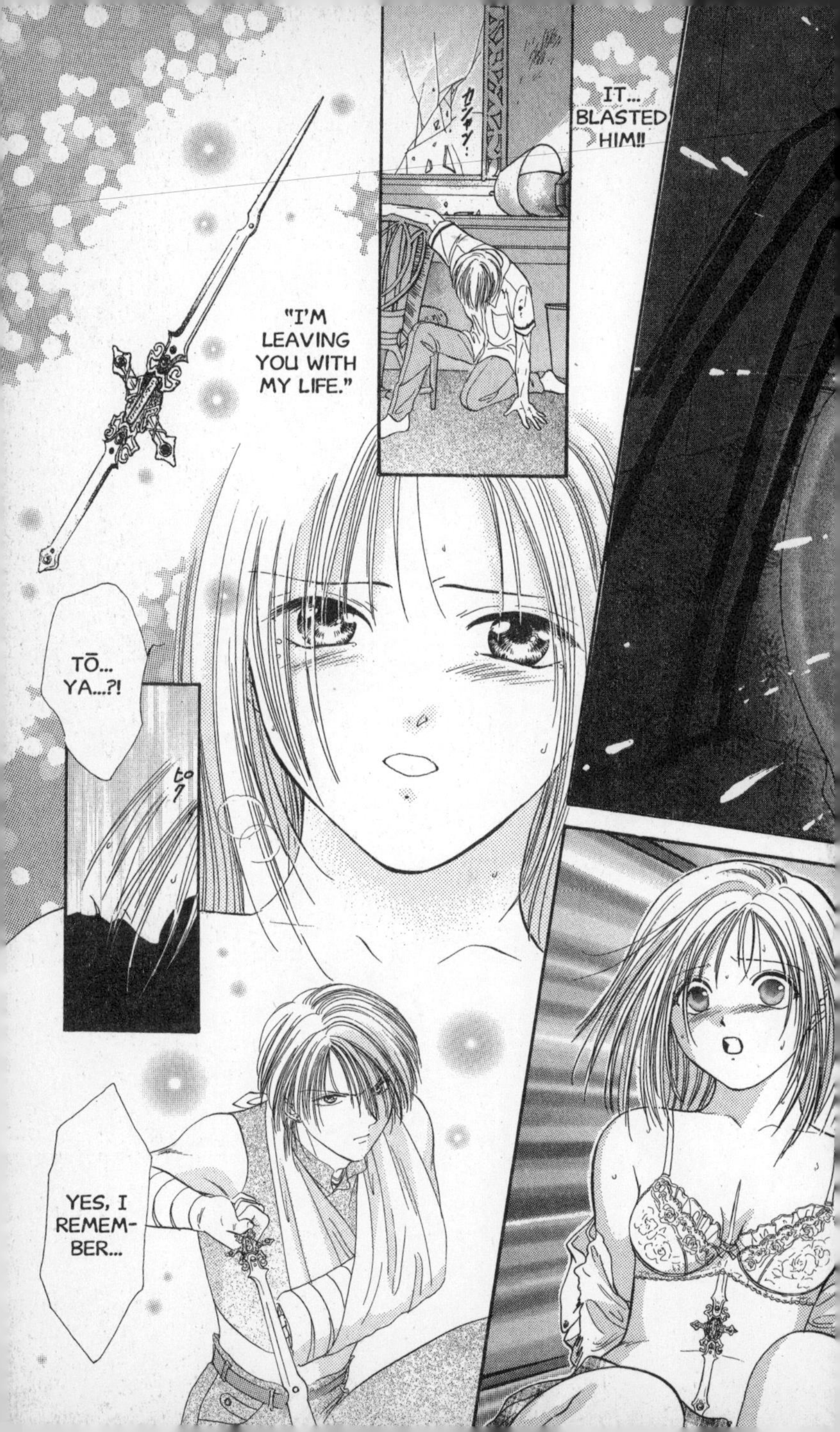
IT... BLASTED HIM!!
"I'M LEAVING YOU WITH MY LIFE."
TŌ... YA...?!
YES, I REMEMBER...

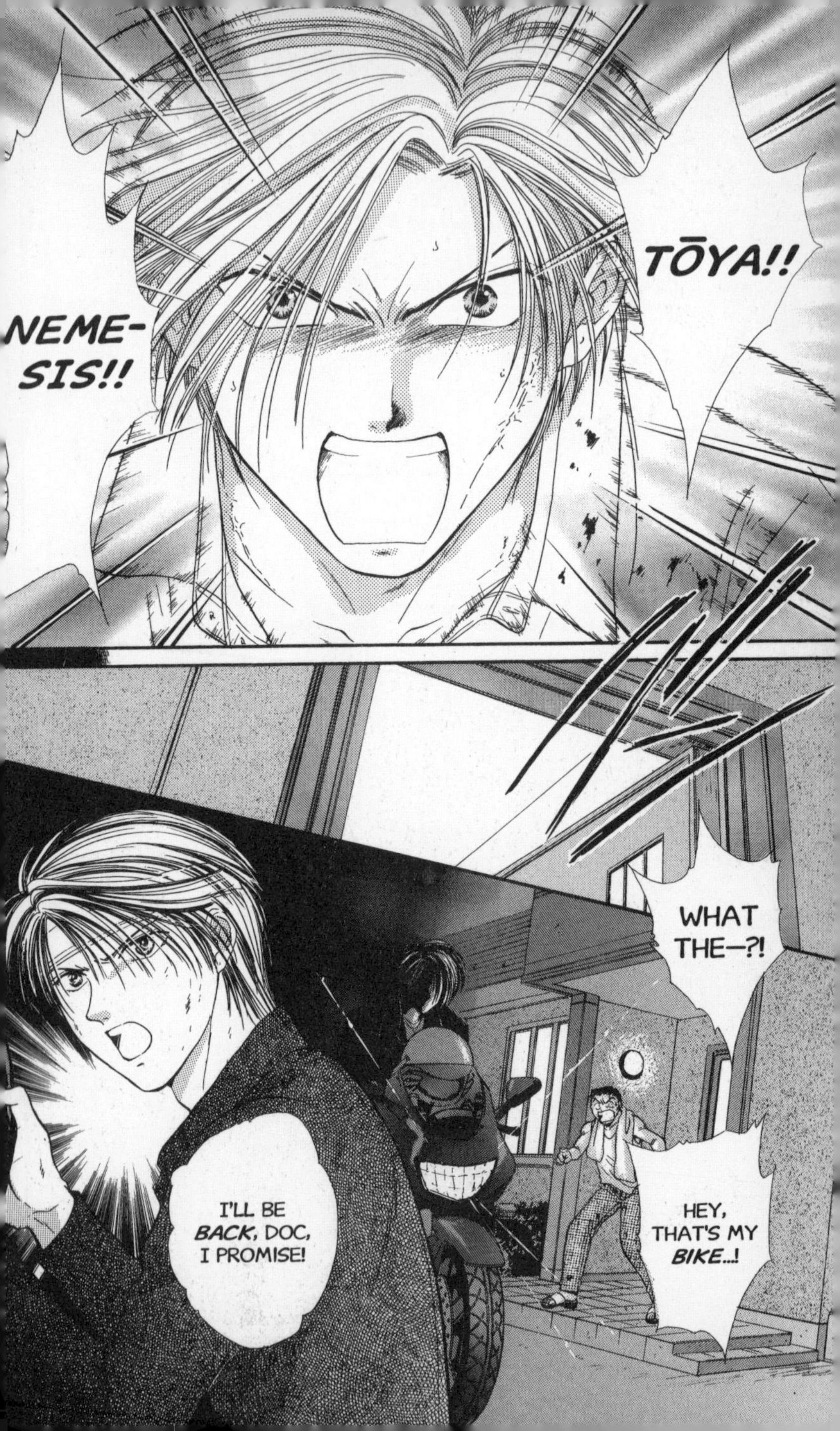
TŌYA!!
NEME-SIS!!
WHAT THE–?!
HEY, THAT'S MY BIKE...!
I'LL BE BACK, DOC, I PROMISE!

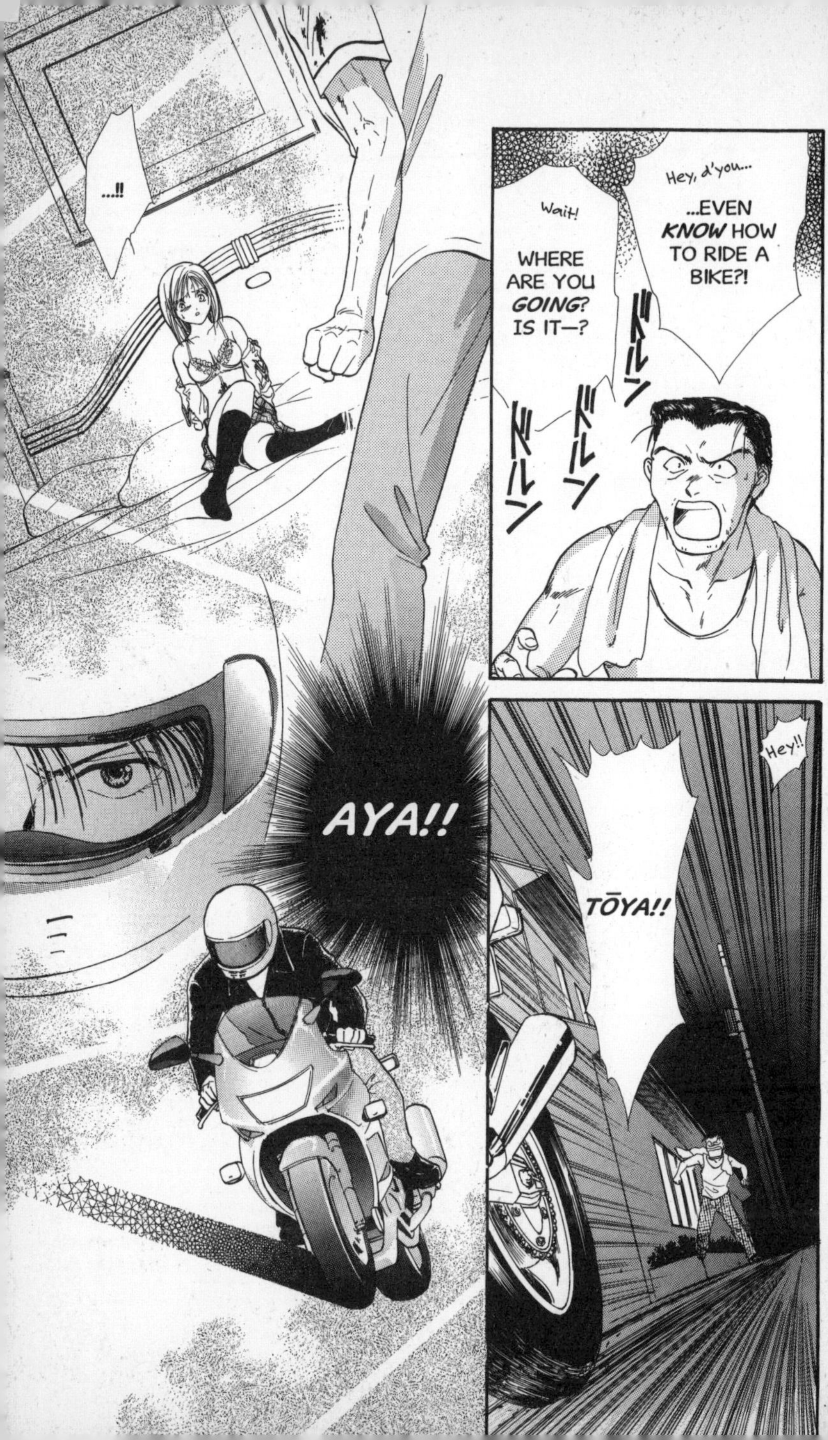
Hey, d'you...
...EVEN KNOW HOW TO RIDE A BIKE?!
Wait!
WHERE ARE YOU GOING? IS IT—?
ドルン
ドルン
ドルン
Hey!!
TŌYA!!
...!!
AYA!!

Who Knows If You're Even Reading This... Call It Filler!

The Maniac's Guide to "Ceres" ②!!

In which we review what's gone before, to help the reader better understand the world of "Ceres"—continued from a previous volume!

CELESTIAL POWERS — Psychic ability that people with celestial genes (C-Genomes) exhibit, catalyzed by the mysterious substance found in Ceres' body. Various manifestations include fire-starting, electromagnetic fields, conjuration (ex., the "white dog" in Miyagi), sound waves, etc. Although all powers were once possessed by the original, ancestral, celestial maidens, they weren't always welcome gifts. Because it is combined with the hatred of all the girls who were murdered, Ceres' power is the strongest of all. In actual legends, celestial powers are rooted in domesticity, such as producing infinite amounts of rice from a single grain, secret sake-making knowledge, or how to ensure a good harvest.

TWINS — Always fraternal, boy-girl twins were considered "taboo" in ancient times. Kagami's words from Volume 4, page 145 are an actual reference—twins were lovers who committed suicide in a previous life...not unlike Aya and Aki (although of course they weren't suicides). Also reflecting the "incest" taboo, in some countries twins were persecuted, along with the mother, and often killed. Looked at another way, many myths describe siblings and their sexual unions as "creation" stories (eg., the Egyptian Osiris and Isis, the Japanese Izanagi and Izanami).

THE MIKAGE FAMILY — Descendants of the ten'nyo or "celestial maiden" Ceres, the Mikage are a clan that have held considerable power since ancient times. Believing that it is their protector, they have preserved the mummy of Ceres over generations, and consider themselves to be "special," with their practice of consanguineous marriage to preserve the purity of their celestial blood. Their lineage extends far back into antiquity; another name for them is the "Shadow Imperial Family." Currently taking the form of a corporate conglomerate, "Mikage International" has established branch-offices all over the world, its influence extending to the political world. Even the police are under their thumb.

MIKAGE SUBORDINATES — As the power of the Mikage is based in the "dark" side of society, their influence sometimes manifests in various, more secretive ways. Discretion always a prerogative, any activity in the "public eye" is shunned. They are especially wary of becoming involved with persons of social and/or economic clout, such as the Aogiri family.

MUMMIFIED CERES — Long enshrined within the basement of the Main House as an object of worship, the mummified Ceres is interpreted by Kagami to be preventing the soul of Ceres from properly resting in peace—thereby forcing her repeated reincarnations as girls within the Mikage family. Although her body may have protected Mikage descendants, ironically, her soul is trying to destroy them. So fixated are the Mikage upon receiving this celestial protection that only the leader of each clan, each generation, is told of its existence (Kagami and the others were not at first aware of it; when it was discovered, it led to the detection of the mystery vector and its eventual, national distribution).

THE PROGENITOR — The man who made Ceres his wife. Kagami and the others call him this because he is the founding father of the Mikage family. Currently reincarnated as Aki Mikage, his personality was awakened by the sight of Ceres' mummy. Obsessed with Ceres, he shared a womb with her as Aya's twin, emerged at the mere sight of the mummy, and desires total dominion over her. The Progenitor is fiercely jealous (obviously), and is hostile to all other men, retaining the wild nature of an ancient people, and exhibiting the male psyche in the worst ways possible. Aware of the hagoromo or "celestial robes," he yet refuses to divulge any information concerning it...perhaps because of Ceres.

To Continue in ③!

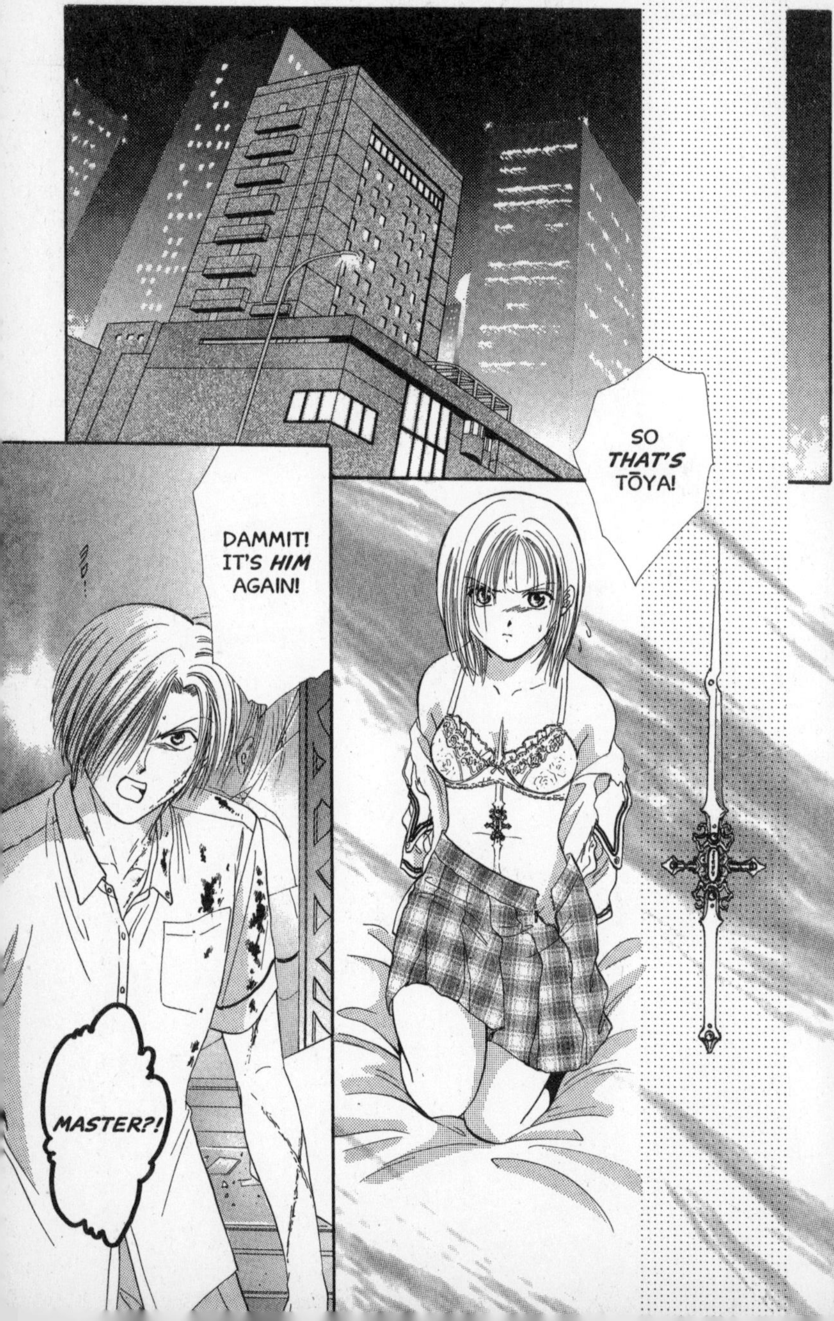
SO *THAT'S* TŌYA!
DAMMIT! IT'S *HIM* AGAIN!
MASTER?!

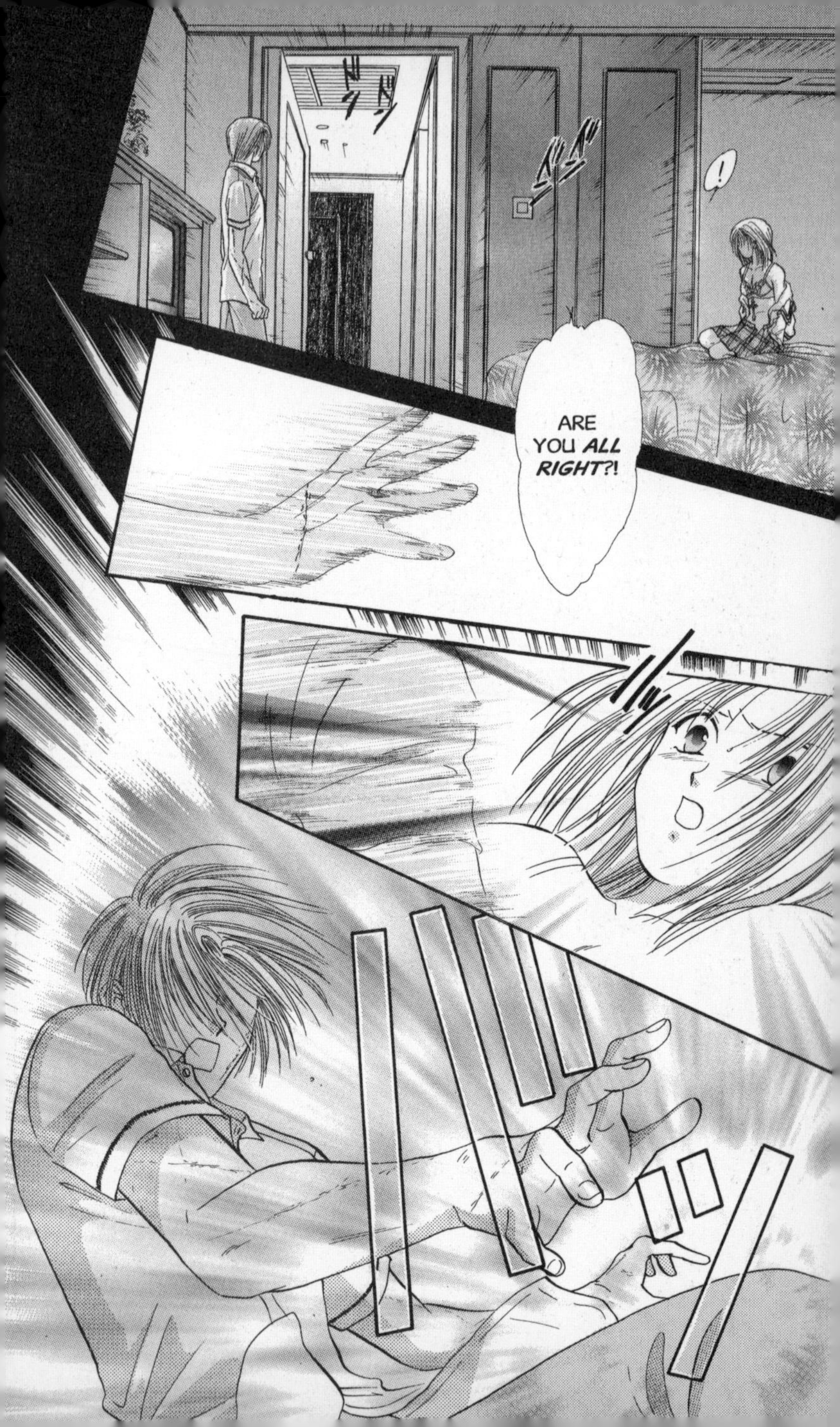
!
ARE YOU *ALL RIGHT*?!

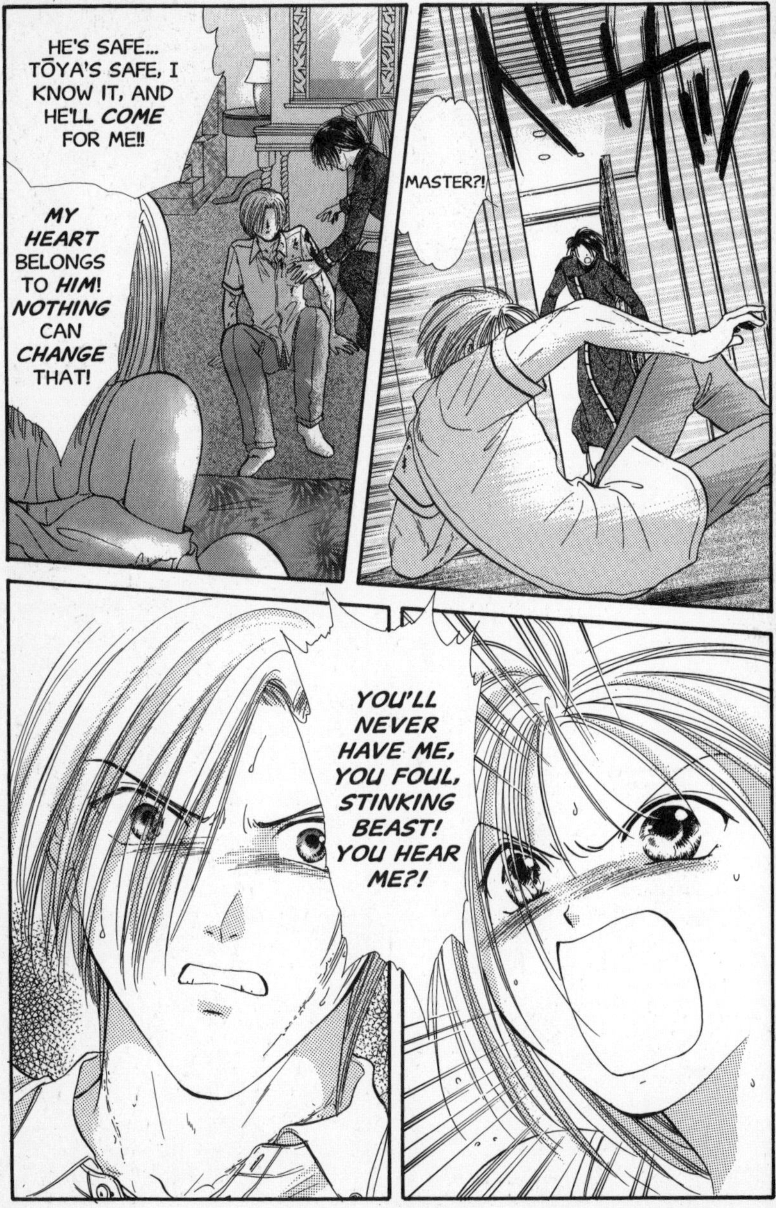
MASTER?!
HE'S SAFE... TŌYA'S SAFE, I KNOW IT, AND HE'LL *COME* FOR ME!!
MY HEART BELONGS TO *HIM*! *NOTHING* CAN *CHANGE* THAT!
YOU'LL NEVER HAVE ME, YOU FOUL, STINKING BEAST! YOU HEAR ME?!

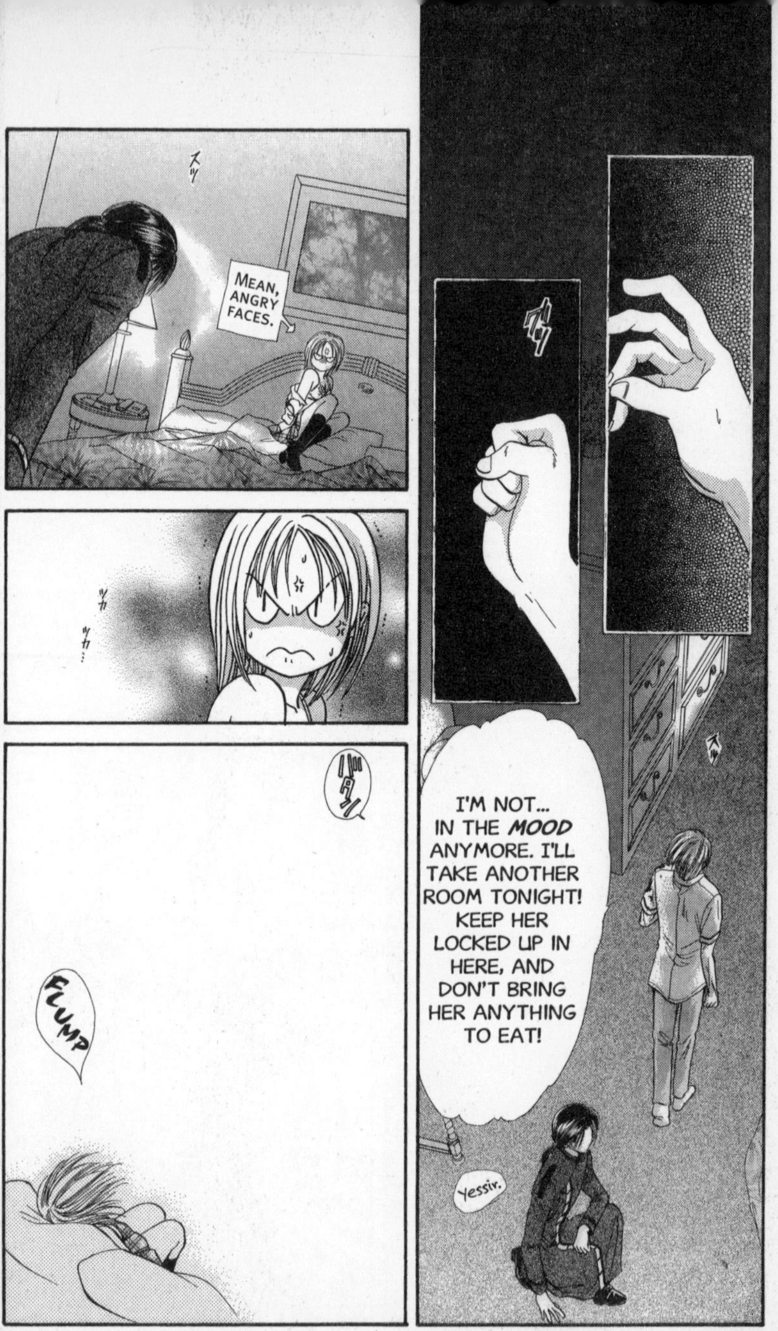
I'M NOT... IN THE *MOOD* ANYMORE. I'LL TAKE ANOTHER ROOM TONIGHT! KEEP HER LOCKED UP IN HERE, AND DON'T BRING HER ANYTHING TO EAT!
Yessir.
MEAN, ANGRY FACES.
FLUMP

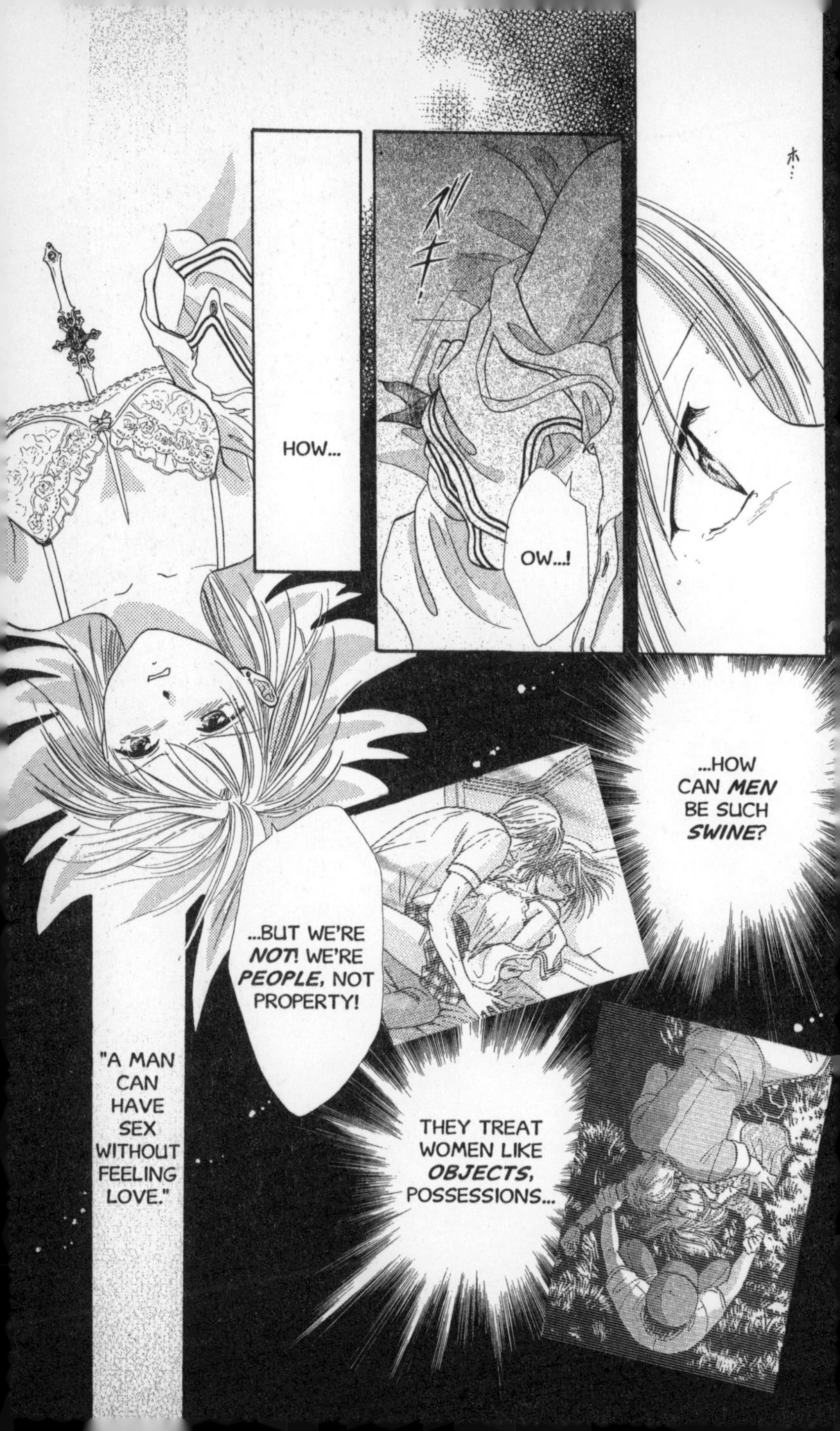
OW...!
HOW...
...HOW CAN *MEN* BE SUCH *SWINE*?
THEY TREAT WOMEN LIKE *OBJECTS*, POSSESSIONS...
...BUT WE'RE *NOT*! WE'RE *PEOPLE*, NOT PROPERTY!
"A MAN CAN HAVE SEX WITHOUT FEELING LOVE."

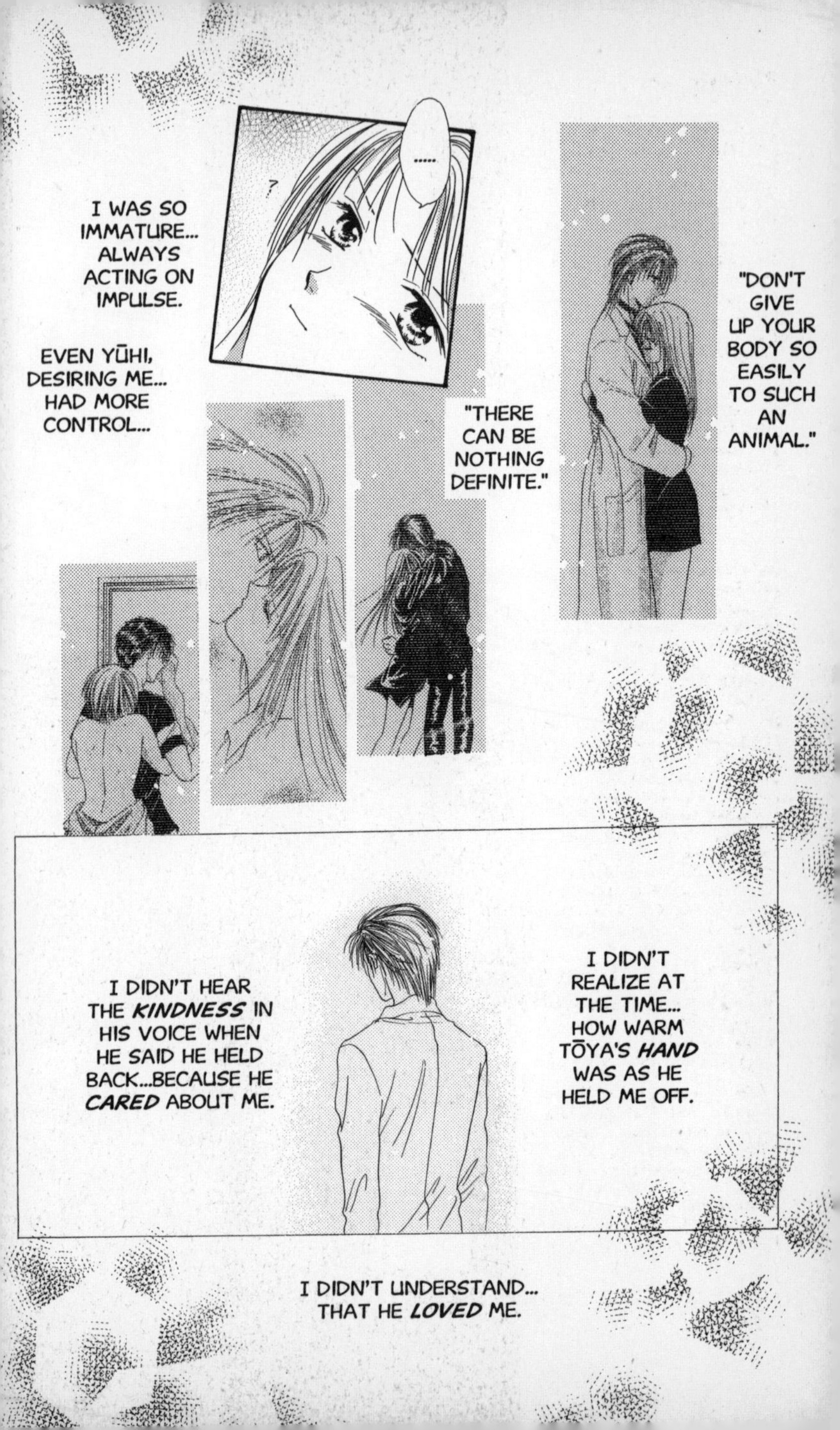
"DON'T GIVE UP YOUR BODY SO EASILY TO SUCH AN ANIMAL."
.....
?
I WAS SO IMMATURE... ALWAYS ACTING ON IMPULSE.
"THERE CAN BE NOTHING DEFINITE."
EVEN YŪHI, DESIRING ME... HAD MORE CONTROL...
I DIDN'T REALIZE AT THE TIME... HOW WARM TŌYA'S *HAND* WAS AS HE HELD ME OFF.
I DIDN'T HEAR THE *KINDNESS* IN HIS VOICE WHEN HE SAID HE HELD BACK...BECAUSE HE *CARED* ABOUT ME.
I DIDN'T UNDERSTAND... THAT HE *LOVED* ME.

Ceres: 10

...And now we change the subject to Tango. Of course, since most of the events took place at the school, we didn't get to see much of the area. ◊ I even climbed Mineyama, 'cause there's a pond there where a ten'nyo is said to have descended, and a monument at the summit (I wrote some comments and scribbled a picture of Ceres in their guest book). There were celestial maidens everywhere in Mineyama Town. They have celestial souvenirs, the monument at City Hall was a celestial maiden, and every summer they have a festival called the "Hagoromo Summit," where they gather the legends from the country, and celebrate with descendants. Nakayama-san at the Financial/PR Dept., thanks for your assistance with the local dialect, etc. ◊

By the way, the story about the flooded shrine was a true one—something I heard during my research. The site is now the sports field for a high school, so close to what I'd imagined that I was like, "Whoa!" It was a nice place, all surrounded by mountains. Other spots had their own legends, with contests for "Miss Hagoromo"? or was it "Miss Ten'nyo"...? I've never seen a whole town so into promoting the legend like this. "Tenten," their celestial maiden mascot character, was really cute. ☺ ...Oh, the local paper interviewed me, too, while I was there for research, and ran an article. ☺ If you ever travel there, be sure to climb Mineyama. There's 1,010 steps total, so it's a killer! The view, though, is fantastic. Just remember to bring your own drinks and snacks, 'cause you won't find any vending machines.

On to a new topic—I've received even more mail from people who want to become manga artists. (The trend used to be toward writers and voice-actors, at least for a while.) "I'd like to be a manga artist, but I'm not sure if I could do it." "It feels pointless to go to school (or college)."

To be continued.

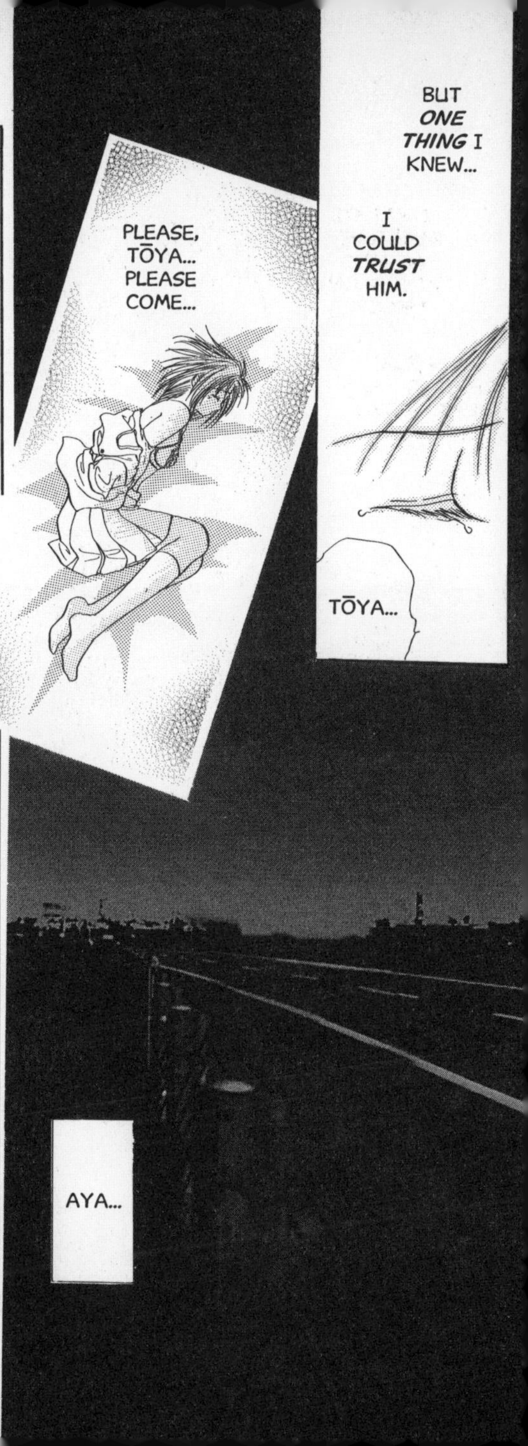
BUT ONE THING I KNEW...
I COULD TRUST HIM.
TŌYA...
PLEASE, TŌYA... PLEASE COME...
AYA...

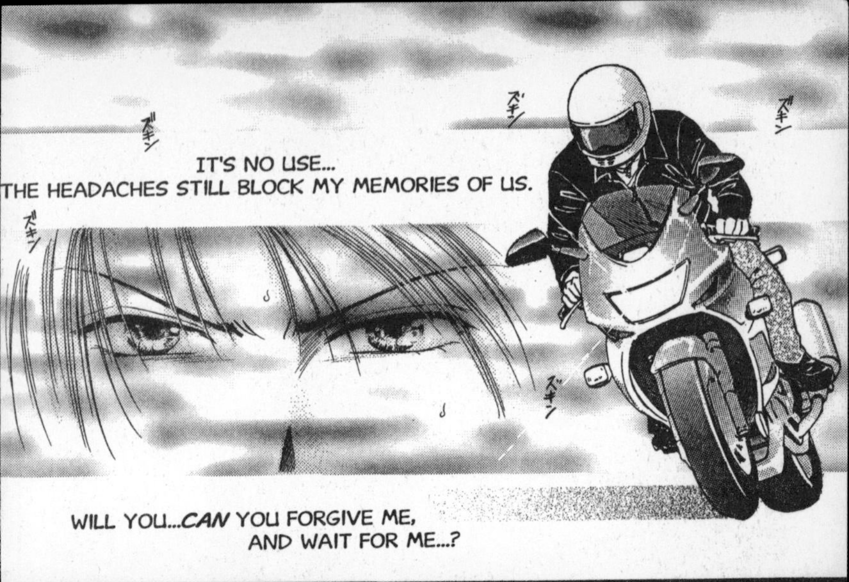
ズキン
ズキン
ズキン
IT'S NO USE...
THE HEADACHES STILL BLOCK MY MEMORIES OF US.
ズキン
ズキン
WILL YOU...*CAN* YOU FORGIVE ME,
AND WAIT FOR ME...?
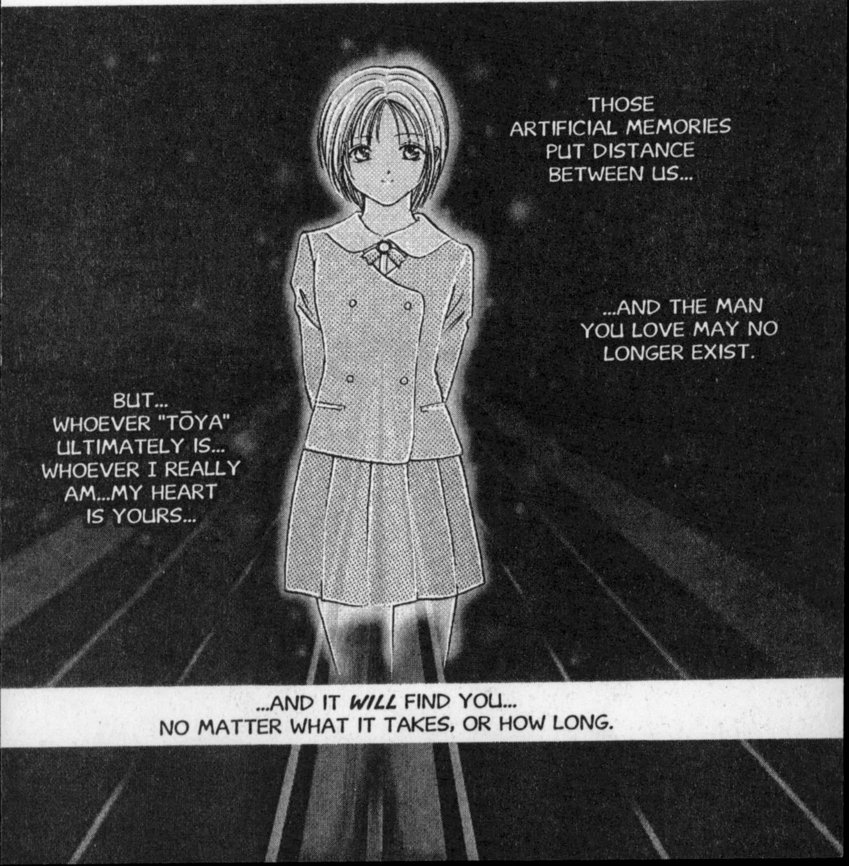
THOSE ARTIFICIAL MEMORIES PUT DISTANCE BETWEEN US...
...AND THE MAN YOU LOVE MAY NO LONGER EXIST.
BUT... WHOEVER "TŌYA" ULTIMATELY IS... WHOEVER I REALLY AM...MY HEART IS YOURS...
...AND IT *WILL* FIND YOU...
NO MATTER WHAT IT TAKES, OR HOW LONG.

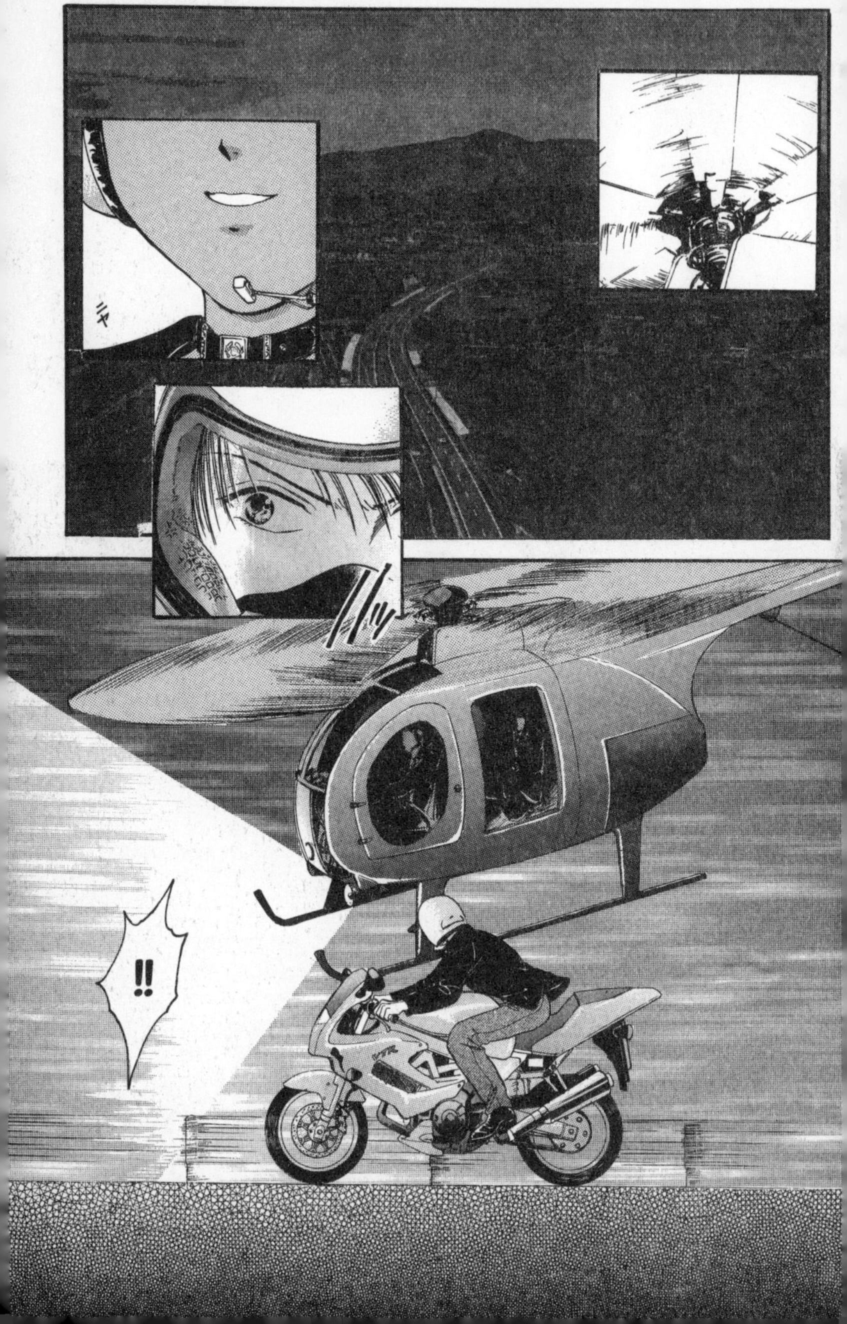
ニヤ
!!

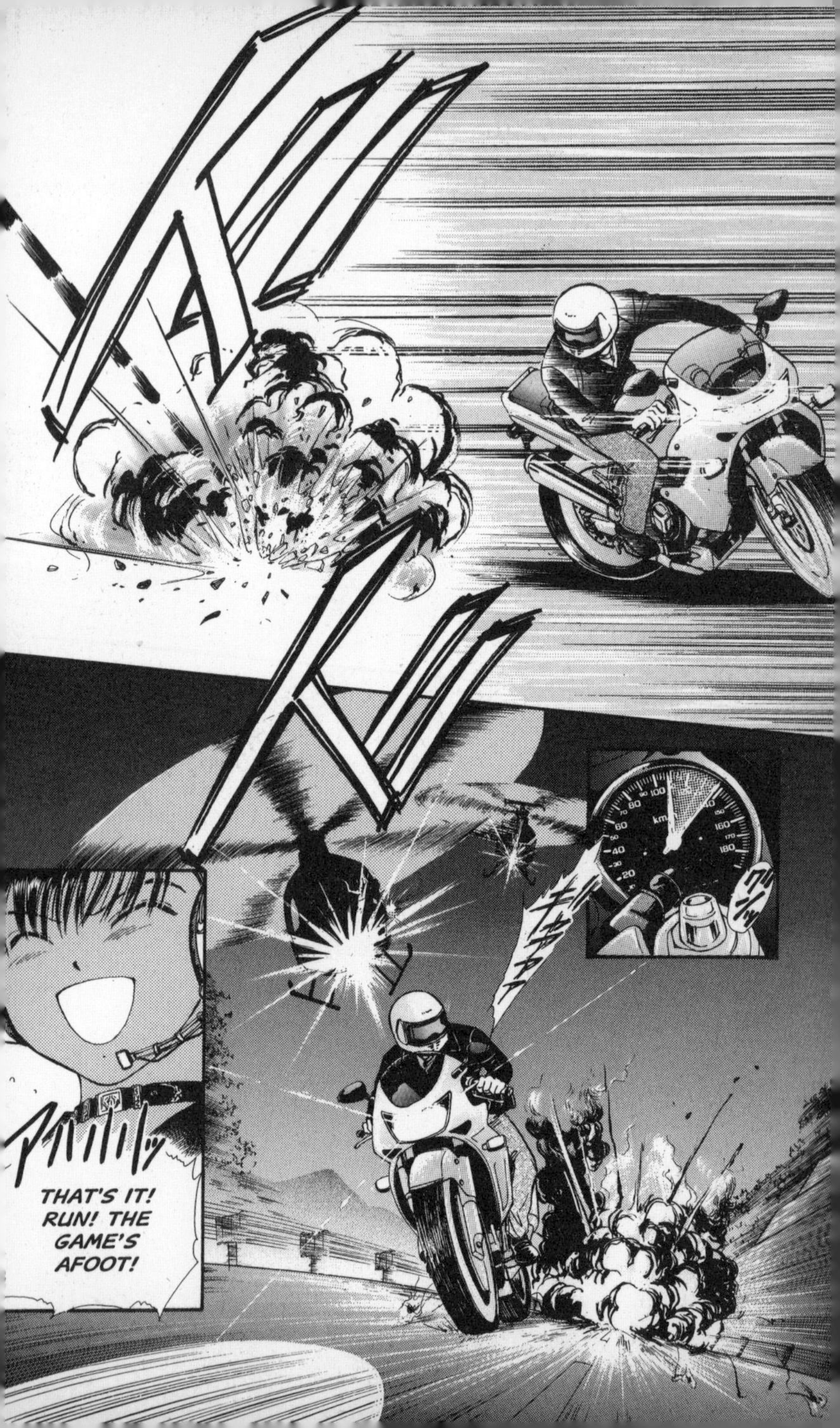
THAT'S IT! RUN! THE GAME'S AFOOT!

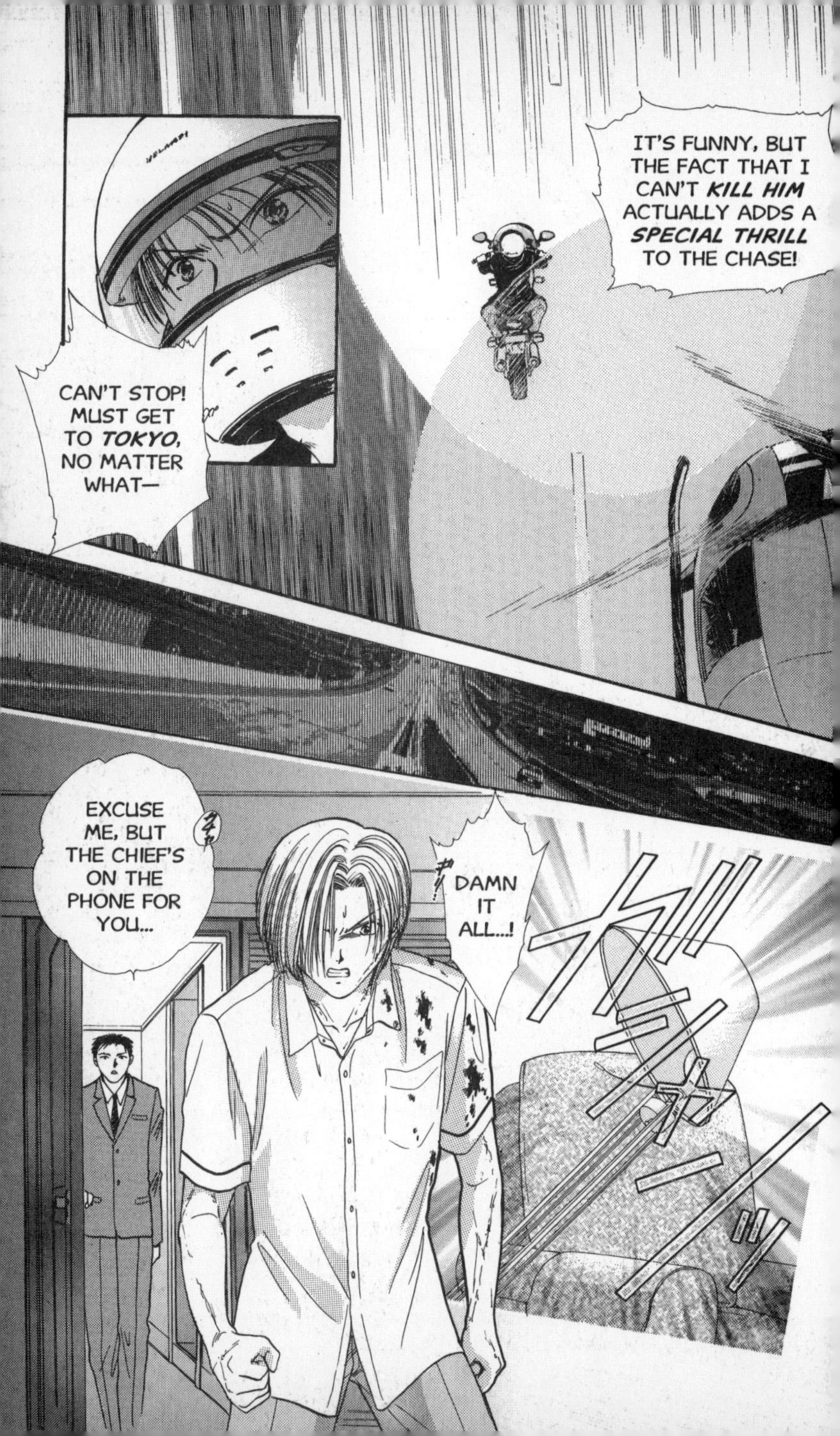
IT'S FUNNY, BUT THE FACT THAT I CAN'T ***KILL HIM*** ACTUALLY ADDS A ***SPECIAL THRILL*** TO THE CHASE!
CAN'T STOP! MUST GET TO *TOKYO,* NO MATTER WHAT—
DAMN IT ALL...!
EXCUSE ME, BUT THE CHIEF'S ON THE PHONE FOR YOU...

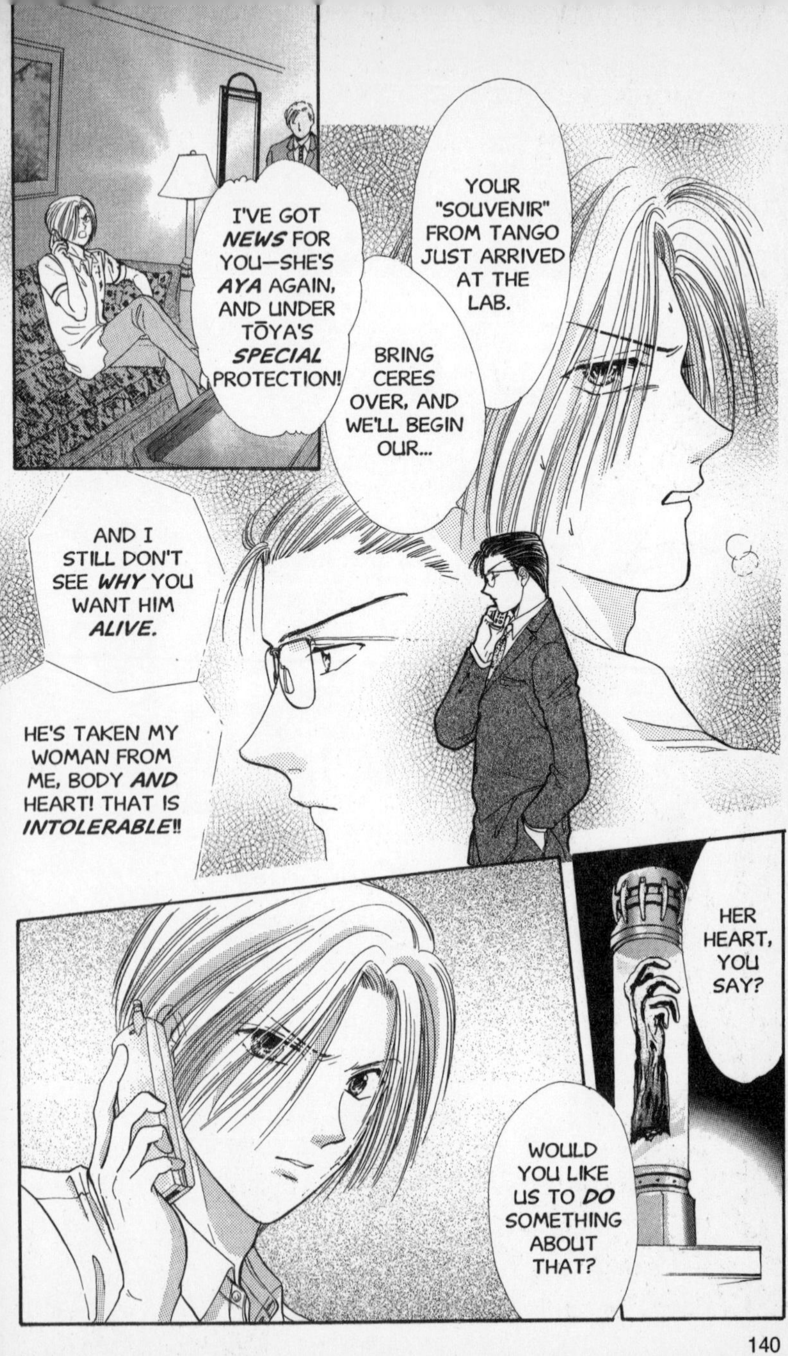
YOUR "SOUVENIR" FROM TANGO JUST ARRIVED AT THE LAB.
BRING CERES OVER, AND WE'LL BEGIN OUR...
I'VE GOT *NEWS* FOR YOU—SHE'S *AYA* AGAIN, AND UNDER TŌYA'S *SPECIAL* PROTECTION!
AND I STILL DON'T SEE *WHY* YOU WANT HIM *ALIVE.*
HE'S TAKEN MY WOMAN FROM ME, BODY *AND* HEART! THAT IS *INTOLERABLE*!!
HER HEART, YOU SAY?
WOULD YOU LIKE US TO *DO* SOMETHING ABOUT THAT?

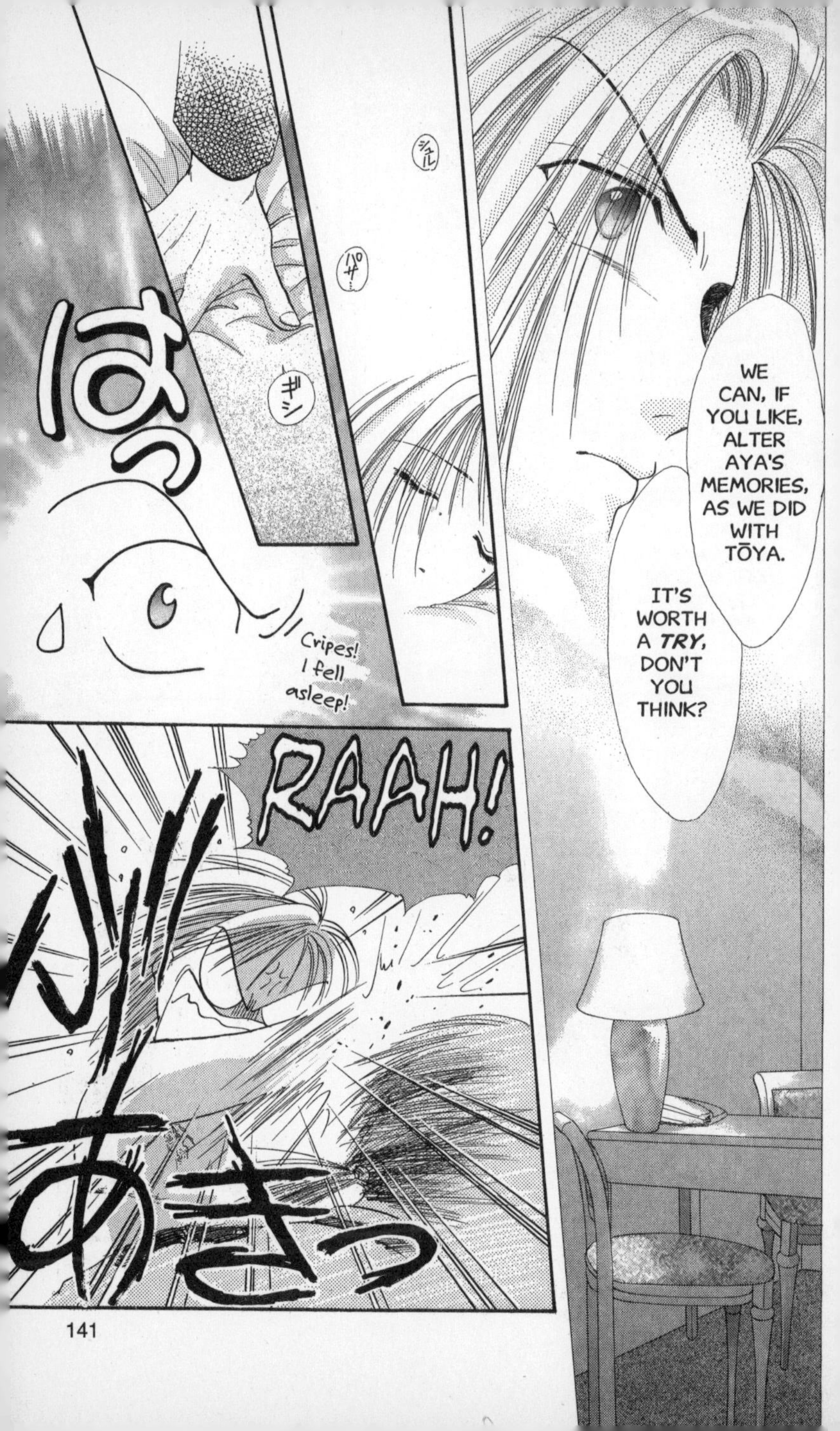
WE CAN, IF YOU LIKE, ALTER AYA'S MEMORIES, AS WE DID WITH TŌYA.
IT'S WORTH A *TRY*, DON'T YOU THINK?
シュル
パサ…
ギシ
はっ
Cripes! I fell asleep!
RAAH!

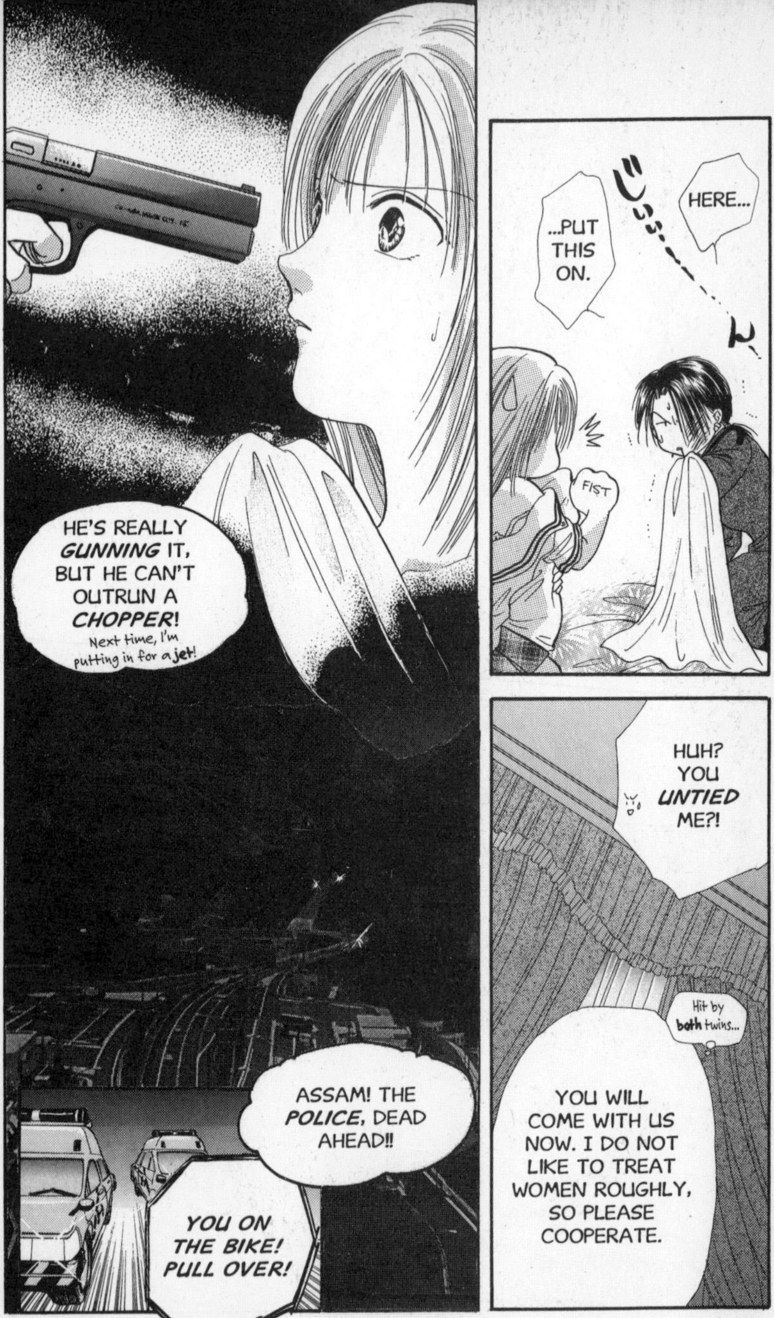
HERE...
...PUT THIS ON.
FIST
HUH? YOU *UNTIED* ME?!
Hit by **both** twins...
YOU WILL COME WITH US NOW. I DO NOT LIKE TO TREAT WOMEN ROUGHLY, SO PLEASE COOPERATE.
HE'S REALLY *GUNNING* IT, BUT HE CAN'T OUTRUN A *CHOPPER*!
Next time, I'm putting in for a **jet**!
ASSAM! THE *POLICE*, DEAD AHEAD!!
YOU ON THE BIKE! PULL OVER!

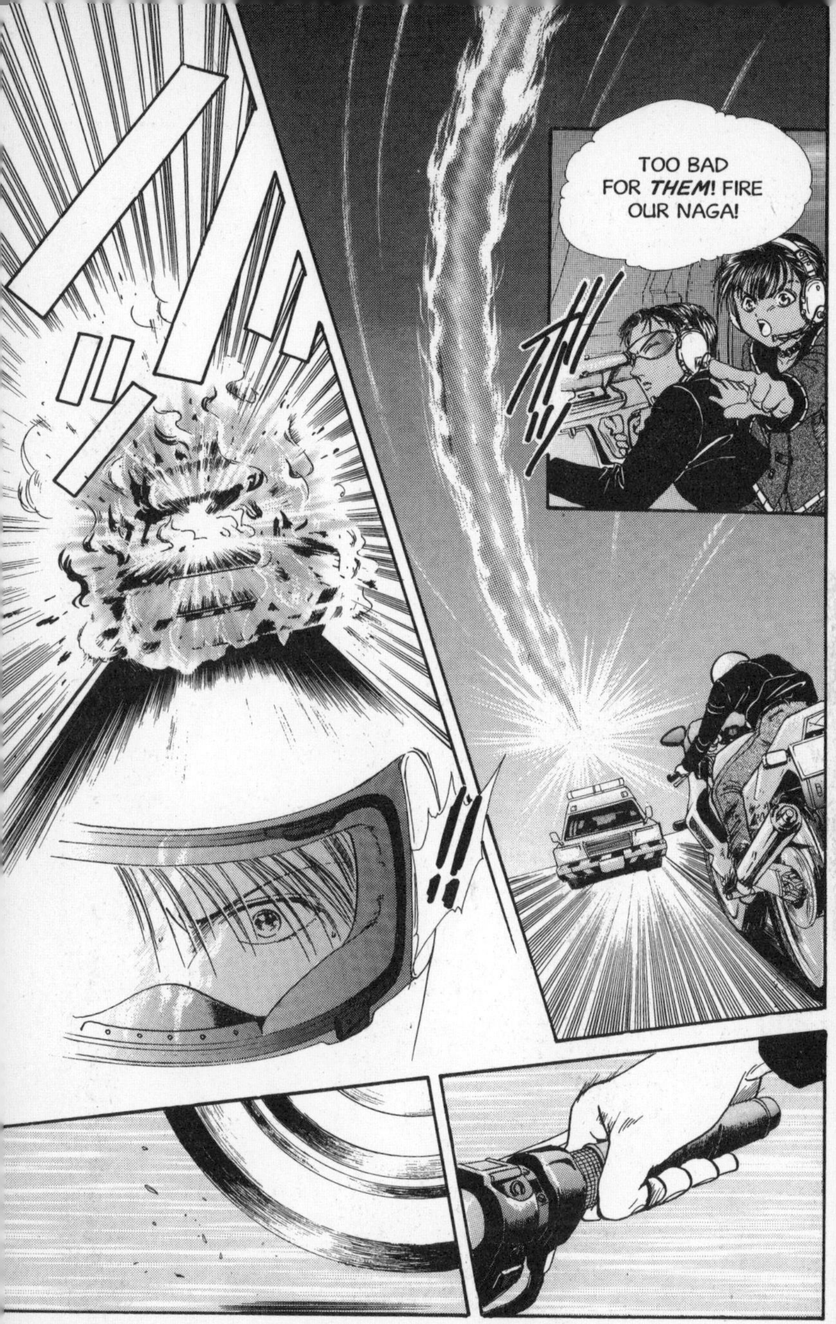
TOO BAD FOR *THEM*! FIRE OUR NAGA!

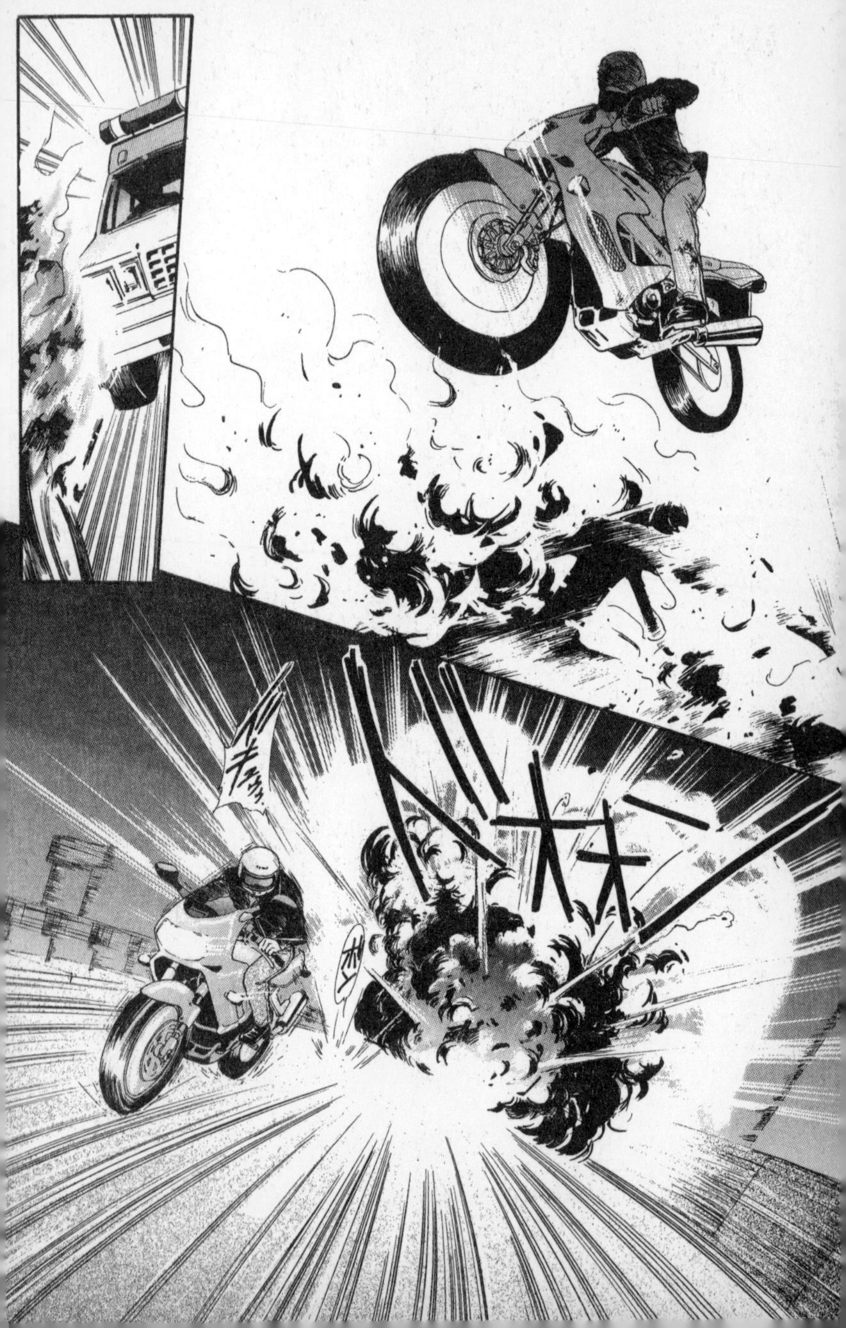
ドオオー
ボッ

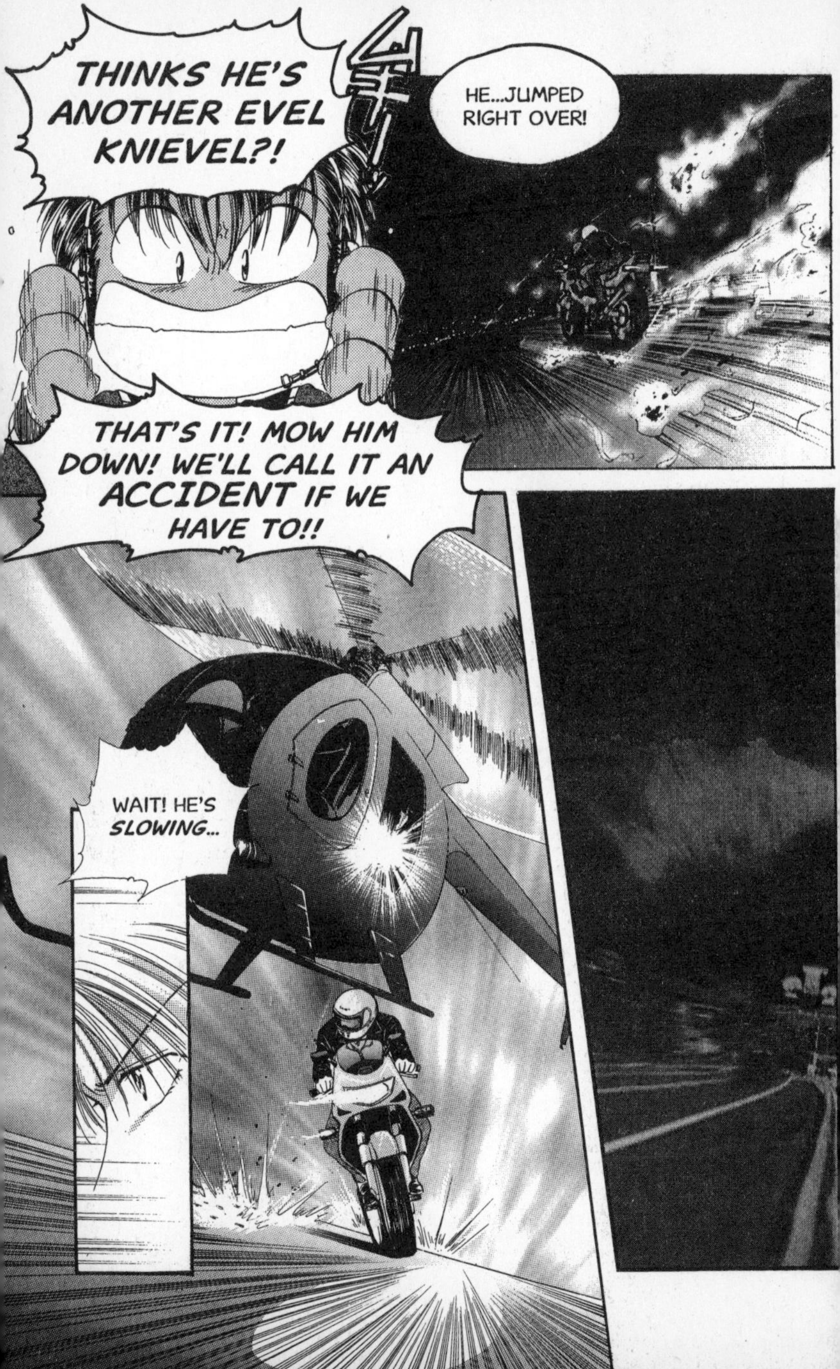
HE...JUMPED RIGHT OVER!
THINKS HE'S ANOTHER EVEL KNIEVEL?!
THAT'S IT! MOW HIM DOWN! WE'LL CALL IT AN ACCIDENT IF WE HAVE TO!!
WAIT! HE'S SLOWING...

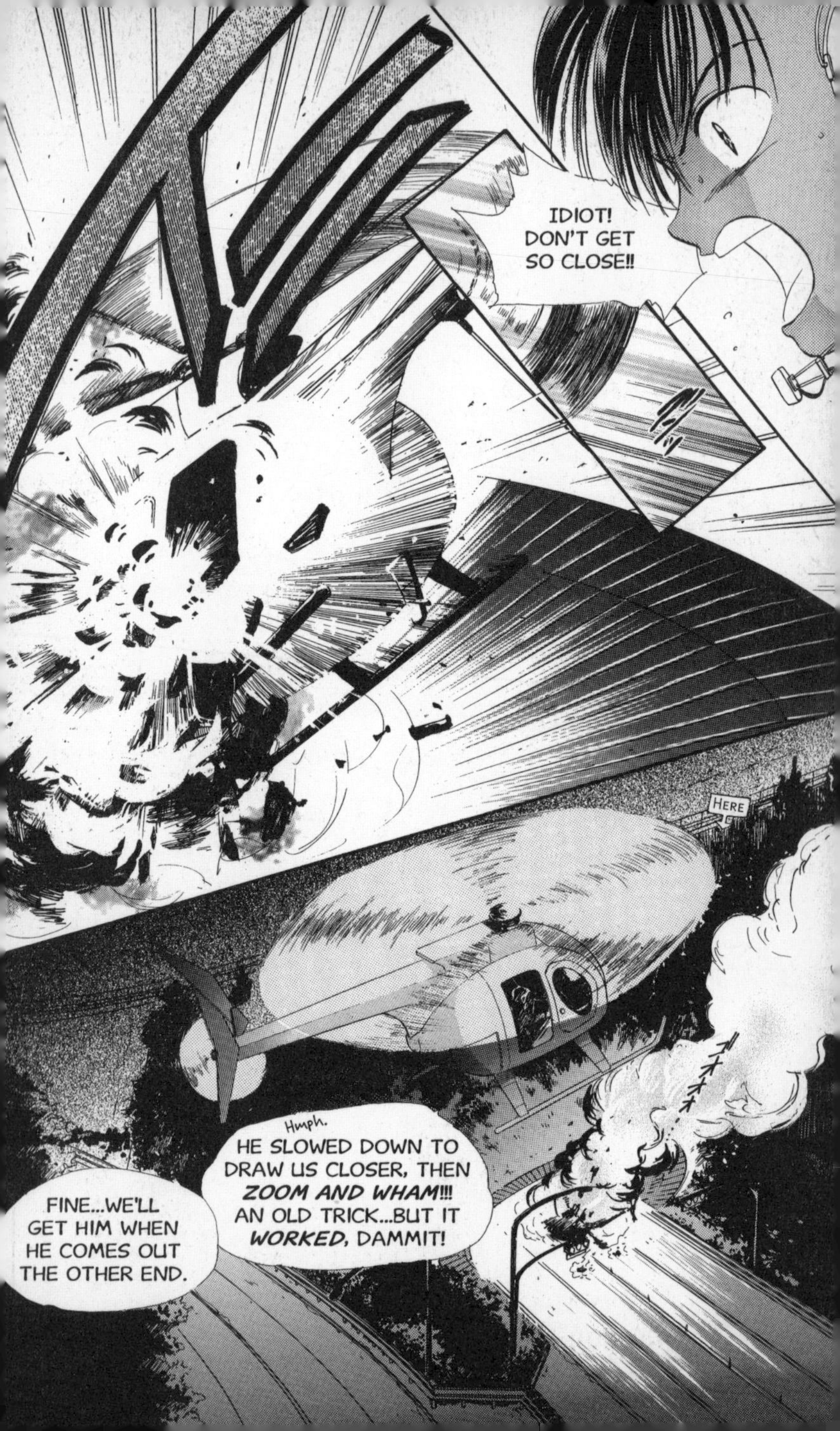
IDIOT! DON'T GET SO CLOSE!!
HERE
Hmph.
HE SLOWED DOWN TO DRAW US CLOSER, THEN ZOOM AND WHAM!!! AN OLD TRICK...BUT IT WORKED, DAMMIT!
FINE...WE'LL GET HIM WHEN HE COMES OUT THE OTHER END.

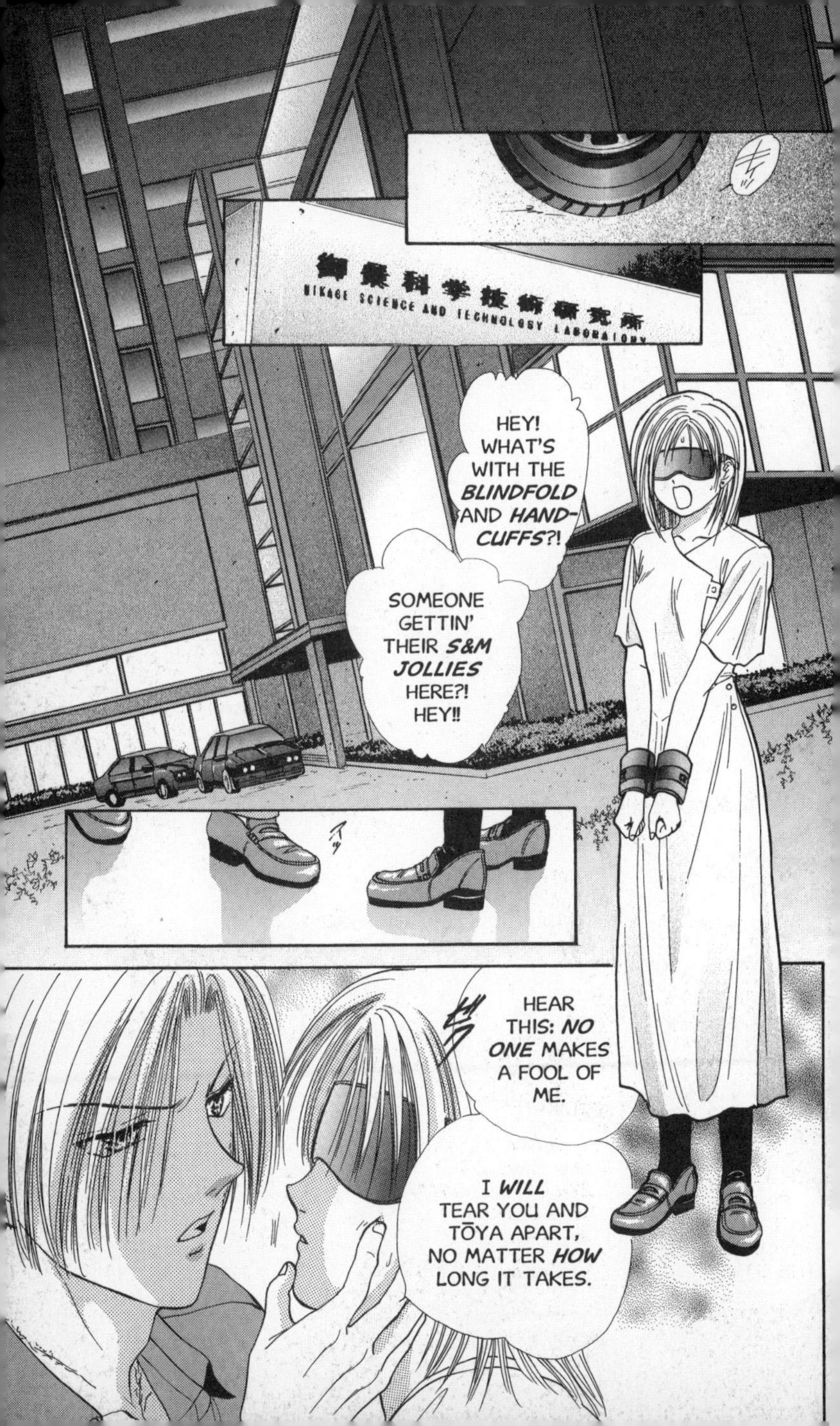
御影科学技術研究所
MIKAGE SCIENCE AND TECHNOLOGY LABORATORY
HEY! WHAT'S WITH THE BLINDFOLD AND HAND-CUFFS?!
SOMEONE GETTIN' THEIR S&M JOLLIES HERE?! HEY!!
HEAR THIS: NO ONE MAKES A FOOL OF ME.
I WILL TEAR YOU AND TŌYA APART, NO MATTER HOW LONG IT TAKES.

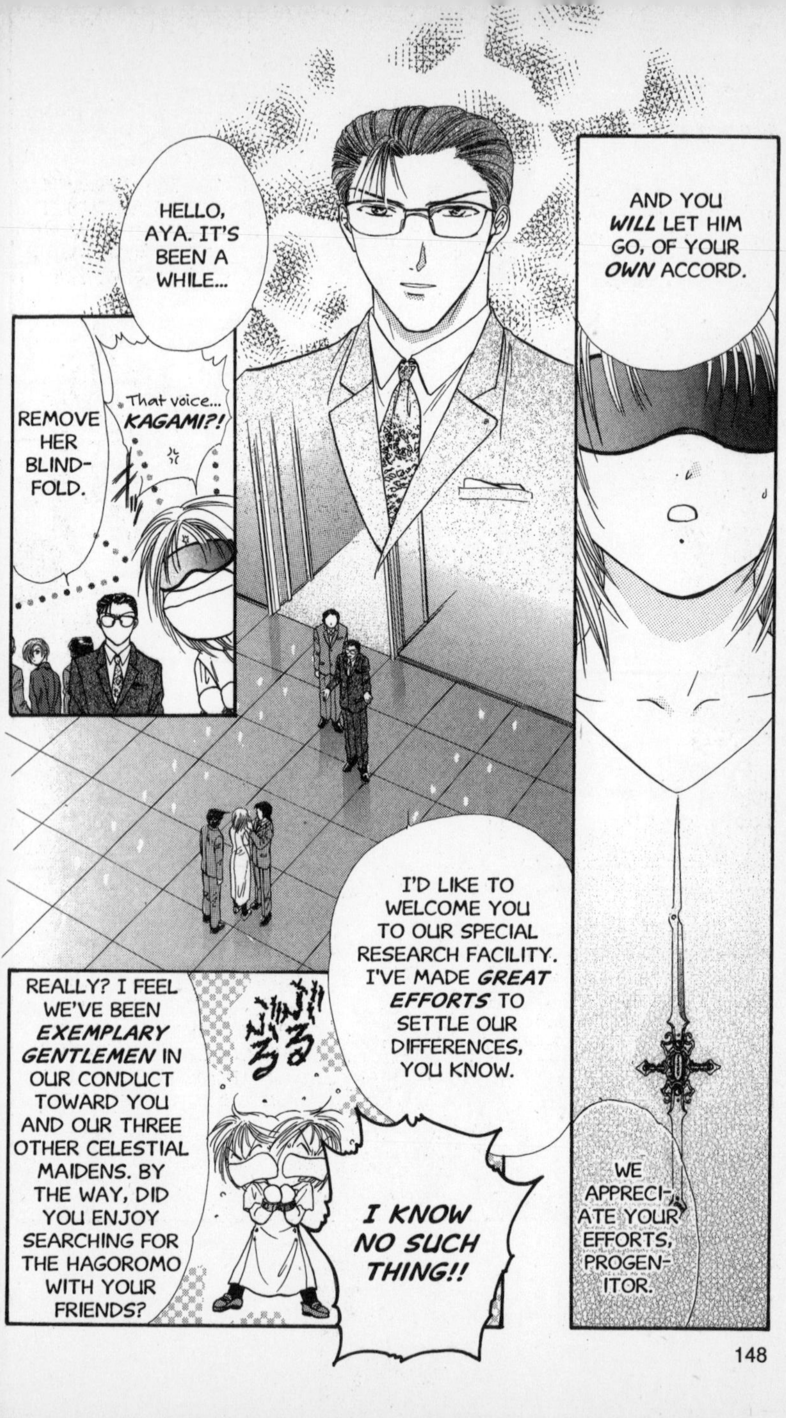
HELLO, AYA. IT'S BEEN A WHILE...
That voice... *KAGAMI?!*
REMOVE HER BLINDFOLD.
I'D LIKE TO WELCOME YOU TO OUR SPECIAL RESEARCH FACILITY. I'VE MADE *GREAT EFFORTS* TO SETTLE OUR DIFFERENCES, YOU KNOW.
WE APPRECIATE YOUR EFFORTS, PROGENITOR.
REALLY? I FEEL WE'VE BEEN *EXEMPLARY GENTLEMEN* IN OUR CONDUCT TOWARD YOU AND OUR THREE OTHER CELESTIAL MAIDENS. BY THE WAY, DID YOU ENJOY SEARCHING FOR THE HAGOROMO WITH YOUR FRIENDS?
I KNOW NO SUCH THING!!
AND YOU *WILL* LET HIM GO, OF YOUR *OWN* ACCORD.

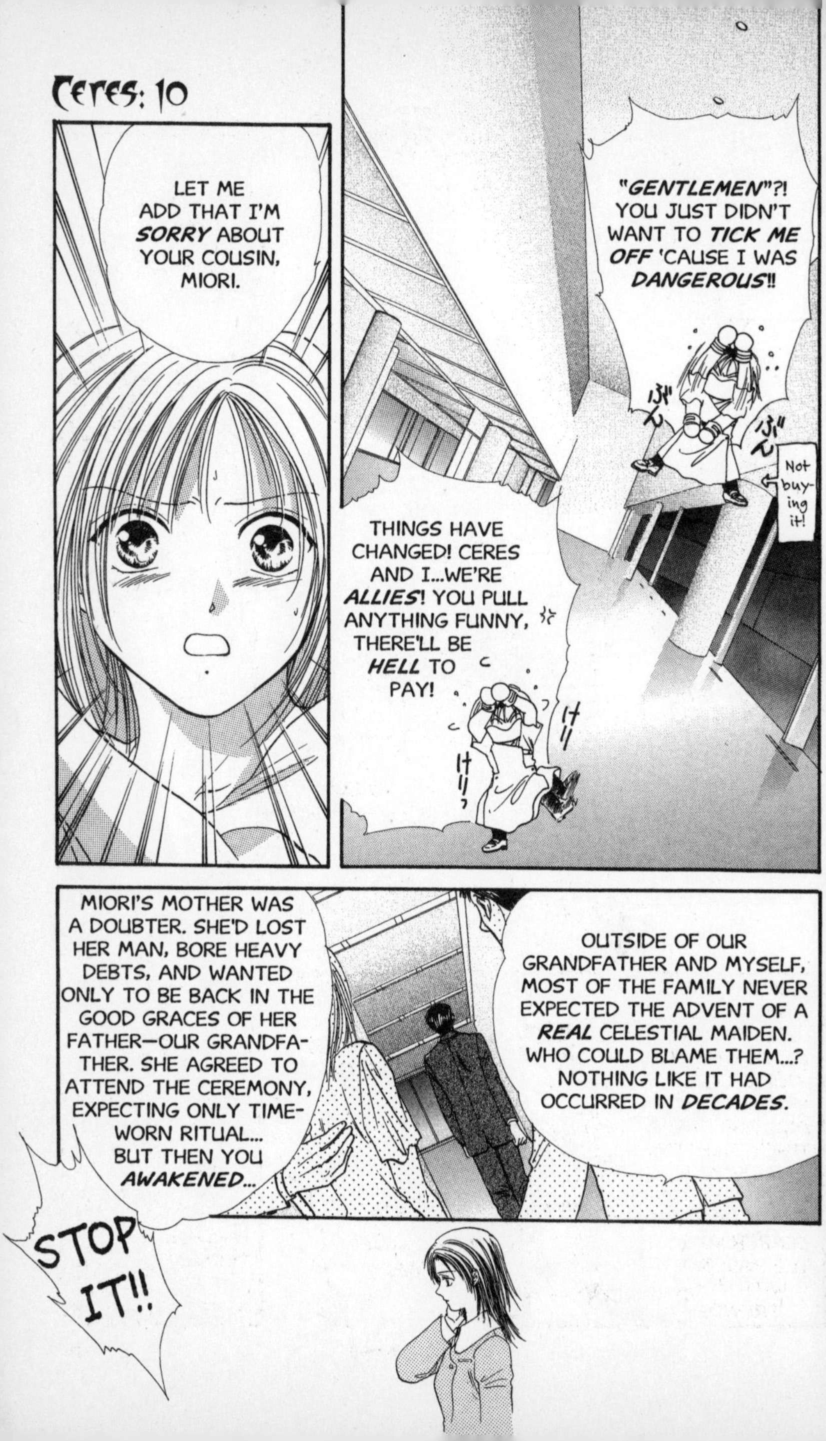
"GENTLEMEN"?! YOU JUST DIDN'T WANT TO TICK ME OFF 'CAUSE I WAS DANGEROUS!!
Not buying it!
THINGS HAVE CHANGED! CERES AND I...WE'RE ALLIES! YOU PULL ANYTHING FUNNY, THERE'LL BE HELL TO PAY!
LET ME ADD THAT I'M SORRY ABOUT YOUR COUSIN, MIORI.
OUTSIDE OF OUR GRANDFATHER AND MYSELF, MOST OF THE FAMILY NEVER EXPECTED THE ADVENT OF A REAL CELESTIAL MAIDEN. WHO COULD BLAME THEM...? NOTHING LIKE IT HAD OCCURRED IN DECADES.
MIORI'S MOTHER WAS A DOUBTER. SHE'D LOST HER MAN, BORE HEAVY DEBTS, AND WANTED ONLY TO BE BACK IN THE GOOD GRACES OF HER FATHER—OUR GRANDFATHER. SHE AGREED TO ATTEND THE CEREMONY, EXPECTING ONLY TIME-WORN RITUAL... BUT THEN YOU AWAKENED...
STOP IT!!

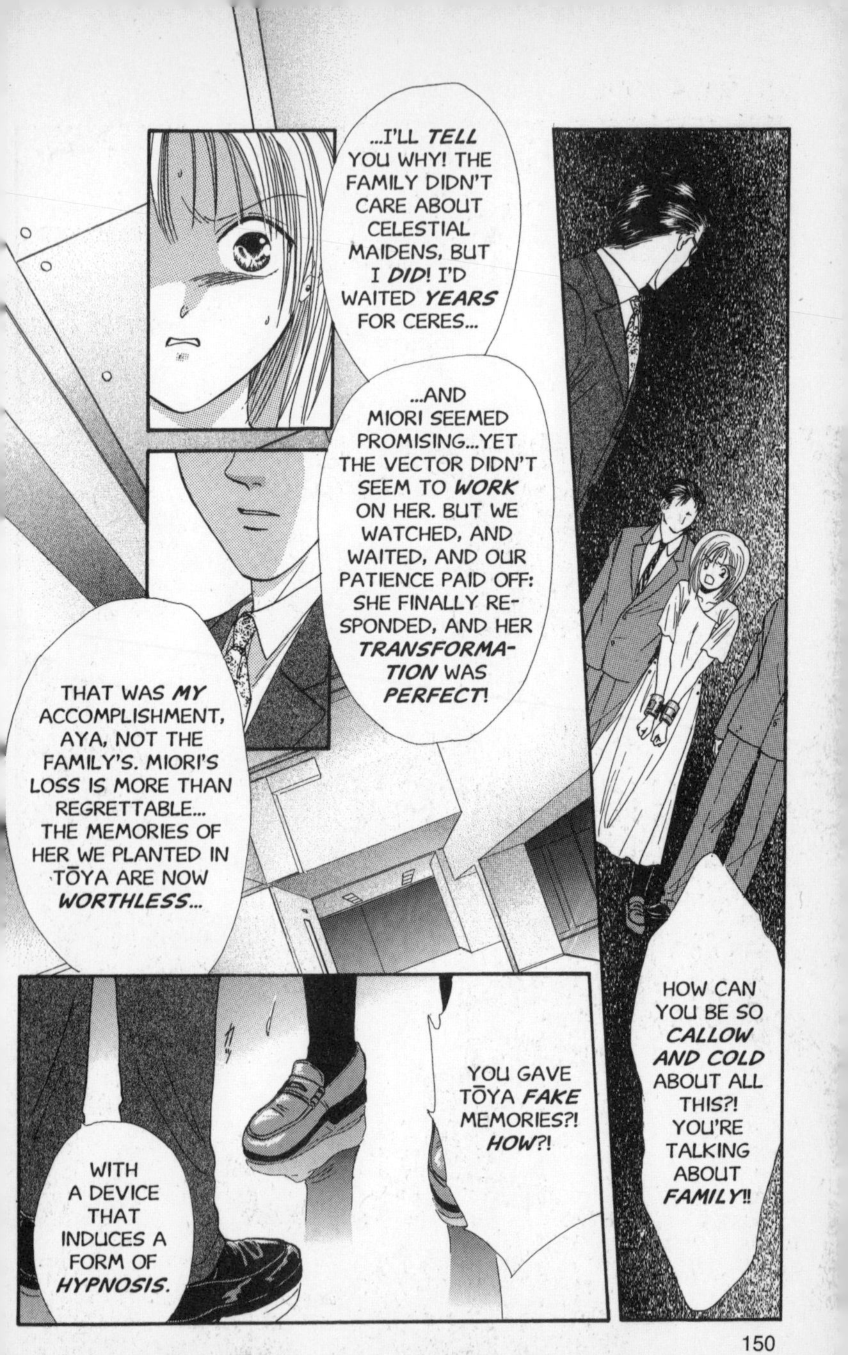

...I'LL TELL YOU WHY! THE FAMILY DIDN'T CARE ABOUT CELESTIAL MAIDENS, BUT I DID! I'D WAITED YEARS FOR CERES...
...AND MIORI SEEMED PROMISING...YET THE VECTOR DIDN'T SEEM TO WORK ON HER. BUT WE WATCHED, AND WAITED, AND OUR PATIENCE PAID OFF: SHE FINALLY RE-SPONDED, AND HER TRANSFORMA-TION WAS PERFECT!
THAT WAS MY ACCOMPLISHMENT, AYA, NOT THE FAMILY'S. MIORI'S LOSS IS MORE THAN REGRETTABLE... THE MEMORIES OF HER WE PLANTED IN TŌYA ARE NOW WORTHLESS...
HOW CAN YOU BE SO CALLOW AND COLD ABOUT ALL THIS?! YOU'RE TALKING ABOUT FAMILY!!
YOU GAVE TŌYA FAKE MEMORIES?! HOW?!
WITH A DEVICE THAT INDUCES A FORM OF HYPNOSIS.

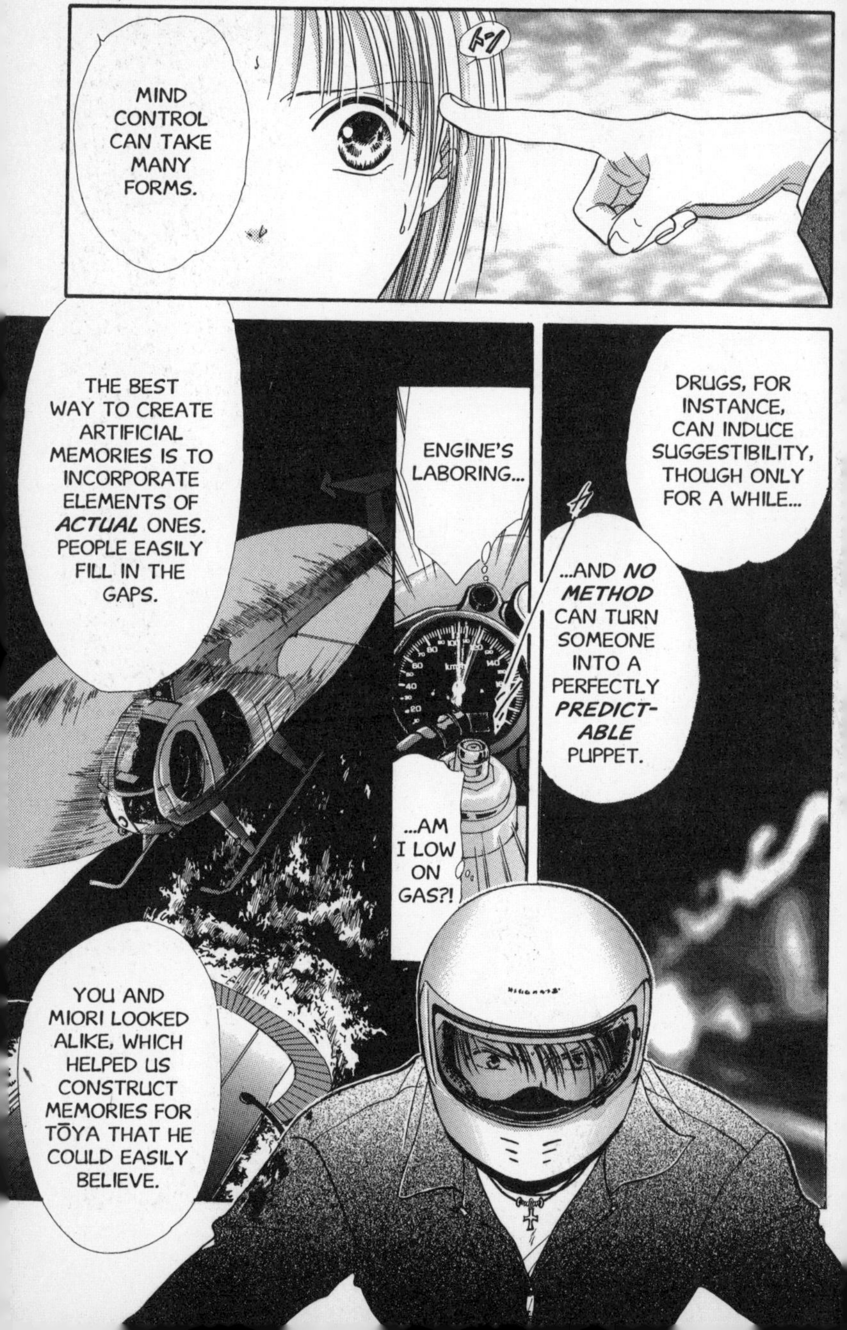
MIND CONTROL CAN TAKE MANY FORMS.
DRUGS, FOR INSTANCE, CAN INDUCE SUGGESTIBILITY, THOUGH ONLY FOR A WHILE...
...AND *NO METHOD* CAN TURN SOMEONE INTO A PERFECTLY *PREDICTABLE* PUPPET.
ENGINE'S LABORING...
...AM I LOW ON GAS?!
THE BEST WAY TO CREATE ARTIFICIAL MEMORIES IS TO INCORPORATE ELEMENTS OF *ACTUAL* ONES. PEOPLE EASILY FILL IN THE GAPS.
YOU AND MIORI LOOKED ALIKE, WHICH HELPED US CONSTRUCT MEMORIES FOR TŌYA THAT HE COULD EASILY BELIEVE.

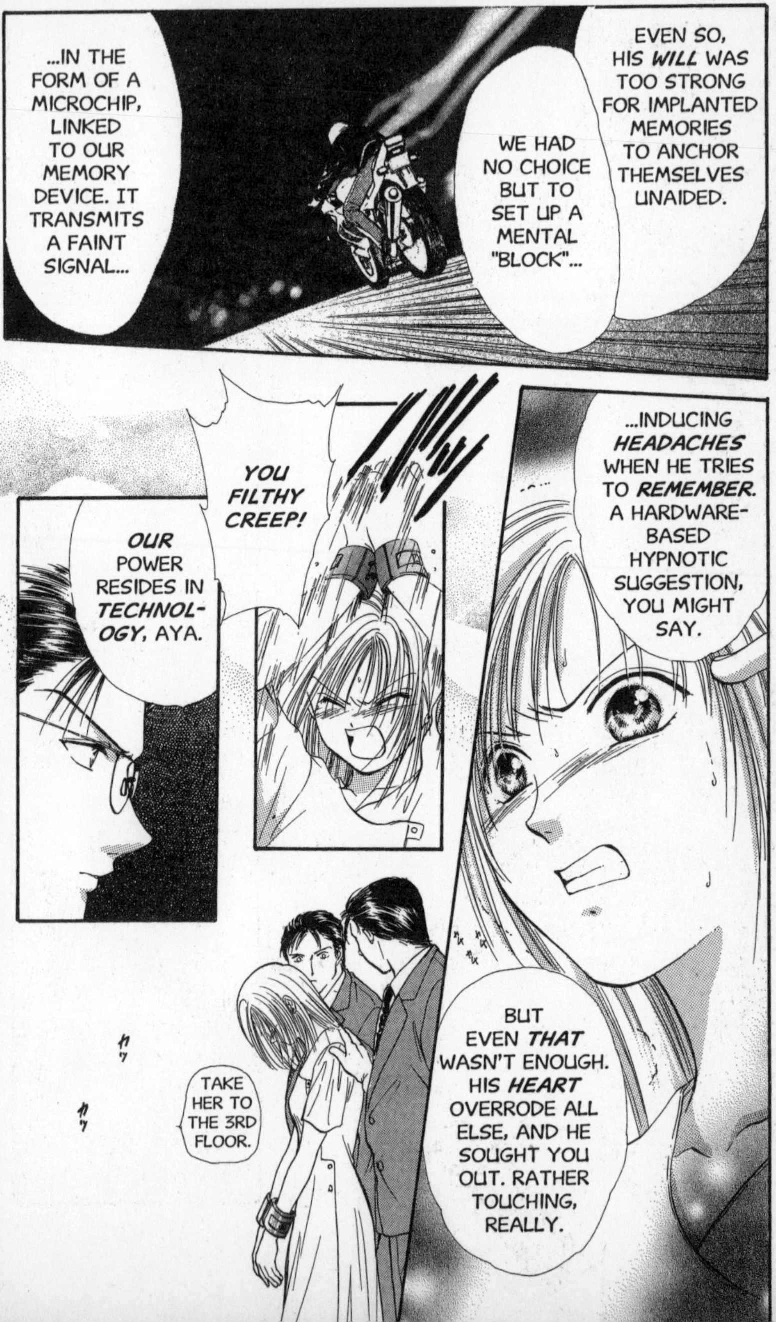
EVEN SO, HIS *WILL* WAS TOO STRONG FOR IMPLANTED MEMORIES TO ANCHOR THEMSELVES UNAIDED.
WE HAD NO CHOICE BUT TO SET UP A MENTAL "BLOCK"...
...IN THE FORM OF A MICROCHIP, LINKED TO OUR MEMORY DEVICE. IT TRANSMITS A FAINT SIGNAL...
...INDUCING *HEADACHES* WHEN HE TRIES TO *REMEMBER.* A HARDWARE-BASED HYPNOTIC SUGGESTION, YOU MIGHT SAY.
...
YOU FILTHY CREEP!
OUR POWER RESIDES IN *TECHNOLOGY*, AYA.
BUT EVEN *THAT* WASN'T ENOUGH. HIS *HEART* OVERRODE ALL ELSE, AND HE SOUGHT YOU OUT. RATHER TOUCHING, REALLY.
TAKE HER TO THE 3RD FLOOR.

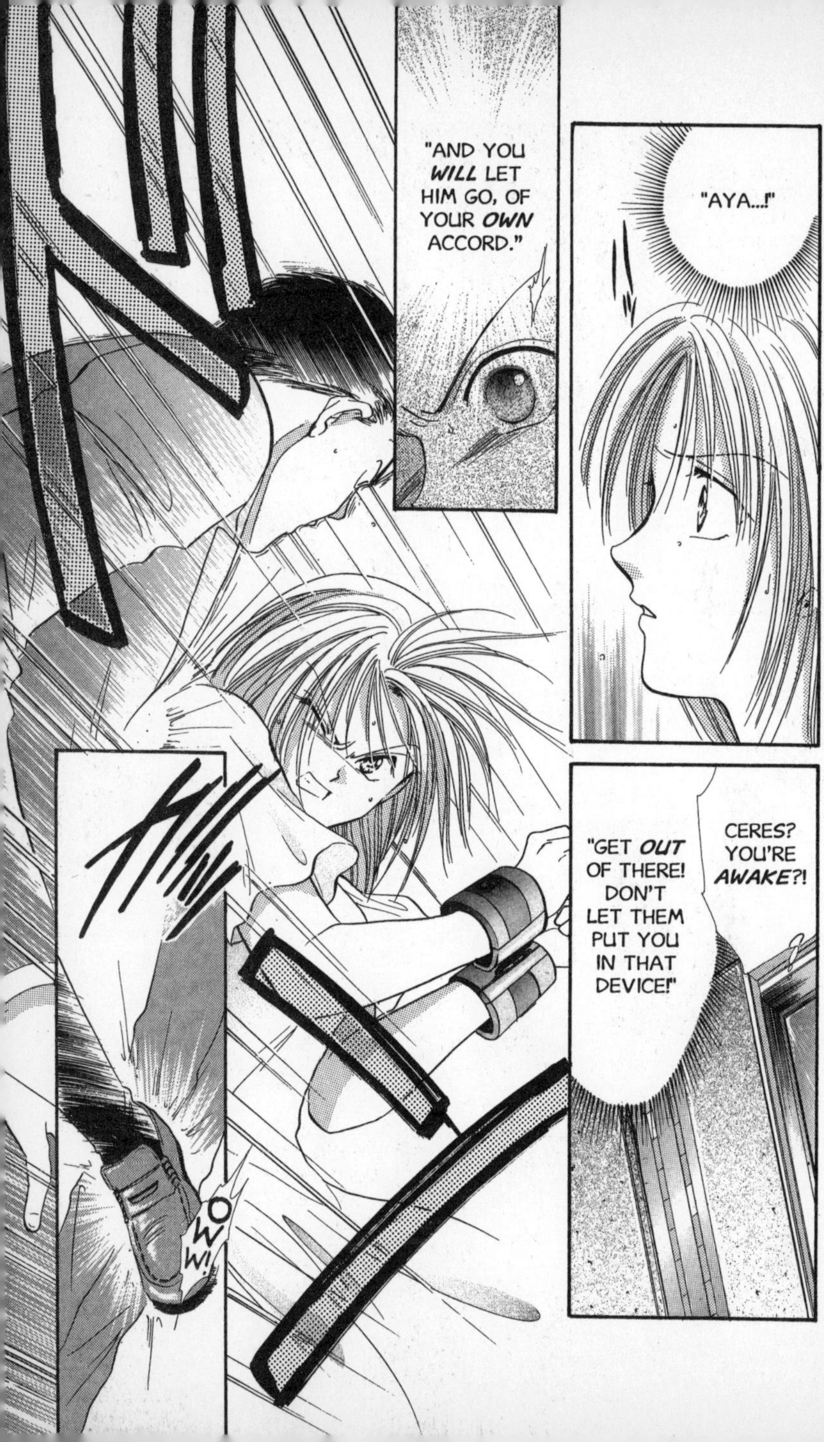
"AND YOU WILL LET HIM GO, OF YOUR OWN ACCORD."
"AYA...!"
CERES? YOU'RE AWAKE?!
"GET OUT OF THERE! DON'T LET THEM PUT YOU IN THAT DEVICE!"
OWW!

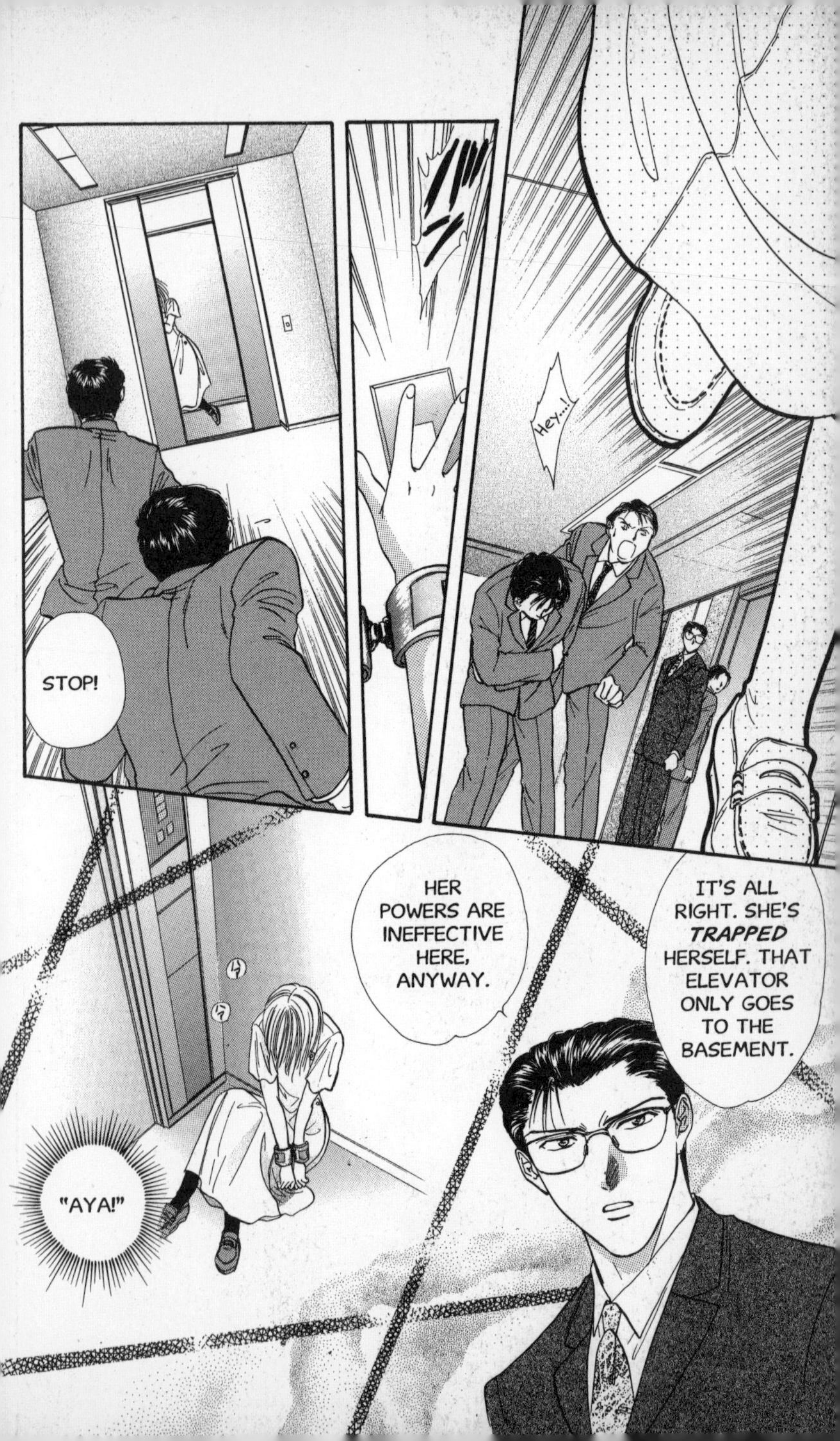
Hey...!
STOP!
IT'S ALL RIGHT. SHE'S *TRAPPED* HERSELF. THAT ELEVATOR ONLY GOES TO THE BASEMENT.
HER POWERS ARE INEFFECTIVE HERE, ANYWAY.
"AYA!"

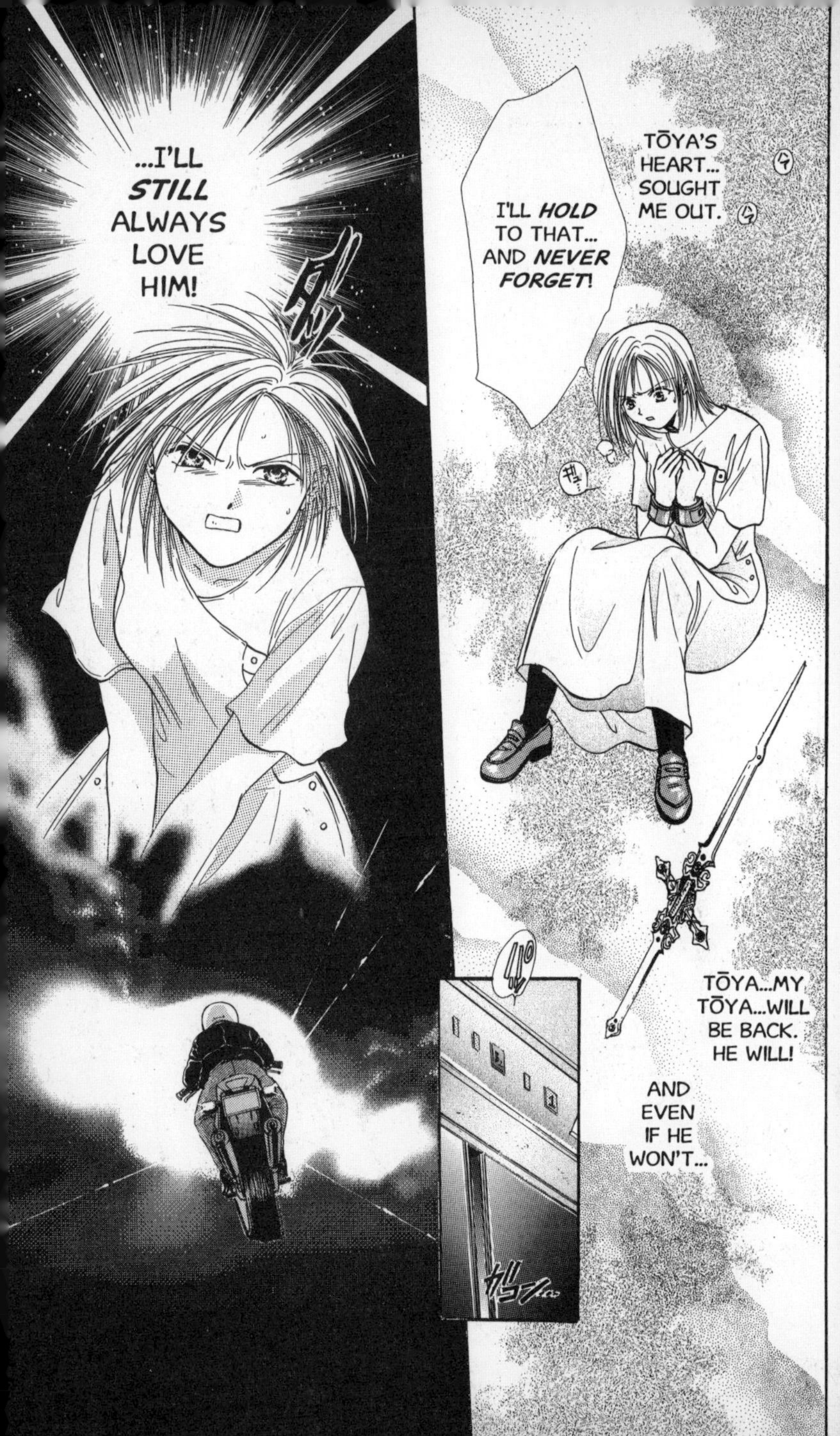
TŌYA'S HEART... SOUGHT ME OUT.
I'LL *HOLD* TO THAT... AND *NEVER FORGET*!
TŌYA...MY TŌYA...WILL BE BACK. HE WILL!
AND EVEN IF HE WON'T...
...I'LL *STILL* ALWAYS LOVE HIM!

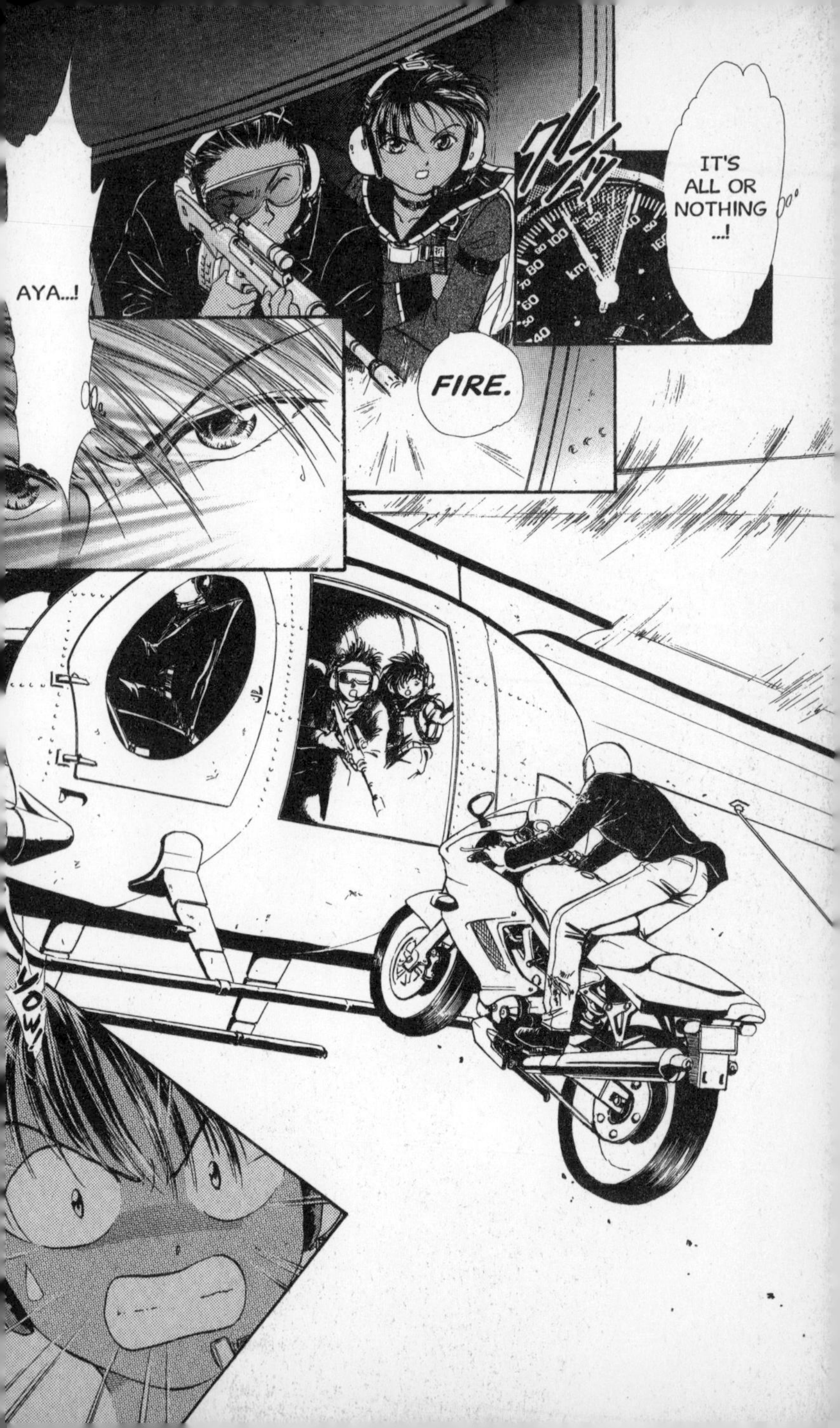
IT'S ALL OR NOTHING ...!
FIRE.
AYA...!
YOW!

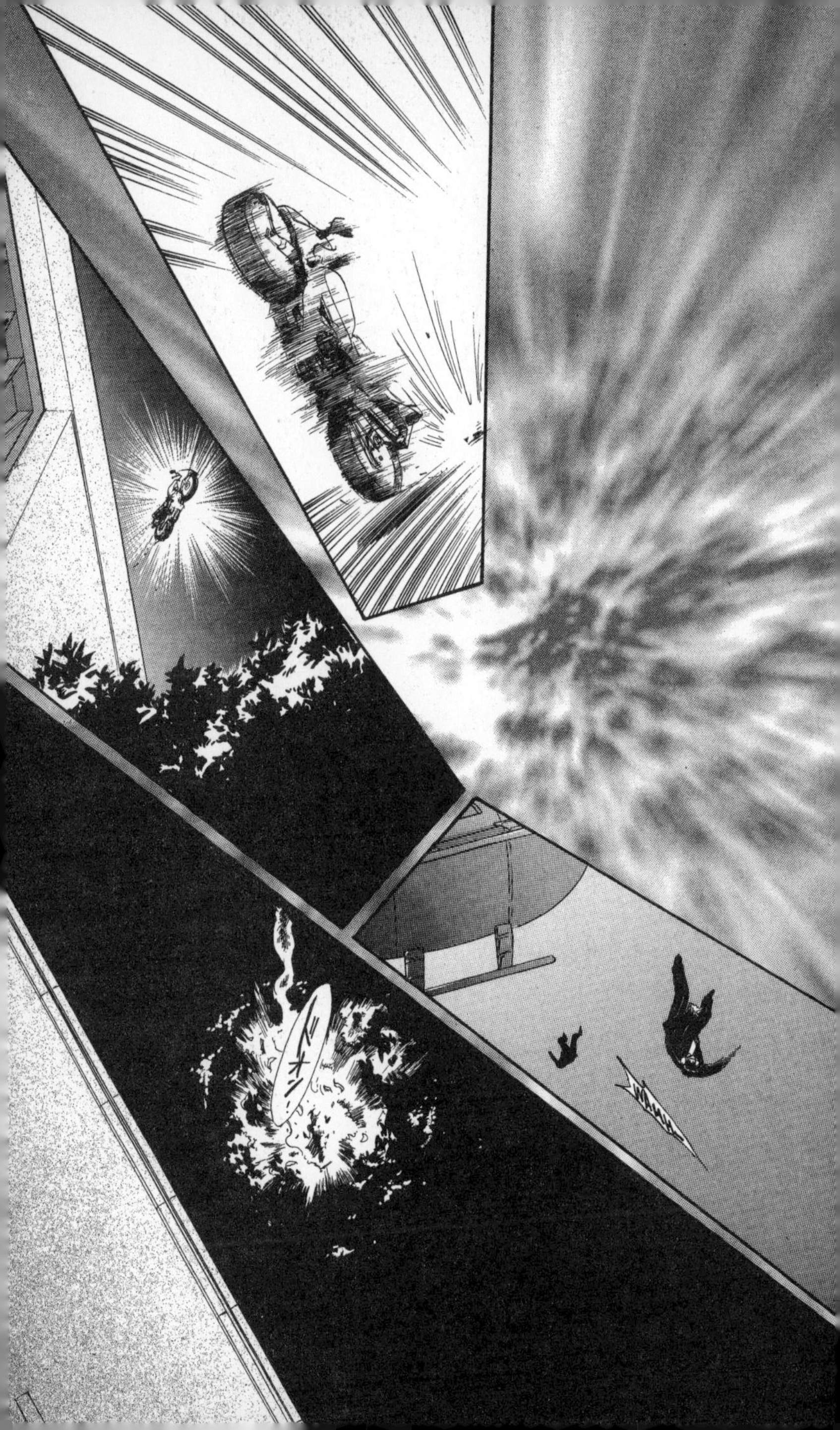
ドオン!
WAAAH

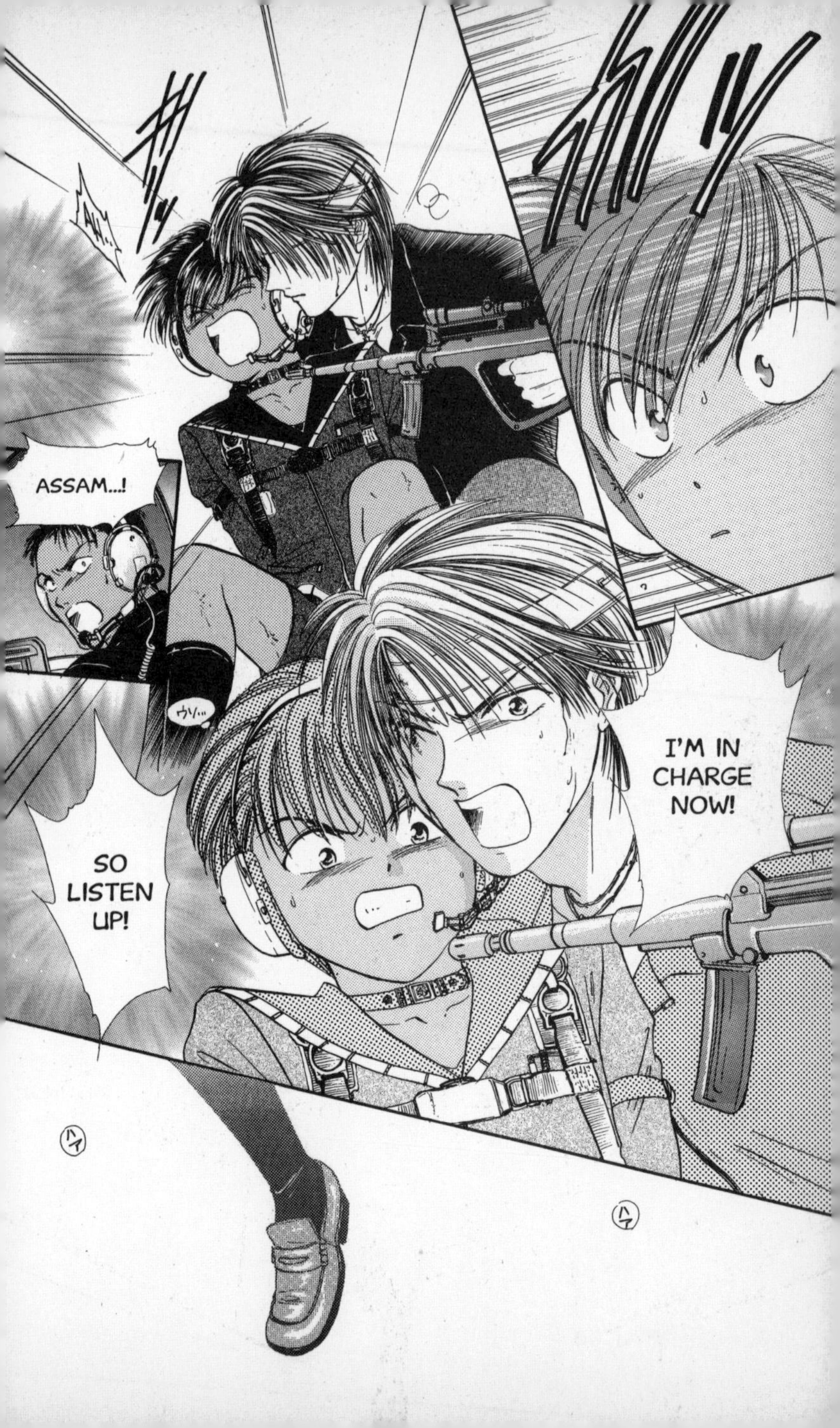
AH...!
ASSAM...!
ウ…
I'M IN CHARGE NOW!
SO LISTEN UP!
ハァ
ハァ

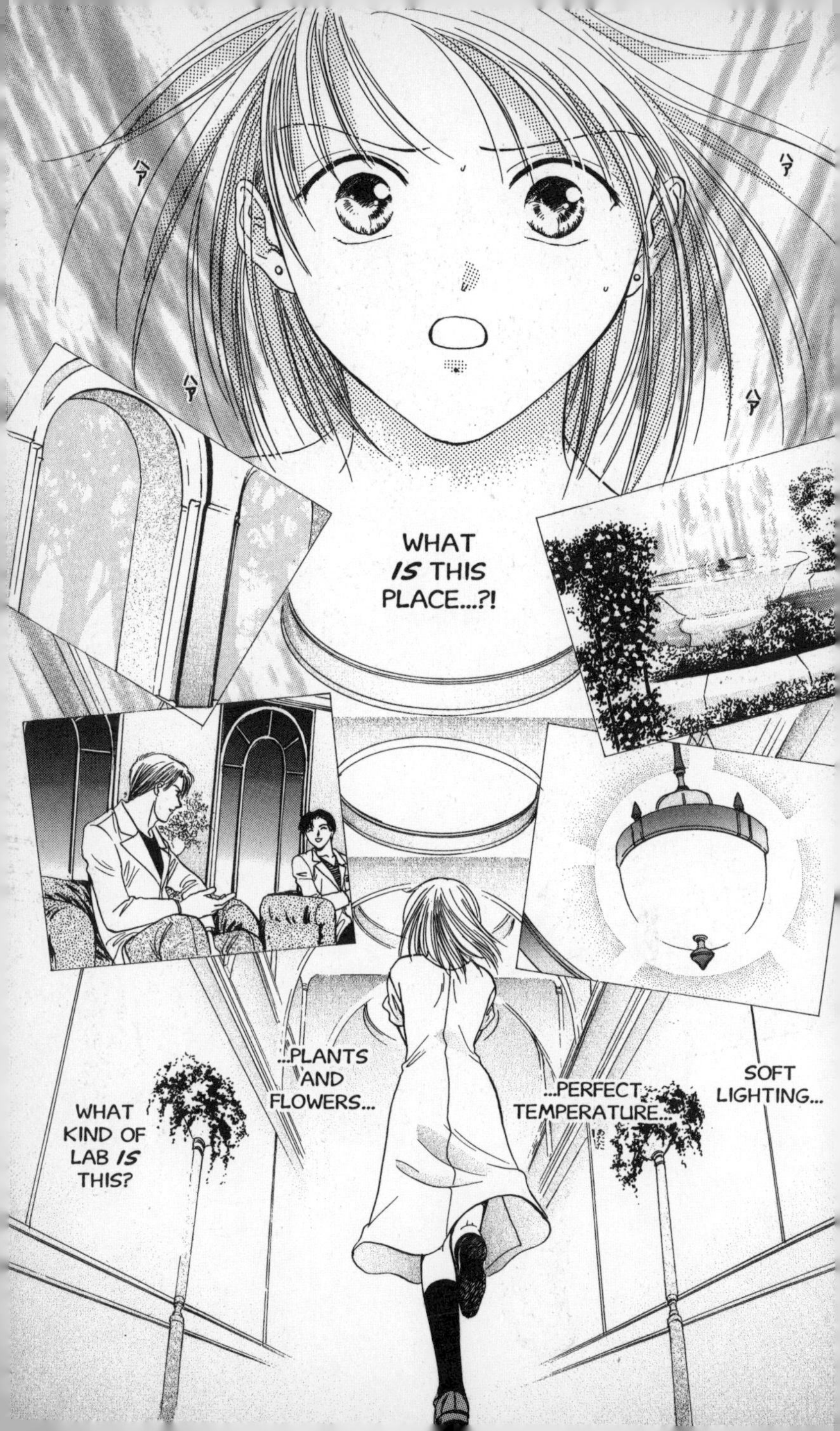
WHAT *IS* THIS PLACE...?!
SOFT LIGHTING...
...PERFECT TEMPERATURE...
...PLANTS AND FLOWERS...
WHAT KIND OF LAB *IS* THIS?

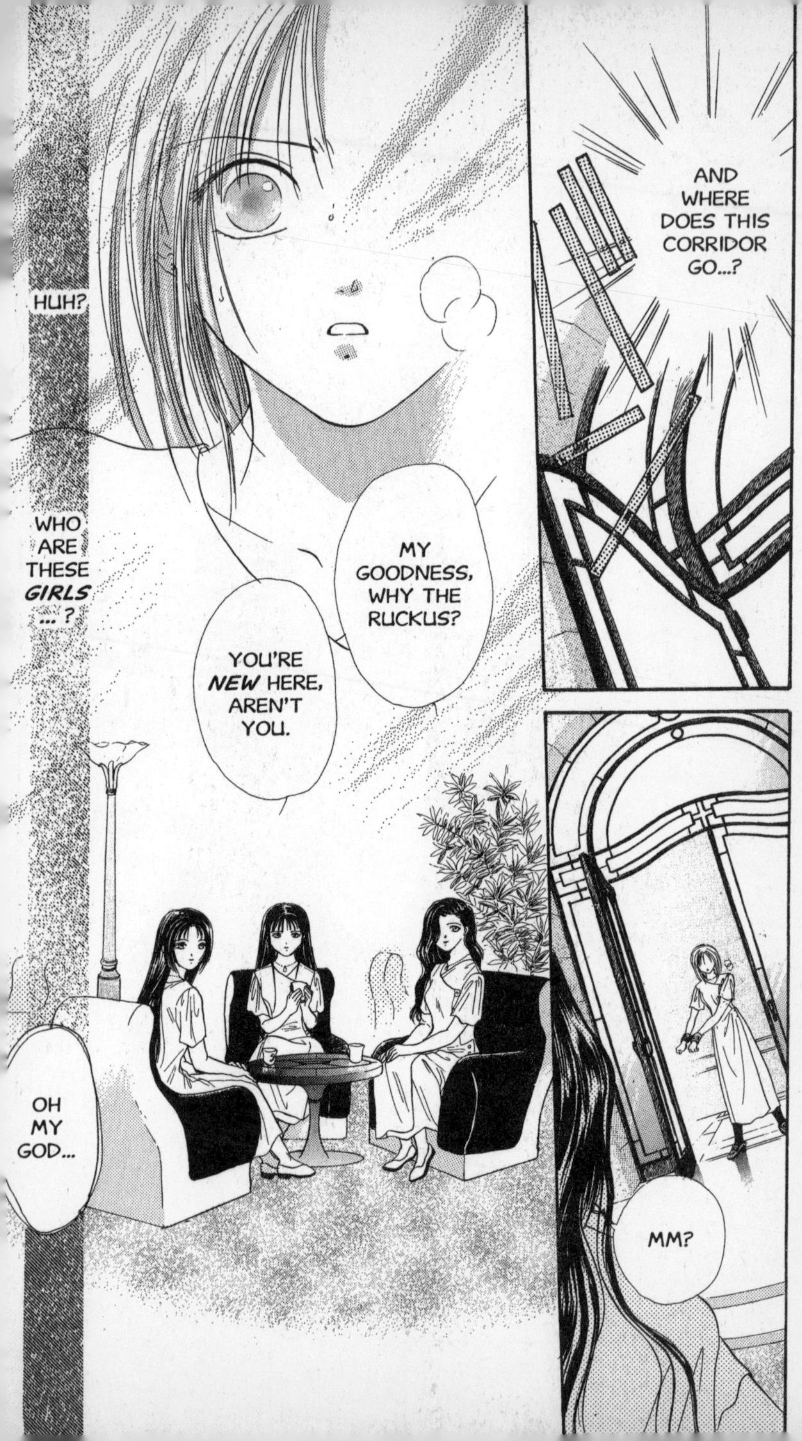
AND WHERE DOES THIS CORRIDOR GO...?
MM?
HUH?
MY GOODNESS, WHY THE RUCKUS?
YOU'RE *NEW* HERE, AREN'T YOU.
WHO ARE THESE *GIRLS* ...?
OH MY GOD...

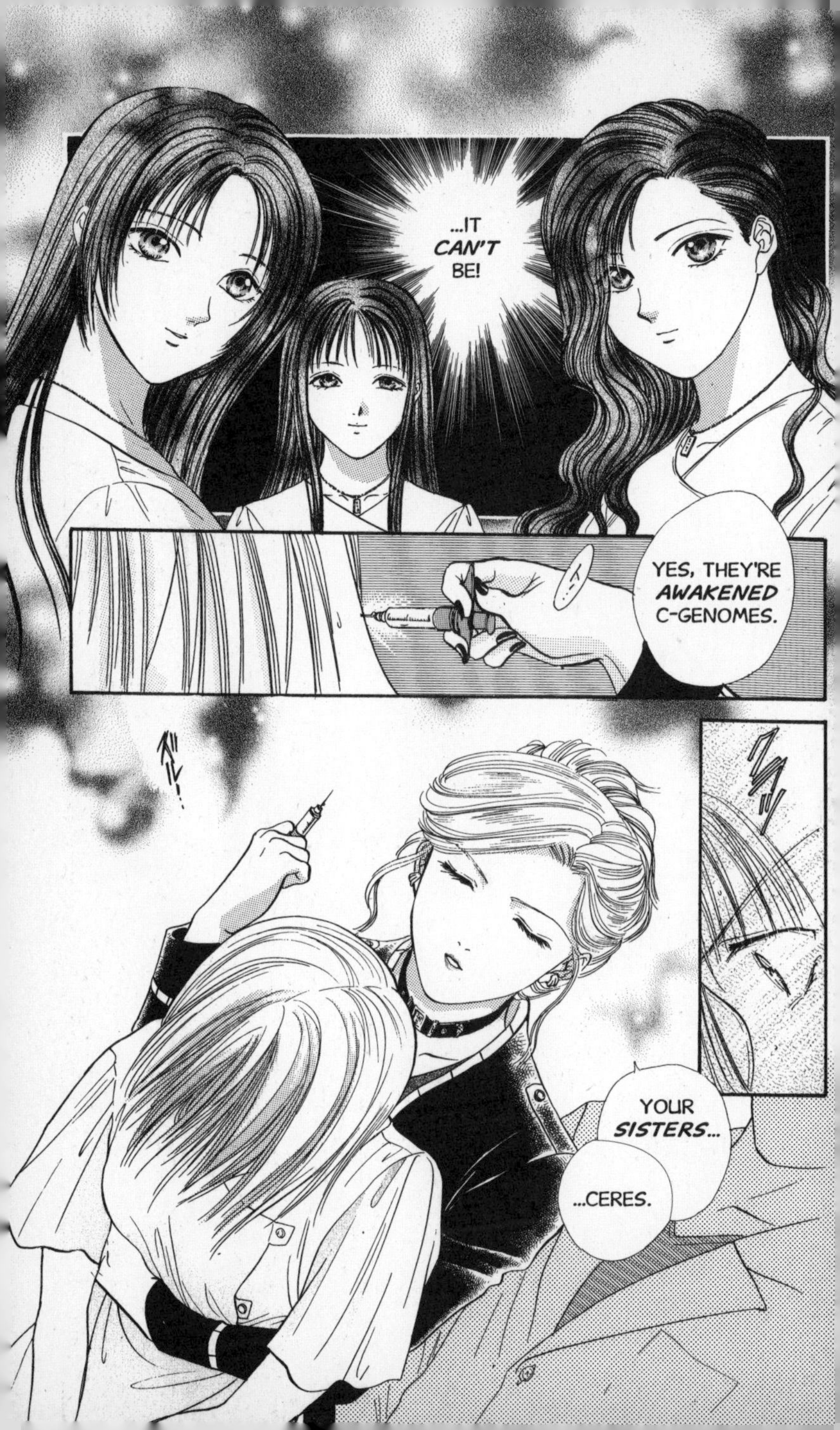
...IT *CAN'T* BE!
YES, THEY'RE ***AWAKENED*** C-GENOMES.
YOUR ***SISTERS...***
...CERES.

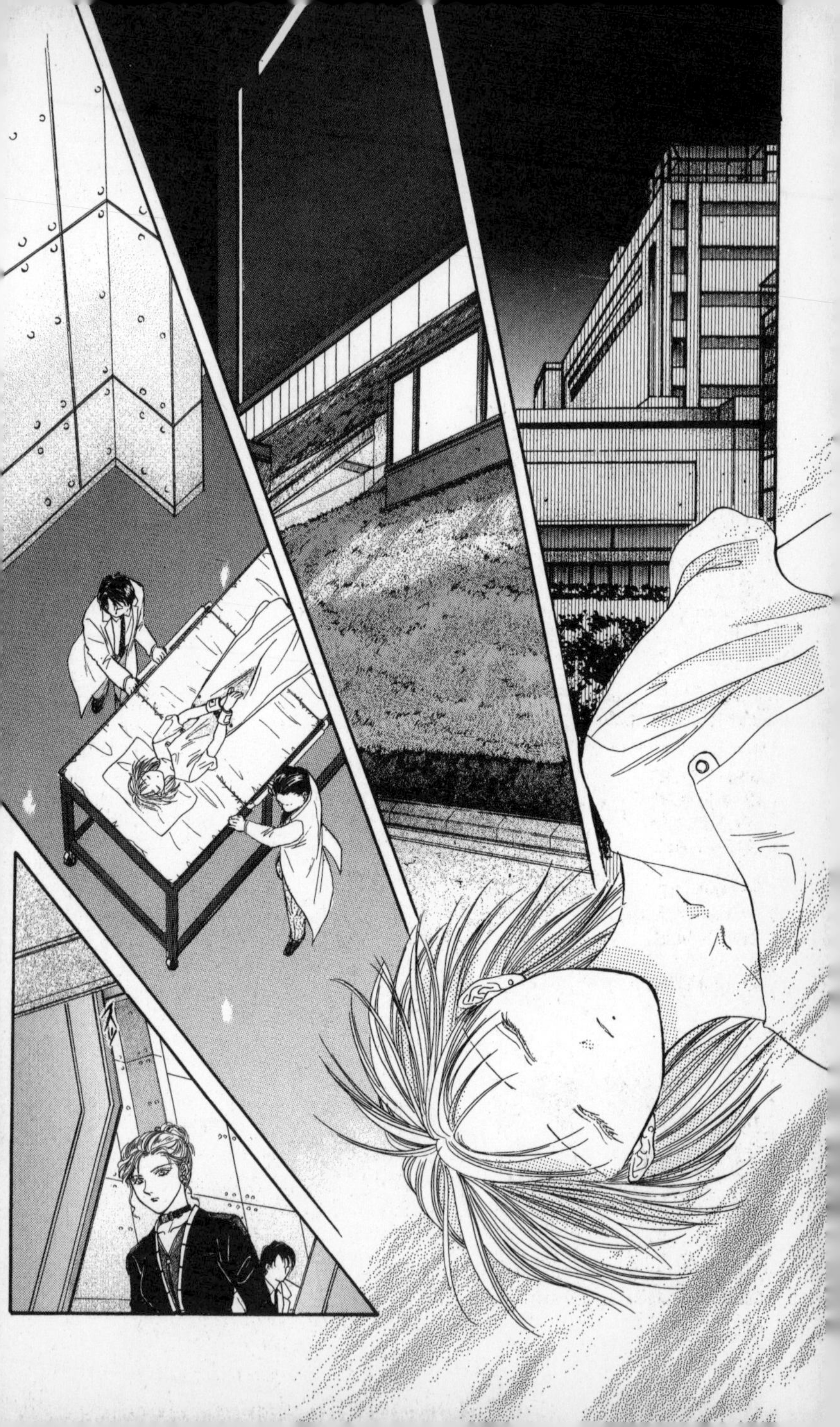
スッ

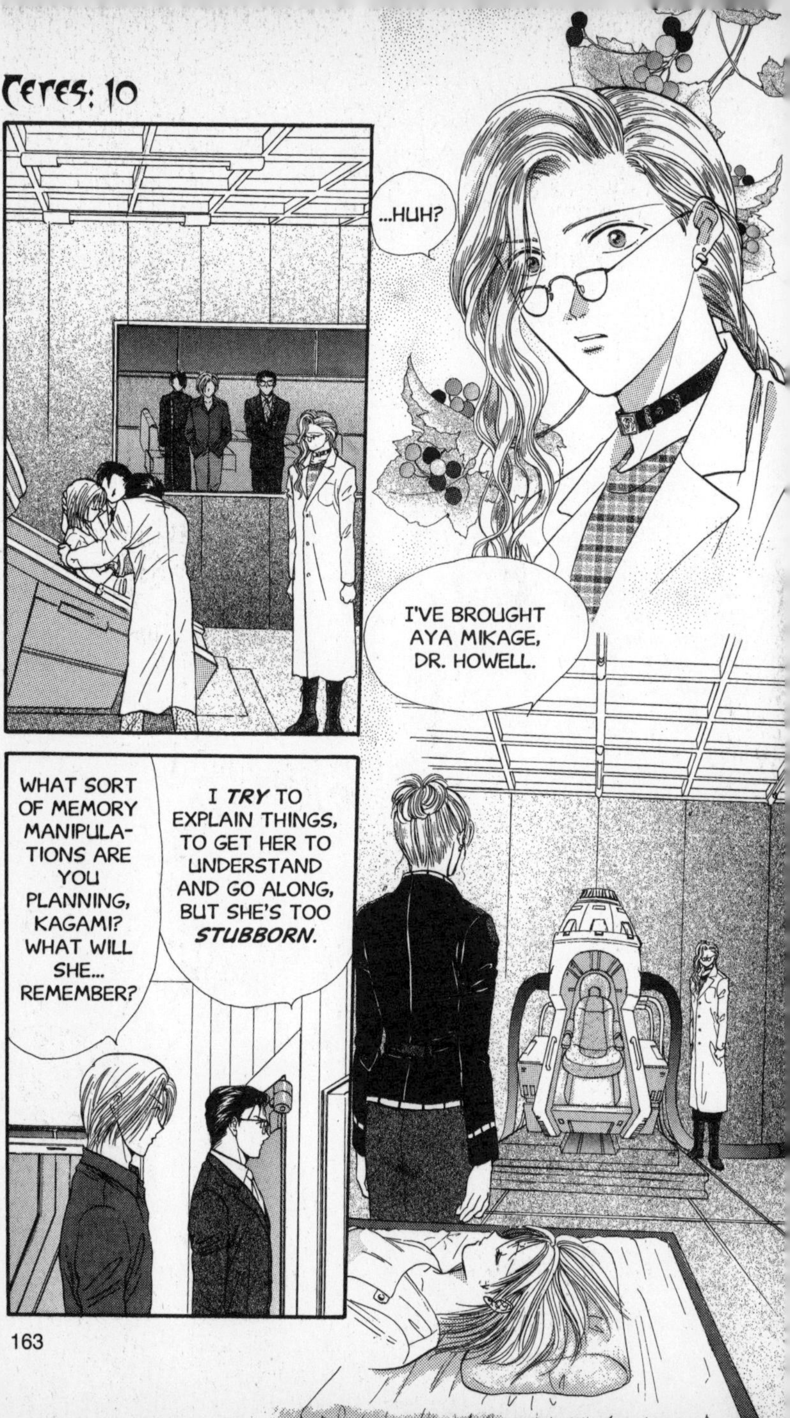
...HUH?
I'VE BROUGHT AYA MIKAGE, DR. HOWELL.
I *TRY* TO EXPLAIN THINGS, TO GET HER TO UNDERSTAND AND GO ALONG, BUT SHE'S TOO ***STUBBORN***.
WHAT SORT OF MEMORY MANIPULATIONS ARE YOU PLANNING, KAGAMI? WHAT WILL SHE... REMEMBER?

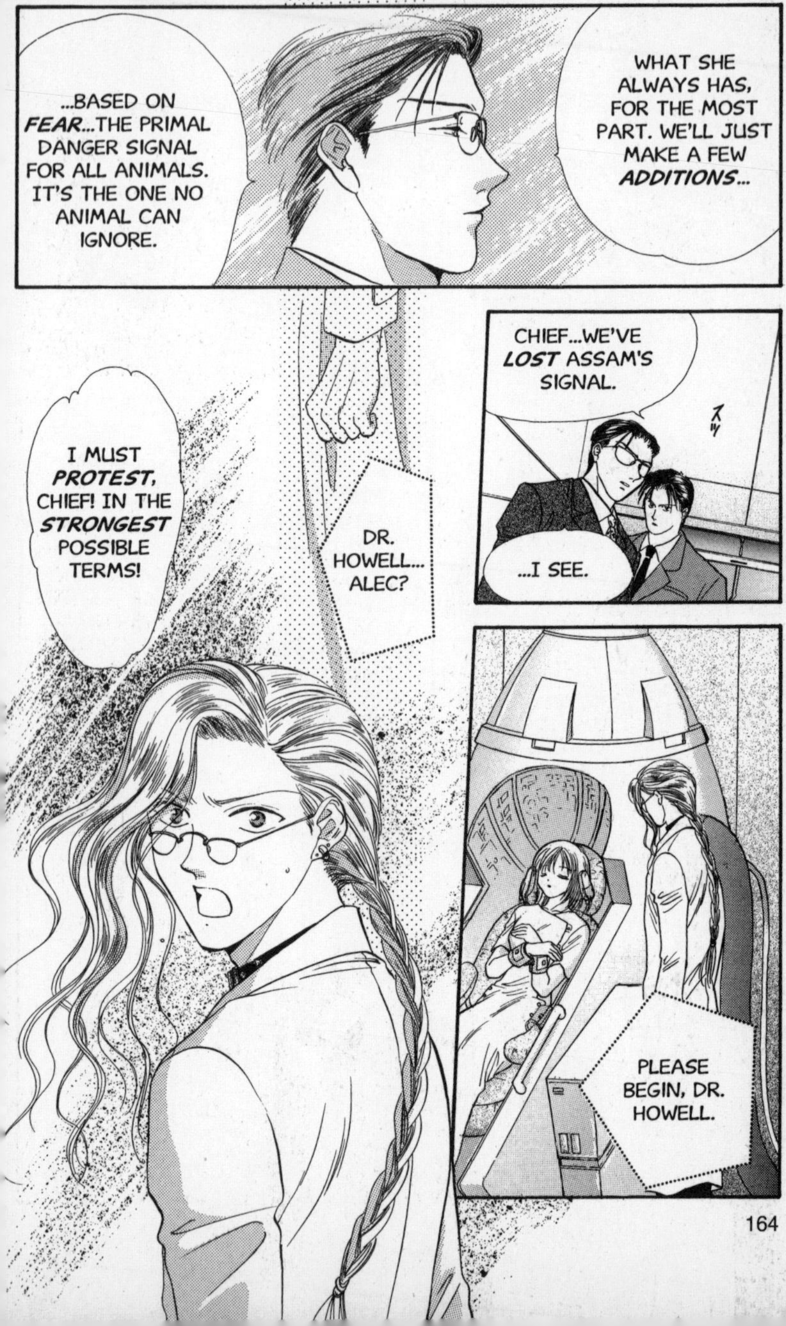
WHAT SHE ALWAYS HAS, FOR THE MOST PART. WE'LL JUST MAKE A FEW *ADDITIONS*...
...BASED ON *FEAR*...THE PRIMAL DANGER SIGNAL FOR ALL ANIMALS. IT'S THE ONE NO ANIMAL CAN IGNORE.
CHIEF...WE'VE *LOST* ASSAM'S SIGNAL.
スッ
...I SEE.
PLEASE BEGIN, DR. HOWELL.
DR. HOWELL... ALEC?
I MUST *PROTEST*, CHIEF! IN THE *STRONGEST* POSSIBLE TERMS!

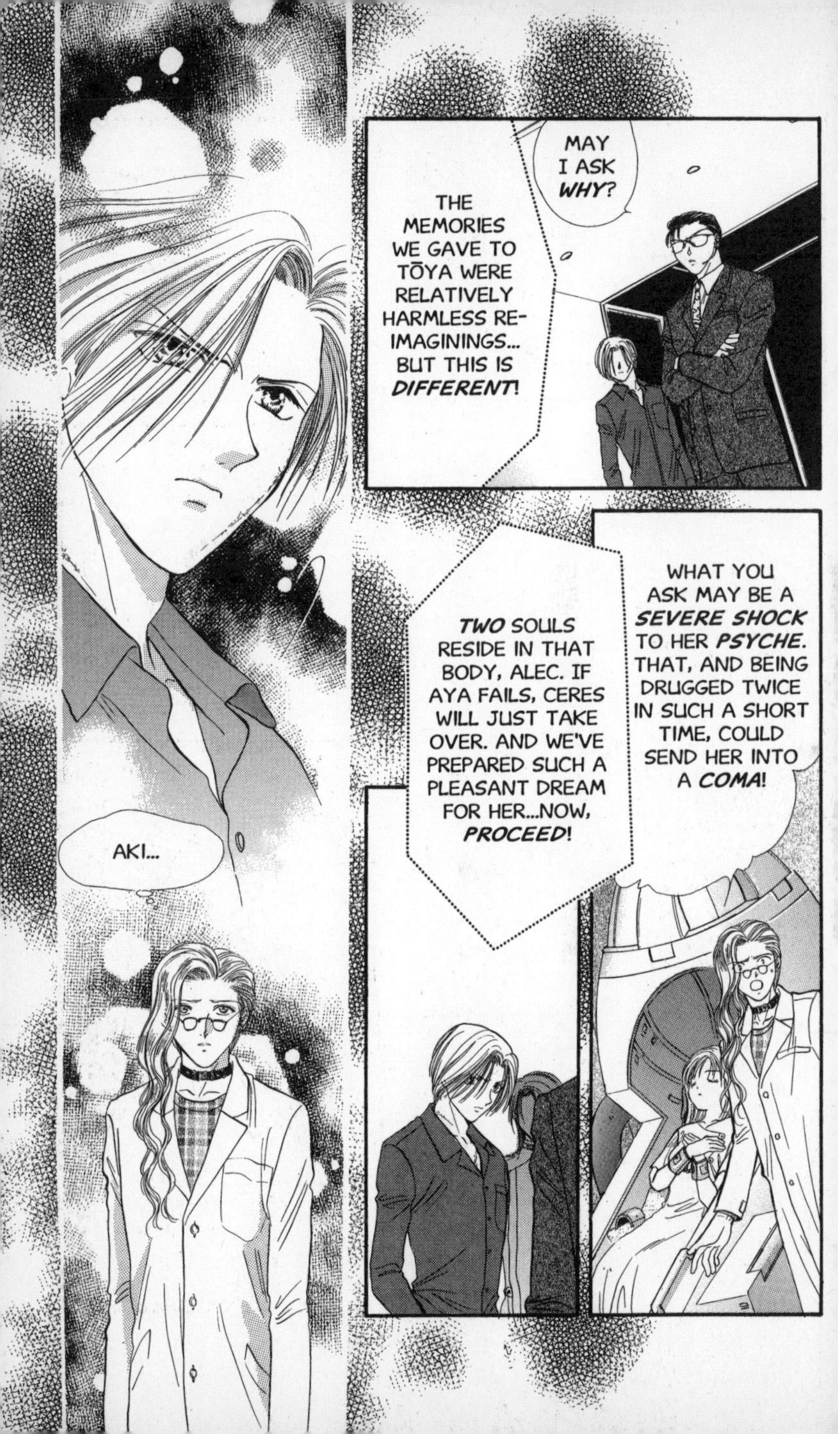
MAY I ASK *WHY*?
THE MEMORIES WE GAVE TO TŌYA WERE RELATIVELY HARMLESS RE-IMAGININGS... BUT THIS IS *DIFFERENT*!
WHAT YOU ASK MAY BE A *SEVERE SHOCK* TO HER *PSYCHE*. THAT, AND BEING DRUGGED TWICE IN SUCH A SHORT TIME, COULD SEND HER INTO A *COMA*!
TWO SOULS RESIDE IN THAT BODY, ALEC. IF AYA FAILS, CERES WILL JUST TAKE OVER. AND WE'VE PREPARED SUCH A PLEASANT DREAM FOR HER...NOW, *PROCEED*!
AKI...

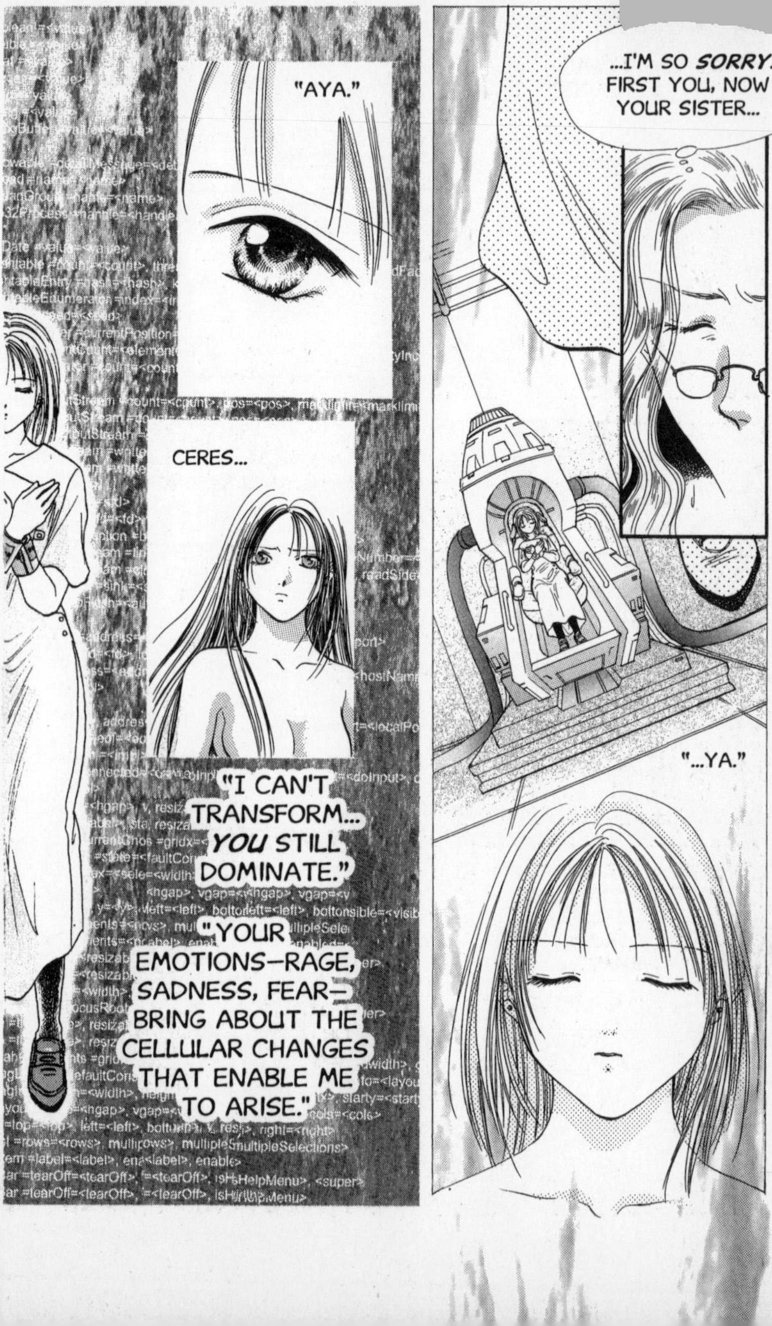
...I'M SO *SORRY*. FIRST YOU, NOW YOUR SISTER...
"...YA."
"AYA."
CERES...
"I CAN'T TRANSFORM... *YOU* STILL DOMINATE."
"YOUR EMOTIONS—RAGE, SADNESS, FEAR—BRING ABOUT THE CELLULAR CHANGES THAT ENABLE ME TO ARISE."

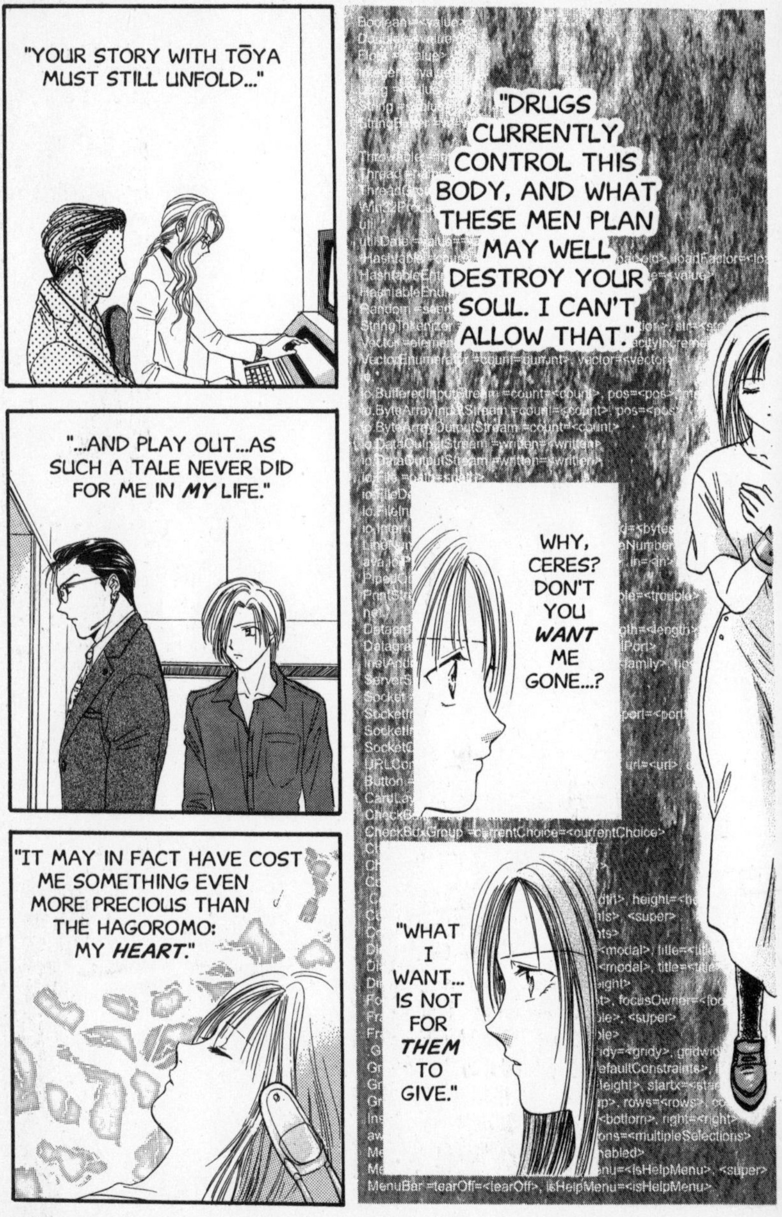
"DRUGS CURRENTLY CONTROL THIS BODY, AND WHAT THESE MEN PLAN MAY WELL DESTROY YOUR SOUL. I CAN'T ALLOW THAT."
WHY, CERES? DON'T YOU *WANT* ME GONE...?
"WHAT I WANT... IS NOT FOR *THEM* TO GIVE."
"YOUR STORY WITH TŌYA MUST STILL UNFOLD..."
"...AND PLAY OUT...AS SUCH A TALE NEVER DID FOR ME IN *MY* LIFE."
"IT MAY IN FACT HAVE COST ME SOMETHING EVEN MORE PRECIOUS THAN THE HAGOROMO: MY *HEART*."

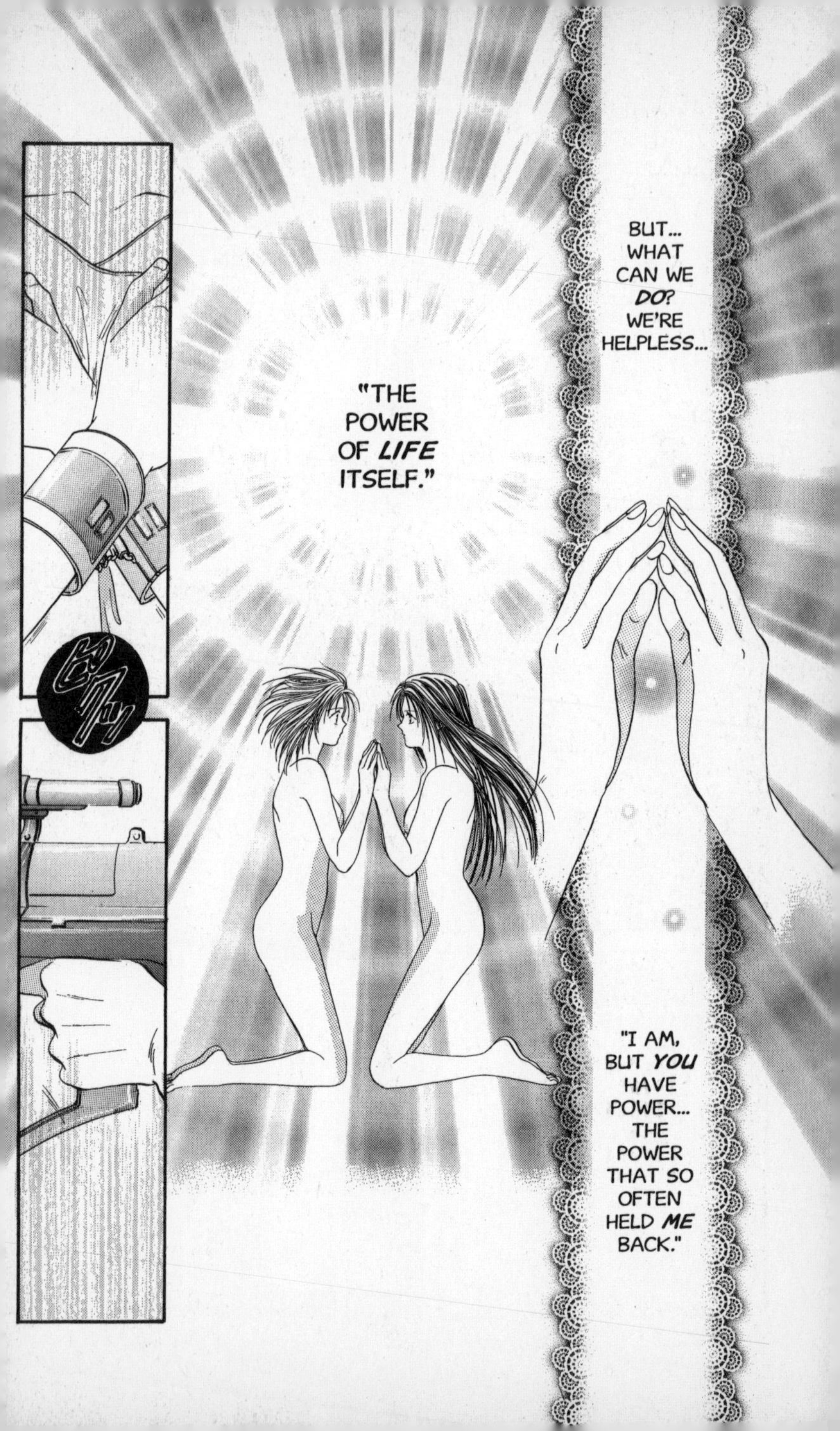
BUT... WHAT CAN WE DO? WE'RE HELPLESS...
"I AM, BUT YOU HAVE POWER... THE POWER THAT SO OFTEN HELD ME BACK."
"THE POWER OF LIFE ITSELF."

Ceres: 10

...I get it, I do. The thing is, you really don't even need to be at an art school—the things you learn at regular school will be enough, for any creative thing you need it to. Think of interpersonal relationships as learning experiences. You'll learn to flesh out different characters in your mind, and being more well-rounded yourself will help you when creating manga. As I've said before about romantic relationships, they'll reflect your own, human, nature. Uh-oh. ◡̈ Your life is what you make of it. "There's no hope" is a self-fulfilling prophecy. ...Well, we'll leave the rest for next time. Hang in there, everyone.

The third **Fushigi Yûgi** novel is on sale! The fourth'll be out before the summer—it'll be about Amiboshi & Suboshi (that's the plan for now, anyway). ...Oh, and I got a copy of the American version of the TV series. It's titled "The Mysterious Play." The packaging looks quite good—CG composite over the Japanese graphics. It comes with character cards, and they're all speaking English! ◡̈ Tamahome's voice is so-o-o deep. ◡̈ Watching it might even help you learn some English, huh? I want to see the Taiwanese version too, since the story is in China. ◡̈ It's already been on TV over there a couple of times. Also, I keep hearing from people who want **FY** merchandise, but I think they've stopped production, so it's gonna be tough to get hold of any. Probably all that's available is what's left in anime stores across the country. I'm not the one responsible for putting it out, so ask the merchandising companies—not me. (I doubt they'll be making any more, though, as the series has ended.) The number of CD books out there is also whatever's left in stock, so if you really want them, try going to Taiwan. They make all sorts of stuff there, even without any kind of official endorsement. ◡̈ I know only because my Taiwanese fans sometimes send me the stuff along with their letters. I guess it's okay, since it's not in Japan.... ◡̈

Ceres may also become novelized (it's not definite yet). I hope I'll be able to make various announcements in the next volume.

Sa~yo~nara! 2/99

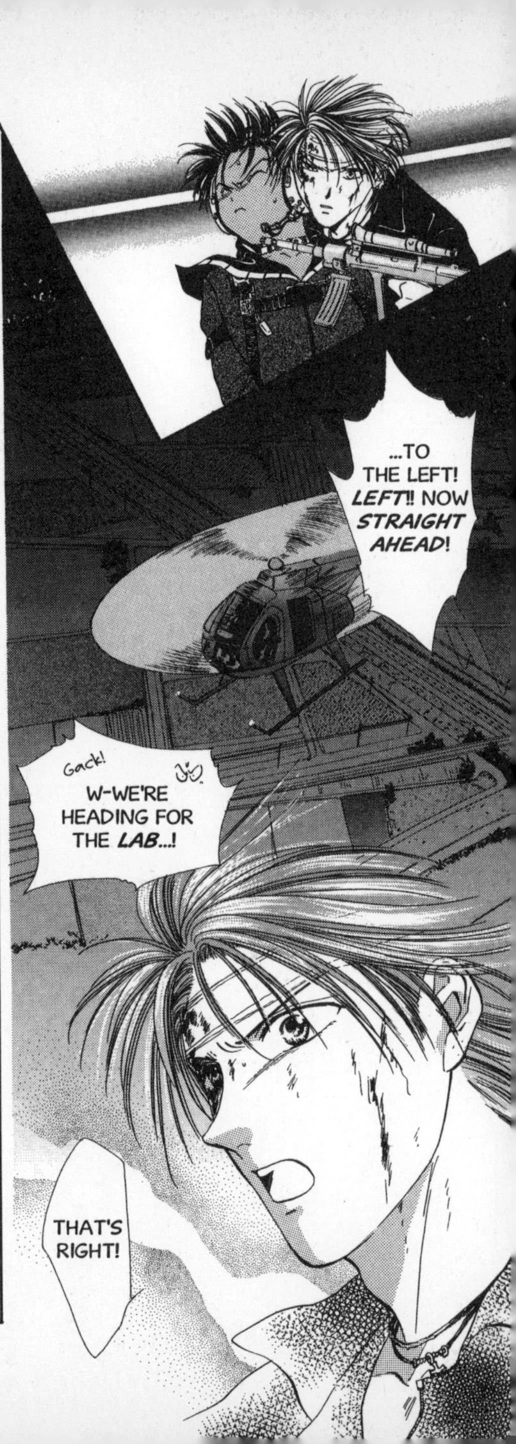
...TO THE LEFT! *LEFT*!! NOW *STRAIGHT AHEAD*!
Gack!
W-WE'RE HEADING FOR THE *LAB*...!
THAT'S RIGHT!

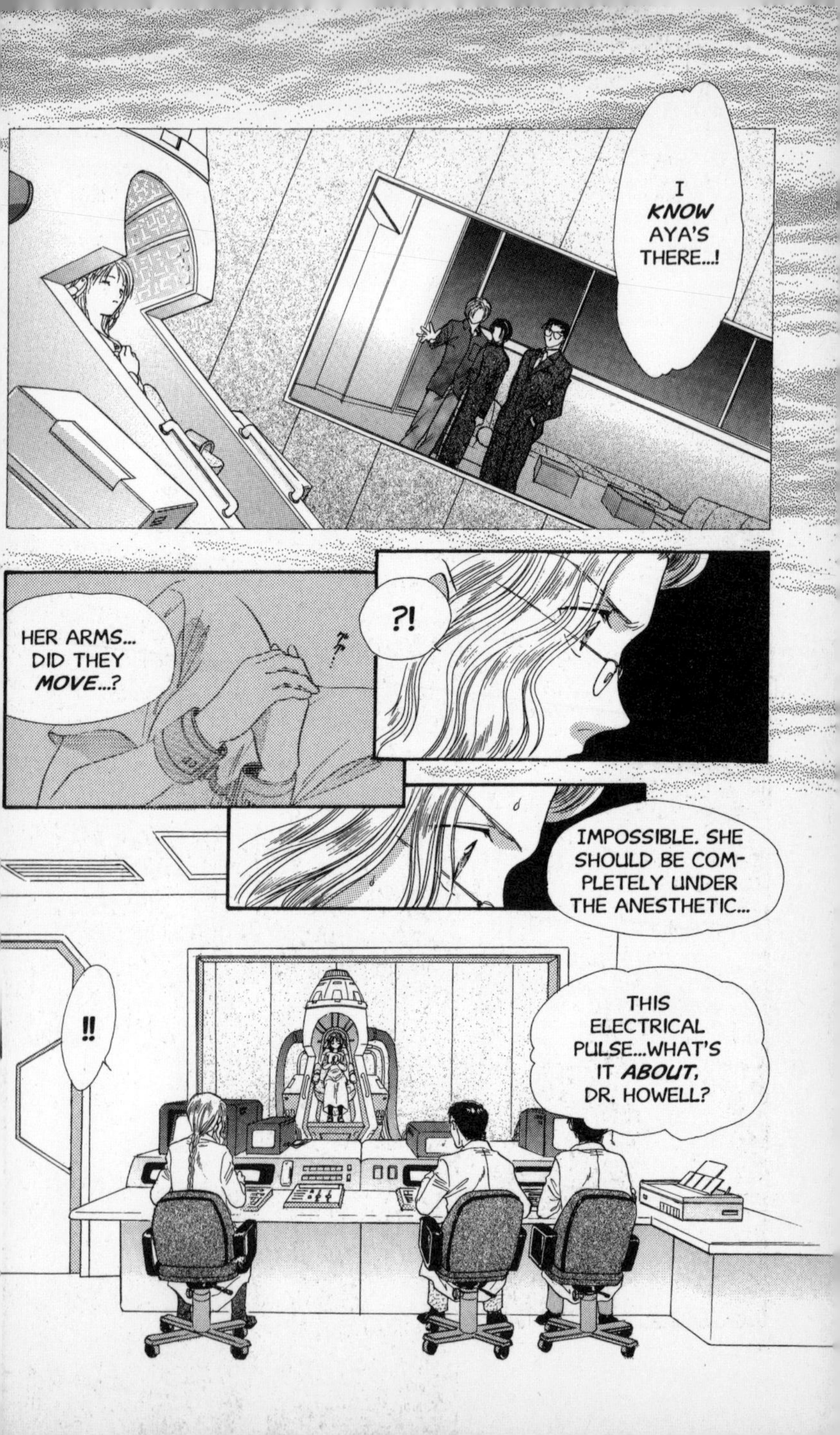

I *KNOW* AYA'S THERE...!
?!
HER ARMS... DID THEY *MOVE*...?
IMPOSSIBLE. SHE SHOULD BE COM-PLETELY UNDER THE ANESTHETIC...
THIS ELECTRICAL PULSE...WHAT'S IT *ABOUT*, DR. HOWELL?
!!

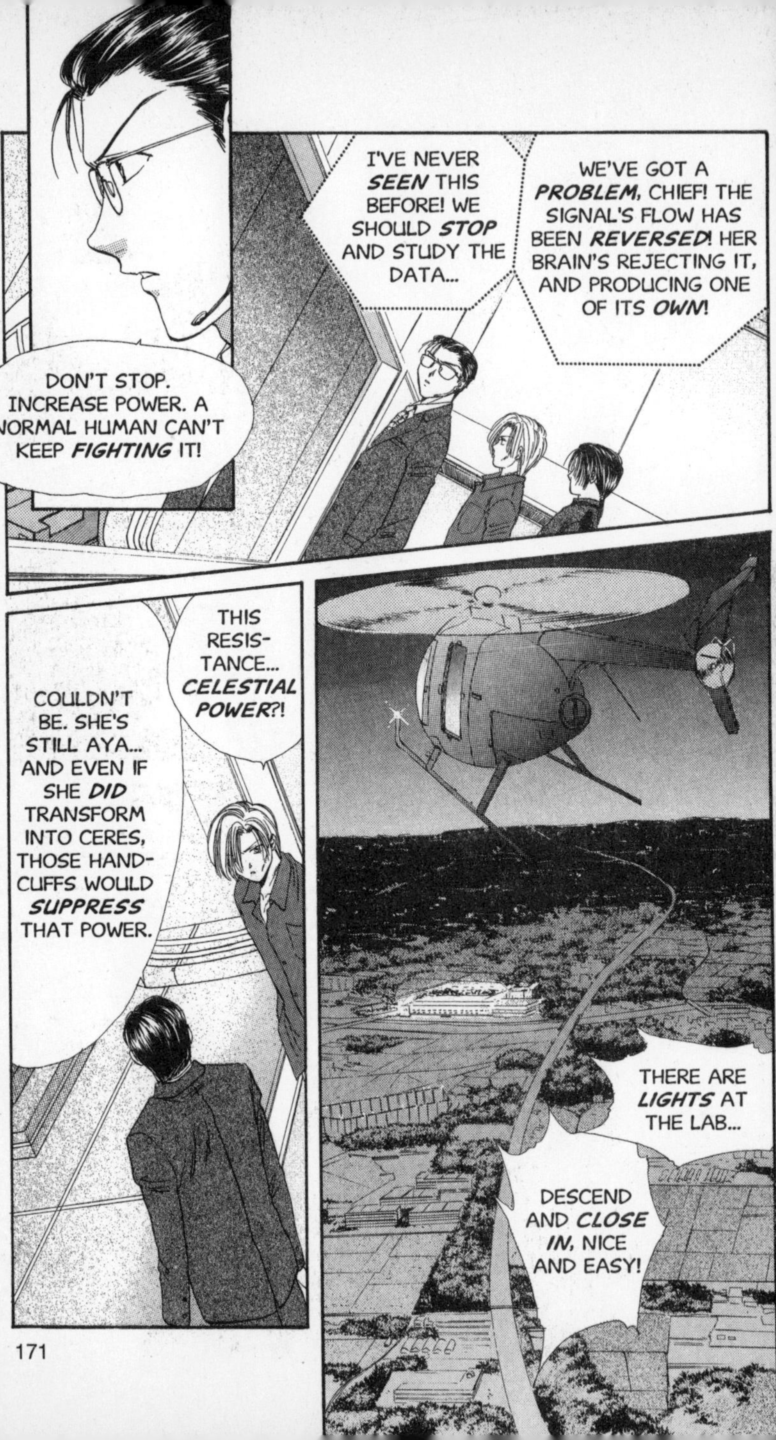
WE'VE GOT A PROBLEM, CHIEF! THE SIGNAL'S FLOW HAS BEEN REVERSED! HER BRAIN'S REJECTING IT, AND PRODUCING ONE OF ITS OWN!
I'VE NEVER SEEN THIS BEFORE! WE SHOULD STOP AND STUDY THE DATA...
DON'T STOP. INCREASE POWER. A NORMAL HUMAN CAN'T KEEP FIGHTING IT!
THERE ARE LIGHTS AT THE LAB...
DESCEND AND CLOSE IN, NICE AND EASY!
THIS RESIS-TANCE... CELESTIAL POWER?!
COULDN'T BE. SHE'S STILL AYA... AND EVEN IF SHE DID TRANSFORM INTO CERES, THOSE HAND-CUFFS WOULD SUPPRESS THAT POWER.

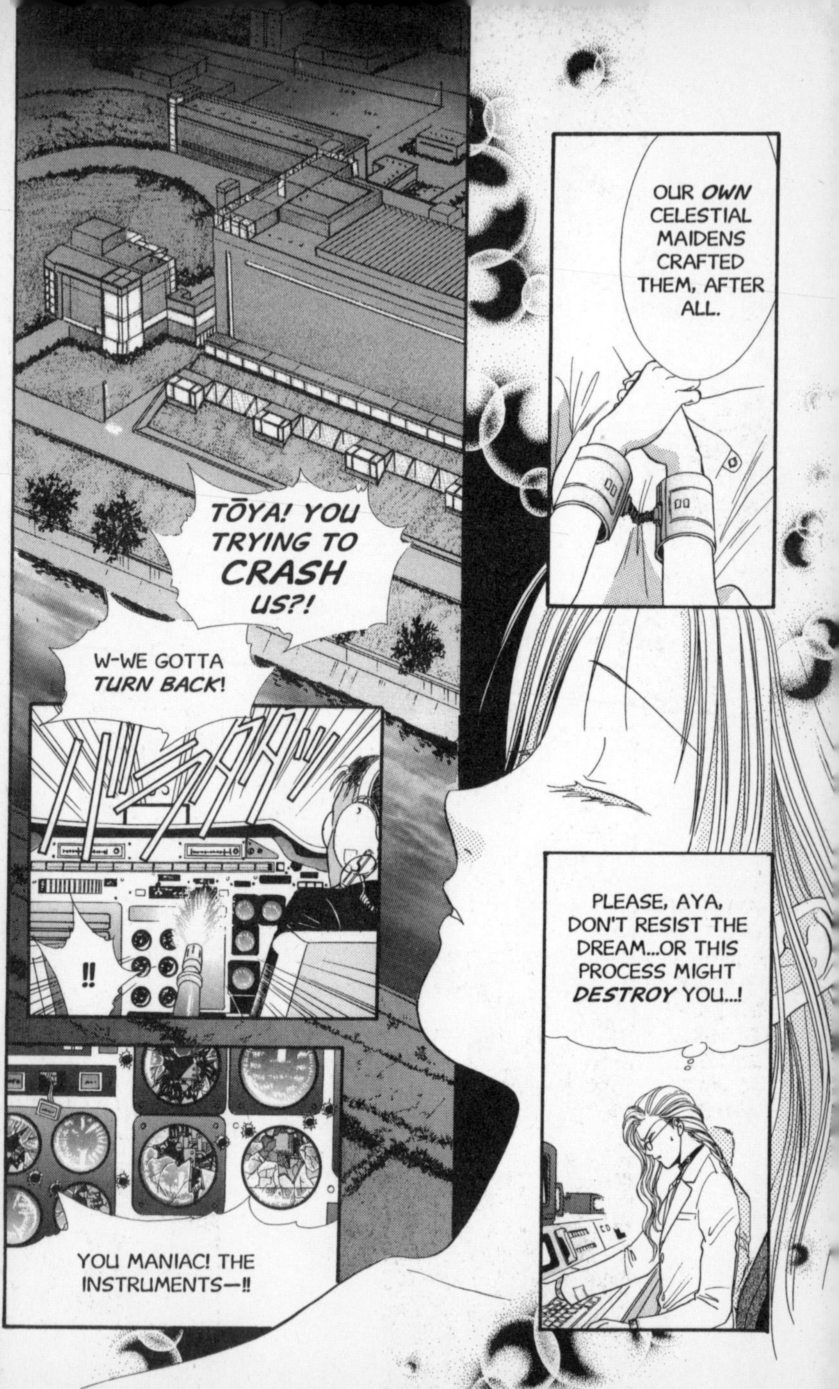
OUR *OWN* CELESTIAL MAIDENS CRAFTED THEM, AFTER ALL.
PLEASE, AYA, DON'T RESIST THE DREAM...OR THIS PROCESS MIGHT *DESTROY* YOU...!
TŌYA! YOU TRYING TO CRASH US?!
W-WE GOTTA *TURN BACK!*
!!
YOU MANIAC! THE INSTRUMENTS—!!

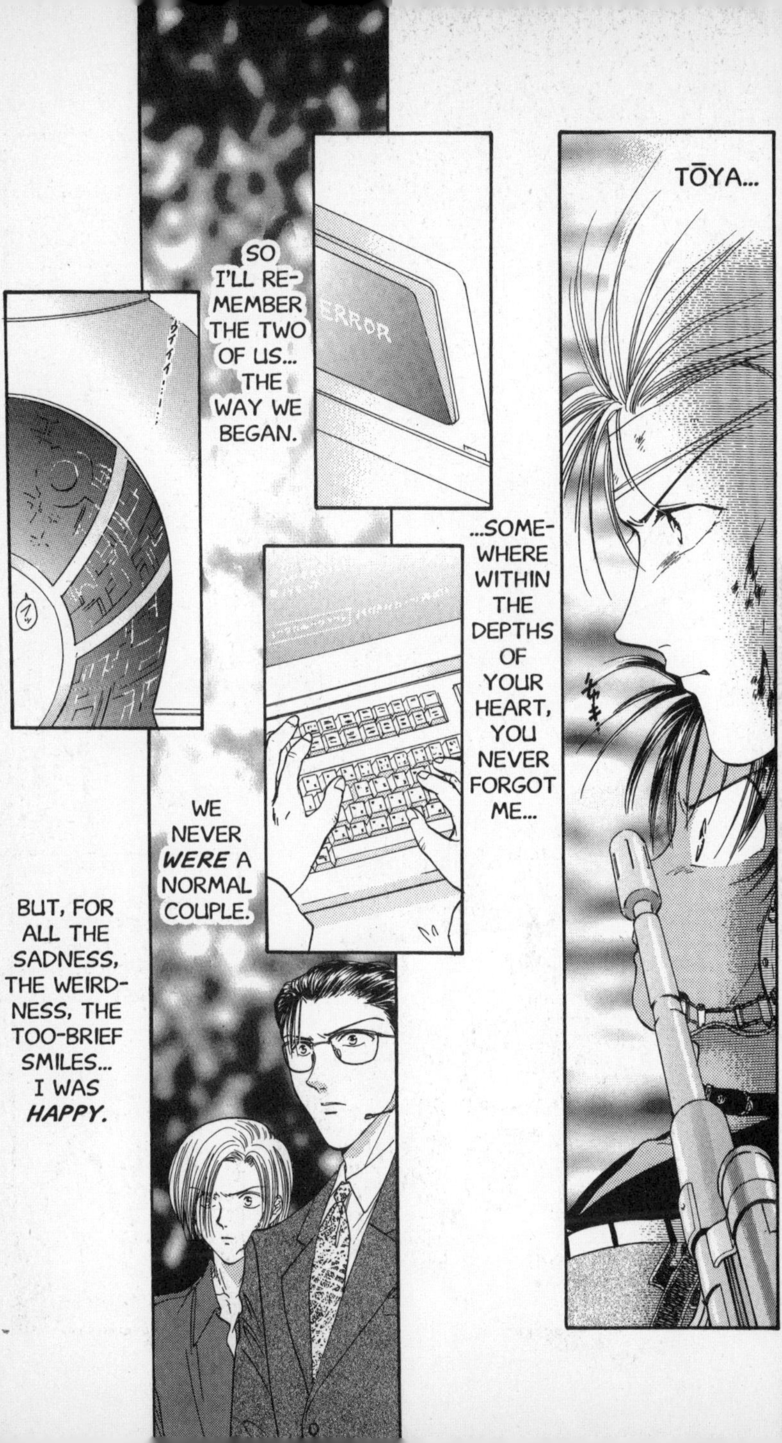
TŌYA...
...SOME-WHERE WITHIN THE DEPTHS OF YOUR HEART, YOU NEVER FORGOT ME...
SO I'LL RE-MEMBER THE TWO OF US... THE WAY WE BEGAN.
ERROR
WE NEVER *WERE* A NORMAL COUPLE.
BUT, FOR ALL THE SADNESS, THE WEIRD-NESS, THE TOO-BRIEF SMILES... I WAS *HAPPY*.

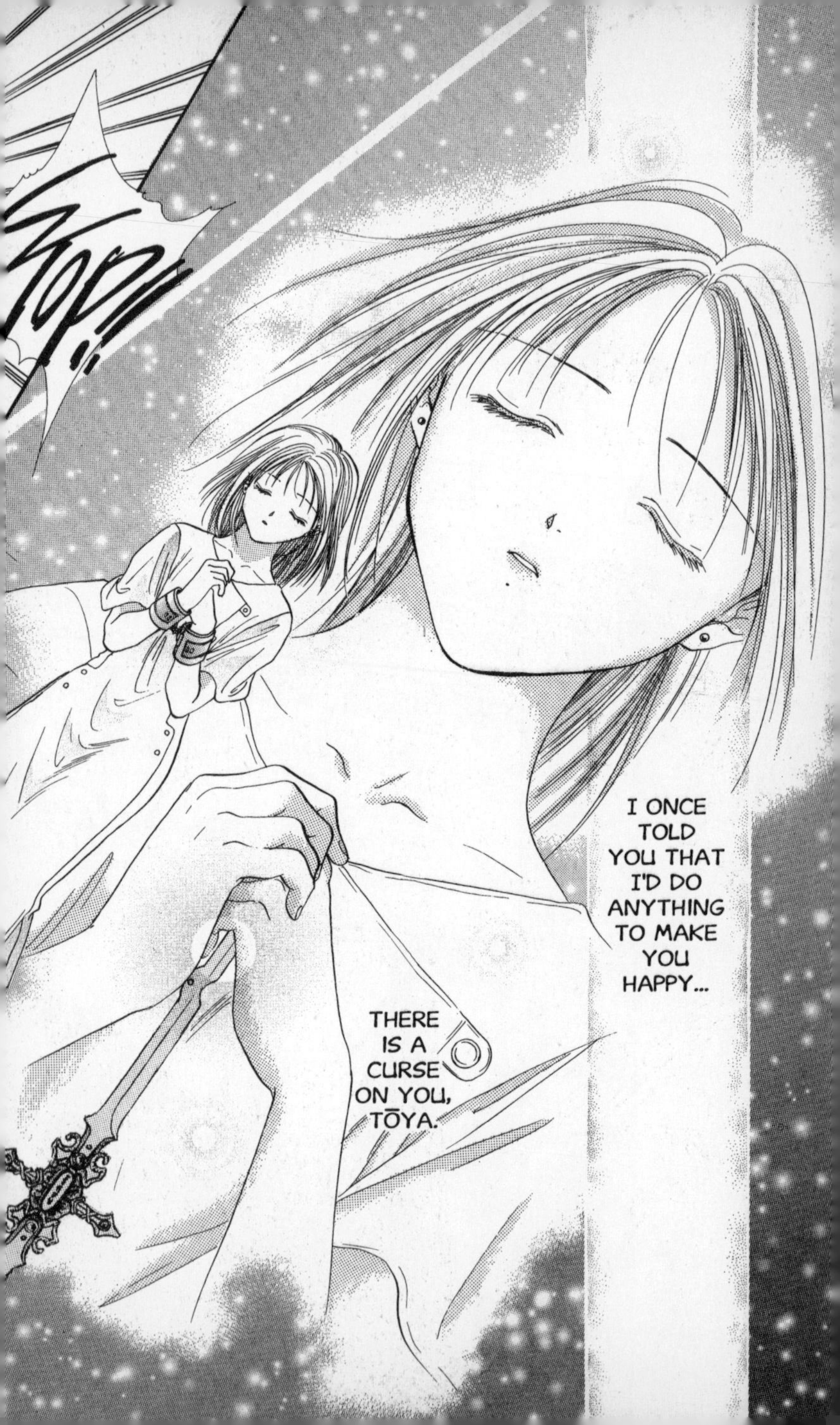
I ONCE TOLD YOU THAT I'D DO ANYTHING TO MAKE YOU HAPPY...
THERE IS A CURSE ON YOU, TŌYA.
TOYA!!

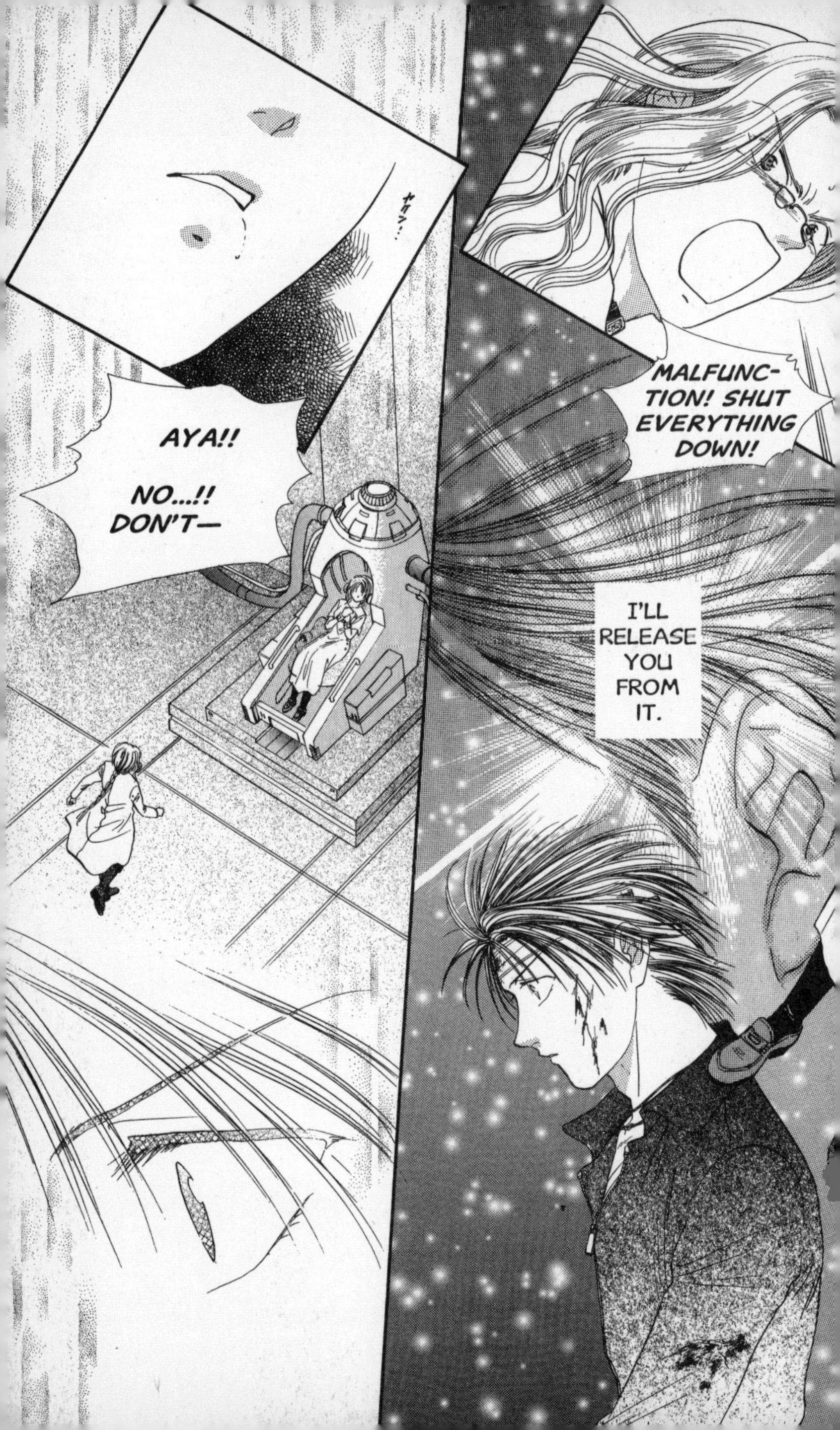
MALFUNCTION! SHUT EVERYTHING DOWN!
I'LL RELEASE YOU FROM IT.
AYA!!
NO...!! DON'T—

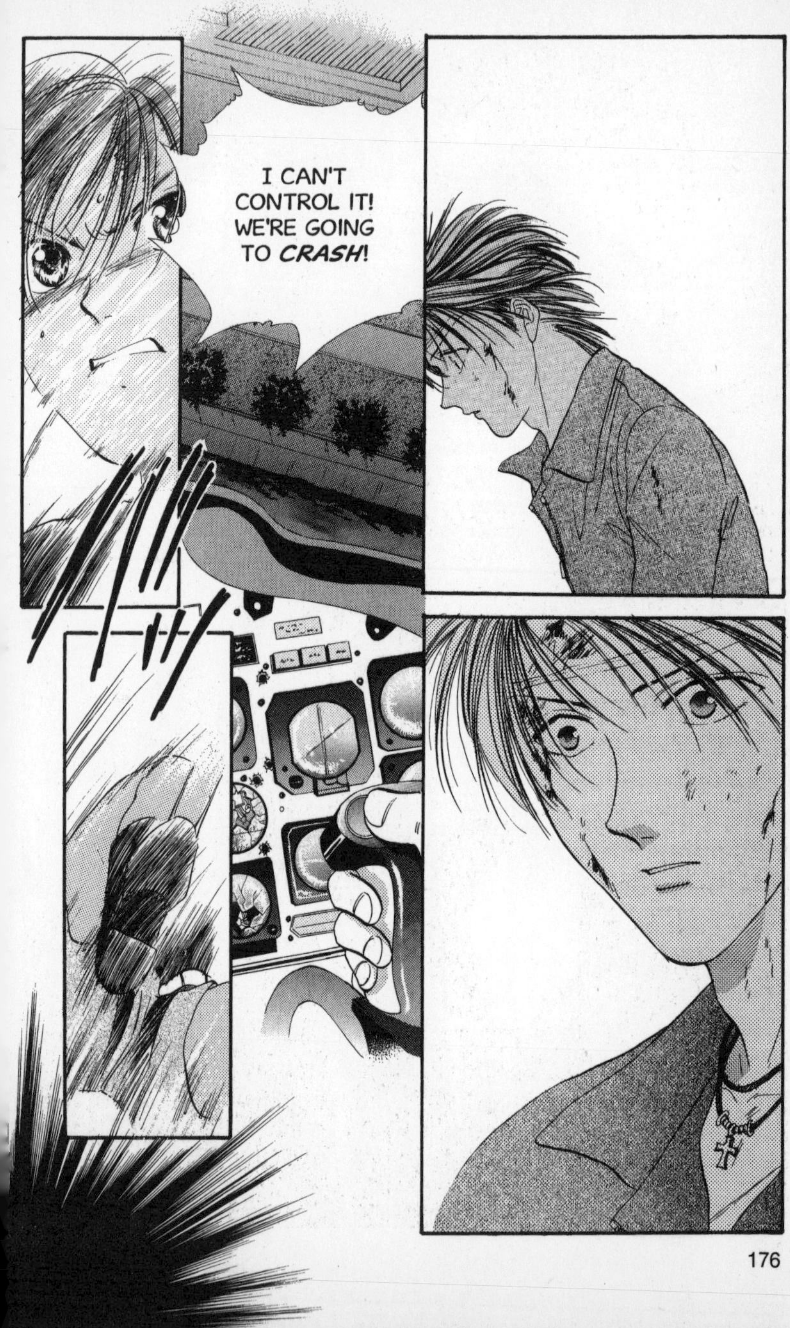
I CAN'T CONTROL IT! WE'RE GOING TO *CRASH*!

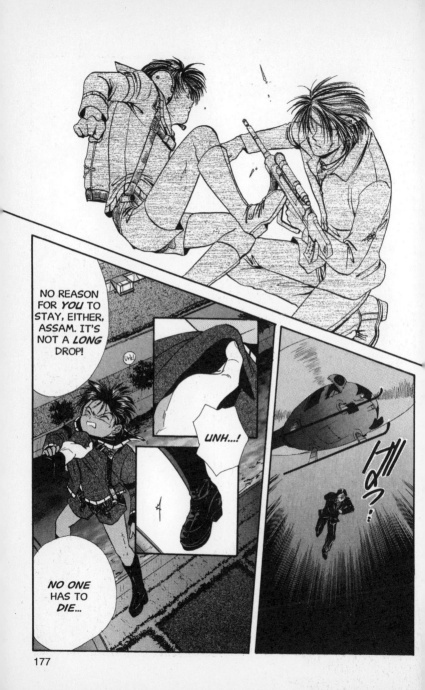

NO REASON FOR *YOU* TO STAY, EITHER, ASSAM. IT'S NOT A *LONG* DROP!

Unk!

UNH....!

NO ONE HAS TO *DIE*...

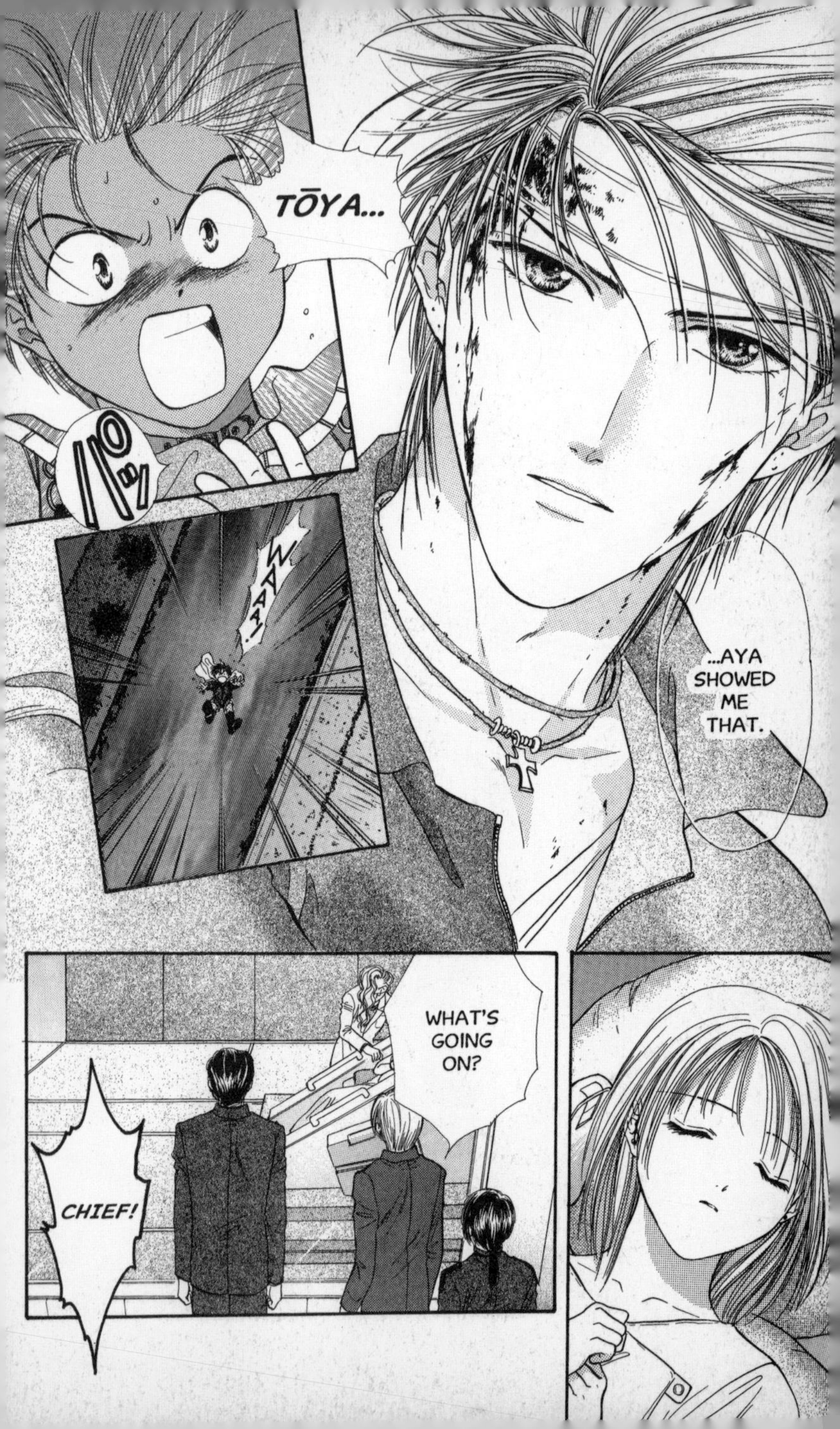
...AYA SHOWED ME THAT.
TŌYA...
WAAA!
WHAT'S GOING ON?
CHIEF!

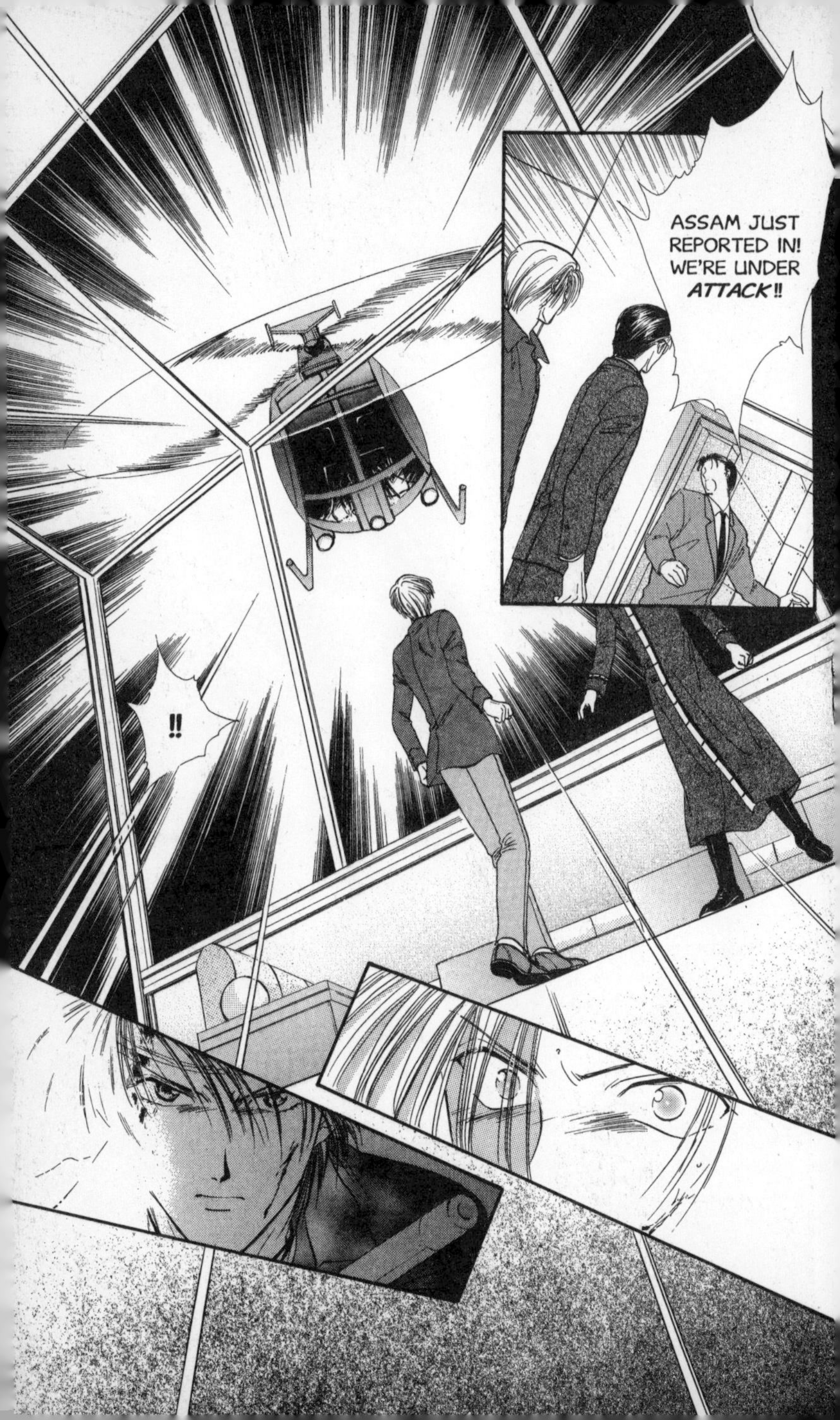
ASSAM JUST REPORTED IN! WE'RE UNDER *ATTACK*!!
!!

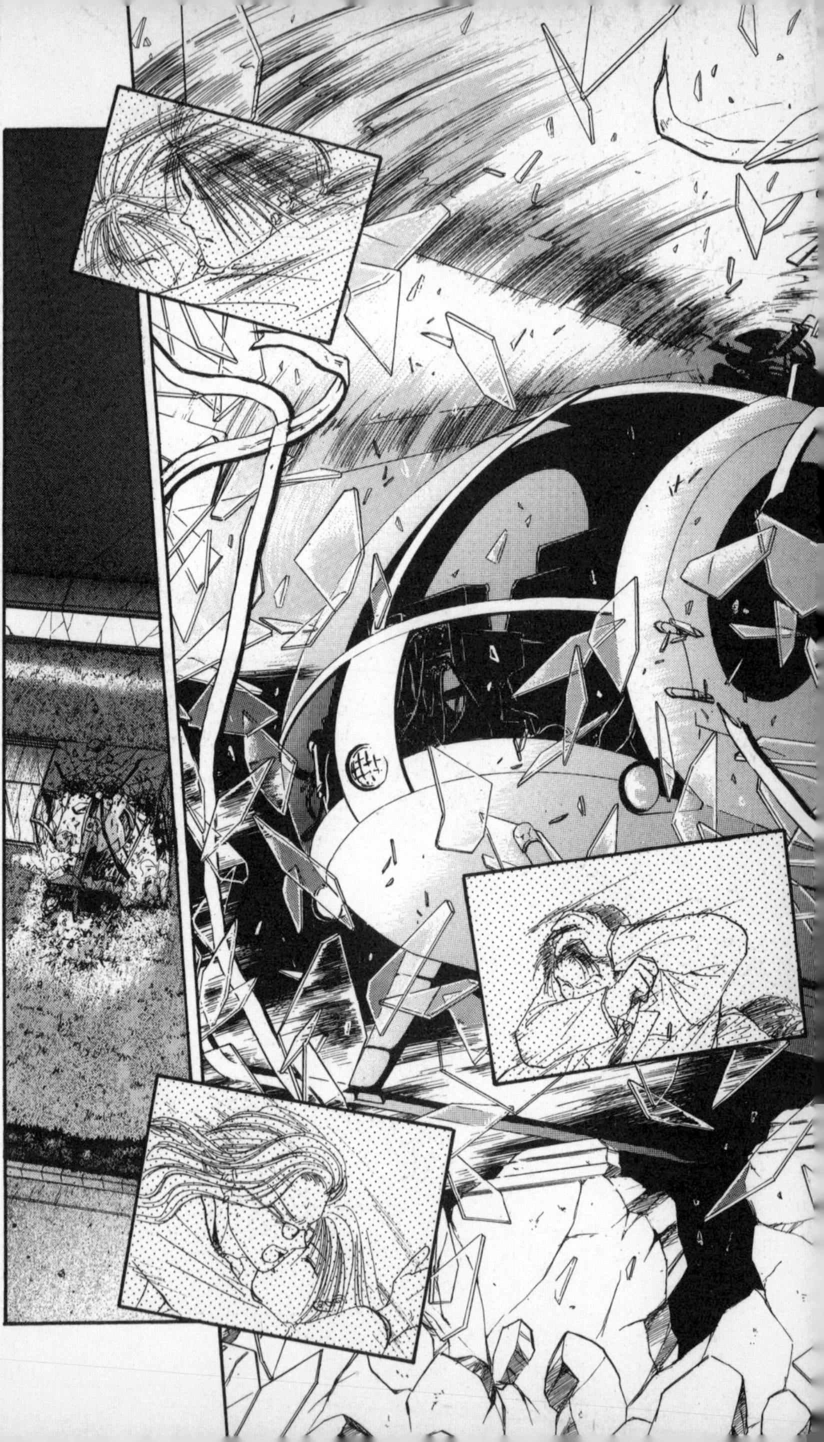

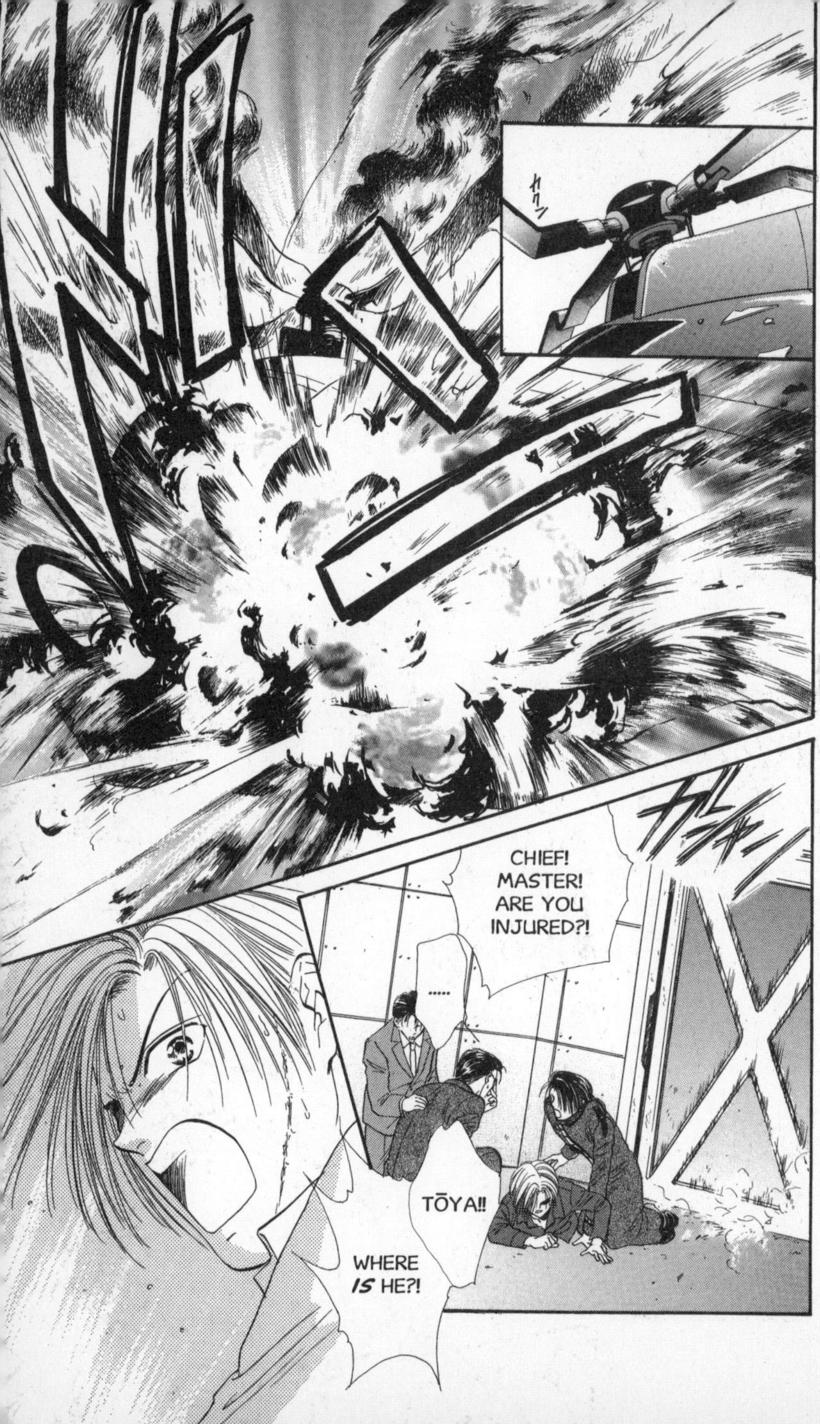
CHIEF! MASTER! ARE YOU INJURED?!
......
TŌYA!!
WHERE *IS* HE?!

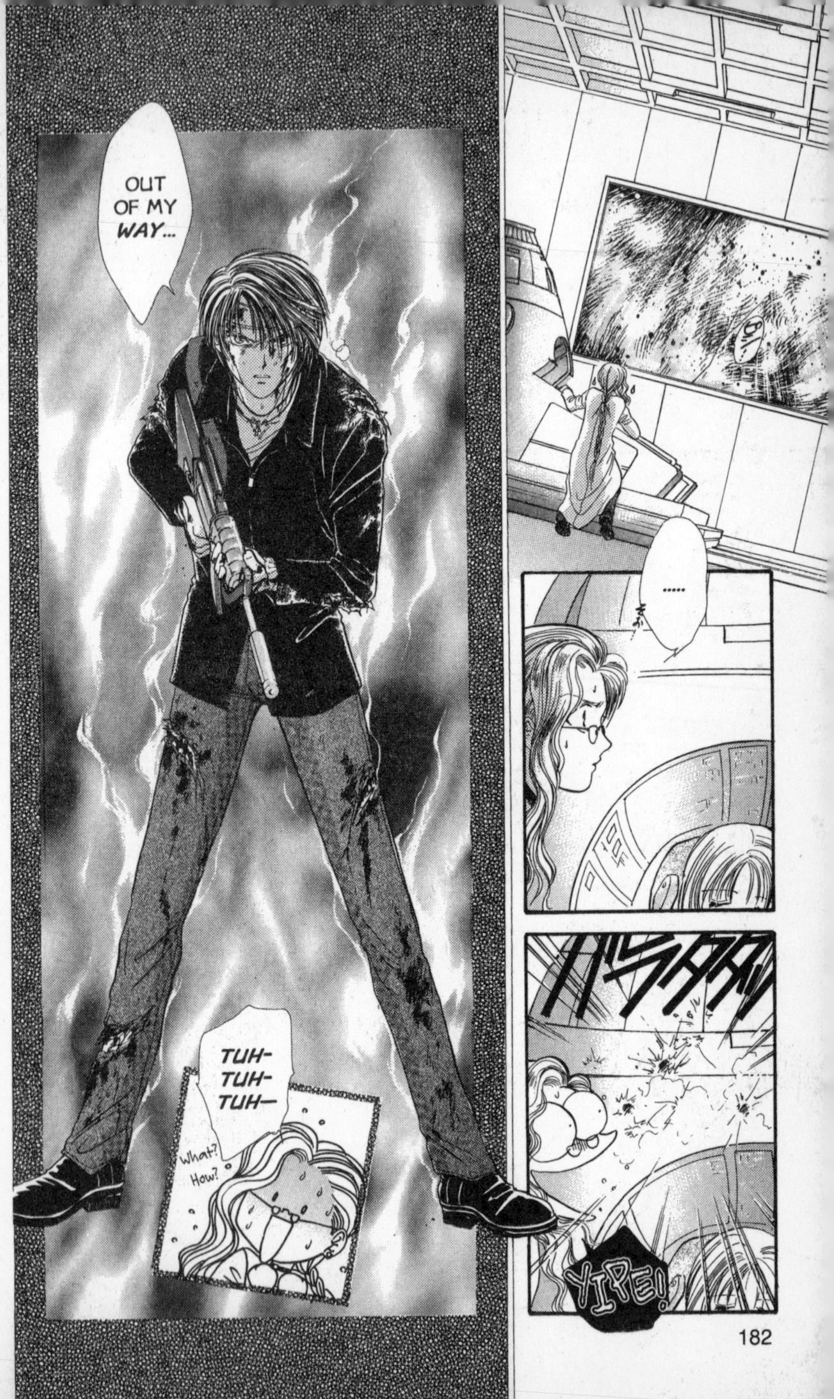

Bi...
......
YIPE!
OUT OF MY WAY...
TUH-TUH-TUH—
What? How?

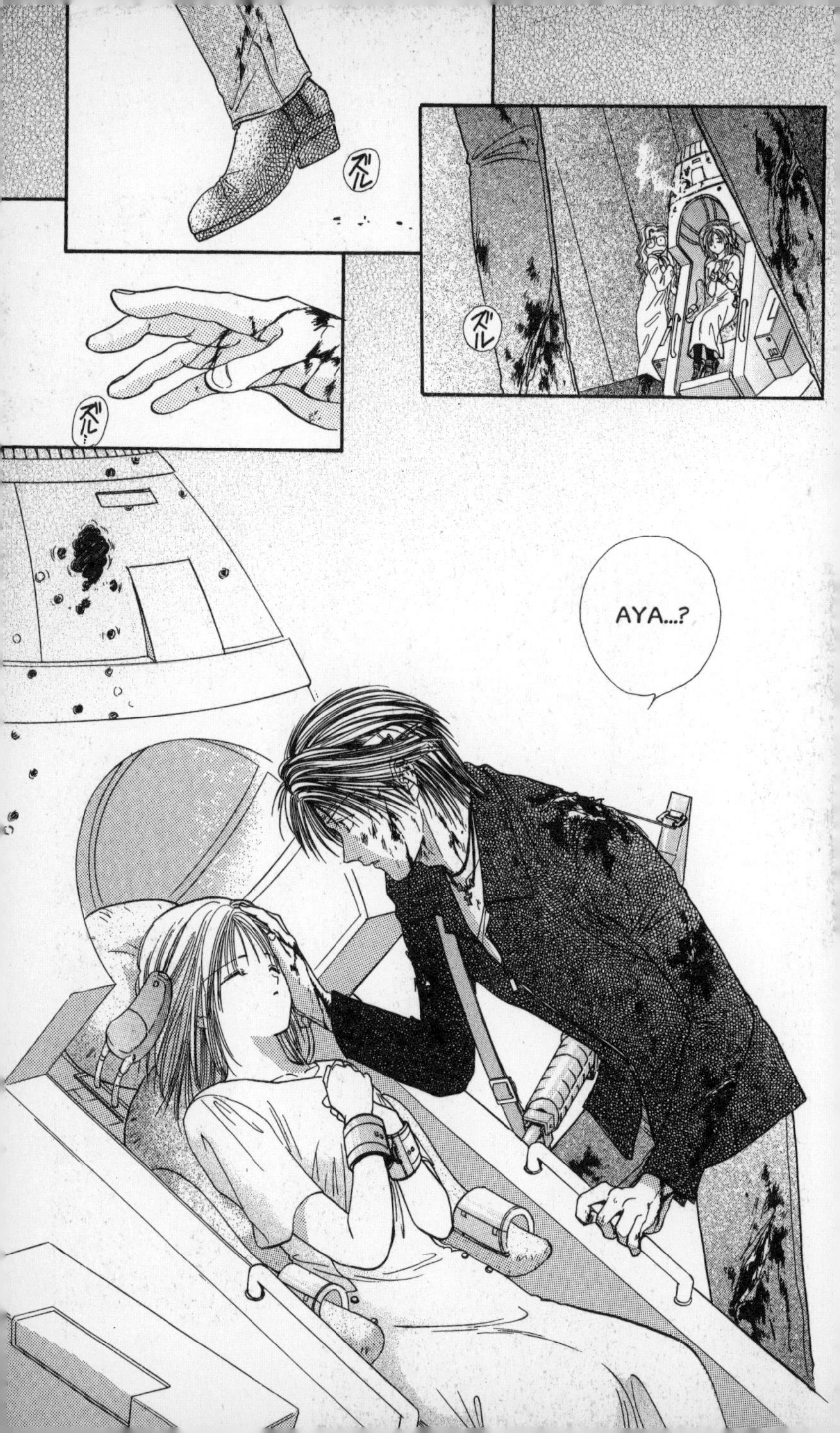
ズル
ズル
ズル…
AYA...?

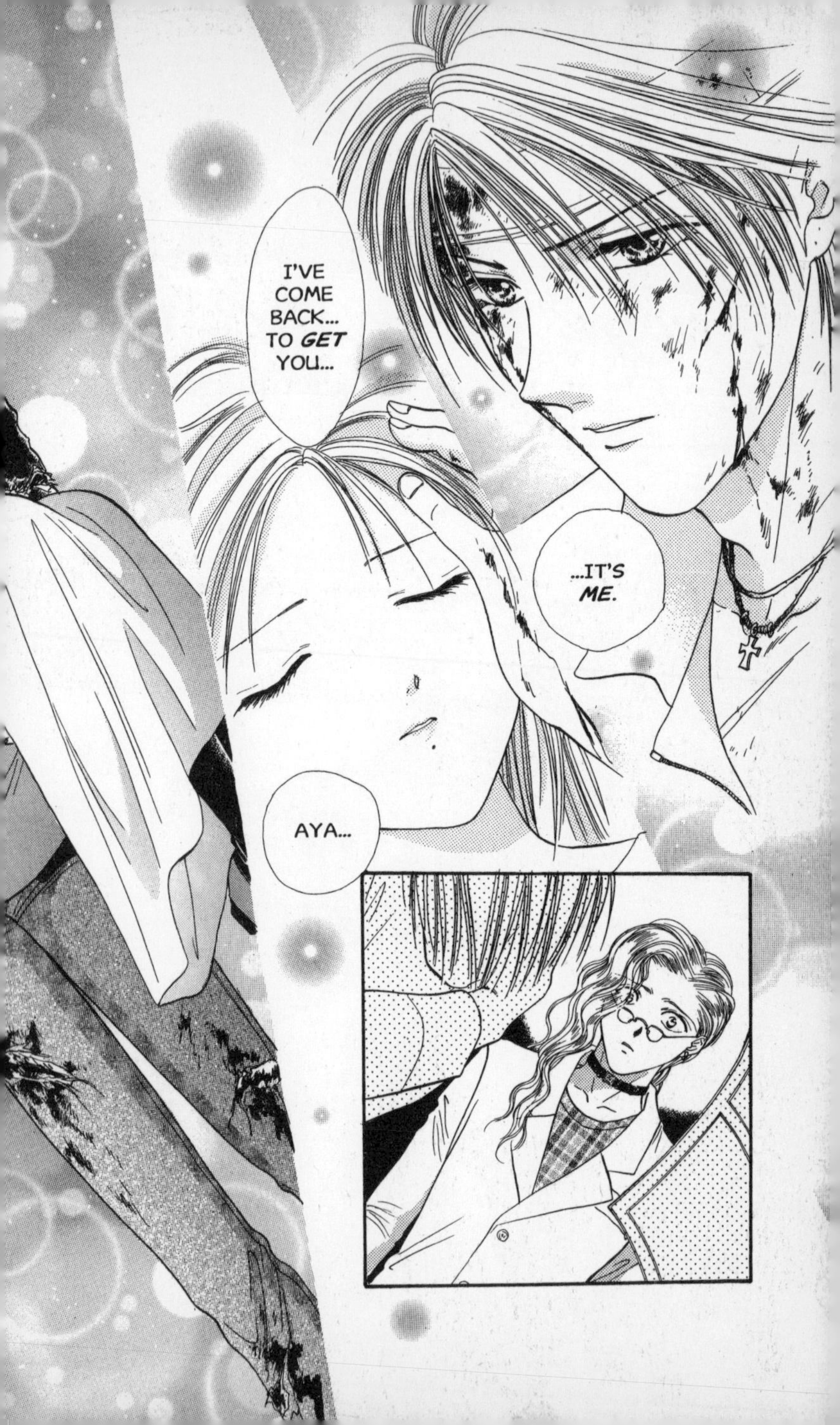
I'VE COME BACK... TO *GET* YOU...
...IT'S *ME*.
AYA...

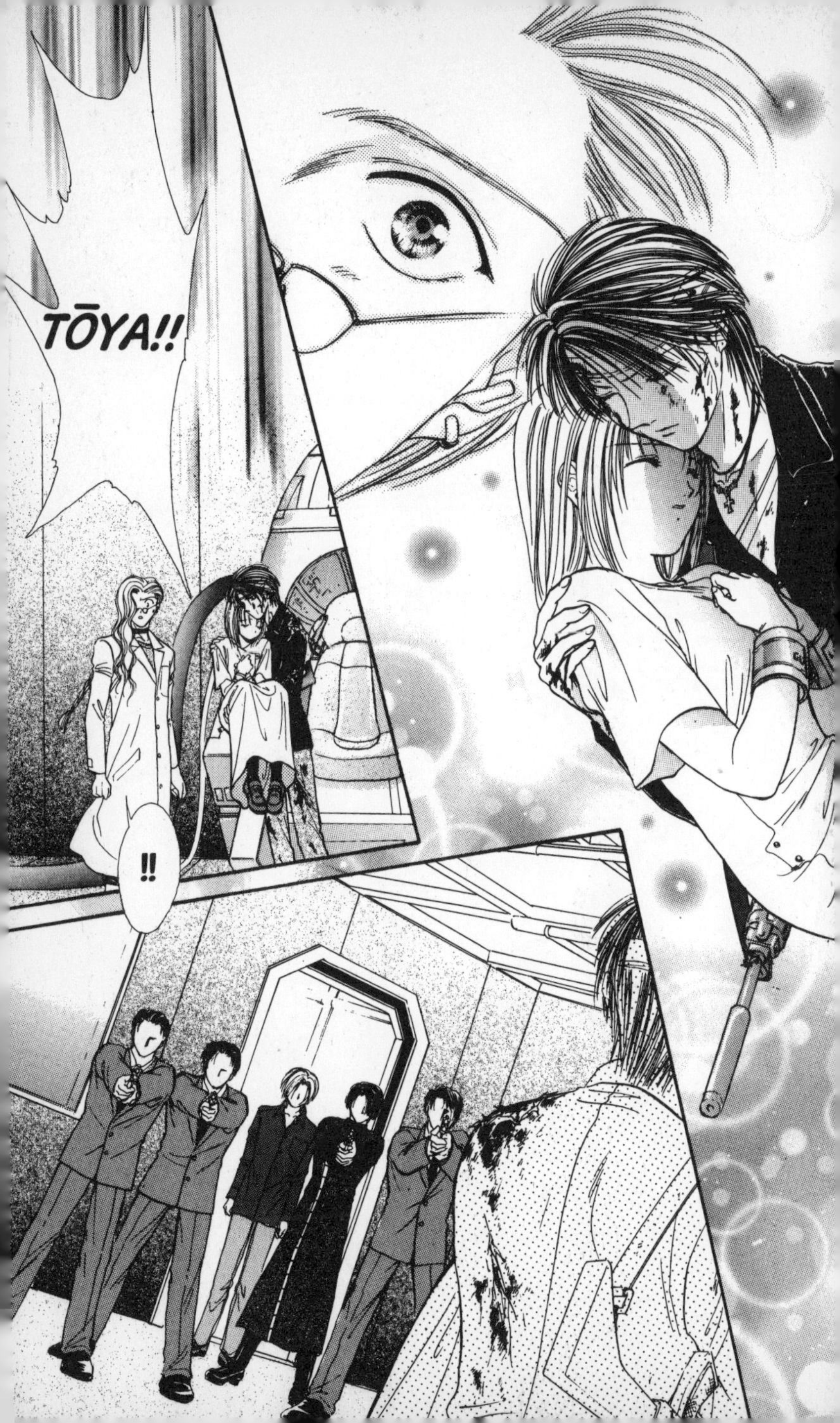
TŌYA!!
!!

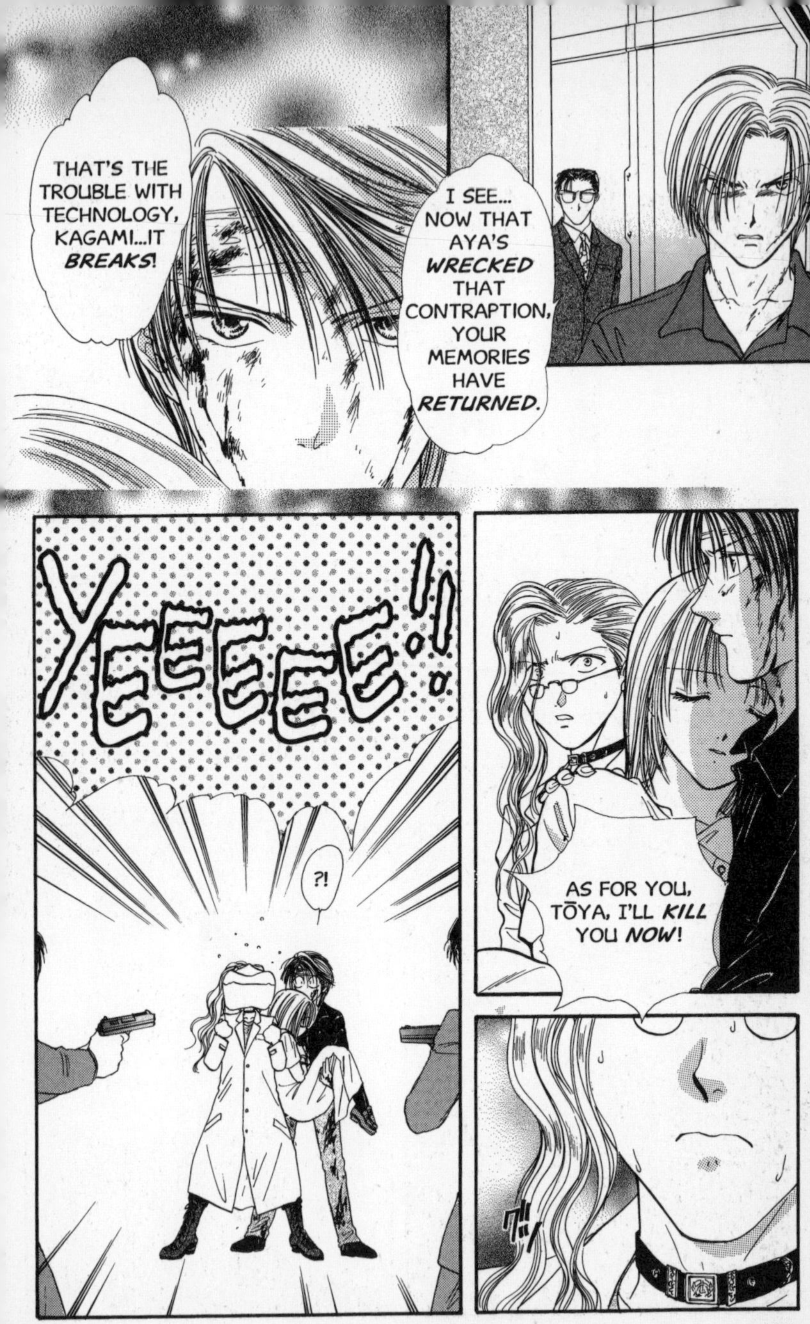
I SEE... NOW THAT AYA'S *WRECKED* THAT CONTRAPTION, YOUR MEMORIES HAVE *RETURNED*.
THAT'S THE TROUBLE WITH TECHNOLOGY, KAGAMI...IT *BREAKS*!
AS FOR YOU, TŌYA, I'LL *KILL* YOU *NOW*!
YEEEEE!!
?!

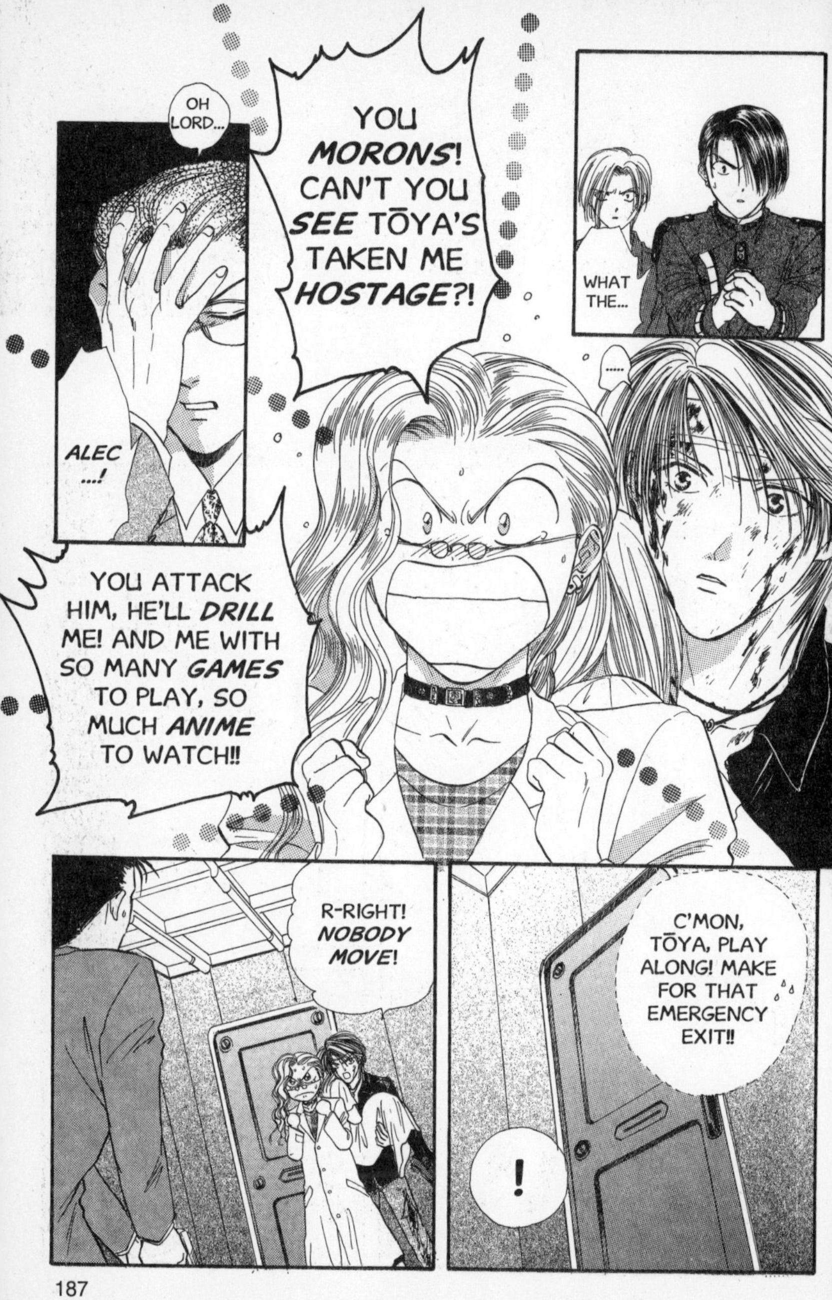
WHAT THE...
YOU *MORONS*! CAN'T YOU *SEE* TŌYA'S TAKEN ME *HOSTAGE*?!
OH LORD...
ALEC ...!
.....
YOU ATTACK HIM, HE'LL *DRILL* ME! AND ME WITH SO MANY *GAMES* TO PLAY, SO MUCH *ANIME* TO WATCH!!
C'MON, TŌYA, PLAY ALONG! MAKE FOR THAT EMERGENCY EXIT!!
!
R-RIGHT! *NOBODY MOVE*!

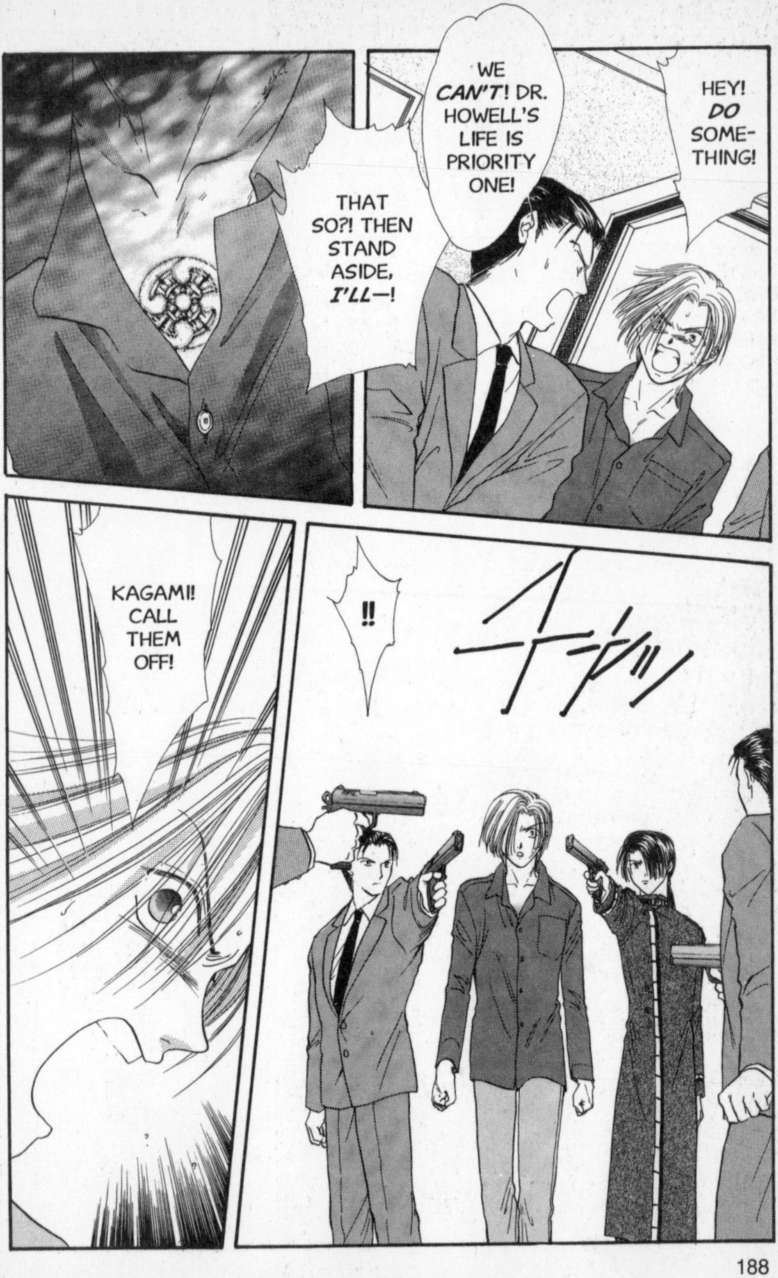
HEY! DO SOME-THING!
WE CAN'T! DR. HOWELL'S LIFE IS PRIORITY ONE!
THAT SO?! THEN STAND ASIDE, I'LL—!
!!
KAGAMI! CALL THEM OFF!

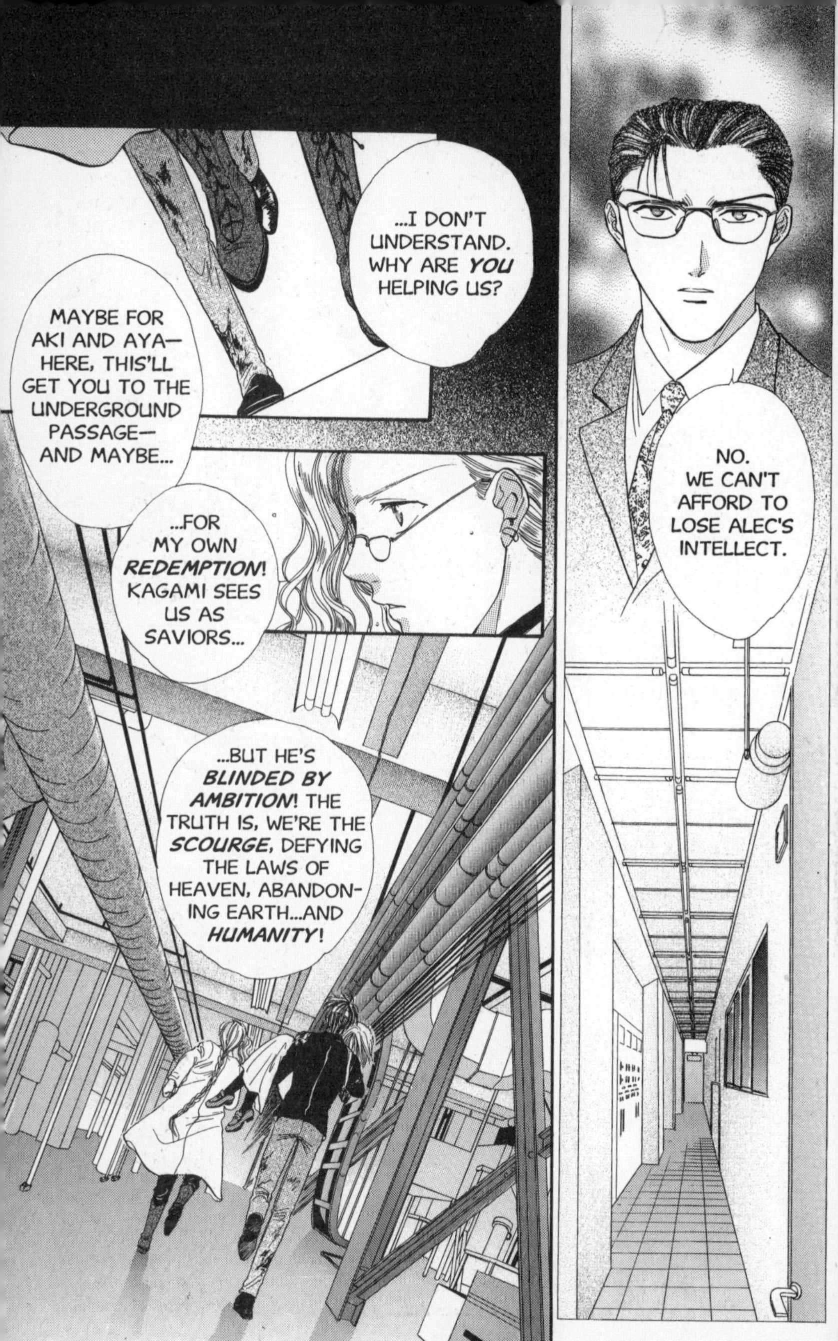
NO. WE CAN'T AFFORD TO LOSE ALEC'S INTELLECT.
...I DON'T UNDERSTAND. WHY ARE *YOU* HELPING US?
MAYBE FOR AKI AND AYA— HERE, THIS'LL GET YOU TO THE UNDERGROUND PASSAGE— AND MAYBE...
...FOR MY OWN *REDEMPTION*! KAGAMI SEES US AS SAVIORS...
...BUT HE'S *BLINDED BY AMBITION*! THE TRUTH IS, WE'RE THE *SCOURGE*, DEFYING THE LAWS OF HEAVEN, ABANDONING EARTH...AND *HUMANITY*!

TO BE CONTINUED...

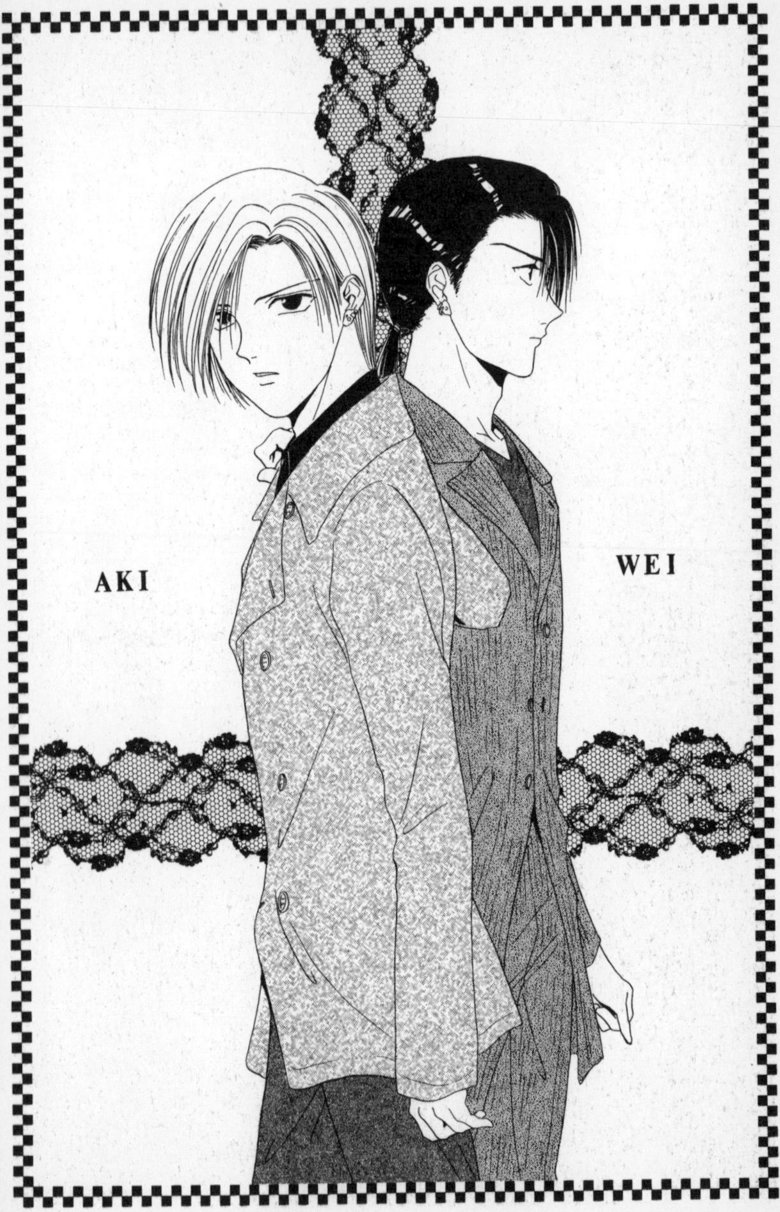
AKI
WEI

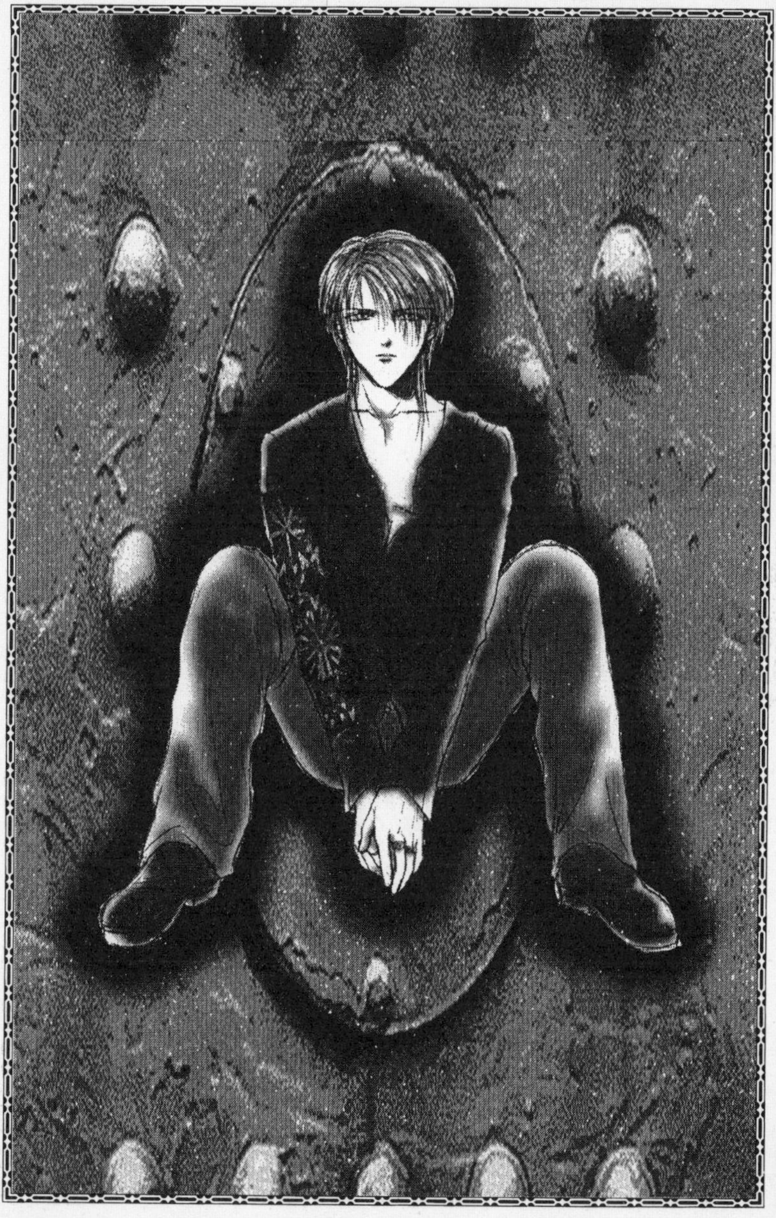

The CERES Guide to Sound Effects

We've left most of the sound effects in CERES as Yû Watase originally created them–in Japanese. VIZ has created this glossary to help you decipher, page-by-page and panel-by-panel, what all those foreign words and background noises mean. Use this guide to impress your friends with your new Japanese vocabulary. The glossary lists the page number then panel. For example, 3.1 indicates page 3, panel 1.

006.2 FX: Garan (noisy clatter)
006.4 FX: Gata ("klunk" of rising from chair)
007.1 FX: Suko—n (hollow "klonk" of bucket against head)
007.2 FX: Gara (rattle of door)
007.4 FX: Dota dota dota ("stomp, stomp, stomp")
007.4 FX: Pata (light sound of slipper)
009.4 FX: Zuru (something shuffling, or dragging)
011.3 FX: Ha? ("huh?")
011.4 FX: Muka (angry growl, "grrr!")
012.2 FX: Zuka zuka zuka (angry "stomp, stomp, stomp")
013.3 FX: Ga (abrupt grab)
014.2 FX: Paku paku (speechless flapping of mouth)
014.3 FX: Piku (a twitching)
015.1 FX: Baki doka gasu bishi ("whack! bam! pow!")
015.5 FX: Bata bata bata (running footsteps, coming closer)
016.1 FX: Ba (abrupt grab)
020.3 FX: Gyu (squeeze)
020.4 FX: Ha ("gasp")
021.5 FX: Gu (firm, clenching tug)
022.2 FX: Ba (Aki's invasion of Aya's space)
023.5 FX: Gasa (rustling, as of leaves)
024.2 FX: Bisha (brushing-up of mop against Aya)
024.3 FX: Kyahaha (mocking, oblivious laughter)
025.3 FX: Pera (flip of page)
026.2 FX: Shaka shaka (music from headphones)
026.5 FX: Pa (abrupt blinking-on of light)
027.2 FX: Kachi ("click")
027.3 FX: Pa (light pointed directly into Aya's face)
028.1 FX: Pa (invasive shining of light)
028.2 FX: Pa (invasive shining of light)
028.4 FX: Don (shove exert)
030.1 FX: Ha— Ha— (breathing exerts)
030.4 FX: Zaza (displaced ground cover)
031.3 FX: Gi gi gi (rusty creaking)
031.4 FX: Zu— zu— (heavy dragging)
033.3 FX: Fu— fu— (hissing breath)
033.3 FX: Zuru (dragging)
035.2 FX: Bashi (slap impact)
037.4 FX: Zuru (dragging)
038.4 FX: Pita (mid-step pause)
039.1 FX: Para (dirt sprinkling into hole)
039.2 FX: Biku (startled flinch)
039.5 FX: Za ("dash")
040.1 FX: Ri— ri— (crickets' cry)
040.4 FX: Gyu (clutching torn clothing)
041.4 FX: Cha (click of door)
042.1 FX: Biku (startled reaction)
042.5 FX: Gu ("clench")
044.3 FX: Don (slam of Mrs. Q's door)
044.3 FX: Bechi (Yûhi going face-first into wall)
045.1 FX: Patan (Aya's door closing with finality)
046.1 FX: Ha ("gasp")
048.4 FX: Don ("bump")
048.4 FX: Basa basa (papers scattering)
049.4 FX: Jiro (pointed stare)
050.1 FX: Ban ("bam" impact)
050.5 FX: Giku (startled, unpleasant flinch)
051.1 FX: Za (taking fighting/ defensive stance)
051.3 FX: Giku (startled, unpleasant flinch)

052.1 FX: Doka ("whack!")
052.3 FX: Ban ("bam" impact)
052.3 FX: Zuru (slow slide to floor)
052.3 FX: Ga (abrupt grab)
052.4 FX: Bogi (splintering, as of bones)
054.2 FX: Ta (light tread on stairs)
055.1 FX: Ha ("gasp")
055.1 FX: Gu (scalp being tugged)
055.3 FX: Doka ("whack!")
055.4 FX: Dogu ("pow!")
055.4 FX: Gyu (clenching fist)
055.4 FX: Zuga (violent kick)
055.5 FX: Ga (impact)
057.2 FX: Ku (snort of derisive laughter)
057.3 FX: Haha (laughter)
059.1 FX: Doki (quickening heartbeat)
059.2 FX: Kyu kyu ("squik" of Aki's shoes on floor)
061.4 FX: Gasa (undeterminable rustling)
062.4 FX: Ka ka ka (footsteps)
063.4 FX: Giku (startled, unpleasant flinch)
064.3 FX: Fu— fu— (hissing breath)
064.3 FX: Pa (flash of light)
066.1 FX: Ta (light footstep)
066.3 FX: Zaza (rustling of foliage)
068.2 FX: Doku doku doku (quickening pulse)
068.3 FX: Ba (snapping)
069.1 FX: Za (Aki moving to forefront)
069.2 FX: Fu— fu— (hissing breath)
069.3 FX: Ha ("gasp")
069.5 FX: Bishi (whipping impact of appendage)
070.1 FX: Bashi (strong "smack" impact)
070.4 FX: Za (heavy knock-back)
071.1 FX: Koro (rolling of flashlight)
071.4 FX: Ga (forceful grab)
072.1 FX: Do (heavy impact)
072.2 FX: Beki ("crack")
072.3 FX: Ka (flash of celestial sigil)
072.4 FX: Butsu (snapping of arm)
074.1 FX: Za (Aki's foot touching ground)
074.1 FX: Piku piku (severed hand twitching)
074.3 FX: Zuki zuki (pained throb of Yûhi's arm)
075.1 FX: Chika (clicking on of flashlight)
075.1 FX: Piku (flinch of monster)
075.2 FX: Sha— (monster's hissing move forward)
075.2 FX: Dosu dosu (stomp forward)
076.1 FX: Ha ("gasp")
076.3 FX: Yoro (staggering)
076.3 FX: Fu— fu— (hissing breath)
079.2 FX: Su (Ceres' slip into unconsciousness)
079.2 FX: Zuru (Ceres' slump)
079.3 FX: Bishi ("whap" of Wei's weapon)
079.4 FX: Ja (jangle of chain)
079.4 FX: Zuru (Yûhi's slump)
081.1 FX: Dosu (stomp of shoe)
082.2 FX: Ha— ha— (labored breathing)
082.3 FX: Ha— (labored breathing)
082.4 FX: Ha— ha— (labored breathing)
082.5 FX: Ha— (labored breathing)
082.6 FX: Ha— ha— (labored breathing)
083.1 FX: Zuki (throb of Yûhi's arm)
083.2 FX: Ha— ha— (labored breathing)
084.3 FX: Katsu katsu (clicking of footsteps)
084.4 FX: Katsu (clicking of footsteps)
085.1 FX: Patan ("clunk" of door)
086.1 FX: Su (Aki's gentle touch)
086.4 FX: Bashi (Aki's slap)
087.3 FX: Patan (door closing with a "clunk")
087.4 FX: Gishi ("creak")
088.1 FX: Sara (silky slide of hair)
088.2 FX: Tokun tokun... (steady heartbeats)
088.4 FX: Ha ("gasp")
091.1 FX: Ba (sudden lunge)
091.2 FX: Do (impact of falling back into bed)
091.4 FX: Ba (arms forced back against pillow)
092.2 FX: Zoku (shudder of distaste)
092.5 FX: Gari ("chomp")
093.1 FX: Bashi (impact of slap)

093.2 FX: Shuru
(necktie sliding against shirt)
094.4 FX: Pita (momentary pause)
095.2 FX: Dokun dokun dokun
(strengthening heartbeats)
095.3 FX: Dokun dokun (strengthening heartbeats)
096.4 FX: Zan (crash of waves)
097.1 FX: Za (faint waves)
099.2 FX: Ba (sitting bolt upright)
099.3 FX: Ha ("gasp")
101.1 FX: Peta (bare foot on floor)
101.2 FX: Bafu (pillow hitting face)
101.3 FX: Bata bata (wrestling flail)
102.4 FX: Bishi
(violently outthrust finger)
104.3 FX: Bicha
("splat" of ice-cream cone)
106.3 FX: Tokun (steady heartbeat)
106.4 FX: Tokun Tokun...
(steady heartbeats)
107.2 FX: Za-za—n (move and crash of waves)
107.3 FX: Zan (crash of waves)
108.2 FX: Ba ba ba ba
(gunfire hitting ground)
108.3 FX: Za (roll into "crouch")
108.4 FX: Hyu ("whizz" of projectiles)
109.1 FX: Do do (explosions)
110.2 FX: Ka (flash of light)
110.3 FX: Chika chika (glint of light)
110.4 FX: Gya— ("vrrrm" of engine)
111.2 FX: Su (slipping away)
111.2 FX: Pokan ("duh-h-h...")
114.3 FX: Za-za—n
(move and crash of waves)
114.4 FX: Pachin pachin ("clik" of game pieces on board)
116.1 FX: Pachin ("clik" of game piece)
116.2 FX: Pachin pachin
("clik" of game pieces)
117.4 FX: Pachin ("clik" of game piece)
117.4 FX: Pachin pachin...
("clik, clik" of game pieces)
118.1 FX: Kururi (flip of game piece)
118.2 FX: Pachin ("clik" of game piece)
119.2 FX: Tokun tokun...
(steady heartbeats)
119.3 FX: Dokun dokun...
(strengthening heartbeats)
119.4 FX: Dokun dokun...
(strengthening heartbeats)
120.1 FX: Doka ("whack" of impact)
120.2 FX: Bishi (striking out of foot)
120.3 FX: Ha— ha—
(labored breathing)
120.3 FX: Ji—in (sting of earlier kick)
120.5 FX: Shuru (loosening of knot)
121.1 FX: Kusu kusu
(snickery little laugh)
121.2 FX: Kusu kusu
(snickery little laugh)
121.2 FX: Gishi ("creak")
121.3 FX: Dokun dokun...
(strengthening heartbeats)
122.2 FX: Biri (tearing away of clothing)
123.1 FX: Bi (smaller "tear" sound)
123.2 FX: Su (light movement of finger)
124.1 FX: Bashii ("zap")
124.2 FX: Ban (slamming into wall)
125.4 FX: Kashan (shattering glass)
125.6 FX: Piku (startled reaction)
126.2 FX: Ban (slamming of door)
127.1 FX: Dorun dorun...
("vroom, vroom" of bike)
129.3 FX: Yoro ("stagger")
130.1 FX: Don don... (rapping on door)
130.3 FX: Ha ("gasp")
130.4 FX: Ba (recoiling at "zap")
131.1 FX: Dosa (uncoordinated "thud")
132.2 FX: Gu (clenching fist)
132.3 FX: Su
(Aki walking smoothly away)
132.4 FX: Su (incline of Wei's bow)
132.5 FX: Tsuka tsuka
(departing footsteps)
132.6 FX: Batan (slamming of door)
133.1 FX: Ho (relieved exhale)
133.2 FX: Zuki (throb of pain)
134.2 FX: Fu (rueful exhale)
136.1 FX: Zukin zukin...
(throb of his headache)
137.2 FX: Niya (an easy grin)
137.3 FX: Ha ("gasp")
138.1 FX: Do do (explosions)
138.2 FX: Gun (revving accelerator)

138.3 FX: Gya— ("vrrrm" of engine)
138.4 FX: Ahahaha (laughter)
139.4 FX: Gashan ("crash")
139.5 FX: Giri (gnashing of teeth)
139.5 FX: Gacha ("clik" of opening door)
141.2 FX: Shuru (loosening of bonds)
141.2 FX: Pasa (bonds falling to bed)
141.3 FX: Gishi ("creak")
141.4 FX: Ha ("gasp")
141.5 FX: Buaki ("whuppah!")
142.1 FX: Jii—in (stinging pain)
143.1 FX: Bo (launching of weapon)
143.3 FX: Ba ("fwoosh" of explosion)
144.3 FX: Do—n ("kaboom!")
144.3 FX: Dokyu— (screech of tires)
145.1 FX: Muki— (shriek of outrage)
146.2 FX: Gun (revving accelerator)
146.3 FX: Do (big "boom")
146.4 FX: Go— (roaring of fire)
147.1 FX: Kii (screeching of brakes)
147.4 FX: Su (soft move forward)
147.5 FX: Biku (startled reaction)
148.3 FX: Ki (angry cry)
148.4 FX: Buru buru (trembling shake)
149.1 FX: Bun bun (flailing of fists)
149.1 FX: Keri keri (kicking of feet)
150.3 FX: Ka (Kagami's footstep)
151.1 FX: Ton ("tap")
151.2 FX: Ka—an (engine distress)
152.2 FX: Kachi kachi... (chattering of teeth)
152.3 FX: Ba (upswing of Aya's bound hands)
152.5 FX: Ka ka (footsteps)
153.1 FX: Ha ("gasp")
153.4 FX: Don (shoulder-slam)
153.5 FX: Ga ("whack" into knee)
154.2 FX: Ban (hand slapping button)
154.4 FX: Ha— ha— (labored breathing)
155.1 FX: Ha— ha— (labored breathing)
155.1 FX: Gyu (squeezing hands around dagger)
155.2 FX: Pa ("blip" of changing elevator light)
155.2 FX: Gakon ("whirr" of elevator door)
155.3 FX: Da (Aya's dash forward)
156.1 FX: Gun (revving accelerator)
157.5 FX: Do—n (booming explosion)
158.1 FX: Ga (Assam being grabbed)
158.2 FX: Giri (Assam, pulled toward Tôya)
158.5 FX: Ha— ha— (labored breathing)
159.1 FX: Ha— ha— ha— ha— (labored breathing)
160.1 FX: Ban (slam of opening door)
161.2 FX: To (touch of needle against skin)
161.3 FX: Kura (swooning sensation)
161.4 FX: Zuru (slide downward)
162.4 FX: Su (soft move forward)
164.2 FX: Su (heads tilting)
168.3 FX: Piku ("twitch")
170.3 FX: Gugu (hands straining)
172.5 FX: Baratata ("rat-tat-tat" of gun)
173.1 FX: Chaki ("chk" of gun)
173.6 FX: Uiii (whirring whine)
173.6 FX: Fu ("fft")
174.5 FX: Kakun (yielding)
176.4 FX: Ba (jerking of control stick)
177.2 FX: Ba (leap from helicopter)
178.2 FX: Pa (sudden release of grip/hold)
181.1 FX: Kakun ("clunk" of bent rotor)
181.2 FX: Don (big explosion)
181.3 FX: Gashan (clanging down of security door)
182.1 FX: Pishi (crack appearing in glass)
182.2 FX: So— (stealthy peek)
182.3 FX: Baratata ("rat-tat-tat")
183.1 FX: Zuru (dragging forward)
183.2 FX: Zuru (dragging forward)
183.3 FX: Zuru (dragging forward)
186.4 FX: Gu (nervous gulp)
188.3 FX: Cha (cocking of guns)

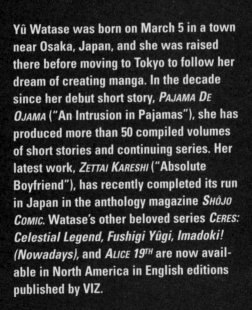

Yū Watase was born on March 5 in a town near Osaka, Japan, and she was raised there before moving to Tokyo to follow her dream of creating manga. In the decade since her debut short story, *PAJAMA DE OJAMA* ("An Intrusion in Pajamas"), she has produced more than 50 compiled volumes of short stories and continuing series. Her latest work, *ZETTAI KARESHI* ("Absolute Boyfriend"), has recently completed its run in Japan in the anthology magazine *SHŌJO COMIC*. Watase's other beloved series *CERES: Celestial Legend, Fushigi Yûgi, Imadoki! (Nowadays),* and *ALICE 19TH* are now available in North America in English editions published by VIZ.

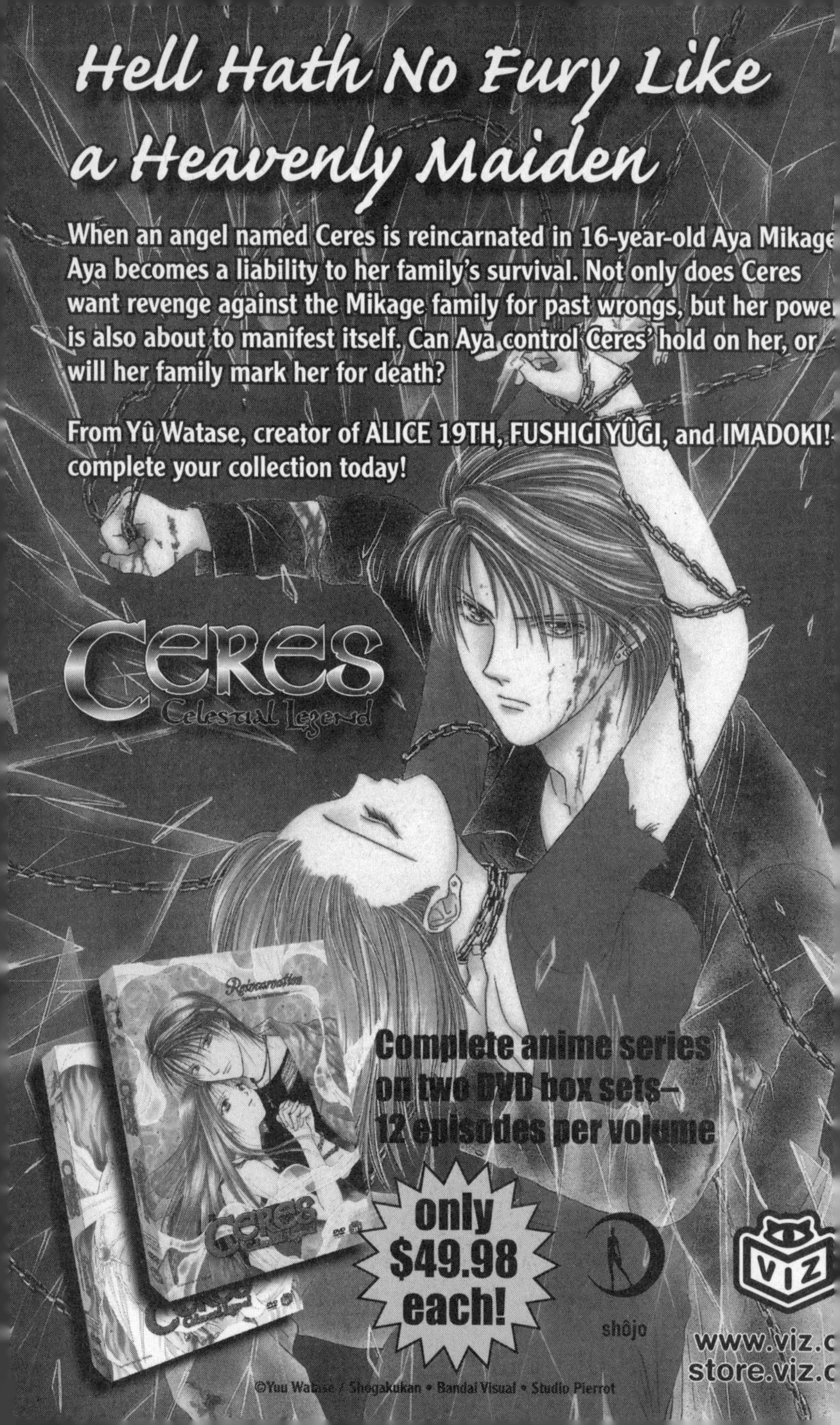
Hell Hath No Fury Like a Heavenly Maiden
When an angel named Ceres is reincarnated in 16-year-old Aya Mikage Aya becomes a liability to her family's survival. Not only does Ceres want revenge against the Mikage family for past wrongs, but her powe is also about to manifest itself. Can Aya control Ceres' hold on her, or will her family mark her for death?
From Yû Watase, creator of ALICE 19TH, FUSHIGI YÛGI, and IMADOKI! complete your collection today!
CERES
Celestial Legend
Complete anime series on two DVD box sets– 12 episodes per volume
only $49.98 each!
shôjo
VIZ
www.viz.c
store.viz.c
©Yuu Watase / Shogakukan • Bandai Visual • Studio Pierrot

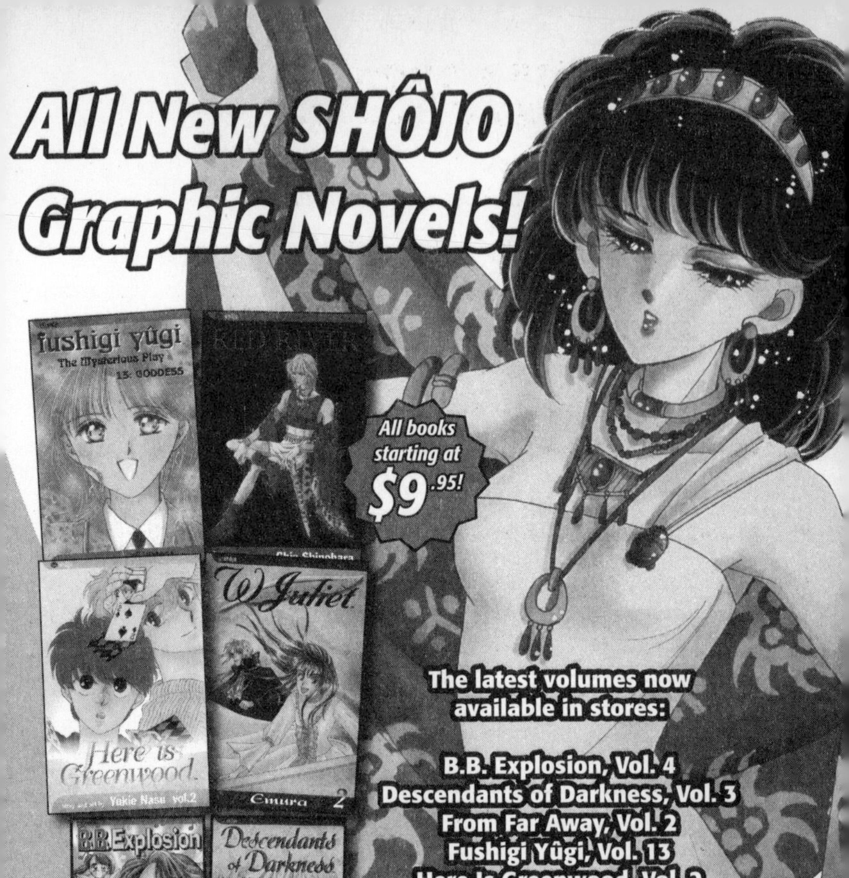
All New SHÔJO Graphic Novels!
All books starting at $9.95!
The latest volumes now available in stores:
B.B. Explosion, Vol. 4
Descendants of Darkness, Vol. 3
From Far Away, Vol. 2
Fushigi Yûgi, Vol. 13
Here Is Greenwood, Vol. 2
Imadoki!, Vol. 4
Please Save MY Earth, Vol. 8 *
Red River, Vol. 4
W Juliet, Vol. 2
store.viz.com
www.viz.com
* Also available on DVD from VIZ

COMPLETE OUR SURVEY AND LET US KNOW WHAT YOU THINK!

☐ Please do NOT send me information about VIZ products, news and events, special offers, or other information.

☐ Please do NOT send me information from VIZ's trusted business partners.

Name: _____

Address: _____

City: _____ **State:** _____ **Zip:** _____

E-mail: _____

☐ Male ☐ Female **Date of Birth** (mm/dd/yyyy): ___/___/___ (Under 13? Parental consent required)

What race/ethnicity do you consider yourself? (please check one)

☐ Asian/Pacific Islander ☐ Black/African American ☐ Hispanic/Latino

☐ Native American/Alaskan Native ☐ White/Caucasian ☐ Other: _____

What VIZ product did you purchase? (check all that apply and indicate title purchased)

☐ DVD/VHS _____

☐ Graphic Novel _____

☐ Magazines _____

☐ Merchandise _____

Reason for purchase: (check all that apply)

☐ Special offer ☐ Favorite title ☐ Gift

☐ Recommendation ☐ Other _____

Where did you make your purchase? (please check one)

☐ Comic store ☐ Bookstore ☐ Mass/Grocery Store

☐ Newsstand ☐ Video/Video Game Store ☐ Other: _____

☐ Online (site: _____)

What other VIZ properties have you purchased/own? _____

_____

How many anime and/or manga titles have you purchased in the last year? How many were VIZ titles? **(please check one from each column)**

ANIME	MANGA	VIZ
☐ None	☐ None	☐ None
☐ 1-4	☐ 1-4	☐ 1-4
☐ 5-10	☐ 5-10	☐ 5-10
☐ 11+	☐ 11+	☐ 11+

I find the pricing of VIZ products to be: **(please check one)**

☐ Cheap ☐ Reasonable ☐ Expensive

What genre of manga and anime would you like to see from VIZ? **(please check two)**

☐ Adventure ☐ Comic Strip ☐ Science Fiction ☐ Fighting

☐ Horror ☐ Romance ☐ Fantasy ☐ Sports

What do you think of VIZ's new look?

☐ Love It ☐ It's OK ☐ Hate It ☐ Didn't Notice ☐ No Opinion

Which do you prefer? **(please check one)**

☐ Reading right-to-left

☐ Reading left-to-right

Which do you prefer? **(please check one)**

☐ Sound effects in English

☐ Sound effects in Japanese with English captions

☐ Sound effects in Japanese only with a glossary at the back

THANK YOU! Please send the completed form to:

NJW Research
42 Catharine St.
Poughkeepsie, NY 12601

All information provided will be used for internal purposes only. We promise not to sell or otherwise divulge your information.